VICTOR

VICTOR
MY JOURNEY

VICTOR MATFIELD
WITH DE JONGH BORCHARDT

Published by Zebra Press
an imprint of Random House Struik (Pty) Ltd
Reg. No. 1966/003153/07
Wembley Square, First Floor, Solan Road, Gardens, Cape Town, 8001
PO Box 1144, Cape Town, 8000 South Africa

www.zebrapress.co.za

First published 2011
Reprinted before publication

3 5 7 9 10 8 6 4 2

Publication © Zebra Press 2011
Text © Victor Matfield 2011

Front cover photograph: Matthys van Lill
Insets: Gallo Images (spine); Gallo Images; Gallo Images/AFP;
Carl Fourie (back cover, top row)
Author photograph: Christiaan Kotze, Foto24

PUBLISHER: Marlene Fryer
MANAGING EDITOR: Robert Plummer
TRANSLATOR: Pieter Redelinghuys
EDITOR: Ronel Richter-Herbert
PROOFREADER: Mark Ronan
COVER DESIGNER: Sean Robertson
TEXT DESIGNER: Monique Oberholzer
TYPESETTER: Monique van den Berg
INDEXER: Sanet le Roux
PHOTO RESEARCHER: Colette Stott

Set in 11 pt on 14.5 Adobe Garamond

Printed and bound by CTP Book Printers, Duminy Street, Parow, 7500, South Africa

ISBN 978 1 77022 144 4 (print)
ISBN 978 1 77022 264 9 (ePub)
ISBN 978 1 77022 265 6 (PDF)

Contents

Foreword

In 2001, the year after I finished matric, I was a shy, quiet junior at the Blue Bulls when I met Victor during a rugby week in Port Elizabeth. At that stage, he was already one of the more senior guys at the union and had just received his call-up for the Bok squad to play against Italy.

We 'met' in passing, but for the following two years, I had little interaction with him. He was in the Currie Cup and Super 12 squads, and I was working my way up from the junior ranks. However, from that very first meeting, something struck me about Victor. I would eventually find out what it was, because when I made my Super 12 debut in 2003, Victor was the captain of the Bulls that day.

We did not become immediate friends in the first two seasons we played in the light-blue jersey together. He was a Springbok and a firm supporter of Rudy Joubert, while my loyalties lay with the Currie Cup side of 2003 and our coach, Heyneke Meyer. Besides, Victor was a senior in the squad and five years older than me, so I never imagined us becoming such close friends in years to come.

If truth be told, I was a youngster who thought I knew everything about rugby and that Victor's knowledge of the game left a lot to be desired. But Victor never treated me – or any other member of the team, for that matter – with anything but grace, respect and integrity.

We became friendlier during the Tri Nations tournament in 2004, when two isolated incidents – one between Victor and Jake White, and another between Jake and me – got us talking, mainly because the Bulls players in the Bok squad spent a lot of time together.

Later that year, back at the Bulls and with Anton Leonard captaining the side, we formed a really tight unit and helped make decisions on the field. We realised that as far as rugby was concerned, we were on the same wavelength. Yes, we sometimes had different viewpoints and engaged in constructive arguments, but Victor is a good listener and our conversations always ended in agreement on some point or another, or where we were satisfied with the plans we had developed together.

At the end of the 2007 Super 14 season, we beat the Sharks in Durban to win the title. When the team lined up afterwards to receive their little replica trophies, Victor held me back and said I should join him on stage when the actual trophy was handed over. I was very surprised, but this was also the moment I realised what a wonderful person and captain he was. It was the first of three Super Rugby trophies we lifted together, and we also won the Currie Cup in 2009 – without a doubt the four highlights of my career.

Victor is not the kind of guy who likes to receive accolades. He is the one who works the hardest to make the team stronger, but when the limelight shines, he stands back and lets everyone else involved experience it.

I know no one who understands rugby as well as he does. Yes, he is a master in the line-outs, but his knowledge goes way beyond that to attacking play, defence and tactical kicking. And he has a particular ability to inspire teammates to perform to the best of their abilities. Rugby is about winning trophies, and Victor knew a team could not win if each player did not deliver his best performance.

Victor is steadfast in his beliefs and will always stand up for his principles, but he is also a reasonable man who will listen when someone has something to say. Thanks to him, a family culture was created within the Bulls and Bok squads, which became the foundation of our many successes over the years.

Victor is an incredible friend who has meant a great deal to me. I don't think anyone else has taught me as much about life or rugby as he has.

Vic, thanks for every minute of every practice session and game. Thanks for the coffee, beers, braais and team meals. And thanks for golf on Thursdays and your (unwilling) contribution towards my son's education one day!

I believe you will make a brilliant coach – it is a talent you have already exhibited without actually being one! I hope we have a long and fruitful journey together into the future.

FOURIE DU PREEZ

Foreword

'As iron sharpens iron, so one man sharpens another.'

Proverbs 27:17

The best sportsmen rise above their peers for several reasons. Victor Matfield stood out above the rest because of his knowledge of the game, and his ability to interpret a game or situation and make the right decisions. You wanted him in your team when you had your back against the wall, as he was at his best when a lot was at stake. I can only imagine how difficult it must have been for coaches to prepare their players for an encounter with Victor Matfield.

Many pundits and opponents regard Victor as one of the best line-out jumpers in world rugby. Those who have played with or coached Victor understand and appreciate his genius more than others. He was rare among rugby players because of his ability to pinpoint, analyse and take advantage of the weak links in his opponents' line-outs. He spent hours studying video footage of teams to learn their patterns and tactics in order to find small, but often significant, clues that would give his team the advantage.

Victor's leadership positively influenced the behaviour of his team-mates, and always elicited their best performances. And he had a burning ambition for success. His biggest legacy at the Bulls union is the way in which he set new standards for many facets of our game.

But what impressed me most about Victor was his easy and consistent ability to be a complete person, player and captain.

FRANS LUDEKE

Acknowledgements

So many people have meant so much to me over the years, on and off the field, that it is impossible to name them all. I want to thank each and every player with whom I shared the rugby field, as well as all the coaches who guided my career. Thanks from the bottom of my heart. Each one of you, in your own, unique way, had an influence on my life.

Still, there are a few people I want to single out:

Swys de Bruin: Back in the days at Griquas, you had an unwavering belief in me. It was under your guidance that I became a Springbok, and for that I am forever thankful.

Heyneke Meyer: Of all the coaches I played under, you probably had the biggest influence on my rugby career. Thank you for 'raising' me and a whole bunch of my teammates – and not just on the field. Thank you for all the great anecdotes and invaluable life lessons. I was one of many Blue Bulls players to achieve success because of the cornerstones you laid.

Frans Ludeke: In my last three years at the Bulls, we worked very closely together. You are the person in world rugby I respect the most, because you always treat people with compassion and respect. I have not met anyone more humble than you, but still you were in control of things, leading with an iron fist from the front line.

Peter de Villiers: Thank you for the last four years of my career. We experienced tough times together, but nevertheless these were the most enjoyable years of my Springbok career. Thanks also for the life lessons you taught us off the field, Coach.

Basil Carzis: When I started at the Blue Bulls, you were their fitness instructor, but you were so much more than that. You were a motivator, a true friend and a confidant. Thanks for keeping me fit and on form, especially over the last couple of years, when this old body really started feeling the pain.

Johann van Graan: Thanks for the good times and the work you did with me at the Blue Bulls. Although this was mostly behind the scenes, we made lots of plans and I learnt a lot from you. We still have big dreams, which I hope we can make come true.

John Smit: For years we stood shoulder to shoulder, working together through the good and the bad times, but also the fun times. Thanks, I've learnt so much from you. For eight years you were a pillar of strength for the Boks, and for that I salute and thank you.

Fourie du Preez: As captain of the Bulls, I was given a lot of the credit for the successes we achieved over the past few years, but you were always there beside me, ready with words of advice or to take action so that we could make the best decision possible. Without you, my task as captain would have been much more difficult. Thanks for all the long talks about the game and about life. Thanks for being such an unbelievable friend. Make sure you save enough money in Japan, because we still have a lot of golf to play – and, after all, you know who usually takes your money!

My parents: Dad, Mom ... thanks for the best education a child could hope for. A solid home is built on a strong foundation, and thanks to you I have a steady base on which I can build my life. Dad, thanks for the long hours you shared with me in my sporting life, whether in the cricket nets, on the golf course or in the backyard when, as a little boy, I climbed up and down a pole to strengthen my muscles for rugby.

Mom, no matter what I was going through, you were always there with a word of advice, offering unconditional support. Thanks for making me study for all those long hours and for all the times you sat next to my bed when I was sick. Mom, you taught me what love and discipline are. Thanks for the thousands of kilometres both you and Dad travelled to support me on the playing fields, from Pietersburg to Kimberley and beyond. It was always comforting to know that you were there. In times of disappointment, you always lifted my spirits. It really meant the world to me. And it was very special to have both of you in Paris in 2007 when we won the World Cup.

My sister, Trudie: Thanks for the love and support and the sacrifices you had to make for me to become successful. It could not always have been easy being my sister, but you wished me only the best. And thank you for always being there to look after Mom and Dad.

My dearest Monja: It must have been difficult to let this young, arrogant rugby player into your life. You made me wait a long time before you let me take you out, but the wait was worth it. Who knows what would have happened to me if you hadn't come along to straighten me out. You brought calmness and balance to my life, and showed me that there is more to life than just rugby. It could not have been easy being married to a rugby player, especially after the births of Jaime and Giselle, as you were often left at home alone and had to deal with the girls on your own, through sickness and tantrums. You often slept with them in another room the day before a game, just so I could get a decent night's sleep. How can you thank someone properly for making so many sacrifices?

On days following a disappointing performance on the field, I often just wanted to stay at home and cry. You were always there to cry with me, or to try to lift my spirits. And what about the times after we'd won a tournament when the whole team would come to our house to celebrate? At those times you were always calm and relaxed, making sure that everyone was happy and content – and this while we were celebrating and acting silly.

There were many other sacrifices you made so that I could be successful. I cannot begin to tell you how much I appreciate your support. I am looking forward to all the wonderful things we as a family will now be able to do.

Last but not least, my two princesses, Jaime and Giselle: You are the biggest gifts a dad could ask for. I love you so very much. Never again do you have to count the days until your daddy comes home. I will try my very best to be the best dad in the world for you both.

VICTOR MATFIELD
PRETORIA
OCTOBER 2011

Author's note

After the 2011 World Cup, the Springbok captain, John Smit, said Victor Matfield was probably the best Bok rugby player of all time. I agree.

Having said that, I must add that I do not possess an extensive frame of reference. I vaguely remember how, when I was very little, my dad and I tuned into a radio station to listen to commentary of the 1981 Springbok tour to New Zealand, and how, later, we went to Loftus Saturday after Saturday to support the Blue Bulls. So my rugby recollections do not go back much further than the time of Naas Botha, Danie Gerber and Carel du Plessis. And this is the thing: one tends to remember the big point-scorers, the try maestros, the guys with true flair.

Victor will forgive me for not putting him in one of these categories. But he will always stand out as one of South Africa's rugby geniuses, a player with an unmatched work ethic, a guy who early on in his career realised that raw talent alone is not good enough if you want to become the best and stay the best.

I remember my very first interview with Victor vividly. It was in 2001, after a Blue Bulls training session at Loftus. He was in an ice bath – a wheelie bin filled with water and ice cubes. I asked him about the rumours that he was considering moving from Pretoria to Cape Town. He had a bemused look on his face when he answered: 'Ag no, I'm not going anywhere. There's work that needs to be done here.' Prophetic words, indeed.

Firstly, I want to thank Victor. When he asked me if I wanted to write this book, I was taken by surprise, as I never expected this honour to come my way. Thanks for trusting me to tackle this project with you. I hope you like the end product. I will always look back fondly on the 16 months between June 2010 and October 2011 when we worked on the book. (And I'm ready for the next one … you've got my number!)

Monja, Jaime and Giselle: thanks for inviting me into your home and sharing Victor with me over so many weekends. It was always a pleasure to visit your home!

Thanks, Oom Fai and Tannie Hettie (Victor's parents), who, together with Monja, shared so many stories and memories with me. Tannie Hettie's comprehensive scrapbooks made it so much easier for me to research Victor's early rugby career.

I was lucky to learn a lot from a whole bunch of colleagues at Rugby365.com, *Beeld*, *Rapport* and the South African Rugby Union (SARU). It is impossible to name everyone, but I'll try my best (in alphabetical order). If I've left someone out, please forgive me; it was not intentional: Rayaan Adriaanse, Hennie Brandt, Shelley Carmichael, Andy Colquhoun, Jan de Koning, Wilhelm de Swardt, Louis de Villiers, Paul Dobson, Bokkie Gerber, Morris Gilbert, JJ Harmse, Howard Kahn, Rudolph Lake, Brenden Nel, Stephen Nell, Vata Ngobeni, Herbert Pretorius, Craig Ray, Gert van der Westhuizen and Simnikiwe Xabanisa.

Victor's agent, Gerrie Swart, thank you for all your good advice. I would also like to thank the staff of Zebra Press – Marlene Fryer, Ronel Richter-Herbert, Robert Plummer and Kim Taylor – for their help and support, as well as my editor with the sharp eye and tons of patience, Tobie Wiese, and translator, Pieter Redelinghuys.

To my parents, the late Niek and Isabel Borchardt, who set the perfect example for the unbelievable journey that my life has become, as well as my two wonderful sisters, Carin and Nina: I cannot thank you enough for the belief you had in me, and all your support over the years. Without you, I would not be sitting here typing. I hope I have made you proud.

Last, but certainly not least, I would like to thank the most patient woman on earth, my wife, Zelda. Without you, I would not have completed this project. Thanks for your unconditional love, for believing in me, and for the inspiration and willingness to share me with Victor and my computer – and all this while our newborn, Tiaan, was becoming a feisty little live wire with a mind of his own.

I dedicate this book to you both.

DE JONGH BORCHARDT
CAPE TOWN
OCTOBER 2011

1

An early lesson

It's a cold winter's morning on the Highveld and the rugby field behind the Pietersburg Golf Club, where we'll be running on any moment, is covered in a crisp, white layer of frost. Groups of parents, warming themselves with steaming cups of coffee, have gathered to watch their youngsters play in an important match.

It's not pleasant running barefoot onto an icy field, but rugby is, after all, a game for tough guys. So we're not complaining. Besides, I'm the captain and eighthman of Noordskool's (Pietersburg North Primary) under-8 team. I have to set the example. I look down at my feet – bigger than most of the guys on my team. I'm also taller and stronger than my peers, and I realise that on this day I have to be a true leader.

We are playing our arch-enemy from the other side of town – Oosskool, as Pietersburg East Primary was commonly known. I size up our opponents. They look bigger than the lot of us, and I know they play good rugby. But we're not too shabby either.

But before long we're behind our own posts for the umpteenth time as Oosskool's flyhalf places the ball to convert yet another try. His teammates all sport happy smiles. There's no scoreboard, but I know we're trailing by at least 30 to 40 points.

I call the guys to form a circle. I am the captain, and the captain needs to say something, right now.

'Boys, when that final whistle goes, we run,' I command. 'We run over there, behind the pavilion. We don't shake their hands, we just go.'

I couldn't think of anything else to say. To lose is a terrible thing. And it doesn't help that your dad is a big shot in Far North schoolboy rugby and principal of the primary school you attend.

When the whistle eventually goes, we make a beeline for the cover of the pavilion. I'm leading, with the team hot on my heels. A feeling of freedom and intense relief fills me as I make my getaway. My plan has saved us from further humiliation.

But I'm not fast enough. And it's not the referee or supporters of Oosskool that chase after us. It's my mom, Hettie. She's furious and speeding towards me like a fleet-footed winger, her target all too obvious: my right ear.

She grabs hold of it and gives it a good pinch before the lecture begins. 'Victor, you turn back this instant, go and find each player on that team, shake their hand and tell them they played well. The same goes for their coach. And then you thank the referee for the game. If you don't go back right now, I'll see to it that you never play rugby again.'

Bit of an overreaction, I think, but I know Mom when she's this serious. And above all, I know she is right. So I turn back and start looking for the Oosskool team.

I'm still down in the dumps when my parents drive me home later that day. Not my best day – first a massive pummelling on the field, then a proper dressing-down from my mother. But there is one more unpleasant surprise in store.

As soon as we arrive home, I am told to go to the bathroom. I know all too well what this means. A hiding on the rugby field isn't pleasant, but this is going to be in a different league altogether. No running away from this one; I have to face a thorough spanking, dished out by my dad.

Moments like these stay with you for a lifetime. Although I didn't realise it then, I learnt a valuable lesson on that fateful day: sportsmanship is more important than winning or losing. In rugby, it's as important to win graciously as it is to lose with dignity.

Thanks, Mom!

***

I was born on 11 May 1977 in Pietersburg (now Polokwane). My dad, Fai, was a primary-school teacher, and our family stayed in the school hostel on the grounds. Ever since I can remember, I went to watch rugby games with my dad or played rugby with my school buddies. As I wasn't in secondary school yet and was younger than most of the other boys who'd been playing rugby for Noordskool, every now and then I was the target of bullies. Sometimes the bullying was quite heavy, but I never complained. Who wants to be called a softie anyway?

Besides, I wasn't really all that small. I shot up at an early age and quickly outgrew boys my own age. Even when I was in Grade 1, I was ready to use my mitts when other boys wanted to bully me. I always stood my ground and remember socking one of the troublemakers on one occasion. For this, my sister, Trudie, a prefect in Standard 5 (now Grade 7), had to take me to the headmaster's office. But I was much faster than her, so that was one tanning I managed to dodge.

Sport played an important role in our household. Both my parents excelled at it and believed a healthy body hosted a healthy mind. I didn't complain because it meant that my friends and I could play outside all day long. Pietersburg had an ideal climate for active youngsters. It was seldom so cold or wet that you had to stay indoors. Toy cars and *He-Man* or *A-Team* figurines were never my bag. I was perfectly happy with my Super Springbok rugby ball, Gray-Nicolls cricket bat and ProKennex tennis racket. That was how my leisure time was spent.

My dad encouraged me to form my own opinions. Whether on a sports field or on holiday, we always discussed various issues. I had the right to disagree with him, but I had to come up with a solid argument if I wanted to convince him. We debated like friends, not like father and son.

People from Pietersburg were commonly thought to be country bumpkins. Even though the town had no big shopping malls or cinemas, I was certainly not a yokel. Yes, we shot air guns and wielded clay sticks, but sport was the number-one priority.

I played cricket with my dad and tennis with my mother. Or my buddies and I kicked and passed a rugby ball and teased Trudie. That's all I knew and understood. But sport was my dream. That was all I was really interested in.

In primary school I played eighthman, but I also enjoyed cricket. And tennis. And athletics. And golf. Any sport, really. Growing up next to a sports field had its advantages. Holidays were long and packed with sports. My dad even installed a cricket net and a bowling machine in our backyard. It wasn't unusual for us to spend four to five hours in the nets, just my dad and me. Breakfast, nets, lunch, nets. What a pleasure and a privilege!

Birthday presents always consisted of a new cricket bat, rugby ball or tennis racket, and it was much the same at Christmas time. I was good at sport and had excellent ball sense. But there was that rivalry with the guys from Oosskool. We just couldn't beat them. We were now the under-11 team and had an away game against them – the biggest game of the season. This time we held our own, and at half-time the score was still 0-all. I knew I had to do something to break the dead-lock, but I wasn't sure what. Forwards usually drive and maul with the ball, but I decided if Naas Botha could do it, so could I – even as an eighthman. We were awarded a free kick, and I took a quick tap and, like a proper flyhalf, let rip with a mighty drop kick. The ball sailed high and straight and cleared the crossbar by some distance. Over! We were in the lead. Now we had to defend like never before.

To this day I don't know how it happened. In the dying seconds, Oosskool somehow crashed over for a try to claim victory. I was gutted. We'd lost again, this time 3-4. 'I hate this feeling,' I thought as I walked over to shake hands with their coach, the referee and the *whole* damn Oosskool team.

***

I was playing good rugby, and I enjoyed athletics as well. As shot-putter in the under-11 and under-12 age groups, I even secured a podium place at the South African nationals. Cricket, though, was my big passion. I was a batsman who could bowl fast and a fast bowler who could bat well. I was the star of the team and was awarded provincial colours in Grades 6 and 7.

Still, I was a nervous wreck when it came to the announcement of the Craven Week rugby squad. I had heard that people were saying things behind my back. As a teacher, my dad was involved with school sport in Pietersburg, and he was also the convener of the selection committee.

When they announced Far North's under-13 Craven Week squad, my name wasn't on the list as eighthman. I was stunned. It was true that the other boys in my age group had caught up with me in size, but I knew that I was good enough to have been picked. Earlier that season, in the nationals, I had finished last in the shot put, a discipline I usually dominated because of my bigger physique. But now, something else was going on.

Perhaps I didn't make the team because of professional rivalry over my dad's position. But I just couldn't understand why I hadn't been selected. All I knew for certain was that I was in the squad as the reserve hooker. Number 18.

Some people whispered that I was in the squad only because my dad was the coach. And, they said, I was the head prefect because my dad was the headmaster of the school. This upset me a great deal. I had always been a quiet boy; I knew my place and didn't even date yet. But this experience led me to make a decision: I would prove the gossip-mongers wrong, even if it took me 20 years.

***

My mom was a teacher at Tom Naudé, the technical high school in Pietersburg. Tom Naudé's boys played in brown rugby jerseys and for years were almost unbeatable. A boy called Frans Ludeke captained the first team. At the end of Grade 7, I pleaded with my parents to enrol me at the school. As primary-school boys, we had all supported the teams of Tom Naudé.

However, after only a week's attendance, I realised that this wasn't the school for me. I was out of my depth at a technical school. To this day I can't even fix a faulty wall plug. When it comes to that sort of thing, I've got 10 thumbs! So instead I enrolled at Pietersburg High School, or PHS, as it was known then.

All the boys from the Oosskool side who'd beaten us year after year also attended PHS. And even though I had been the head prefect in primary school, suddenly I was a nobody – the Oosskool guys were the big shots. We were 13, 14 years old, but the Oosskool boys were young men by then. My voice hadn't even broken yet.

In those years, I wasn't much of a rugby player. There was nothing wrong with my skills – I was just too small. First I was moved from eighthman to lock, even though I was one of the smallest forwards.

I wasn't strong enough to play in the front row, and I was too slow for the backline.

Luckily, there was cricket. I was the opening bowler and batsman of the A-side. I was also picked for the Far North provincial side – this time for the under-15 squad. In Grade 10, I was picked again, and also in Grade 11 and matric. My last year of playing in the Country Districts Tournament went really well, as the runs were flowing and the wickets were falling. As a result, my nerves were shot by the time they announced the national Country Districts side. I knew I had a good chance to play in the Nuffield Week.

But, yet again, I didn't make the final squad. How was that possible?

Some people alleged that I hadn't been picked because I'd played in a rugby match on Transvaal Unions Day, when I'd accepted an offer to move to Pretoria after matric to play for the Blue Bulls. This was incorrect, but there was nothing I could do to set the record straight. And maybe the 'people' had a point. I had injured my back and couldn't bowl to my full potential. Rugby was the logical alternative, even though this didn't make me feel any less disappointed.

On the rugby front, things were also changing. I had gone through a growth spurt and was now bigger than the boys who'd been bigger than me. However, I didn't captain the team any more, as Oosskool's Walter Campbell-McGeachy had assumed that role since Grade 8. We had played against each other at primary-school level, but now we were teammates. As the captain of the team, he was the fast one, the one who scored most of the tries. Those were the deciding factors when a captain was picked.

Our under-15 side at PHS played good rugby. Most of the team consisted of the guys from Oosskool, but a few of us from Noordskool also made the side. Luckily, my teammates didn't remember what I'd done after that fateful game as under-8 captain!

After a great season in 1992, we reached the semi-finals of the Director's Trophy Tournament – not too shabby for a small-town school that had to play against big, prestigious schools from Johannesburg and Pretoria.

Because my birthday is in May, I was too old for the under-15 side in my Grade 10 year in 1993, so I had to take a step up to senior level.

I'd lie if I said I was looking forward to battling it out with the matrics in the side. For a while I was only making PHS's third and fourth teams. The thirds lacked a decent lock – height wasn't such an important requirement – and I decided that that was going to be my position. It was a great year and I enjoyed my rugby tremendously.

At the end of Grade 10, I went through another major physical change. I bulked up quite a bit, thanks to lots of *pap* and hard training, and I acquired the ideal height and weight for a sturdy No. 4 lock (the stronger and less athletic of the two), and made the first team. That year, PHS had another great run at the Director's Trophy Tournament, but lost against Affies (Afrikaanse Hoër Seunskool in Pretoria) in the finals. Quite a number of the guys who played against us in that match would later become my teammates at Tukkies and the Blue Bulls. But this was still 1994 – a very enjoyable year for me. I was once again picked for the Far North side, but this time as No. 4, not No. 18!

***

My matric year kicked off in the usual way: athletics, cricket and, of course, a bit of schoolwork. Even though I considered sport to be the cornerstone of my existence, my parents always emphasised the importance of a good education. I had a knack for figures – I just 'got' them. Maths came naturally, just as deciding on and deciphering line-out codes would. Languages, on the other hand, were not my cup of tea. Nevertheless, no one complained about my academic results.

I probably did well because I wasn't distracted by the average matric boy's interests – parties and girls. They weren't high on my priority list – yet. Make no mistake, there were parties, and I hardly spent a Saturday evening alone at home, but I was innocence personified. When there was a party and my buddies downed beers and ciders to impress the girls, I was the responsible one that drove them around. Those days were filled with good, clean fun; even a shy bloke like me had a good time.

I passed matric with distinctions in mathematics, science and accountancy. Working hard wasn't a foreign concept to me and I enjoyed the challenge. But rugby ruled my world. Although I still played cricket, a back injury had forced me to concentrate more on batting. It didn't bother me, though, because all I really wanted to do was play rugby.

In 1995 PHS had a super season and gave some strong performances in the Far North league, but the wheels came off against Potgietersrus in the semi-finals. It was quite disappointing, as the year before we had made it all the way to the final of the Director's Trophy.

The Far North trials were up next, and in those days all the schools gathered on a Saturday to compete in a normal league fixture, after which six trial squads were announced. The previous year, in Grade 11, I was chosen for the Craven Week side, but this time I was only good enough for the Far North's D-side. How did this happen?

It seemed that there were a lot of complaints about my game: I played too loose; I was constantly in the backline; I didn't do the hard yards expected from a lock forward. The tears flowed, as I was extremely disappointed, but my parents continued to encourage me. 'A place in the D-side is better than nothing. Go and do what you know you can do,' was their advice.

That was exactly what I did. And, as they say, all's well that ends well. Before long, I was in the B-side. When the final Craven Week squad was eventually announced, I was picked – not as a hooker, but as a reserve lock. And again at No. 18! For me, 18 was becoming a 'lucky unlucky' number.

Were it not for Piet Oberholzer, our first-team coach, I would probably not have made the squad. Again, as in previous years, some people thought I didn't deserve a place in the side, but Piet believed in me and fought hard to get me into the Far North squad. Thanks to him, 18 was my lucky number this time round.

Shortly before the start of Craven Week, during the annual Unions Day Tournament, I had made an impression on the late Zandberg Jansen, in those days a flamboyant television rugby commentator. He was the guy who coined the phrase 'nag, ou grote' (goodnight, old chap) and was the first rugby pundit to predict that I had a bright future as a player. Zandberg even said that I could be a blindside flanker for the Springboks one day!

For one of South Africa's most respected students of the game to say this about me was a tremendous boost. Every youngster who's ever picked up a rugby ball in this country dreams of playing for the Boks one day. So when Zandberg spotted me, I realised that fulfilling the dream might be a possibility.

That year, in the Craven Week in Bloemfontein, I made the starting line-up in most of the games, and I played well. As a result, I was picked for the Northern Unions side, followed by a place in the SA Academy squad. So, in the end, it was indeed a case of all's well that ends well – even though I wasn't selected for the SA Schools side. The SA Schools locks in 1995 were Northern Free State's Jaco Barnard and Western Transvaal's Gerrie Theron, while Northern Transvaal's Chrisjan van der Westhuizen was picked as the reserve. Morné Engelbrecht, also from Western Transvaal, was my lock partner in the Academy and Unions sides.

Here I also met up with an old cricket buddy of mine: a nippy and attacking flyhalf from South Eastern Transvaal called Jaco van der Westhuyzen. We'd met each other in passing before, but became firm friends after this. We were both quite shy, but as a brilliant flyhalf, he got more attention than me. He was also the better-looking one. I wasn't the first guy the girls ogled – at two metres tall and weighing in at 112 kilograms. Even though I gained a reputation for being a bit of a 'pretty boy' in later years, this wasn't the case at all in my matric year.

With the Northern Unions side about to take on the SA Schools side at Newlands, we set off for Cape Town, all wide-eyed and innocent. We narrowly lost the game 0-5. That evening we went to the Waterfront to watch a movie and play video games. While we drank soft drinks and milkshakes, some of the boys were hitting the bottle hard. On the way back to the hotel, Jaco and I sat at the front of the bus. At the back, the other guys were partying like there was no tomorrow. Most of them were Lions players, and the hooker, André van Niekerk, and eighthman, Sean Raubenheimer, were the ringleaders.

When our team manager, Theo Pieterse, told them to behave, they just swore at him. Jaco and I were speechless. How could matric boys drink so much and swear at an adult? That was just wrong. With the aftertaste of milkshake and waffles still in my mouth, my eyes were opened that night in Cape Town.

I was a dedicated child. I worked hard at school and on the sports field and was always considered the responsible one, even by my friends' parents. I never danced at parties, preferring to stand on the sidelines with a Coke in my hand.

I had my parents to thank for my good behaviour, although my dad also taught me to be competitive, whether it be on the golf course in Port Edward, in a game of table tennis at the TO holiday resort on the Natal South Coast or in a game of pool at the local café. We even competed for the best waves whenever we were able to enjoy a bit of surfing. My mother, on the other hand, kept me fit and active with swimming and athletics. And my parents accompanied me to every sporting event; they were always on the sidelines when I competed. I'll never forget how they once fried an ostrich egg right next to the field when we were on a cricket tour to Oudtshoorn – there was enough to feed the whole team.

Those were good days. Much like the day we had run away after being beaten by Oosskool's under-8s, I also learnt a valuable lesson in high school. To inspire us, Mr Tiaan Lee, our third-team coach at PHS, quoted legendary heavyweight boxing champ Muhammad Ali: 'Champions train when the others rest.' Years later, this would become the foundation of my sporting philosophy.

But before I could start thinking like a true champion, I had to prepare myself to leave the nest in Pietersburg.

2

Headed for bigger things

The Blue Bulls Rugby Union approached me shortly after the 1995 Unions Day Tournament at Loftus Versfeld and asked me to join the franchise after I finished matric. Although most of my friends were considering 'normal' jobs, I had realised that sport was also an option as a career.

In those days, the newspapers were reporting on guys like François Pienaar, Joost van der Westhuizen and Sean Fitzpatrick, who would soon be playing rugby for serious money. The Springboks had just won the World Cup and, according to reports, all the players were to become overnight millionaires. There was even talk about rebel leagues as rugby outgrew its amateur status and rapidly embraced the professional era.

South Africa had been swept away by rugby euphoria. I had watched the World Cup final with a few buddies from school, as well as Fred van Rheede from Oudtshoorn and Eugene Henning, who would later work as a lawyer for the commercial arm of the South African Rugby Players' Association (SARPA). We'd all got together at the house of a friend, Imke Lombard, in Pietersburg. As a serious rugby player who dreamt of becoming a Springbok one day, I was ecstatic when President Nelson Mandela handed François Pienaar the William Webb Ellis Cup.

Like the rest of the country, we took to the streets, waving our flags and partying till all hours. For the first time I saw whites and blacks join hands as fellow South Africans in celebration of this gigantic sporting moment. This was only a year after our first democratic elections of 1994, but the signs seemed to indicate that we'd be all right. It was also about a year after many Afrikaners had started hoarding tinned food in case of a civil war breaking out if the ANC won the general elections. Who would have thought that in the future I, too, would become involved in similar acts of nation building in another World Cup?

In between festivities and studying for my final exams, the Bulls offered me a very enticing deal, though I didn't know exactly what they expected me to deliver in return. I was, however, more than willing to listen to what they had to say.

I was offered a junior contract that included a full study bursary from the University of Pretoria and a salary of R500 a month, which wasn't quite what the Pienaars and Van der Westhuizens of the world were earning. For a young matriculant from PHS, however, it was a small fortune. I accepted their offer and, after matriculating, set off for Pretoria. I enrolled for a B.Comm. degree in accounting and took up residence in Huis Boekenhout, which was on campus. In those years, Boekenhout dominated student rugby at Tuks and also offered preferential accommodation to boys from Pietersburg.

Early in 1996 it felt like I had the world at my feet. I had big dreams and couldn't wait to find out what varsity life was all about. I had been a quiet, reserved child at school who never touched alcohol. This state of affairs, however, would soon change. On arrival at Boekenhout, I was cut down to size in no time at all. The targets of the seniors were the first-year students who had played for SA Schools or the SA Academy sides, and it was no use trying to hide – especially someone like me, who stood two metres tall! Initiation was as much a part of res life as the idle chit-chat around the tea urn and lazing on campus lawns between classes.

On the first day, while we were preparing ourselves for initiation, I met Bossie, a bloke from Pretoria. Bossie was quite rowdy for a first-year. He smirked at the seniors and wasn't fazed when they barked out orders. At one stage we all had to do push-ups, but Bossie stood to one side and smoked a cigarette. As this got us into even more trouble with the seniors, we weren't very pleased with Bossie, to say the least.

The first chance we got, my room-mate, François du Randt, and I got hold of Bossie and told him to 'get with the programme' or suffer the consequences. I weighed almost 120 kilograms and François was a bulky provincial flanker from South Eastern Transvaal (later the Mpumalanga

Pumas), so we weren't exactly the smallest guys in the res. We would sort Bossie out in a flash if he carried on taunting the seniors.

To our amazement, we saw Bossie the following morning chilling with the seniors in Hall B2. This was the turf of all the big blokes and the rugby players who were initiating the first-years. Bossie called me over and in no uncertain terms explained whom I was actually talking to. His real name was Riaan Boshoff and he wasn't a first-year student, but a senior in Boekenhout. I got an earful from him, and to add insult to injury, I was accused of having tried to chat up his girlfriend during the matric holidays!

Bossie was, in fact, a second-year student who had been 'planted' among the first-years to cause trouble for us. Much later Bossie and I both stayed in B2 and formed a friendship that lasts to this day. He even introduced me to my future wife. Apart from Bossie's troublemaking, the initiation period was a great deal of fun, as it should be. We were given a hard time, but it was all in good spirit.

I really enjoyed my days as a student. My parents had bought me a cellphone – one of those old bricks – and I chatted to them three or four times a week. They were still important people in my life, even though I'd left the nest. I was excited about my studies, and because I had a head for numbers, I was keen to learn accountancy and study business finance.

I hadn't moved to Pretoria only to study, though – I also wanted to play rugby. As a kid growing up in the protected environment of Pietersburg, I'd been excited but also a bit apprehensive about leaving home; but getting involved with the Blue Bulls was a massive drawing card. My whole life I had passionately supported the Bulls, and now I had the chance to wear the famous light-blue jersey with the red Barberton daisy.

I also joined Boekenhout's rugby team and soon played my first game in their turquoise jersey. The whole res packed one side of the field, while the opposing team's supporters watched from the other side. I was quickly nicknamed 'No. 11' by some wisecracking senior, and not because of the number on my back, but because I had such skinny legs!

As a former Craven Week player and a contracted player for the Blue Bulls, it was interesting for me to see what student rugby was all about. Even though I would never play for Boekenhout again, as I was called up for Tuks under-21 duty after that game, the spirit of student rugby was so contagious that I seldom missed a res game as a spectator over the next three years. And as a supporter on the sideline, I also had the opportunity to chirp the players on the field.

I found it a massive step to go almost directly from schoolboy rugby to the Tuks under-21 side. Our first match was against Potchefstroom's Pukke, and my nerves were shattered the night before the encounter. But before I could ponder the challenge ahead, a senior nicknamed 'Botter' and a couple of guys from B2 were at my door. They were in a foul mood. And hungry.

I was ordered to go and buy 'ballas chips' (literally, scrotum chips) for them. This heavily spiced, deep-fried 'delicacy' was sold at Cool Cats Café in Lynnwood Road. It was close to the res, so I shook a leg. After finishing their meal, Botter and the boys weren't impressed enough, so they decided to further initiate this 'arrogant rugby player'.

I was ordered to do the notorious 'duck walk', which basically entailed a person going down on his haunches and shuffling forward up and down the hallway – 50 metres there, 50 metres back. I had to repeat this five or six times until the seniors were happy and I was allowed to go and get some sleep, aching muscles and all.

Game day – whether you are playing for the Tuks under-21 side or the Boks – is a major event, and you have to be focused, mentally alert and in peak physical condition, or you simply won't be able to perform at your best. But I could hardly walk the next morning, let alone run or jump in the line-outs. On the bus on the way to Potch I knew that I had a big problem and tried my best to massage the stiffness from my thighs, but of course it was of no use and my first game for Tuks was not exactly a great success.

The result was that I was dropped to the under-21 B-side, but not before my very first 'rugby kontiki', or initiation. The 'ceremony' was held at the Impala Hotel in Potchefstroom, where I was forced to down a few glasses of either a salt-and-soap-water mixture or beer. So I drank beer for the first time in my life. And it was really nice. I had two beers that evening and felt fantastic. I must have been a bit tipsy, because I even made my debut on a club dance floor that evening.

I played a number of games for the Tuks under-21 B-side, but because I was under contract with the Bulls, I still had to report for practice at Loftus Versfeld as well. Then I was picked for the provincial under-21 A-side. I guess I was lucky because Morné Engelbrecht, who had been my teammate in the Union and SA Academy sides in 1995, was the SA under-19 lock at that stage. While Morné was doing national duty, I had the chance to stake my claim in the Bulls under-21 side, so that I was already settled in the starting line-up when he came back. It was the start of three good years with the Bulls under-21s, and I played in all the matches.

Steve Butler was the coach for the under-21 As and he liked my style of playing. Although I only ran out for the Tuks B-side, he didn't hesitate to pick me for his A-team. Those days, weighing 120 kilograms, I was the biggest guy in the front row, and the heavier of the lock forwards is traditionally the one who jumps at the front and takes the quick, low line-out throws and is not lifted as high as the middle jumper.

But Stephen Temple was my lock partner in the under-21 side, and although we were both typical No. 4 locks, he'd been in the squad longer than me and jumped at the front of the line-out. I therefore had to exchange my beloved No. 4 jersey for No. 5 and move to the middle of the line-out.

I learnt a great deal from the senior players. There was also the tough Carlton League – a physical training school where you quickly got to know what senior rugby was all about. Your opponents were big, hard men who took great pleasure in teaching the young, 'clever' university boys a lesson or two. Luckily, we had two Blue Bull props, Pierre Ribbens and Piet Boer, for protection, but it still wasn't easy. I had to take on guys like Police Rugby Club locks Johan Ackerman and Casper Oosthuizen, and Ralph Schroeder and Botha Rossouw of Normaal Kollege Pretoria (NKP).

My debut game for the Tuks first team was against NKP, where I had to compete against Botha, who'd played for the Springboks, and Ralph, a massive fellow who reputedly enjoyed unnerving his opponents with his physical approach. Before the game, Pierre and Piet told me, 'Don't worry.' That was the full extent of their advice. Years later Ralph and I would play against each other again, but I showed him then that I wasn't the kid from 1997 any more.

Pierre dubbed me Victor 'Hatfield', either because he had misheard my surname or confused me with the Pretoria suburb of the same name, where we often went to party. I looked up to Pierre, and in later years we became good mates.

Although rugby was a big priority in my first year at Tuks, I also studied hard. Besides one or two subjects I carried over in my first two years at varsity, everything went swimmingly.

In my third year I was called up to the Blue Bulls senior side. We had practice between eight and ten o'clock every morning for the Vodacom Cup competition; then I went to class, after which I had Bulls under-21 practice in the afternoon. And, after that, Tuks rugby practice. So it was practice, practice, practice!

Although I was the Boekenhout house-committee member for sport and stayed in B2, I never attended a class in my third year. I wanted to pursue rugby as a career, which meant that I had to choose rugby above completing my final-year studies. I couldn't excel at both rugby and studying. As a 20-year-old, it was an easy decision to make, but if I look back now, perhaps I should rather have completed my studies. It's a mistake many young rugby players make. Setting your studies aside may be the easier option at the time, but it's not necessarily the right one.

Having said that, I didn't just stroll into the Bulls Vodacom Cup team. I was a talented under-21 lock, but I was up for selection against the hardened warhorses of the Carlton League. Although I'd already run out for the Bulls under-21s, it was my dream to be selected for the senior side, and playing in my first game for the Vodacom Cup team was, therefore, a major moment in my life. The Bulls had been my team ever since I could remember, and it was very special to slip on that light-blue jersey.

Sometimes the under-21s had to join the senior guys at practice, among them old hands like Ruben Kruger and Joost van der West-huizen. They were seasoned Boks and tough guys, and we were pretty apprehensive. They didn't take any nonsense from the youngsters. The difference in status between senior and junior rugby was very clear. Although we seldom played against the senior players, they often sum-moned us for practice sessions and trials.

During one of those practice sessions, shortly after the SA under-21 trials, they wanted me to do fitness training with them. I protested. I'd just played 80 minutes of rugby and was tired. But Ruben and Joost wouldn't take no for an answer and gave me a good talking-to.

Mondays were set aside for trials. Two days after a tough league game – whether for the senior side or the under-21s – and you had to play another 80 minutes of full-contact rugby, but nobody held back. As youngsters, we quite often had to stand in for injured senior players, and in many instances the trials were tougher than league matches, as everyone had something to prove. Fists would fly …

In one line-out session against the senior side, Jaco Barnard and I were doing really well against our opposing locks, Krynauw Otto and Wium Basson. I managed to steal a couple of Krynauw's line-out balls and was getting quite chuffed with myself. Krynauw, on the other hand, didn't take kindly to this. When I nicked the next throw-in, it was the final straw. My feet barely touched the playing surface before Krynauw let rip with an uppercut. The message was clear: know your place, youngster.

That's just how it was.

Those exhausting sessions contributed to my decision to give up my studies. I stayed on in Boekenhout, but just played rugby. I had more money than my friends in the res (never enough, though – typical student), without the stress of studying. What a wonderful life for a young man! I was paid R1 000 a month – soon increased to R1 500 – for playing in the Vodacom Cup, which was a lot of disposable cash for a 'student'. Add to this the match fees for Tuks and the Bulls under-21s … I also had few expenses, as my studies and accommodation were paid for.

Money opened doors, and my friends shared in my wealth. I liked to spoil them, and the nickname Victor 'Hatfield' finally rang true. Although I knew my limitations and never partied during the week, weekends were a different story altogether, especially after a rugby game, when I could really relax. Then the evenings would start off with tequila and Ströh rum, just to get into the spirit of things … I always tried to be responsible, though – as a professional rugby player, you just had to be.

Riaan Olckers, my big buddy at the time and a Blue Bulls teammate, and I quickly perfected the art of attracting the attention of the fairer sex. After weekend games we'd hit the town in our formal team colours and, as soon as the girls showed an interest, we'd give them one of our Blue Bulls ties. We had to ask the team manager for a new tie every second week. He complained, of course, that his whole budget was being blown on replacing our ties.

I met my first steady girlfriend at the Sports Frog, a pub in Hatfield. If Therese le Clus had known then how badly I would behave at times, she would not have given me the time of day. Back then I didn't know much about girls, but Pretoria was a strange place: if you played rugby for the Bulls – even if it was only for the under-21 team – the girls were interested in you. Of course, later on I found out that Pretoria wasn't unique in that regard.

Initially, Therese wasn't very keen on me, but a few days after our introduction at the Sports Frog we bumped into each other again, and this time she showed more interest. I thought she was the prettiest girl in the world, but of course there were other beauties as well …

Poor Therese had to endure a lot. She once drove from Pretoria to Cape Town to support me in an SA under-21 game, but afterwards I left her at the hotel and went out to party with the rest of the team. In later years, I could hardly believe that I'd done such a thing.

Therese was a flight attendant, so she was away a lot. Whenever she was out of town, other girls provided some distraction. Eventually Therese got wind of my shenanigans and confronted me. We were in a park in Lynnwood and sat down to have a chat. I was ready to deny everything and cut her down to size, but while Therese bombarded me with questions, she wasn't antagonistic at all.

'I'm not angry,' she said, 'just disappointed. I hope you don't treat your future girlfriends or your wife the way you treated me.' It completely took the wind out of my sails. Therese was very sad and ended our relationship of five years there and then. It broke my heart, but I could hardly blame her, as I was the one who had treated her badly. To this day I regret what I did to her and still feel bad about it.

Therese's words that day in the park in Pretoria made me realise that I couldn't just treat women – or anyone else, for that matter – without consideration. Your conscience won't allow it. I learnt a sad and costly lesson; one that I'll never forget. When I look back on those days, I can see how badly I behaved. It's often difficult for a young player who is barely out of matric and suddenly in the 'limelight' to keep a level head. You've got more money than your buddies, and beautiful girls pay you a lot of attention, but you're not properly equipped or mature enough to deal with it all. A great many young players completely lose the plot early on in their careers because of this.

We always used to laugh whenever the senior guys gave us the 'Springbok speech', a lecture on the pitfalls we, as youngsters, should avoid. Still, it seemed as if most of them had also learnt these lessons the hard way. Years later, I would be the one giving the 'Springbok speech' to the next generation of youngsters.

During Rag at the beginning of my third year, I'd noticed a beautiful blonde girl by the name of Monja Bekker, a first-year student in the Jasmyn residence. Although we were introduced, nothing further happened at the time ...

***

More rugby also meant more games, and more travelling locally and, eventually, abroad. By 1997 I'd played for the SA under-21s, along with guys like Bob Skinstad, John Smit, Hottie Louw, Breyton Paulse, Jaco van der Westhuyzen, Lawrence Sephaka, Shaun Sowerby, Danie Coetzee, Boela du Plooy, André Pretorius, Conrad Jantjes and Johan Roets.

In 1997, I also embarked on my first overseas tour as a member of Bob Skinstad's under-21 side to compete in a southern hemisphere tournament in Australia. Bob became our tour leader Down Under, as he was more experienced in the ways of the world than the rest of the group. Our first encounter was a warm-up game against Western Australia's senior team in Perth, which we won easily (44-18). I even scored one of our five tries! The rest of the tour, however, was a disaster. We lost all our games in Sydney – against Argentina, New Zealand and Australia. Fortunately, the excitement of touring overseas for the first time partly made up for the poor results.

I also experienced the New Zealand *haka* for the first time when we played the under-21 All Blacks. Like the 1995 World Cup Boks, we also faced the Kiwis head-on. The *haka* was very impressive, though I reminded myself that it was only a war cry. But the next moment, their hooker, Ace Tiatia, took a step forward and headbutted me right on the nose. I couldn't believe it – the game hadn't even started! In those years I was the big lock – the enforcer – a role in which Bakkies Botha would later excel, so I assumed that this was the Kiwis' way of trying to unnerve the big guy in the team.

We quickly realised just how important the *haka* was to New Zealand. Nothing you did while the players performed this ritual could distract them. You just had to get used to it, but you could also use it to motivate yourself. Unfortunately, on that day we were no match for the New Zealanders, and they thumped us 46-20.

A year later, at the 1998 SANZAR/UAR under-21 tournament in Stellenbosch, my path crossed with that of a Cape Town lock named Daniel Vickerman. I was injured and had missed the under-21 trials, while Dan had delivered some great performances. However, when the national side was announced, my name was called out and not his.

Dan was quite miffed about his omission and asked me if I thought it was fair that I had made the side and he had not. I didn't really have an answer for him. I didn't pick the squad. From that day on, Dan and I regularly locked horns. He decided to leave South Africa soon afterwards and relocated to Australia, where he joined the Waratahs in Sydney. Dan eventually became a Wallaby and we often competed at Test level. He was one of the best locks I ever played against and our rivalry was always intense.

During that under-21 tournament in Stellenbosch, fairness did prevail. I was named the best forward, which I think justified my inclusion over Dan in the national side. Nevertheless, our tournament started with a bit of a wobble in typical Cape winter weather. Our first performance, against the Australians, was pathetic and we lost 6-41. During the video session afterwards, our coach, Dawie Snyman, singled me out for criticism because I had sidestepped the mud puddles as we ran onto the field so that I could start the game with dry boots and socks.

After that we got our rears in gear and finished on a high note, smashing England 41-12, drawing 15-all with Australia and shaving through 18-16 against New Zealand. With John Smit at tighthead, we drained the young All Blacks in the scrums, and André Pretorius was superb at flyhalf, chalking up all our points with his boot.

My biggest rival was the Kiwi Chris Jack. At 21 you're full of bravado – you provoke opponents at every opportunity and take a swing whenever you can. Chris regularly got a working over during our under-21 days. I remember giving him a bloody nose with my knee on one occasion – unsighted by the referee, of course. Chris didn't forget the incident and would get his revenge years later.

At the end of 1998, with the Currie Cup final rapidly approaching, a serious lock crisis forced the Bulls selectors to call up players like Gerhard Laufs and Wium Basson. I saw this as an indication that my stakes in the senior side weren't that high, so I was left with a difficult decision: should I stay on at the Bulls and focus on club rugby, where I could learn the tricks of the trade from hardened guys like Krynauw Otto, or should I move to a smaller union where I'd get more opportunities to prove my worth at senior level?

Eventually I decided to leave Pretoria, as I thought I'd benefit more by getting playing opportunities at a higher level. My future as a player was the deciding factor. The Bulls' structures weren't as good in those days as they would become under the watchful eyes of Heyneke Meyer and Frans Ludeke. Also, my relationships with Bulls forward coach Chris Buitendach and senior coach Eugene van Wyk weren't close, as I mostly played for the under-21s or in the Vodacom Cup competition.

But I had a lot of respect for Swys de Bruin, then still the Sharks' under-21 coach, who would soon take over as head coach of Griquas, in Kimberley. Swys and I had known each other since our junior years. I first met him when I played for the Bulls against Natal's under-21 team, which he was coaching, and he appreciated my style of playing. We always had a good chat after games and got to know each other well.

In 1998, Griquas had a good team. They'd won the first Vodacom Cup tournament earlier that year and had had a super Currie Cup season as well, even though they'd lost against Western Province in the semi-final. So Griquas were by no means a lightweight team. Guys like Luther Bakkes, Boeta Wessels, Albert van den Berg, Edrich Lubbe and Philip Smit – all very competent players – were in the side.

Another factor that influenced my decision was that Riaan Olckers – for three years my teammate in the Tuks and Bulls junior teams – had just signed a contract with Griquas. Although Free State were also showing interest in me, I felt it would be nice to tackle something new with Swys.

All of these factors made my decision to leave my beloved province a little easier.

Still, it was hard to pack up and go, as I had wanted to play for the Bulls my entire life. Also, my parents were in Polokwane, just a few hundred kilometres away, and my girlfriend lived in Pretoria. And the Bulls didn't even really want me to go. It was an emotional time for me. If I could have chosen, I would've stayed in Pretoria, but it didn't work out that way. I'd had three solid years at Loftus, and it wasn't easy to leave it all behind.

So, after many games for the under-21s and seven turnouts in 1998 for the Vodacom Cup side, I made my way to Kimberley. The intention was to stay there for a few seasons and hope that my performance at Griquas would show what I had to offer. It was a big risk, which I was prepared to take only because I wanted more game time.

I traded my Nissan Langley for a new VW Polo and left Pretoria with a suitcase full of clothes, my togs and my mouth-guard. Kimberley was somewhat of a culture shock. Suddenly I was a biggish fish in a smallish pond, even in the early days of the professional era. In rugby terms I was still relatively young, and although I was a big signing for Griquas, big houses and fancy cars weren't the way things were done in the Northern Cape.

Riaan and I diligently set off to find accommodation, along with two other new Griquas players – an Englishman from Durban named Morné Snyman and an Afrikaans teacher from Pinetown, Tom Cameron, who represented Natal at hooker in the Vodacom Cup competition. Tom and I played golf together and had similar interests, like hunting and enjoying a good braai, so we became firm friends very quickly. The first month we all stayed in a hostel, and then we rented a miner's house. For the next two years, this was to be our humble abode – the 'Genotgrot' (Cave of Pleasure), as we dubbed it.

One morning, after a practice match between Griquas and the Cats

Super 12 side, my phone rang. It was André Markgraaff, former Bok coach, who was now in charge of the Cats franchise. He wanted me in his team.

You don't let such an opportunity slip by, especially not if you're a 21-year-old tight forward, and I got my 'call-up instructions'. The Cats consisted of players from the Golden Lions, Free State, Griquas and Northern Free State, so the decision was made to set up base at a resort outside Vanderbijlpark, on the banks of the Vaal River. Again I had to pack the Polo and hit the road.

Of course it was a huge surprise to be roped in by Markgraaff, and thanks to him I made my Super Rugby debut at the age of 21, without a single Currie Cup game on my résumé. But I was unable at that point to cement my place in the Cats team – I never expected it to happen in my first season in the Super 12, anyway. So I commuted between Vanderbijlpark and Kimberley, where I still played Vodacom Cup rugby for Griquas.

Being in the presence of living legends and Springbok players left me wide-eyed when I joined the Cats. One player who immediately made me feel welcome and put me at ease was the naughty boy of South African rugby, James Small. He was the only one who extended a hand of friendship. And he was the big shot over there.

My eyes popped with amazement each time I joined James and company on a night on the town. With the ties I'd handed out in 1998, I thought myself a bit of a Casanova, but the attention James and his friends got from the fairer sex, the number of autographs he had to sign and the way he was given VIP treatment wherever he went, thanks to his status as a World Cup winner, were something to behold.

Regardless of his star status, James made the effort to help me as a young outsider. He'd join me at team lunch and, just to make me feel at ease, we'd chat about this, that and the other. This was not the typical behaviour of a senior player and it made a big impression on me, especially because I was used to the Bulls hierarchy, where senior and junior players didn't mingle.

The first few months in Kimberley were over in a flash. I played two Super 12 games for the Cats and a handful of Vodacom Cup games for Griquas. We managed to reach the final of the competition, in which a very strong Lions side completely outplayed us. They would also win the Currie Cup in 1999.

The advent of the 1999 Currie Cup season was a big moment for me. Every South African rugby player dreams of participating in this competition, and although I was in Griquas colours, it was still a massive honour to be part of it.

Games come and go, but two Currie Cup encounters against the Blue Bulls in my two years at Griquas will always stand out. In 1999 we faced the defending champions – fielding a full-strength side – in Pretoria and beat them 32-26. The next year, the Bulls travelled to Kimberley for their opening encounter of the season, again with veterans (and childhood heroes) like Ruben Kruger in the line-up. This time round we trounced them 58-37.

Although I respected Swys as a coach and enjoyed winning big games like these, I knew it would be difficult for me to play serious rugby at Griquas. I had to show my mettle at Super 12 level, but players from the smaller unions didn't get as many opportunities as the guys contracted by the Lions or the Cheetahs.

Even though it's all good and well to reach the semis of the Currie Cup competition, it will always be difficult to get your hands on this sought-after trophy at a union like Griquas, as it lacks the depth of the bigger provinces. When three or four key players are injured – and it happens often – the coaching staff have to turn to the clubs to find replacements, and the stronger teams in the competition easily expose those weak spots. We were a group of 26 contracted players, which was small for a Currie Cup squad, and injuries in the team meant that we were often sitting ducks for the bigger teams in the competition.

Besides Swys, I also looked up to our captain, Luther Bakkes. He was an incredible guy, who went above and beyond the call of duty for the team, never serving his own interests. The example he set on and off the field made a huge impression on me. Luther was soft-spoken and reserved, but when he spoke, everyone listened. And if something bothered him, he sorted it out.

I was a typical young, impetuous player, and I talked a lot on the field. With two victories over the Bulls, it was easy to have a go at my friends in Pretoria. Every opportunity I got, I laid into them. I also targeted Derick Grobbelaar, an experienced lock playing in my position at the Bulls. He was older and heavier than me, and I let him know in no uncertain terms that I thought his playing days were numbered. Typical of a youngster moving up in the ranks: a big mouth and full of bravado. All aimed at 'my team'. Ruben Kruger, Krynauw Otto, Pote Fourie and, of course, Naas Botha were my heroes. Playing against them all of a sudden was a massive psychological challenge, but I also wanted to prove a point – the Bulls union, after all, didn't think I was good enough for them.

But not only the Bulls got a piece of my mind. Mark Andrews, World Cup, Tri Nations and Currie Cup winner, was also one of my targets.

'Old man, don't you think it's time you retired?' I asked him during a Currie Cup game in 2000. A South African rugby legend getting a mouthful from a pipsqueak! Mark never forgot this encounter. Senior players didn't take kindly to boastful youngsters, I would realise afterwards. Later, as a senior myself, I learnt to ignore comments such as these and just get on with the game.

More and more young players were coming through the ranks. One of them was a young flank forward from the Falcons, Bakkies Botha. He'd finished matric a year before and was already making an impression in the senior side. Bakkies was skinny – just about 100 kilograms – but you could immediately see he had a big heart. We all wondered about him: who was this lad? He was barely 19, but didn't shy away from taking on bigger or older players. He held nothing back.

But Bakkies irritated me tremendously. He didn't seem like a nice guy, and that was all I needed to know about him.

***

My second season at Griquas, in 2000, was just as enjoyable as the first. I also played a few more games for the Cats, but didn't make the side once they'd reached the semis of the Super 12. Laurie Mains was the Cats' new coach, and that was an experience in itself. He'd coached the Lions in 1999 when they won the Currie Cup final in a one-sided encounter against the Sharks. Laurie was an eccentric New Zealander and the perfect candidate to coach the Cats. His no-nonsense approach to discipline was the cornerstone of the franchise's campaign in 2000.

A lot was said about Laurie's working relationship with Cheetahs players like Rassie Erasmus and Werner (Smiley) Swanepoel, but I stayed out of the controversy. It was obvious that Laurie paid more attention to the Lions players in the squad, but it didn't bother me, as I wasn't involved with the Cats for the whole season, and in the long run I benefited a great deal from playing Super 12 rugby.

One morning I was receiving treatment in the physio's room when I heard Rassie and Smiley discussing how they planned to get the Free State and Griquas players to revolt against Laurie. Rassie worked hard and put in many extra hours analysing video recordings of games, but Laurie didn't like it one bit when Rassie made suggestions during team meetings. I learnt a lot from Rassie about the value of video sessions, and they certainly helped in later years to improve my line-out technique and strategy.

Laurie was very strict on fitness and diet. He was a fitness fanatic and the only coach who drilled me so hard that I actually considered faking an injury just to get some rest. At 120 kilograms, I was a big chap and had a tough time keeping up during fitness training.

Two other big and experienced guys in our team, Willie Meyer and Leon Boshoff, learnt in a hard – and bizarre – way not to mess with Laurie. On the Wednesday before our Super 12 encounter in Canberra, Willie and Leon each had a scoop of ice cream at dinner. That Saturday, we lost 0-64 against the Brumbies.

Laurie singled out the two of them at our team meeting, grilling them on their lack of discipline, and he almost sacked them from the team. He said we had lost that game because they had had ice cream on the Wednesday! Of course, you didn't dare laugh during a team meeting – Laurie would send you packing. I always sat at the back, trying my best to avoid making eye contact with him. I was too scared I'd start giggling.

Laurie expected all the players in the changing room to have sat down before he walked in. He would enter, take off his blazer and hang it over a chair. Then he would take out his notes, place them on a table and quietly and carefully read through them. After that he'd look up and meet each player's eyes. Only after this ritual would he start his team talk.

All my experiences with the Cats came in handy later in the season. After we returned from our tour, I went back to Kimberley, where I thoroughly enjoyed playing in the Vodacom Cup for Griquas. Later in 2000, I was also selected for the SA under-23 side to participate in an African series, where we massacred the Test sides of Namibia and Zimbabwe.

With our regular captain and my lock partner, Boela du Plooy, being injured, I captained the under-23s later that year against a South African Barbarians side in a curtain-raiser for the Boks against the All Blacks at Ellis Park. It was my first taste of captaincy at this level, and afterwards I made sure we shook hands with our opponents, their coach and the ref. I found this much easier to do than I had years before at Noordskool, because this time round we'd won easily (62-34).

Griquas had a middling performance in the Currie Cup competition in 2000, though we managed to reach the top eight, something not even the Blue Bulls could do. In a way, this was a personal triumph for me, even though we had struggled in the competition and finished stone-last in the top group.

Round about this time, I heard my name being mentioned as a possible member of the Springbok squad for a tour of Argentina and Britain. Then the Blue Bulls contacted me about a move back to Pretoria. Although I was grateful for the experience I had gained in Kimberley and the things I'd learnt, my plan had always been to make Loftus my home again. So when opportunity knocked, it was an easy decision to make.

At the end of 2000 I packed my bags for the big city. But before I could join the Bulls, a pleasant surprise awaited me.

3

I become a Bok!

'And the locks are: Mark Andrews, Natal; Albert van den Berg, Natal; Hottie Louw, WP; Quinton Davids, WP; and Victor Matfield, Griquas.'

I was in Pretoria visiting my two big mates from Boekenhout, Riaan 'Bossie' Boshoff and François du Randt, when my name was read out as one of 13 newcomers who would join the Springbok squad at the end of 2000 on a tour to Argentina and Britain.

To call this a dream come true would have been the understatement of the year. It was unbelievable to hear my name being read out during the announcement. My phone didn't stop ringing, nor did my parents' at their home in Polokwane – everyone wanted to congratulate me. It was a very special moment – a feeling I can't easily describe. You may believe that you can become a Springbok, but you're never sure until it actually happens. And to accomplish this feat as a player for one of the so-called smaller unions made it an even bigger honour.

The year before, rumours had done the rounds that Nick Mallett was considering me for his World Cup squad, but the talk had come to nothing, with the selectors choosing more experienced players instead. At that stage I was still a greenhorn at senior level. Now, though, we had to prepare for a long, exhausting tour of nine matches – four Tests, four weekday games and an encounter with the Barbarians – and I had no illusions about my position in the rank and file. I knew I would play only in the weekday games, but that was fine with me. From now on, I would always be Springbok No. 705!

When we drove from our hotel in Johannesburg to the practice field, the new guys sat in the front of the bus, as tradition dictated.

Senior players like Joost van der Westhuizen, Mark Andrews and Percy Montgomery each had their own seat in the back. Because there wasn't enough space up front, we were squeezed in like sardines. I couldn't help wondering whether I'd ever have a single seat at the back of the bus. I wasn't sure what the future held.

We were a large group of 40 players, and Harry Viljoen, having recently been appointed in Nick Mallett's place, was coaching the Boks. I looked forward to going on tour with guys like Johan Wasserman and Gavin Passens, who, like me, were also contracted to play for the Blue Bulls in 2001, as I was keen to get to know them.

From a logistical point of view, the tour set unique demands. Three days after the Test against Argentina, the weekday team had to play Ireland A in Limerick. It meant that the dirt trackers could almost never practise with a complete team of players, as we were sent out to the next venue in advance. It was weird to be on a Springbok tour and never see the senior Boks play in any of the Tests.

I played my first game for the Boks as a replacement against Argentina A in Tucumán. Afterwards, the debutants – among them me, Craig Davidson, Delarey du Preez and Thando Manana – had to be initiated. Although I'd been through similar rituals before, I was still quite nervous. I'd lived with initiations since my days as a resident at Boekenhout and had been initiated into numerous rugby teams, but I didn't know quite what to expect in the Bok set-up. We debutants suspected that we would have to tell a joke, so I tried to remember a funny story. I wasn't much of a comedian.

We walked nervously into the team room of our hotel in Tucumán, and Mark Andrews, André Venter and Joost van der Westhuizen were sitting up front. We rolled out the jokes one by one, but there was hardly a ripple of laughter. And nobody had told us to learn the words of the Springbok team song, which we now had to sing. For this oversight, we had to down a few beers.

Then Mark, at that stage one of the most experienced Boks of all time, looked me straight in the eye and asked if I remembered what I had said to him a few months earlier in Kimberley. My only defence was to play dumb, so I said I had no idea what he was talking about. Of course Mark remembered, and he reminded me that I'd told him that he should think about retiring. So, as luck would have it, it was his task to tan my hide with those big paws of his. The ritual was concluded with the reading of the Springbok code of honour, the real reason for the initiation. Yes, we had to down a few beers and the senior players tanned our backsides, but the most important part of the process was imparting what an enormous responsibility it was to be a Springbok.

I was filled with tremendous pride. It was the first time the debutants would recite the code of honour, while the initiated players had the opportunity to listen to the words and be reminded of what it meant to be a Bok.

I recited the following words out loud:

'I, Victor Matfield, hereby undertake and pledge my word of honour in support thereof, to honour and abide by the following code:

'That I shall at all times, and on every occasion, conduct myself in a dignified manner and with pride, so as to ensure that all my actions are worthy of the proud traditions of Springbok rugby.

'That whilst wearing this jersey, I shall at all times remain gracious in victory and honourable in defeat, yet never shall I surrender whilst enjoying the privilege of wearing the green and gold.

'That the Springbok team and its interests shall always be placed above my own ambitions, and my contribution will serve only to enhance the proud history of Springbok rugby.'

***

With throbbing backsides and hearts full of hope, we then set off for Ireland. Although our 'midweek group' was small, I still felt like a Springbok and was geared for a tough game against Ireland A at Thomond Park. The dirt-tracker coaches were Allister Coetzee and Frans Ludeke.

I knew very little about Allister, but it was an honour to be coached by Frans. In part, he had inspired me to attend Tom Naudé Technical High School – if only for a week! Frans had been the head prefect at the time, and my mom was his teacher. She always said he was the best head prefect the school had ever produced. I got along well with Allister and Frans, and enjoyed playing under their leadership. Over the years our relationship would deepen and result in many successes on the rugby field.

In the meantime, the Springboks were playing the Pumas, and we watched the Test on TV. It was very strange watching Harry's new game plan unfold, with the Boks not kicking the ball for about 70 minutes of the game. In the end they had to dig deep to beat the Pumas 37-33.

Unfortunately, though, we lost 11-28 against Ireland A in Limerick. It was a small town, yet thousands of spectators turned out to pack the stadium. In that game, whenever a place-kicker of either team took aim at the posts, the whole crowd would fall silent. It was a new and special experience for me. I wish all rugby-loving nations across the globe would emulate the Limerick supporters. Then again, some place-kickers say they prefer the noise, as they've grown accustomed to it.

Just three days after the Test in Dublin against Ireland, we were off to Cardiff, again ahead of the rest of the squad, for a game against Wales A in the Millennium Stadium. We made good on our loss against Ireland A and chalked up a 34-15 victory.

As the tour progressed, it became increasingly apparent that we were no longer one Bok team. Instead we were more like two touring sides travelling separately who now and then met up for a couple of days before the smaller group would depart for another destination. Two days after the third Test of the tour, against Wales in Cardiff, we played an English League XV in Worcester. I captained the team, but we lost again: 30-35.

On this tour I had my first encounter with Ollie le Roux, who had captained the midweek side against Ireland A. Afterwards he blamed the younger players for the defeat, claiming that we hadn't been focused and just wanted to party before the game. But he wasn't even in Limerick at the time, as he had stayed on longer with the Test team in Argentina.

'How can he talk such nonsense?' I wondered. Maybe he wanted to take the pressure off himself, as he had been the captain and we had lost the match. I knew immediately that he and I would never be friends.

Even though our results weren't that good – in the last Test, we lost 17-25 against England at Twickenham – I felt honoured as a young player to have been part of the tour. Yes, it had been somewhat chaotic, and yes, we'd hardly had a decent practice session, but I still preferred sitting squashed together in the front of the bus, keeping my mouth shut, to watching the games on TV in South Africa.

* * *

The idea of returning to Pretoria had actually come about in George earlier in 2000, when Griquas were playing South Western Districts at Outeniqua Park in the Currie Cup. Heyneke Meyer was SWD's former coach, and in 1999 he had taken the Eagles to the competition's semi-finals. He was also an assistant coach with the Stormers franchise. In the first half of 2000, he had coached the Bulls in the Super 12 competition, and although I'd heard his name before, I didn't know much about him and had never met him in person.

We talked for the first time at a players' function at Outeniqua Park and soon realised that we shared the same rugby aspirations. His first coaching stint in Pretoria hadn't been very successful (in 2000, the Bulls finished 11th on the Super 12 log), but the Blue Bulls Rugby Union had appointed him to take over the reins as Blue Bulls coach for the 2001 Currie Cup and Vodacom Cup competitions.

Griquas and SWD were two of the strongest small unions, and on that day the Eagles gave us a big hiding. Ironically, Frans Ludeke had taken over the SWD coaching duties from Heyneke in 2000 and had worked wonders with a young, inexperienced outfit, even though they didn't make the semis again.

Heyneke's plan for the Blue Bulls in 2001 was to get rid of the dead wood and build a team around young, keen players. When I started negotiating my contract with the Blue Bulls Rugby Union at the end of the 2000 Currie Cup season, I'd actually already made up my mind to return to Pretoria. But then Free State also came to the party. Oom Tat Botha, who had coached me in the SA under-21 side in 1997, wanted me in Bloemfontein. However, with Braam Els and Ryno Opperman established as the Cheetahs locks and with Boela du Plooy knocking on the door, I decided not to sign up with them. In 1999, my first year with Griquas, I had had to compete against two Boks in the form of Albert van den Berg and Philip Smit, but fortunately Swys always picked me, often fielding Philip as a flanker.

But at the end of 2000, after two seasons in Kimberley, I was back in Blue Bulls country. However, it was probably not the best time for anyone to join the franchise, as the Bulls had gone downhill in a big way after winning the Currie Cup in 1998. The union was in disarray, without a firm plan or a fixed structure for the future, a situation that was apparent in the endlessly rotating coaching staff. From 1999 to 2001, Eugene van Wyk, Heyneke Meyer and Phil Pretorius were all head coaches at some stage, with a change of staff sometimes implemented halfway through a season. Furthermore, each coach did things his own way, as was evidenced in the playing style of the under-19s, the under-21s and the senior level. There was also very little consistency between the Super 12, Currie Cup and Vodacom Cup teams. Added to this, almost all the players were in a comfort zone, earning good salaries. Stories even surfaced of players lighting up cigarettes in the changing room with Coach Eugene van Wyk, who was a heavy smoker, after losing a match.

In the 2000 season, under Eugene's guidance, the Bulls couldn't even reach the top eight in the Currie Cup and were relegated to the ABSA Cup competition, nowadays known as the First League Cup. This trophy eventually ended up in the display cabinet at Loftus, but it would've been a shame if the Bulls had lost to Eastern Province in the final.

Irate Blue Bulls supporters wrote letters to *Beeld* newspaper, questioning the state of affairs at the union, and before long, Loftus had more empty seats than spectators. Heyneke, who took over from Eugene as Vodacom and Currie Cup coach at the end of 2000, believed that the rudderless ship could be steadied again. He wanted all the teams to share the same vision and play a similar style of rugby.

Phil Pretorius replaced Heyneke as Super 12 coach for the 2001 season, but not before Heyneke had enticed a handful of younger players to move to Pretoria. Johan Wasserman, Gavin Passens, Richard Bands, Danie Coetzee, Anton Leonard, Tiaan Joubert and Dries Scholtz joined me in the move to Loftus that year.

More players followed suit – Bakkies Botha, Frikkie Welsh and Jaco van der Westhuyzen – but times were still tough for the Bulls. Despite this, we were excited with Heyneke's plans and the calibre of youngsters he'd brought to Pretoria. Even though he was coaching Vodacom and Currie Cup rugby in 2001, his forward planning in 2000 hadn't been completely in vain.

My first day back at Loftus was like a homecoming. Yes, the Bulls' Super 12 results of the previous few years hadn't been great (more about that later), but there was a hunger for success among the younger players – most of whom were unknowns in their early 20s – that was contagious.

Heyneke started his rebuilding process in earnest only after the 2001 Super 12 competition, in which we'd also struggled. Before we could even touch a rugby ball, we were carted off to a farm outside Warmbaths for a two-day planning session. When Heyneke said that he wanted to make the Bulls the best rugby brand on the planet, I was astounded. What he said might have been wishful thinking, but we nevertheless listened intently to his plans.

Heyneke drew a diagram with four quadrants. The first one, he said, was where we were now, where 'nobody knows you'. The second quadrant was where success started. Quadrant three was the pinnacle of your success, but this was also where the warning lights started flashing, because in the fourth quadrant everyone was content and wealthy, and had nothing but personal gain in mind. Years later, when the team was doing really well, Heyneke constantly reminded us of that diagram and how important it was to stay in the third quadrant.

Joost van der Westhuizen, who had attended FH Odendaal High School in Pretoria, where Heyneke had coached years ago, was one of the senior players in the squad. The players respected him, and he was almost on the same level as the coach. When he spoke, we all listened. Besides Joost, Danie van Schalkwyk was the only other player considered to be a senior.

Heyneke won his first trophy for the union when the Bulls were victorious in the Vodacom Cup competition in 2001. I was playing in the Super 12 team, but we all took notice of what was happening down the ranks. It was good to see things getting pulled back into shape at the Bulls, even though I couldn't be directly involved.

During the Vodacom Cup, I started realising what a good player Bakkies Botha was. He was one of the top try-scorers for the Bulls in the competition that year, which impressed me as a lock. Suddenly it seemed like a great prospect to play next to him.

***

My first year in the Bulls Super 12 team was 'interesting', to put it mildly. Phil Pretorius was the coach, and Peter de Villiers (from the Falcons) and Chris Grobler (from the Pumas) were his assistants.

Phil had his own way of coaching. He and I got on well, but some of the players struggled to cope with his short fuse and impulsive nature. Very few people know this, but in 2001, two years before the Springboks, the Bulls experienced their own Kamp Staaldraad (Camp Steel Wire). This intense and physical penalty drill, which had been Phil's idea, was designed to build team spirit and unity.

A few of my future Bok associates also attended the camp: assistant coach Peter de Villiers, fitness trainer Neels Liebel and sports psychologist Henning Gericke, a former Springbok middle-distance runner. At the camp, I was astonished when Naka Drotské, one of the senior players in the team, complained about cramps in his calf muscles after two hours of hiking. He refused to continue walking and got onto the back of a pick-up truck.

Phil was livid and immediately sent Naka home. Then he called up veteran hooker James Dalton, at that stage contracted by the Falcons, to join the squad. In the first couple of matches Naka had been the man in the driving seat, but James replaced him for the last six games and even took over the Bulls captaincy in the last two encounters of the season. It summed up Phil's way of running the operation: if you didn't do as he said, he would hold it against you.

Henning was a firm believer in the mental preparation the camp provided, but it didn't do much for me. 'This camp will make your head strong and take you to a new level,' Henning said at one stage. 'Well, I think it's a load of nonsense,' was my response. Henning wasn't impressed.

One of our tasks was to carry a 'beertjie' (literally, a teddy bear), which was a piece of railway track tied to a rugby ball. I heard that it was an exercise used in training by the defence force, but I never did military service. Henning used beertjie as a means to inspire us. Whenever we were struggling during a game, someone had to shout 'beertjie!', and that would apparently motivate us to fight back.

But Kamp Staaldraad – beertjies or not – didn't help us much in the Super 12. We lost our first game, against the Sharks in Durban

(17-30), and directly afterwards flew to Wellington, where the Hurricanes awaited us.

We arrived in New Zealand's capital around midnight and went straight to bed. The next morning, the coaches were in a foul mood. There was no time to acclimatise or recover from the long flight. Instead, we had to gear up for a three-hour contact session in which we had to run at full speed and crash into our teammates with maximum power. This sort of training after a long flight was unheard of, but we knew our place and said nothing. Years later we discovered that the best way to recover from jet lag is not to be on your feet too much in the first week.

Then, later on the tour and shortly before kick-off against the Brumbies in Canberra, Phil tried to ignite our spirits in the tunnel by saying, 'If you want, I'll go and *bliksem* Eddie Jones [the Brumbies coach] before the game starts. You must slaughter these guys.'

We were stunned and could only hope that our coach wouldn't do something stupid. Phil was a difficult guy. He didn't hesitate to bawl out players, or to shout and throw chairs in the changing room. At half-time during one game he told our outside centre, Wynand Lourens, to bugger off. Wynand had to watch the rest of the game on TV at home.

We had some tough months. I had just returned from Kimberley, where I had enjoyed my rugby and had played well. I knew that Phil was a good coach, but he was unreasonably strict and lost his temper very quickly. As a young player you accept this behaviour as normal, but it isn't. I also believe that too much emphasis was put on the psychological aspects of the game.

It was as if the whole season was just one big mind game, from Kamp Staaldraad to the excessive emotional incitement. In his way, Phil tried to inspire us to victory, but he failed miserably. We won only two games in the 2001 Super 12, and those happened right at the end of the season, against the Blues (28-25) at Loftus and the Cats (21-19) at Ellis Park. Nevertheless, I was satisfied with my game and had even experienced a personal highlight against the Waratahs in Sydney. Although we lost 7-53, I scored an individual try after chipping the ball over Wallaby fullback Matt Burke's head, fielding it and planting it between the posts.

Our last Super 12 game of the season was against the Cats at Ellis

Park, after which the Bok squad was to be announced for a home series against France and Italy. During warm-up before kick-off, Danie van Schalkwyk jokingly said that it would be terrible if a Bok contender got seriously injured in a game that had no significant bearing on the log. What happens if you tear your knee ligaments, for instance, and you've been picked for the Bok squad?

I was quite annoyed with Danie for making such a cynical joke. But, lo and behold, just as he had predicted, this was exactly what happened. In a tackle, my knee ligaments tore. And yes, afterwards my name was read out as a member of the Bok squad. So I had no choice but to withdraw.

I've learnt over the years that disappointments are a part of life. What's more important is how you overcome them. I had missed the opportunity to play in my first Test for the Boks, but, although the disappointment was massive, I accepted my fate.

Danie felt really terrible about his 'prophetic words', but I couldn't really blame him. Injuries come with the territory.

***

After recovering, I joined the Blue Bulls in Port Elizabeth for SAIL Week, a short rugby tournament contested by all teams in which South African Investment Limited have shares. We used the tournament as preparation for the Currie Cup season. I wasn't 100 per cent fit yet and was given a 30-minute spell in the third game, against Border.

The Sunday morning after the game, I received a call from Harry Viljoen, the Bok coach. 'Victor, I want you to report to the Boks' hotel as soon as possible.'

I was ecstatic. I was being given a second chance to make my debut in a Bok Test. As luck would have it, the Boks were preparing in Port Elizabeth, so I was there in a flash.

Earlier in the week, Rassie Erasmus, a former teammate with the Cats, had told me that he didn't think he would be fit for the first Test and that I should prepare myself for a call-up. He eventually did withdraw from the squad. When Albert van den Berg was also injured, I was picked on the bench for the first Test, against Italy. Harry had controversially appointed Bob Skinstad as captain in place of André Vos.

In stepped Ollie le Roux again, with whom I had to share a room in Port Elizabeth for a week. Although we didn't really know each other, after that incident in Ireland the year before, I didn't like him much. But as a young player you grab every opportunity to wear the green and gold, so the last thing on my mind was questioning the allocation of rooms. I took my luggage and moved in with him.

As soon as Ollie closed the hotel-room door behind him, he changed into a Beau Brummel of sorts, stripping off every item of clothing. It wasn't exactly a pretty sight if you wanted to relax in your room!

Luckily, Jaco van der Westhuyzen was also in the team, and although I didn't move out, I spent most of my free time in his room. Jaco didn't have a room-mate for some reason.

Ollie was quite demanding, even in a team context. He was very out-spoken, which went against my grain. And he talked a *lot*. Supporters thought he was a jovial bloke – the 'hamburger man' – but in fact he was the one who complained the most when we had to sign autographs or attend social events. He also had a special request for lunch: spaghetti bolognaise without onions, every day. And if he didn't have it his way, the tantrums escalated.

Then things happened very quickly. André Markgraaff, Harry's assist-ant, whom I'd got to know at Griquas, was impressed with my line-out knowledge, and at a practice session he asked me to explain a strategy we had used in Kimberley to the forwards – many of them experienced Boks. I felt quite shy, as I had to give advice to guys like Mark Andrews, a player I admired and who not long ago had initiated me into the Springboks.

That Saturday I reached another milestone when I made my Test debut as a replacement for Johan Ackermann in the 68th minute against Italy in Port Elizabeth. It was a wonderful feeling. Finally, I was a fully fledged Springbok and, to top it all, we won 60-14. Now I could finally wear my Springbok blazer and not carry it draped over my arm, as is the tradition for players without Test experience.

But the 12 minutes against Italy was just the prelude to greater things. Although Harry had brought the younger guys into the Bok squad for a reason, I was still surprised when, three weeks later, he picked me as Mark Andrews's lock partner for the Test against the All Blacks at Newlands.

Mark was a superb player. He played with confidence, even though a hard session in the gym was not his thing. Every time he pulled that green-and-gold jersey over his head, he was focused on nothing but the task ahead. To be in my first starting line-up for the Boks with Mark was very special.

I had a serious bout of bronchitis the week before the Test, but I didn't tell anyone, as I didn't want to blow my chances of playing. I spent most of the night before the Test in the bathroom so that I wouldn't wake up my room-mate, Cobus Visagie, with my constant coughing. Cobus knew what I was going through and even prayed for my recovery.

My parents travelled to Cape Town to be there for the occasion, but I was still in the grip of the bronchitis. Nevertheless, standing there while the All Blacks performed the *haka* was a momentous experience, even with suppressed coughing fits. During the game I had to use an asthma pump at almost every scrum or line-out.

Besides my breathing problems, I didn't enjoy the match itself. Typical wet winter weather in Cape Town had soaked the Newlands pitch, and Harry's young guns – Lukas van Biljon, Marius Joubert, Butch James, Dean Hall, Joe van Niekerk and I – couldn't tip the scales in our favour. Our place-kickers, Percy Montgomery and Butch, also missed quite a few scoring opportunities.

Shortly before half-time, Anton Oliver tried to hand me off in a tackle and I got a finger stuck in my eye. The impact cracked the eye socket and broke a bone behind my eye. The pain was excruciating – probably the worst I'd experienced on a rugby field until then.

By the way I was stumbling around after the incident, the spectators probably thought I had concussion. I couldn't stand up straight and eventually had to leave the field. Our team doctor, Frans Verster, raced me to hospital for scans and X-rays. Later that evening, while everyone was relaxing, and guys like Lukas, Marius and Joe were celebrating their Test debuts, I was in my hotel bed, curled up in pain.

Jonah Lomu played for the All Blacks that day. On the pitch he was even scarier than on TV. He was quick, massive and strong – unstoppable. It was almost impossible to tackle him on your own. Every time the ball was kicked downfield in his direction, we formed a defensive line and tried to look as big and menacing as possible so that he wouldn't pick us as the target to run at. A big lock would look like a complete idiot if a winger ran all over him.

Mark and I managed to get hold of him a couple of times, though. Working in unison, I would break Lomu's momentum with a swinging arm while Mark moved in to wrestle him to the ground. André Venter, on the other hand, relished the opportunity to get hold of Lomu. He tracked him all over the pitch in an attempt to take the big Kiwi down.

What does it say about the Springbok defence knowing that Lomu never scored a try against us? He didn't score against Wales either, but then he played in more games against us than against the Red Dragons.

The Test was over in a flash. Former Springboks always tell you to enjoy your first Test because you're back in the changing room before you know it. I remember pinching two All Black throw-ins at the line-out – with my old under-21 rival, Norm Maxwell, in the team – and was quite chuffed with my performance afterwards, despite the injury. Harry, Bob and the rugby writers seemed pleased as well.

Unfortunately, though, we lost 3-12 in the first Tri Nations game, in which no tries were scored and no points were chalked up in the second half. I guess we could've clinched it had our goal-kicking not let us down.

Many people criticised Harry for his methods, but he was an innovator and one of the first to realise that the Bok coach's role involves more than just training the team. The coach must also be involved in managing the side in order to motivate his players and ensure that they are happy. Harry appointed quite a few people who had to cover all aspects of our preparation.

At one stage, André Markgraaff was in charge of the forwards, and Ian McIntosh, another former Bok coach, assisted with our attacking game plan. At different times, Harry also roped in three Australians, Tim Lane, Les Kiss and Michael Byrne. It was unheard of at the time to involve other nationalities in the Bok set-up, but Tim, Les and Mick were used respectively as backline coach, defence specialist and kicking coach. Les went on to achieve big success with the Waratahs and Ireland. Harry probably made one big mistake, and that was to involve *too* many coaches. When there are too many voices, there is more opportunity for people to disagree, which is very disadvantageous for a rugby team.

Although I had toured with the Boks the previous year and had made my debut against Italy, for me the Test against the All Blacks at Newlands had been my real debut. Coupled with the joy of a Test against the Kiwis, there was also the disappointment of my eye injury, which caused me to miss the next Test, against Australia in Pretoria. That's just how the dice rolls for a rugby player.

There was an advantage to the injury, though … a lifelong advantage. I spent a week at home recuperating, and during that time I attended a girl's 21st birthday party with my friend Bossie, which is where I once again met up with the cute blonde girl from Bethal, Monja Bekker – the same one who had turned my knees to jelly a few years earlier on the Tuks campus. Back then, I couldn't get her to show any interest in me.

That Wednesday evening, however, the situation was different, despite my swollen eye! I didn't mention anything about my Springbok endeavours, which turned out to be a good call, as rugby talk doesn't impress Monja at all. I had been quite arrogant the first time we'd met, but this time I listened – I really wanted to get to know her better. It actually suited me that she wasn't interested in rugby stories, as it gave me the opportunity to show her that I was just a decent, humble boy from Limpopo Province.

Monja was different from the girls I'd dated before. Usually it wasn't difficult to persuade a girl to go out with a Springbok rugby player, but Monja made it clear from the start that I'd have to work hard and make a serious effort if I wanted to impress her. So it took numerous bouquets of flowers – and even more emails, SMSes and phone calls – to persuade her to go out with me. My friends convinced me that I should take Monja out for dinner before the Boks departed on a Tri Nations tour to Australasia. She said yes, and I took her to Pachas, one of Pretoria's finest restaurants.

I was rather disappointed at the end of the evening when I leant in for a goodnight kiss and she gently refused! During the tour I sent her messages every day, but she didn't reply to all of them. Playing hard to get, as they say … But it worked!

However, Monja didn't approve of my social habits. After we'd been dating for a few months, she broke up with me, as she said I wanted to party all the time and enjoyed the attention of other girls too much. I realised then that it was time for me to get back on track. Fortunately, Monja gave me another chance. I had to decide how I wanted to live my life, and in the end it really wasn't that difficult to sort myself out. The good, chilled Victor had always been there – just as well Monja was around to help me find that guy again.

Monja had a calming influence on me and gave me a purpose in life. I'd always been a Christian, but at that stage I'd lost my way due to my hectic social life. Monja helped me put things in perspective again. I had found it difficult to handle all the fame at the beginning, as temptations were around every corner. You had to be strong and learn to appreciate the value of a good relationship, or that unbridled life could catch up with you.

***

Before the Wallaby Test in 2001, I had to fulfil my first public-speaking obligation, in Pretoria. I was invited to a corporate breakfast and had to answer questions from the audience. And all I'd ever wanted was to play rugby!

People who attended the event had bought an entertainment package that included Test tickets and a breakfast with past and present Springboks. As I was injured at the time, my agent, Jason Smith, arranged for me to attend the occasion, in spite of the fact that I don't enjoy speaking in front of an audience. My parents had always encouraged me to participate in debating competitions at school, but I always used my busy sport schedule as an excuse to get out of it.

Fortunately, the event took place in Pretoria, so at least I could speak Afrikaans. Languages were not my strong suit and back then my English was almost non-existent – you didn't need it much in Pietersburg! Thanks to numerous international press conferences and TV interviews, my English is now more or less up to scratch and I can hold my own.

A week later, it wasn't much fun for me to watch the Boks beat the Wallabies at Loftus from the bench, complete with swollen black eye and without my rugby gear. I wanted to get back into the team as soon as possible, but it would be almost a month before the next Test. However, this gave me enough time to recover, and fortunately I was included in the touring side for the Tri Nations games in Perth and Auckland.

Harry kept me in the loop throughout my recovery period. He told me that he was happy with my performance and that I would be included in his touring side, so I wasn't worried that I'd have to fight my way back into the team and could concentrate on my recovery instead.

The first Test, against Australia, ended in a draw (14-all), and I think I competed well against the experienced John Eales and Justin Harrison. This was my first and only Test against Eales, and I was stoked when I managed to steal three of Australia's line-out throws, as I rated Eales as the best lock forward ever. For me, this was also the start of a big rivalry with the Wallabies, a team against which I always enjoyed playing.

Then we were off to Auckland to take on the All Blacks, but we lost 15-26. Mark and I were starting to form a solid lock combination and I was learning a lot from him. Now knowing exactly how important the line-outs were, I wanted to make this set-piece my speciality.

I also had a second run-in with Chris Jack, the Kiwi lock I had targeted in our under-21 days. Intense physical rivalry is part of Test rugby, and tempers occasionally flared. It was usually nothing more than pushing and shoving, but this time Chris really had it in for me. During some argy-bargy, he gave me a solid biff on the lip. When he saw the surprised look on my face, he reminded me why he'd hit me: 'I hope you remember what you did to me back in Stellenbosch. Now we're quits.'

I quickly realised that playing against the All Blacks was no walk in the park. You don't get tougher games than these.

My room-mate on this tour was Lukas van Biljon. After bunking down with two props, a hooker was probably the next logical step! Lukas and I were good mates, as we were the two youngsters in the pack, and he was also one of the most talented players I'd ever come across in my career, but unfortunately he never realised his full potential. He struggled with injuries later on, but he also made some poor decisions off the pitch.

It's an unfortunate fact that some rugby players never fulfil their true potential. Rugby is a very taxing sport – not only physically, but also mentally. You simply have to be willing to make sacrifices if you want to play to the best of your ability. Besides having ball sense and being fit, the other key ingredient in any serious rugby player's recipe book has to be dedication.

Take Riaan Olckers, a good friend of mine, as an example. Riaan and I often had a few beers together, but the next day I'd do a few additional kilometres in the gym, while he slept late and tucked into a hamburger for lunch. I knew this wouldn't work for me if I wanted to make a success of my career.

'Champions train while the others rest' is, after all, my motto.

***

After the Tri Nations series it was back to the Blue Bulls, where Heyneke Meyer would coach me for the first time. Our plans for the season were in order and Heyneke worked very hard behind the scenes for his players. He insisted on the best facilities: our own gym at Loftus, a swimming pool for recovery sessions and dedicated physiotherapists. These things were unheard of in 2001.

Now the pressure to perform was on the players. SA Rugby had decided to change the format of the Currie Cup competition, and we would have to finish in the top eight to play in the following year's first league. It was a massive challenge for such a young team, but we were ready for it.

However, we spent most of the season with our backs against the wall, and the guys had to dig deep to make the top eight. We were never one of the title contenders, but we did win a few important games, which allowed us to scrape through in seventh position – enough to survive into Currie Cup 2002.

Western Province and the Sharks made the finals for the second year running, but we couldn't have cared less, because we had reached our goal for the season. Now we would aim for a place in the semi-finals in 2002. Little did we know what lay ahead!

Members of the Bulls board were not in agreement on who should coach the Super 12 side in 2002. Phil Pretorius enjoyed some support, as did Heyneke and Chris Grobler from the Pumas. In the end, thanks to SA Rugby, it was decided that Heyneke would replace

Phil. As players we were very happy, as we could see a brighter future with Heyneke at the helm. Harry Viljoen then also roped in Heyneke as Springbok forward coach for the end-of-year tour to France, England and the US.

The tour started in the worst way possible when France beat us 20-10 in Paris. But a week later, in Genoa, we were back on track when we beat Italy 54-26. I also scored my first Test try in that game.

I don't remember my debut match at Twickenham – also my first against Martin Johnson – fondly. England beat us 29-9, giving us a good wake-up call. The pressure on Harry was mounting because of the team's poor international performances. Although we ended the season by beating the USA 43-20, we had been far from convincing.

On that tour, I was the first South African to initiate a new trick, which would lead to hectic debate afterwards. Whenever the opposition took a long-range penalty kick, I positioned myself under the crossbar, where I was lifted to catch the ball before it could cross the bar. You needed to believe in your abilities to pull it off, because if you fumbled the ball and knocked it on, the opposition would be awarded an attacking scrum on your goal line and what would have been three points could easily turn into seven. I 'saved' the Boks three points a few times, but eventually the IRB disallowed this practice, as the rules stipulate that there can be no interference with a penalty kick to the posts.

Touring in the States, where rugby is only a very minor sport, was a unique experience. Harry let us invite our wives and girlfriends along, and I asked permission from Monja's dad for her to join me. It was quite nerve-wracking. Her dad wasn't keen on the idea, as we'd only been dating for a few months. Eventually, though, he agreed, and Monja came over to visit me. Yet this trip almost spelt the end of our relationship. Monja was under the impression that it would be like a holiday for us, but the team was practising hard every day and, when I wasn't training, all I wanted to do was watch TV in my hotel room. Monja wasn't very impressed, despite the fact that Houston did not have a lot to offer in terms of sightseeing or entertainment.

We did, however, visit the NASA Space Center, home of the famous phrase 'Houston, we have a problem'. It was ironic, because at that stage the Boks – and to a lesser extent, the Bulls – were certainly experiencing some problems.

Although the Bulls hadn't performed very well in either the Super 12 or the Currie Cup, and the Boks ended the season with a winning record of just over 50 per cent, I was named as one of the five finalists for the Player of the Year award. It was a great honour, as I still thought of myself as a young, upcoming player.

Harry promised quite a few of us contracts for 2002. I'd be in the second-highest contract category and stood to make a lot of money. I was ecstatic, as it would have more than doubled my income in a year.

But shortly after the tour, once we had completed a photo session for a new Bulls commercial, a few of us had a braai at the air force base in Centurion, the venue of the shoot. We were discussing the season ahead when someone phoned with the news that Harry had resigned as Bok coach and was to be replaced by Rudolf Straeuli, whose first announcement was that *none* of the players would receive Bok contracts.

To put it mildly, we were flummoxed. Suddenly we had no idea what to expect. Although I was quite happy with my game in 2001, I knew that it would be no guarantee for 2002, and that I would have to prove myself all over again.

4

No more games

Sometimes just when you think you're getting back on your feet, another setback comes along to knock you down. That was the sad reality the Bulls had to deal with in their Super 12 campaign in 2002.

For the first time in many seasons there was consistency in the coaching, with the same coach in charge of both the Currie Cup and Super 12 squads. We had young, exciting players, like Ettienne Botha and Pedrie Wannenburg, who bought into in Heyneke's long-term plan, and felt that we were on our way to an attainable target. After a few lean years, Blue Bulls rugby had to rise up again, and we were ready for the challenge.

Heyneke wanted three years' grace to win the Currie Cup. That was our goal. In those years we used the Super 12 as preparation for the Currie Cup, but later on it would be the other way round.

Heyneke prepared frantically before the start of the Super 12. We trained locally and were ready for the season, but rugby is a funny game. You can be as ready as you possibly can be, but if you don't have world-class players with lots of experience – guys that can handle pressure situations – you're staring down the barrel of disappointment.

We had a tough training camp at the air force base in Centurion, south of Pretoria. One evening, after a long session on the practice field, we had a braai to relax, which in the end turned into an enjoyable team-building exercise. The guys were chilled, the beers flowed and we excitedly discussed the season ahead.

Quite a few of us, including me, Ettienne, Frikkie Welsh and Bakkies Botha, had an extended evening. When the sun rose that morning, we were still at it, even as the wake-up siren howled. Our first activity of the day was a photo session for the new Bulls marketing campaign, 'Bull Force in Full Force'. We were dressed in air force uniforms and posed next to fighter jets.

Heyneke noticed that not all of us were 100 per cent sharp, and for him, discipline was not negotiable. He changed his plans for the day there and then and sent the photographer packing. Instead, he arranged for an exhausting practice session in which we had to play shadow rugby up and down the field 20 times. The game would start with a line-out or a scrum, the ball would then be passed down the backline, the last player would put it on the deck and the forwards would pile in for the second phase. This carried on and on and on. Every time we dropped the ball, we had to start from scratch.

We were a bit wary of Heyneke and concentrated hard on not making mistakes. It was swelteringly hot, and the last thing we wanted to do was run up and down a field the entire day. Funny how things turn out – that 'punishment' session was one of our best practices ever, even though we'd felt a bit weak.

Heyneke was very straight with us. If you did something that he didn't approve of, he'd let you know straight away. The session had also been a means to shape the younger players, to make them mentally strong, an aspect of paramount importance in rugby. It may sound as if I am contradicting myself after criticising our experience at Kamp Staaldraad, but I believe that psychological preparation does not have to involve breaking down the players. However, the guys have to know that there are ramifications if they disregard the team rules. They also have to know how to conjure up the mental toughness they've acquired when a game goes pear-shaped on the playing field. These skills can be taught without degrading anyone.

Heyneke's philosophy was that character and discipline were even more important than talent. He wanted to properly prepare the human being before working on the player.

At the time, it was quite an issue who would captain the Bulls. Our most senior player in the squad, Joost van der Westhuizen, was injured and would miss the entire season. The 22-year-old eighthman Chris le Roux, one of the younger players in the group, whom Heyneke knew well, was eventually appointed as captain. Although a lot of us doubted whether it was the right decision, we accepted Chris's appointment because he had captained the Vodacom Cup side the previous season and many players from that team were also in the Super 12 squad. However, more experienced players like Franco Smith, Anton Leonard and James Dalton could also have been considered for the captaincy.

The awful truth was that our planning and efforts on the practice field did not immediately deliver results. We started poorly, losing our first five games at Loftus, against the Cats (31-44), the Hurricanes (18-37), the Waratahs (19-51), the Brumbies (35-45) and the Highlanders (17-54). Then having to board an aircraft to take on the Blues, Crusaders, Reds and Chiefs in Australia was simply attempting the impossible. We lost all our games there, and badly too. We leaked 65 points against the Blues in Auckland (24-65) and were actually relieved that it wasn't more. That's how low our self-esteem was.

I was also cited for dirty play for the first time on the tour. Granted, I had no problem throwing a few punches during a game – as any lock tends to do – but I'm not a dirty player. However, a dangerous high tackle against a Blues player resulted in a disciplinary committee hearing – the longest two hours of my life. Luckily, I got off with a warning, but Heyneke gave me a piece of his mind and told me to get with the programme. I was, after all, one of only a handful of Springboks in the Bulls group that year and had to set a good example.

In hindsight, a few factors stood out that season. Heyneke's decision to appoint Chris le Roux as captain was not the best he ever made, and it was also unfair to Chris – it was his first taste of Super 12 rugby, and although he had captained the Vodacom Cup side, there was a massive difference between the level of the two tournaments.

During one of our overseas games, our confidence was at an all-time low, and then Chris stunned us with his team talk. 'It's ridiculous that these guys can come to Loftus and beat us there. In that case, we can beat them here, at their home ground.'

We were completely taken aback. The Super 12 was a tough competition and it was no easy task to win our home games – how on earth did he think we'd win our matches in New Zealand and Australia? We just didn't think it possible to win there. Chris was young, and I think the burden of captaincy and the series of defeats caused him a lot of damage psychologically. Heyneke eventually came to realise this, and when Chris was injured, he asked James Dalton to take over the reins.

I knew James, but right from the start we were at each other's throats. Before the game against the Blues, we had a line-out video session. Even while Chris was the captain, I did the talking when we discussed the line-outs. But suddenly James and I had differing opinions on how this set phase should be executed.

'Who do you think you are … Mark Andrews?' he snapped.

'No, but then you're not really John Smit, are you?' I retaliated. At that stage, John was the number-one hooker in the Bok squad and one of a group of young, up-and-coming players.

It escalated into a big argument. The younger players were astonished that I was taking on James Dalton, a 1995 World Cup–winning Bok, as it was just not done. After our scrap we patched things up, and before long we were treating each other with great respect.

In those years, the Bulls were a regional franchise and Heyneke had to answer to the Blue Bulls, the Pumas and the Falcons. This was no easy task, as the Blue Bulls had finished below the Pumas and Falcons in the 2001 Currie Cup competition. Each union was represented in the management team and had its own mandate. Heyneke was under pressure to pick players from all three unions, even though he had his own plans.

The Bulls' Super 12 record between 1996 and 2002 was sickening – only seven victories in 55 games. We were the laughing stock of the series. People referred to us as an 'easy target' – the team against which other teams were sure to accumulate log points. It hurt. Something drastic had to be done, but Heyneke's position as head coach was now under threat, even though he knew that we urgently had to change our playing style. As a student of the game, he could see that rugby was moving towards a new direction, with counter-attacks from kicks down-field and quick attacks from turned-over possession the new cornerstones of the game.

Whereas retaining the ball at all costs used to be of cardinal import-ance – as the Brumbies tried to do – we were now moving towards a game plan whereby we would force our opponents to make mistakes. We were discarding any elaborate moves and instead were concentrating on the basics. As such, we were taking small, but necessary, steps.

* * *

As if the Super 12 wasn't disappointment enough, Rudolf Straeuli was the new Bok coach. He made it clear from the start that the 'easy' days under Harry Viljoen were something of the past. No contracts, for starters – you had to show your worth if you wanted to play for South Africa.

Rudolf, who had coached the Sharks to the Super 12 final in 2001, quickly made his move and dropped some of Harry's Boks. After trials at Loftus Versfeld and shortly before our Tests against Wales, he picked new caps such as Bolla Conradie, Daan Human, Faan Rautenbach, André Pretorius, Craig Davidson and Brent Russell.

Although I was selected, I knew that Rudolf wasn't one of my biggest fans. I was not your typical Springbok or Blue Bulls lock, and traditionalists were not accustomed to the way I approached the game. Traditionally, locks were there to unnerve the opponents, to soften them up and even hurt them in order to set up the platform for the backline and the rest of the forwards. Lurking in the backline, waiting for an opportunity to run with the ball, was not allowed.

Rudolf was a traditionalist. He was an eighthman in his playing days, and he saw the role of a lock forward just the way I describe it above. No flourishing runs with the ball, nor anything remotely to do with the role of a backline player. You are the hard man of the pack, and that's how you should behave. Rudolf and Kobus Wiese were from a generation of Lions players who used to incite themselves before a game by pushing and shoving each other and running into changing-room walls. That was not my style.

So the new Bok coach tried to stamp his authority in the old-school way by having our first training camp at the Police College in Pretoria. In his days as a player, and even earlier, this was the venue where several Bulls teams were shaped.

The first thing we did together was to sing the (somewhat new) national anthem. Rudolf had the words printed out and we were each given a copy. It was a good start and we enjoyed learning the lyrics.

But then one of his first instructions was for all of us who wore head guards and other protective gear to take them off, as it indicated weakness. As an international player, you couldn't be perceived as soft. His logic baffled me, and I decided to ignore his instruction. I wasn't being a rebel, I just wanted to do what I thought was right. I thought Rudolf was being unreasonable in this case. It would also not be the last time I ignored his orders.

The reason why I started wearing the head guard has an embarrassing twist to it. In my early days with the Bulls, Riaan Olckers and I had gone out on the town one evening in 1998. I had been dropped from the Vodacom Cup team and was playing only for Tuks – all the more reason to down a few beers.

At a popular hangout in Hatfield, a big bouncer stopped us when we wanted to enter the premises with beers in our hands. I had quite an attitude, so I dropped the bottle on the ground in front of him and walked in. I was *the man*, after all.

The next thing I knew, I was waking up in my bed in Boekenhout with a defrosting chicken lying next to me. I had no idea how it had got there, but when I looked in the mirror, I saw that my face was badly swollen. I phoned Riaan, but he was none the wiser.

Minutes later, he phoned back. 'Victor, I have *two* black eyes.'

Then I knew. We phoned a couple of friends who confirmed that we had been 'worked over' by the bouncers at the club. Apparently we had wanted revenge afterwards and went looking for reinforcements, and we found two big guys in the form of Wium Basson and Jaco Barnard at the Rugby House on Tuks campus, but they told us to go home. All I could find at the time to stop my eye from swelling was a frozen chicken in the kitchen's deep-freeze.

That afternoon at Tuks practice I told our coach, Chris Buitendach, that my face was swollen because I had had my wisdom teeth extracted. When Riaan arrived a little later, sporting two black eyes, the coach dryly remarked, 'I see you also had your wisdom teeth removed.' I started playing with a scrum cap that day, to try to avoid any direct contact with a very sore eye. The scrum cap soon became a permanent fixture, as it helps prevent cuts and cauliflower ears. I don't want to lose my wife because I have big, wrinkly ears!

The arm guard I wear is a different story. Kevin Putt, former Sharks coach, alleged that it was a steel plate bound to my arm to injure opponents. The truth, however, is that I broke a small bone in my right arm during an under-21 game and it took a long time for the injury to heal. Initially I just strapped the arm, but later I started using an arm guard one of our equipment suppliers had developed. It is made from the same dense foam rubber as a scrum cap, and I used it not as a weapon to injure players, but as protection. I didn't want to take any risks with my 'weak' arm.

We had to get up at 5 a.m. every morning at the training camp at the Police College, and we'd sweat it out on the infamous hill where coach Brigadier Buurman van Zyl used to toughen up his Northern Transvaal players in the past. We also took part in wrestling sessions – during one such session, Corné Krige injured himself so badly that he missed the Test against Wales in Bloemfontein.

We spent hours working on our scrumming technique, first against the scrum machine and then against the Police pack. These were tough guys who played in the very physical Carlton League in Pretoria, and they gave us a hard time. What can be more enticing than to try to out-scrum the Bok pack? After these sessions, we were dog-tired. All the hard work, however, ensured that we were ready when Wales finally arrived for the two Tests. Although Rudolf's approach to coaching was semi-militaristic, he also did a lot of good.

We won the first Test 34-19, but I wasn't satisfied with my performance and was determined to improve. The next day we left for Cape Town for the second Test against Wales. On arrival, Rudolf summoned me and a few of the other players to his hotel room. We had to wait out in the hallway as he called us in one by one.

When it was my turn, Rudolf told me that I hadn't done a good job in the rucks and mauls and would be dropped for the second Test. I went home the next day, gutted and in tears. It was the first time I had ever been axed from a team. Back in Pretoria I pulled a mattress up to the TV and watched DVDs the whole day. At least Monja was there to feed me and provide a shoulder to cry on.

A day later I realised that it wouldn't help to mope around the house. I had to get back to the practice field, I had to work harder and, above all, I had to regain my spot in the Bok team.

While the Boks were preparing for the second Test against Wales and the one against the Pumas (which they won 19-8 and 49-29, respectively), I had to run on for South Africa A against Argentina in a midweek match in Witbank. Mark Andrews captained our side. Jannes Labuschagne, Quinton Daniels and Hottie Louw were now Rudolf's first-choice locks, and AJ Venter was a backup.

Before the game in Witbank, the South Africa A-side was asked to practise against the Boks in a training session in Johannesburg. We accepted the invitation, but we did point out that we had a game on the Wednesday and thus wouldn't do a full-contact session.

During the practice, AJ Venter and I had a bit of a scrap, and Mark called us aside. With things beginning to get out of hand up front, he realised that it wouldn't be of benefit to anyone to go full tilt two days before taking on a touring Test side. He told Rudolf that we were finished for the day, as we had a big game on the Wednesday evening.

Rudolf lost his temper. 'I'm the fucking Springbok coach! You will stay on this field.' Mark replied, 'I'm sorry, but this is my team and we're playing in two days' time. We're done here.' And that was the end of the practice.

Now that's how a captain should stand up for his players, I thought. Mark knew what was happening wasn't right. He was also aware of the fact that he was in a team with guys who desperately wanted to be in the Bok squad and that they would want to impress the national selectors in the game they were soon to play.

The game in Witbank went without hiccups and we won 42-36, and afterwards I rejoined the Boks for the fourth Test of the season, against Samoa in Pretoria – my first Test at Loftus. Danie Coetzee, my Bulls teammate, made his Bok debut from the bench in that match, and the first time he touched the ball, the big Samoan hooker Trevor Leota almost decapitated him with a full-blown South Sea Island tackle.

It was fantastic to play in front of my home crowd, and fortunately we had no problems beating the Samoans (60-18). We now felt that we were well prepared for the upcoming Tri Nations series.

Even though we lost the first game 20-41 against New Zealand in Wellington, we believed the scoreboard was not a true reflection of the game. A week later, after the Test against the Wallabies at the Gabba in Brisbane, Rudolf and I drifted further apart. We lost 27-38 in a match marred by a big punch-up. Jeremy Paul and Justin Harrison just climbed into a couple of Boks, which led to punches being thrown left, right and centre. Paul and Harrison were subsequently sin-binned.

I tried to break up the free-for-all, and after the game Rudolf accused me of not being a team player, as I didn't take part in the fight. He'd expected me to get involved in the altercation and throw a few punches, but that wasn't the way I played rugby any more. During my days as an under-21 player, I realised that it was better to play within the rules and to focus on the game rather than get involved in off-the-ball distractions. There are plenty of opportunities within the rules where you can get the better of your opponent legally, like going in low and hard for a tackle, and rucking and mauling aggressively.

But Rudolf still believed in old-style intimidation. In some of the games against Australia, he offered a reward of AU$100 for the first player to bring back a dreadlock from George Smith's head.

Back in South Africa, we had a training camp in Durban in preparation for the All Blacks. Rudolf wanted us to hand over our cellphones, but I wasn't so keen. Monja's dad had just died of a stroke and it was important for me to stay in touch with her. So I secretly bought a second cellphone and handed in the other one.

On the Monday before the Test, I asked Rudolf whether I could attend Monja's dad's funeral, and he wasn't too happy with the idea, as it wasn't in the team's best interest if I missed a practice session. He thought that I was putting my interests first instead of the team's, but he did add that it was up to me to decide what I wanted to do.

So the next morning I caught a flight to Johannesburg and was back in Durban that evening – I missed one practice session. Nevertheless, I was dropped from the starting line-ups for the Tests against the All Blacks in Durban and the Wallabies at Ellis Park. AJ Venter and Jannes Labuschagne were the locks in those games. I am convinced that I was dropped for the second time that season because I had decided to attend the funeral, and because I didn't take part in the fight in Brisbane.

I don't think you build discipline by removing players' cellphones and I still don't understand what the point of it was. We all blamed

Rudolf for this silliness, but why did senior players like the captain, Corné Krige, and Bob Skinstad not stand up for the players?

Rugby is important to many of us, but in the end it is just a game, and the player is always more important than the result. But Rudolf didn't see it that way.

***

In Durban, the Boks lost 23-30 to the All Blacks in what would become known as the 'Piet van Zyl Test'. Van Zyl was a Bok supporter from North West who thought the Irish referee, Dave McHugh, was unfairly punishing the Boks, and he lost his temper. Despite not being a very athletic chap, early in the second half he sidestepped two security guards and ran onto the field to let rip with a flying tackle that floored the ref. In the chaos that ensued, some of the players punched Van Zyl a couple of times before he was dragged off the park like a criminal and banned from all rugby games for life. I watched the whole episode from the reserve bench. Although I did eventually get about five minutes' game time when AJ left the field, by then the die was cast.

The local Test season ended on a personal low for me, but at least the Boks concluded their Tri Nations series with an epic victory over the Wallabies at Ellis Park. I was once again on the bench and didn't get any game time. However, it was a fantastic day for the team, thanks to Werner Greeff's try in the dying seconds of the game. He also converted his try to clinch victory by 33-31.

Because of the disappointments of the Bok experience, I was very excited to return to the Blue Bulls camp for the rest of the Currie Cup season. Our aim was to reach the semi-finals, and although the Bulls had struggled in the Super 12, there was always hope for the Blue Bulls.

Heyneke adapted our game plan so that it would focus on the most basic elements of rugby. We had only three set moves, one from the scrum and two from the line-outs. We practised these moves only – nothing else.

In the meantime, Heyneke had also roped in John McFarland, an Englishman specialising in defence patterns. Tactical kicking would be the cornerstone of our strategy, and we had two superb kickers in Jaco van der Westhuyzen and the very young Derick Hougaard.

Joost van der Westhuizen, who by then had recovered from his injury, was instrumental in getting Derick, at 19 one of the youngest players in the squad, more involved in the team. At one practice, Jaco made a few basic errors and Joost called him over and told him to join the backline. As Currie Cup captain, Joost didn't hesitate to take control on the field. In this regard, he was almost on the same level as Heyneke and influenced many of the decisions.

Heyneke subsequently picked Derick for a couple of games, which was all he really needed to start coming into his own. Derick was an excellent kicker, which suited our restricted game plan to a T. Jaco was moved to fullback, where he could utilise his creative attacking abilities. We started dominating our opponents in the line-outs, had a solid driving maul, defended well and managed to keep our mistakes to a minimum.

With such great kickers in the team, I realised how important it was to compete in the line-outs. Although that part of my game was going well, I decided I had to pay even more attention to it. So, armed with a video recorder and a notebook, I studied every opponent's line-out strategy in the lead-up to that weekend's game. I tried to work out their line-out calls and what their body language told me.

Because we were a young team, we tried to keep the game plan as simple as possible. It was 10-man rugby, as in Naas Botha's day. Heyneke wanted a conservative approach. He often had to pull us back when our game grew too creative or experimental. Whenever I tried a new line-out move, he reminded me that there were seven other forwards who had to help me execute it. If one failed, the whole move failed.

It was a case of the simpler, the better: kick for the corner, force a turnover and take it from there. Before we'd even blinked, it seemed, we were in the Currie Cup semi-final. We had worked towards this – it had been our single goal for the season. As we were fourth on the log, we had to travel to Durban to take on the Sharks, who'd lost only one of their seven matches in the top-eight phase of the season. But we had nothing to lose and were very excited at the prospect of playing in a semi.

I had been nursing an ankle injury and had my work cut out play-ing in the knockout rounds, but thanks to the best medical treatment,

I recovered in time for the encounter in the Shark Tank. Bakkies Botha and I would come up against Mark Andrews and Albert van den Berg, two very experienced Bok lock forwards, which was quite a daunting challenge. In fact, the Bulls basically consisted of Joost – the rest of us were a whole lot of 'no-name' brands or up-and-coming youngsters, and we were up against a team chock-a-block with Springboks. I was pumped full of cortisone, but nevertheless my Blue Bull heart was brimming with confidence, as were my teammates'.

And then we beat the Sharks 22-19, a colossal achievement. It was almost too good to be true. For years the Sharks and Western Province had been the leading teams in South African rugby. So when Province lost to the Lions at Newlands in the other semi, the final was scheduled for Ellis Park, just 60 kilometres from Loftus. And we'd be playing against a team we'd beaten earlier that season on their home ground.

The Monday after the semi-final against the Sharks I limped into our team doctor Tommy Smook's office. He presented me with two options: either he could treat the ankle intensively in order for me to make a full recovery and tour with the Springboks in November – but then I would have to miss the Currie Cup final – or he could inject me with cortisone so that I could play in the final, but then I wouldn't be able to go on tour.

I didn't find it a hard decision to make. I didn't have a great relationship with Rudolf Straeuli, and a Currie Cup final didn't come around every year. Although I had 13 Tests under my belt at that stage, I'd never played in a final at senior level. And after beating the Sharks we were so amped that I didn't want to miss the awesome opportunity to play in the final. Joost would remind us: 'Boys, you don't get it … you win the Currie Cup maybe once in your lifetime. This is the one game we simply *have* to win.' We all knew what we had to do.

But the Monday before the final, I couldn't put any weight on my ankle. By the Wednesday, after more injections, I was able to jog (or hobble, at least). I still hadn't told the Bok management team about my injury. After three further cortisone injections, I was ready for the final, and at last we boarded the team bus for the short journey to Johannesburg. The team consisted of Jaco van der Westhuyzen, Wylie Human, Dries Scholtz, Tiaan Joubert, Gavin Passens, Derick Hougaard,

Joost van der Westhuizen (c), Anton Leonard, Johan Wasserman, Pedrie Wannenburg, Victor Matfield, Bakkies Botha, Richard Bands, Danie Coetzee and Wessel Roux. Replacements: Gary Botha, Sias Wagner, Geo Cronjé, Ruan Vermeulen, Norman Jordaan, JP Nel and Johan Roets.

We were the underdogs. The Lions had all the experience *and* they had home advantage. The battle up front was intense, but we never stood back and stuck to our game plan: a tactical-kicking flyhalf and fierce contesting at the line-outs.

Derick was phenomenal. He'd still been in matric the year before, but now he was playing like someone with twice his experience. The 26 points he accumulated that day was a new Currie Cup record and helped us beat the Lions convincingly (31-7). Derick scored a try, converted two and kicked five successful penalties. Pedrie scored the other try, while Joost was also brilliant on the day and got to lift the coveted Currie Cup a second time. André Pretorius's converted try gave the Lions their only points.

The festivities afterwards were something else. Back at Loftus, we partied through the night. The Blue Bulls hadn't won the Currie Cup since 1998, and just the year before we'd struggled to survive in the competition. Our Super 12 effort had been a fiasco, but we had turned the ship around and won the golden trophy. It was more than we could ever have hoped for. And it had all come about in the second year of Heyneke's three-year plan.

***

When my ankle didn't recover in time, I had to withdraw from the Bok squad for the tour to France, Scotland and England. The Boks had a nightmare, losing all three Tests, but four of my Blue Bulls teammates – Bakkies Botha, Norman Jordaan, Wessel Roux and Pedrie Wannenburg – made their debuts for South Africa.

With the Boks away on tour, Jaco van der Westhuyzen and I decided to use our time at home to prepare for 2003. It would, after all, be a World Cup year. For three weeks we did everything by the book: we exercised, we ate the right food, we took the right supplements. We did everything a professional rugby player is supposed to do. Jaco was very driven and he and I inspired each other to aim for something better, further, faster and higher. Together we braved the intense Pretoria heat to become better rugby players.

When I analysed my diet, I quickly realised how badly I was eating – I was scoffing far too many peanut-butter-and-syrup sandwiches. I lost more than 10 kilograms in those three weeks and my weight dropped to 108 kilograms. Since then, I've never strayed from my 'ideal fighting weight'. Jaco and I had heavy workouts in the gym, and we cycled, boxed and rowed. I didn't risk my ankle by jogging, however.

And so my days of ambling along at the back of the pack with the props were finally over. From now on, I belonged with the loose forwards and the backline guys.

My approach towards rugby changed completely during those three weeks. Now that I was more athletic, I would be able to do more on the field; I would get to phases more quickly. It was a watershed moment in my career.

5

Staaldraad, spying and confetti

A new approach, a new hairstyle and – yet again – a new Super 12 coach for the Bulls! Just when we thought things were starting to fall into place at Loftus Versfeld, the South African Rugby Football Union (SARFU) decided that the Bulls needed a new coach.

Although we had lost all 11 games in 2002 under Heyneke, overnight success had never been in his plans, nor was it what he had promised. His goals were long term and when we clinched the Currie Cup, we knew that we were on the right track.

But Rudy Joubert was the man SARFU wanted instead. He had had great success as the Boland coach a few years earlier and at that stage was contracted by Cardiff in Wales. Rumour had it that Rudolf wanted Rudy as the Springboks' assistant coach, replacing the Australian Tim Lane, and that SARFU was, therefore, trying to lure him back to South Africa. As the Bulls were the 'easy targets' of the Super 12 competition, it was the logical place for Rudy to intervene, according to the rugby bosses. Rudy had also previously been connected with Pretoria and Tuks.

Still, none of us, as players, could understand Rudy's appointment, given that the state of affairs had started to improve with Heyneke at the helm. We were a young team, but we all had the same goals and sought success for the union. It would be difficult for us to work with yet another new coach – the fifth Bulls coach in six seasons. Consistency and stability in our camp remained elusive – and they were two of the most vital ingredients for success.

Nevertheless, Rudy and I got along well virtually from the start. His plan for the Bulls was different from the one Heyneke had. Under Heyneke we had tried to keep our game plan as simple and basic as possible, but Rudy preferred the Australian playing style, where positions are quite interchangeable. After one phase, the pack divides, with two forwards on the left side of the field, four in the middle and two on the right, which opens up the game, and you play with ball in hand.

Rudy started his planning early. Before the season had even kicked off, he had drawn up a list of possible Super 12 players. Of the Blue Bulls team that had won the Currie Cup competition a few months earlier, only eight made his first-choice Super 12 team. Derick Hougaard, for example, who had been one of the stars of the Currie Cup final, was now only a second- or third-choice flyhalf, according to Rudy. Perhaps Rudy reckoned that most of the 'Currie Cup Bulls' wouldn't fully support him, and he therefore decided to leave them out of his squad.

Blikkies Groenewald was Rudy's assistant coach, and he also had some new ideas. He focused a great deal on teaching us new skills, like passing the ball with one hand. We weren't used to this kind of trick, but we knuckled down and did our best. We were extremely fit and reckoned that we'd left our struggle years behind us for good. Perhaps we were a tad too optimistic, but we even thought we had a chance of reaching the Super 12 semi-finals.

The season started off with a bang when we beat the Cats 34-26 in Bloemfontein. Louis Koen, who was now the first-choice flyhalf instead of Derick, scored 29 points with the boot that day (a conversion, six penalties and three drop goals). Then we were off to New Zealand for a game against the Hurricanes in Napier. And, in a historic moment, we won a game over there (46-34) for the first time. It was a wonderful feeling.

In those years, South African teams very seldom won overseas, and the Bulls had certainly never done so before. To achieve a victory against the Hurricanes – a team we had always admired – was very special.

Most of the big-name Hurricanes played that day – Jerry Collins, Rodney So'oialo, Ma'a Nonu, Tana Umaga and Christian Cullen. We took them on up front and destroyed them with a tight five that would later that year form the nucleus of the Bok pack at the World Cup: Christo Bezuidenhout (loosehead prop), Danie Coetzee (hooker), Richard Bands (tighthead prop), me and Geo Cronjé (locks), with Bakkies Botha returning a week later after recovering from injury.

It was a very physical game, but for once we didn't hold back against a Super 12 side from the Antipodes. We hit the Hurricanes with rock-hard South African forward play, which they didn't like at all. Our playing style – although somewhat different now that Rudy was in charge – was established, and even though we made greater use of tactical kicking, we concentrated on the basics of the game as much as always.

There were highlights other than rugby on this tour too. At the beginning of the tour, I had a very lucrative evening at the blackjack table. A few of the guys were also playing, and I won NZ$600 from Joost van der Westhuizen, which covered my pocket money for the duration of our visit. I won't ever forget that evening!

But we were by no means the cat's whiskers, as many of us thought. We went on to lose all our other games on tour. The last match, against the Brumbies in Canberra, where we were beaten 26-64, brought us back to earth with a thud. With Joost injured, I captained the side in that game, in which Fourie du Preez made his Super 12 debut for the Bulls at scrumhalf.

Back in Pretoria, we beat the Reds (39-19), Crusaders (32-31), Chiefs (29-26) and Sharks (24-16), and eventually finished sixth on the log. It was the best performance by a South African team that season, and we were only one or two points shy of a place in the semi-finals.

Besides experiencing a reversal of fortune on the rugby field, my personal life also changed for the better. Monja and I were getting serious after dating for a year and a half.

Ettienne Botha and I were room-mates on the Super 12 tour and he was talking about getting engaged to his long-time girlfriend, which made me think that I should perhaps follow suit.

Monja must have read my mind, because soon after our return from the Antipodes, she started dropping hints to that effect. Whenever we were out shopping in Menlyn or Brooklyn, she would linger in jewellery stores and explain in detail which ring she liked the most. Popping the big question was easier said than done, however. For a shy bloke like me, it wasn't an easy task. I was actually more nervous than before a big game, so I decided I'd just throw caution to the wind. I hired a Santa Claus suit and one morning at 5.30 a.m., in the dead of winter, I surprised Monja with a bag stuffed full of goodies while she was still half asleep. I told her that Christmas had come early this year.

The last present I gave her was in a small box. When she opened it to reveal the ring, I went down on one knee, in my fire-engine-red Santa suit, and asked her to marry me. Monja was completely stunned, as she hadn't expected me to ask her so soon. But she said yes, and I just hoped that she was awake enough to mean it! It was a wonderful, blessed feeling. I was looking forward to spending the rest of my life with Monja.

Unfortunately, there was no time for holding hands or celebrating the occasion, as a day later we departed on the Boks' Tri Nations tour. With the World Cup ahead there would be no time to get married, so we picked a date in December 2003, when rugby wouldn't interfere.

Bakkies Botha and I made a bet – whoever had a haircut first would have to take the other one out for lunch. Unfortunately for Bakkies, his hair grows quite wild, almost like a Boere Afro, and he soon after made an appointment at the hairdresser for the usual short back and sides. Monja liked my hair a little longer than I usually wore it, so I let it grow – a seemingly trivial thing that would present its own problems in the coming years.

By the way, that stingy Bakkies still owes me a lunch.

***

After the Bulls' much-improved Super 12 campaign, we could approach the Test season with greater confidence. My relationship with Rudolf Straeuli also seemed to be improving. Perhaps he had seen some things he didn't like during the end-of-year tour in 2002 – when I was not in the squad – and it made him realise that I deserved a place in the team after all. He phoned me up shortly after the Boks' return to tell me that my line-out work would be of great value to the Springboks in the coming season. I had performed well in the Super 12, and he wanted me back in the team. He also offered me a substantial contract.

With a solid Super 12 performance behind me, the woman of my dreams agreeing to marry me and a place in the Bok World Cup squad virtually confirmed, everything was coming up roses!

We practised really hard for the Test series against Scotland, and it gradually became clear that Rudolf was planning on picking quite a few Bulls for the Springbok team – a welcome change for Joost and me, who for years had been just about the only two players from Pretoria who were regularly picked for South Africa.

Bakkies had been one of the new players touring with the Boks in 2002, but I had to wait till 7 June 2003 before the two of us could play in the green and gold together. Ironically, I was the one who was shown a yellow card in the Test against Scotland in Durban! Although we won 29-25, we didn't play well. Even though the Scots had a rather mediocre side, we still struggled against them, and their locks, Scott Murray and Nathan Hines, were two experienced campaigners who gave us a hard time in the line-outs.

A week later, at Ellis Park, we upped our game and won 28-19. Then we travelled to Port Elizabeth to take on Argentina. The Pumas were superb, while we simply couldn't get going. In the end we managed to pull off a one-point victory (26-25) thanks to a try by Brent Russell and a difficult penalty converted by Louis Koen.

The Tri Nations was looming and the World Cup was around the corner, but in the Bok camp, things were not well. Were these the first signs of what would await us in the last six months of 2003? Rudolf had become quite paranoid after appointing Adriaan Heijns – or '007', as we dubbed him – as a security consultant. He was soon Rudolf's right-hand man, and his influence on the coach was plain for all to see.

When Rudolf wanted to speak to senior players like Joost, Corné Krige and John Smit at a training camp in Durban, they had to wade waist-high into the sea so that no one could eavesdrop on their conversation. Adriaan, for his part, turned our team room upside down looking for listening devices. This room had to be locked at all times and we could enter it only by using our special access cards. It was all totally weird and rather silly.

Some of the Sharks players, whom Rudolf had coached to the finals of the Super 12 in 2001, told us that he'd already behaved strangely back then. I knew Adriaan, as we used to bump into each other at the gym in

Pretoria sometimes and have a chat, and outside the Bok environment he was a nice bloke: maybe a bit too serious, but not weird. However, as a 'consultant' for the Boks, it was a completely different story. Maybe he was given too much power and suddenly thought of himself as a bigwig.

At one game, Adriaan sat right next to Rudolf and constantly whispered in his ear. As far as we knew, Adriaan had never played or coached rugby at a high level, so it was strange to see him trying to give rugby advice to the Springbok coach.

After those three unconvincing victories, we had to face the Wallabies in Cape Town. Fortunately, we performed much better in this Test, winning 26-22. I also scored my third try – in my 17th Test!

A week later, against the All Blacks at Loftus, the tables were turned. Nothing that we tried worked, but the All Blacks were sublime. The altitude usually helped us at Loftus, but not this time. Later, this match would be referred to as the 'Jan van Riebeeck Test', as we lost 16-52. It was a sad day.

Usually we'd go out on the town after a game and unwind a bit, but that evening, to hide from the disgruntled Bok supporters, Monja and I, along with a few teammates, just had a quiet dinner at a local restaurant. We couldn't look anyone in the eye, and while we were still eating, the first sarcastic jokes about the Boks were SMSed to us.

Even though we had won four out of our five Tests in 2003, the warning lights were beginning to flash. We had no fixed game plan and no established playing pattern. It was one of our biggest problems with Rudolf: none of us knew what we were supposed to do on the field. One week, Brent Russell was at flyhalf, which meant we had to play wide and pass the ball, but the next week Louis Koen, with his tactical kicking, was at No.10, and then we had to play conservative rugby.

Rudy Joubert, as one of the assistant coaches, had some influence, and during the week we would practise tactics we used at the Bulls or moves that Gert Smal had instituted at the Stormers, but come Friday at the captain's run, Rudolf would change everything. Meetings between the senior players and the coaches to discuss the situation yielded no results, as the players' influence was limited and Rudolf just carried on doing what he thought was right. And we didn't know what that was.

Our next Test took place in Brisbane against the Wallabies, and we lost 9-29. To add insult to injury, their hooker, Brendan Cannon, afterwards claimed that Bakkies had bitten him during the match. It was terrible to hear such an allegation against someone who'd been in the team with me for some time. We all knew Bakkies as a tough and physical customer, but he wouldn't have used his teeth to injure an opponent on the field.

'I feared for my life,' Cannon told Australian journalists.

We thought Cannon was being ridiculous, and his 'injury' also wasn't nearly as bad as he was claiming. The Aussies, in general, are somewhat prone to exaggeration. The newspapers, of course, spread photos of the bite marks on Cannon's shoulder all over their front pages.

Bakkies was very worried that he might miss the World Cup because of the incident. We were room-mates on the tour, and he was very emotional before his disciplinary hearing. Fortunately, Rudolf fully supported Bakkies, and I respected him for backing and defending his player. In the end Bakkies was banned for eight weeks for 'attacking the face' of Cannon. He had to return to South Africa, and Geo Cronjé replaced him the following week against the All Blacks in Dunedin.

Nobody gave us a chance to beat the Kiwis at the House of Pain. Nobody. Bakkies was gone and we'd suffered two successive defeats, against Australia and New Zealand. So we decided to give everything we had against the All Blacks. We would play right in their faces and physically take the game to them up front. The result was that Richard Bands scored an unbelievable try after running 50 metres and handing off Carlos Spencer.

Richard, a late bloomer as a rugby player, was the most explosive prop I ever played with. Heyneke had pulled him from Stellaland's ranks and turned him into a key player in the Bulls set-up. Richard could tackle his opponents into oblivion and was a strong ball carrier, as he later showed in a Super 12 game when he bulldozed Richie McCaw with the ball under his arm. Sadly, his career ended abruptly due to a serious knee injury.

So we did a good job in Dunedin. Whereas the All Blacks had chalked up more than 50 points against us at Loftus, this time they'd barely held on to win 19-11. It gave us a lot of hope for the World Cup. Although we hadn't had a good year up till then, the All Blacks had had their work cut out for them in Dunedin. We now believed we could beat them. Even though they were the best team in the world, our confidence was at a new high after that game.

Rudolf was also quite positive, but he was peeved that we had lost. As players, though, we felt our energy levels being lifted just in time for the World Cup.

* * *

If we wanted to be successful in the World Cup, we had to make personal sacrifices. That was Rudolf's belief, but not all of us completely shared his view. Instead of eating so little and crawling through bushes, as we would do later, why did we not have more intensive fitness or scrum sessions?

The preliminary Bok squad gathered at the Tuks High Performance Centre in Pretoria. Our friends and family weren't allowed at the camp – they were one of the 'sacrifices'. Those of us from Pretoria were quite peeved that we weren't allowed to see our loved ones. It wasn't as if we would miss a practice in order to have coffee with our girlfriends – we just wanted to see them from time to time.

Monja was busy with our wedding arrangements and obviously we had to discuss certain issues. The Tuks cricket field is next to the High Performance Centre, and behind it is a pub called Nick's Place, and Monja and I met there after I slipped out unnoticed. We would soon be away at the World Cup for two months, so it was ridiculous that we weren't allowed to have contact with the people closest to us.

When the members of the initial squad were allocated their rooms, it became apparent that Geo Cronjé and Quinton Davids would have to share, even though Rudolf knew Geo wasn't comfortable with such an arrangement. It was one of Rudolf's little games to get us out of our 'comfort zones'. Earlier that year, he had AJ Venter share a room with me, even though he knew that we didn't get along. As Jaco van der Westhuyzen and Stefan Terblanche were sharing, Stefan and I swapped so that Jaco and I could share and the two Sharks guys could room together. When Rudolf got wind of the swap, he was furious and threatened to send us home if we didn't move back.

Bugger that, I thought. Why must I be in a room with someone who is not my friend? I wanted to share with someone with whom I was comfortable, because your bedroom is basically the only place you can relax on tour. I'm sure that the other players felt much the same. You don't want to share your personal space with just anybody.

So back in Pretoria, Geo decided to move in with Fourie du Preez, one of the youngest players in the squad, who was sharing with Gcobani Bobo. Quinton and Gcobani would then share a room. It was certainly not unusual for players to swap rooms, and Geo was more comfortable sharing with Fourie, his Bulls teammate.

There are many different cultures in South Africa, and each one tends to band together with its own kind. It wasn't unusual for the Afrikaans guys in the team to seek out one another's company, and the players of colour and the English-speaking guys did much the same. But of course this didn't happen *all* the time. So, is someone a racist if he prefers to spend time with his friends?

The morning after the room swapping, all hell broke loose. Joost announced that the players who had swapped rooms had to move back immediately, and Rudolf decided to punish those who had swapped, which involved Geo, Quinton, Bobo, Fourie and Corné Krige repeatedly running up and down the grass embankment of the Tuks rugby field.

Although Corné wasn't involved in the room-swapping affair, Rudolf felt he had to suffer the same fate, because he was the team captain. The punished players were not allowed to wear running shoes. Rudolf always had us train in our rugby boots, which was what they had to wear that day as well. Those who had swapped rooms where race had not been a factor were not punished. Everyone eventually reverted to their original rooms and we continued with our World Cup preparations.

The next morning, before the story hit the newspapers, our media manager, Mark Keohane, told me that the fur would fly that same day. He was right, because that afternoon the incident was splashed across the front page of a newspaper: 'Race bomb explodes in Bok camp'. We soon began to realise that Rudolf's trust in Keo was wearing thin. Many people believed that Keo had leaked the story to the newspapers. Rudolf started leaving him out of conversations, and Keo didn't like that at all.

Quinton and Geo were removed from the squad and taken to a

place near Roodeplaat Dam while SARFU launched an investigation. Before the story hit the headlines, we'd thought nothing of it. Race had never been an issue at either the Bulls or the Boks. It was a simple case of birds of a feather flock together – that's how we saw it at the time. After all, you can't be friends with everyone. Only when the story hit the newspapers did we realise just how sensitive an issue it was.

Hordes of reporters descended on the team, and not just your usual rugby journalists. Rumours abounded that Rudolf might be fired, and a player strike was also mentioned. Joost and Corné, the two most senior members of the squad, called a players' meeting and said that if Rudolf was fired, we would boycott the World Cup. A few of us didn't even consider this as an option. I was definitely not going to sacrifice my first World Cup for a coach I didn't even get along with all that well. Luckily, nothing came of the boycott, as Rudolf stayed on as coach.

* * *

After the training camp in Pretoria, the final World Cup squad was announced during a sports day on the Tuks campus. Geo and Quinton didn't make the final team. Danie Rossouw was included as lock, along with Bakkies, Selborne Boome and me.

I got quite a shock when the official team photograph was taken. Where you are placed in the team photo is determined by two factors: seniority and height. The senior players sit in the front row with the coach, the coach's assistants and the captain. The tall guys make up the back row, and the rest pile in the middle.

As one of the tallest men in the squad, I took up my usual spot in the back row, but I was told to take a seat in the front row instead, with the more experienced players. And this after just 20 Tests! The youth and inexperience of most of the players in the squad was quite disconcerting. Of the 30 picked for the World Cup, 19 had not yet played 10 Tests and four were yet to make their debuts.

Schalk Burger, Jaque Fourie, Derick Hougaard and Danie Rossouw were the four newcomers, while Brent Russell, Jaco van der Westhuyzen and Pedrie Wannenburg were unlucky not to be picked. We later learnt that Pedrie's omission was due to a phone call he had made to his girlfriend from the changing room shortly before a Test at Loftus Versfeld, which Corné observed. He didn't like it at all.

We were aware that we would go on a team-building expedition, and after the announcement of the World Cup squad, we were given an hour to prepare ourselves for the camp. A cap, a red jersey, exercise shorts and running shoes were the only items of clothing we were allowed to take along.

Rudolf had discussed details of Kamp Staaldraad with Joost and Corné, and they thought it was a good idea. When I got wind of what was planned, I told Joost that it wouldn't help us at all. Those of us who had played for the Bulls in the 2001 Super 12 knew exactly what was coming, as we had experienced it before. Nevertheless, we all got on the bus and headed off in the direction of Warmbaths.

Because I'd gone through Kamp Staaldraad before, I smuggled along some toilet paper. I knew the camp would involve a lot of physical activity, and the last thing you needed was chafing between your legs. Of course, the camp 'commanders' busted me, but I explained that I suffered from hay fever, and as the veld would be very dry after the winter, I had to be prepared for a runny nose.

On our arrival, we got off the bus and were loaded onto a truck. The team was still in high spirits and everyone was laughing and joking around, but the camp leaders were most displeased and ordered us to be quiet. They were very aggressive, almost militaristic, and we soon realised that the situation was getting serious.

When we reached our destination, more orders were barked, and the guys in control – they looked like Adriaan Heijns's buddies – were very unfriendly. All at once the good-spirited vibe turned sour and the fooling around stopped immediately.

We were told to pair up to carry a heavy tar pole down a dark dirt road. As Bakkies and I were the same height, we shared this heavy burden. After a couple of minutes we were told to put the poles down and swap partners. This didn't work for us at all, and in the mayhem Bakkies and I made sure we stayed together.

We continued with the exercise until the camp commanders got wind of what we were doing, and then the whole group was punished for our 'transgression'. We were made to leopard-crawl through a scorched veld, which was pretty terrible, but we did it. They probably did this sort of thing back in the days of military service, we thought.

After that, we had boxing matches. We were divided into two groups – those of similar size and height, and those who played in the same position – and were then handed boxing gloves, paired off and told that we would have to hit each other. First up were Thinus Delport and Werner Greeff, and they went at it till the blood flowed. It seemed quite hectic, and I wasn't keen on taking a swing at a teammate.

Bakkies and I were paired again. Bakkies was a far better fighter than me, but he also thought it was a ridiculous exercise. We agreed that we wouldn't hit each other too hard.

Rudolf, however, picked up on this. He was furious and told us to fight properly. He even offered to pit one of the camp commanders against us. I thought it would be interesting to see what would happen to this guy if Bakkies decided to have a proper go!

One of our 'tasks' was to kill and cook a chicken. The city boys weren't very good at killing anything with their bare hands. Not all of us had grown up on a farm. Joe van Niekerk was the first to grab hold of his 'prey'. Having been born and bred in Johannesburg, Joe had never had to 'hunt' for food. In a way it was funny to see him holding the chicken by the neck and slamming it against the ground. The poor bird probably died of shock. When the chicken was cooked, the meat was tough and virtually inedible because of the adrenalin that had pumped through its body as it was being killed.

Another of our 'tasks' was to sit stark naked in a dark pit and sing the national anthem, while a recording of the *haka* was repeatedly played over loudspeakers.

I will always remember Kamp Staaldraad for how extremely cold the water in the dam was that we all had to stand in. I'd never before felt so incredibly cold. Ever since that experience, I have detested cold water – I even refuse to take a dip in the ocean if the water is only slightly too cold.

Every time we did something they didn't like, the camp commanders – most of them armed – fired their pistols into the air to scare us. It was ridiculous. Maybe the Kamp Staaldraad experience meant something to the other players, but it did nothing for me.

Because I had known more or less what to expect, it wasn't so bad. But we were tested to our limits and it was interesting to see how much punishment we could endure. However, I thought that we could have utilised the time we had before the World Cup much better.

Although the physical elements of this camp were the same as the earlier one the Bulls had done under Phil Pretorius, this time they'd tried to break us down mentally. At last, when most of us were covered in cuts and bruises, the ordeal came to an end. We were utterly exhausted. I'd lost five kilograms in the space of a few days – not the ideal situation before a big rugby tournament, one would think.

Team building is a good idea, but there has to be a fun side to it as well. It can't only be about breaking down and punishing people. All of this happened just a few weeks before we were to leave for Australia, and I was really worried.

***

After all the drama of the 'Geogate' debacle and Kamp Staaldraad, we had a few days off before assembling in Durban for our last training camp. This time we were allowed to see our loved ones, but they had to stay in the hotel next to ours, the Elangeni on Durban's Golden Mile.

On a lighter note, on our arrival in Durban, some of the guys decided to shave off their hair in support of a cancer-awareness campaign. Most of them went for the skinhead look, and they exerted a lot of pressure on Schalk Burger and me to shave off our locks too. Although Schalla eventually succumbed, I refused. I knew that Monja would want me to keep my long hair. After all, we would be getting married in a few months' time and she wanted me to look my best on the day. So only a few of us had hair at the World Cup!

At the training camp, Rudolf called us together before breakfast one morning. Dale Santon and Ashwin Willemse were told to come to the front. Apparently the two had been at loggerheads about something Ashwin had done that Dale didn't like, and the coach wanted them to sort it out in front of the squad. We had been completely unaware of the situation. Dale was much older and bigger than Ashwin, but Ashwin was a tough customer who, in his younger days, had run with street gangs in the Cape. Not the kind of guy you messed with. The two went at each other till the blood flowed; Dale had to be stitched up afterwards.

It was a pretty sensational incident, but it was kept under wraps. Odd how a seemingly innocent room-swapping incident in Pretoria had made the headlines, but when two teammates fought till the blood flowed, it was hushed up. I wondered what would have happened if the scrap had occurred between two players of different races.

The militaristic culture in the Bok camp continued throughout the Durban event. If we went for a run on the beach, for instance, we had to do so in formation, like a troop of soldiers. Bystanders gave us many a perplexed look. Most of the players were simply embarrassed. In later years, our senior players would have a say in certain decisions, but at the time it seemed as if our two most experienced team members, Joost and Corné, had no authority to stop the nonsense that was happening to us.

In the weeks leading up to the World Cup, I was the fittest I'd ever been, as were most of the other players. Rudolf's aim was for us to be the fittest team at the tournament – that was how the Boks under coach Kitch Christie had won the World Cup in 1995. We had three practice sessions a day: sparring and running before breakfast, then lifting weights in the gym, and after lunch a field session and more fitness exercises. We worked very hard in Durban.

We were mostly focusing on our game against England, our second, and most important, match in the group stages. Rudolf even had the tackle bags fitted with England rugby jerseys, each sporting a name like 'Wilkinson' or 'Johnson'. He wanted us to visualise how we would beat England. The Boks had lost their last four Tests against them, which included the embarrassing 3-53 hiding at Twickenham at the end of 2002. We weren't allowed to stop until we had tackled all the jerseys from the bags. Then Rudolf would say something like, 'Do you think you've practised hard enough today?' Most of us would say that we had, but then Joost would go, 'No, we can take some more.'

Then we would have to run four 400-metre sprints. I could do it, because I was slim and very fit, but the bigger guys really suffered. It broke a lot of them. There wasn't a lot of positive motivation going around.

As a result of the excessive exercise, quite a few players were struggling with minor injuries. Our team doctor, Uli Schmidt, wasn't very sympathetic. You couldn't show any pain or weakness, so someone like Danie Rossouw, who suffered from severe calf-muscle pain, simply had to strap his own leg and hide the bandages under his rugby socks.

We overdid the training, but Rudolf was very pleased that we could take so much punishment. Head games were his thing, but I'm not convinced that they helped – maybe because I'm not very emotional. The mental stuff worked well on some of the other guys, though, like Joe van Niekerk, for instance. The French are passionate and very emotional, which is why I think Joe played so well for Toulon later on.

***

Fremantle, near Perth, was our base at the start of the World Cup. It's a lovely little place and we enjoyed it there, but we were closely guarded by Adriaan Heijns and his henchmen, which somewhat spoilt the experience. You couldn't even go and have a coffee in town without them following you. We didn't understand this at all. Even when we received phone calls from our girlfriends or family, Adriaan first had to screen the call. Nobody knew why Rudolf behaved like this. Was he afraid our girlfriends or wives would leak the game plan – which nobody knew – to the 'enemy'?

One evening we decided to go out for a meal, but at the last minute our Australian public-relations officer helped us find another restaurant. When we arrived there, Adriaan was furious that we had changed the venue. We had to stay on the bus until he had inspected the place.

Our first World Cup game was a one-sided affair against Uruguay in Perth, which we won 72-6. It wasn't the best preparation for our next encounter, England. As mentioned, we had been on the receiving end in the last four Tests against England, but most of those games were played at Twickenham. We felt we had a better chance in Perth, which was like a home ground to us because of its large South African population. When you are wearing the Bok jersey, you feel as if you can win any game, no matter how good the opponent is. You're a Springbok.

England had the more experienced side and could beat just about any team that crossed their path, but we still thought we could beat them. And we might have, had we not missed so many penalty kicks. After 65 minutes we were still within reach, trailing only 6-12.

But then Louis Koen's line kick was chased down, from which Will Greenwood scored the only try of the game. That was it: game, set and match. England won 25-6, but I didn't think the score was a true reflection of the game. We were an inexperienced team, and although we'd played well, the English had more experience at winning this type of game.

As a result of our loss, the All Blacks now awaited us in the quarter-final. In our next game, we beat Georgia 46-19, and then had to beat Samoa to reach the quarters. It was widely rumoured that the island side had a real chance of upsetting the Boks. However, we left our best for the last group game and completely overpowered them 60-10. Our rolling mauls were magnificent and Derick Hougaard showed awesome courage by getting up after being floored in a shattering tackle by Brian 'The Chiropractor' Lima. It was the biggest tackle I'd ever seen on a rugby field.

The evening after the Samoa game, the theme for our kontiki – the team's initiation ceremony – was 'hat and shirt'. We were under the impression that a funny hat and shirt would do the trick, but when we got there, the senior players told us to take off our pants. We were allowed to wear only the hat and shirt. In all my years of playing Test rugby, this was the first and only time something like this happened. It reminded me of the naked hours at Kamp Staaldraad, and many of the guys were totally embarrassed.

On the Wednesday before our quarter-final match, we were given only a hard-boiled egg and a chicken drumstick for lunch, like we'd had at Kamp Staaldraad. Rudolf was playing some kind of mind game again to prepare us for the big match, but most of the players thought he was being absurd and later slipped away for a hamburger.

In the quarter-final, the All Blacks were just too good for us. With the final score 29-9 in their favour, our World Cup campaign of 2003 came to an end in Melbourne. It was a huge disappointment, but if you take into account what had happened the year before, it shouldn't have come as a surprise. It simply wasn't our year; it was England's moment. They would become the first team from the northern hemisphere to lift the Webb Ellis Cup when they beat the Wallabies in a nail-biting final. Jonny Wilkinson's famous drop kick sealed the game in extra time, with the final score 20-17.

The rugby season was over, but we were still making headlines. Photos of the Springboks at Kamp Staaldraad were in every newspaper, and video clips were shown on the TV programme *Carte Blanche*. Rudolf again summoned us to a secret World Cup squad meeting, this time in Sandton, so that we could discuss the events that had befallen us. But by that time, most of the players just didn't care any more. Us younger Blue Bulls in the Springbok squad drove to Sandton for the meeting, but on the way we stopped for a few beers and arrived only after the meeting had already started.

All we wanted was for a bizarre 2003 season to be over and done with.

***

Fortunately for me, the year ended on a personal high when Monja and I were married on 12 December 2003 at Oakfield Farm in Muldersdrift, west of Johannesburg. About 120 guests – family and close friends, as well as my Blue Bulls mates who had been in the Bok side with me that season – attended the event.

Unfortunately, my old Griquas teammates didn't make the guest list after they'd shaved off my eyebrows at a bachelor's party shortly before the wedding – Monja didn't appreciate the gesture. I tried to draw fake eyebrows with a pen, but it just made me look like the Joker in *Batman*.

As I'd expected, the male guests gave my wedding speech a warm reception. They placed their chairs in a semi-circle right in the front of the room, where I was getting ready to speak, and then the heckling started. One of the guys dared me to sing Monja a love song. He probably thought I wouldn't do it, but I launched into 'Senorita', a Don Williams hit, with gusto. I thought I was brilliant, but I was probably the only one. Fortunately, that took the wind out of the peanut gallery's sails and shut them up for good!

Monja and I opened the dance floor with 'I can't help myself' by The Kelly Family as the guests stood in a circle around the floor with sparklers. My wife looked stunning, and it felt like we were floating on air. It was a very special moment in my life.

We had a great party. One of the highlights of the evening was when Basil Carzis, the Bulls' fitness trainer, performed a traditional Greek dance, complete with the smashing of the plates. One of the plates landed on Monja's toe, but luckily the most important dance of the evening was done and dusted. The Greek theme lent the party an even more jovial atmosphere. It was truly an unforgettable evening.

A day later, Bakkies and Carien Horn got married. Although the rugby hadn't given us any cause for celebration in 2003, we could at least thoroughly celebrate these big personal events.

Monja and I enjoyed a week-long honeymoon in Italy, where we skied, and then we spent two days in Barcelona on the Spanish coast. Here I realised that there were other things besides rugby that could make you happy in life. Although it had not been my best year on the rugby field, on a personal level my life could not have been better. I had married the woman of my dreams, my best friend. I will always be grateful for this blessing.

While we were at the World Cup, the Blue Bulls were going from strength to strength, winning the Currie Cup for a second year in a row when they beat the Sharks at Loftus Versfeld. It gave us a tremendous mental boost for 2004.

Younger players like Gary Botha, Pedrie Wannenburg, Fourie du Preez, Etienne Botha, Wynand Olivier, JP Nel and Johan Roets were settling down in the ranks. In later years, they formed the nucleus of the Bulls teams that would achieve unbelievable success.

6

A look in the mirror

In the wake of the dramas preceding the 2003 World Cup, our failure at the tournament and the subsequent repercussions, Rudolf Straeuli resigned as Springbok coach. Rian Oberholzer, managing director of SA Rugby, followed suit, and Brian van Rooyen was elected as the new president.

I wasn't really concerned about these changes. Although Heyneke Meyer and Rudy Joubert's names were mentioned as possible successors to Rudolf, all we were obsessing about at the start of 2004 in Pretoria was the Super 12.

We had done well in 2003, just missing out on a place in the semi-finals. The Blue Bulls had won the Currie Cup competition for the second successive year, and we should have had loads of confidence for the new season, which would be our second with Rudy at the helm. However, this 'confidence' was nothing but pretence. In our inner circle, we had problems.

While Rudy appointed me to lead the Super 12 team, Anton Leonard was captain of the Currie Cup side. Rudy and I had worked together throughout 2003, first at the Bulls and then at the Boks. We understood each other, and most of the Bulls players in the World Cup Bok squad – guys like Bakkies Botha, Danie Rossouw, Danie Coetzee and Richard Bands – supported him, as did I.

In the other corner were Heyneke, Anton and the team of Currie Cup winners: players like Fourie du Preez, Gary Botha, Gavin Passens, Johan Roets, Pedrie Wannenburg, Wynand Olivier, Frikkie Welsh and

Wessel Roux. We seemed to be split into two camps, which was an unhealthy situation.

To make matters worse, Pretoria's two major newspapers – *Beeld* and *Pretoria News* – weren't really sympathetic towards me. Rudy and I were often criticised, but according to them, Heyneke could do no wrong. Some of my teammates also made things difficult for me as Bulls captain. Right from the beginning, I could sense that we were divided into two camps: the World Cup Boks and the Currie Cup winners. It might never have been said out loud, but the younger players thought that Rudy was partial to the World Cup Boks. Some guys also thought that I had a say in Rudy's selections.

In later years Fourie du Preez and I would become best mates, but at that stage we were not friendly. In his quiet manner he had a huge influence on his teammates, as he's such a strong leader. However, there was never any doubt about his loyalty. He believed that Heyneke and Anton should lead the team, and I knew it.

One can sometimes perceive Fourie as being rather undiplomatic, or his timing can be out – off the playing field, that is! – but he's always honest. In later years his honesty would play a pivotal role in the successes the Boks and the Bulls achieved. Very often people are afraid to say what they think, and then they talk behind your back, but with Fourie, any issues are resolved immediately.

For me, the situation was complicated by Anton's presence. 'Luiperd' (Leopard), as we nicknamed him, is a true gentleman. He will never confront you in the presence of others and always honours his integrity. When Rudy picked Jacques Cronjé instead of him as eighthman, some players interpreted it as an attempt on my part to keep his strong leadership out of the side. But this wasn't the case and, in 2007, when Heyneke called on Anton to support me as captain, it only benefited and strengthened our team.

Although Rudy was opposed from all corners, I thought it was important for a captain to support his coach and I helped him where I could. Years later, Heyneke commended me for the way I had stood by Rudy through these difficult circumstances.

Rudy didn't have a lot of faith in Derick Hougaard, as we'd realised in 2002 when he picked Louis Koen at flyhalf. During the 2003 World

Cup, Louis was ahead of Derick in the Bok ranks for our important group match against England, but later on in the tournament, Derick got the nod to start against the All Blacks in the quarter-finals.

In Pretoria, Derick was hailed as the new Naas Botha. He was the golden boy, but Rudy didn't regard him as the right option at flyhalf for our game plan. He wanted us to play attacking rugby, and he saw Derick as a kicking No. 10. Whereas Heyneke knew exactly how to utilise Derick and how to guide his career, Rudy couldn't, or wouldn't, do it, and, in turn, Derick didn't like the kind of pressure he was under with Rudy.

At the end of the Super 12 season, a newspaper article in *Rapport* alleged that Rudy was trying to sabotage Derick's career. Rumour had it that Rudy had had the floodlights at Loftus switched off while Derick was still practising his place-kicking. Derick's game was going through a bad patch at the time, and the situation got so tense that I found it necessary to voice my strong support for Rudy at the weekly press conference.

The hatchets were buried after that, but it was obvious that we were not a happy, united team, even though we still did pretty well in the Super 12. We won half of our games and drew one, while the Stormers made it to the semi-finals. We once again finished sixth on the log. One of the highlights was when we beat the Reds at Ballymore in Brisbane 23-17, our first victory in Australia.

It had not been an easy Super 12 year for us, but besides the little leaks that threatened to sink the ship, the belief in our ability grew week by week.

***

Early in the 2004 Super 12 season, Rudolf Straeuli's successor as Bok coach was appointed: the former SA under-21 coach and Bok assistant coach, Jake White.

Joost van der Westhuizen announced his retirement and Corné Krige was no longer available for the Boks, and speculation as to who would be the new national captain intensified week after week. My name was mentioned, as were John Smit, Joe van Niekerk and the young Schalk Burger, who at that stage was still a spring chicken at Test level, but a strong leader nonetheless. John was the favourite for the job, but he wasn't sure of his place in the national team, as my Bulls teammates Danie Coetzee and Gary Botha were both playing exceptional rugby. Rudy supported me as possible Bok skipper, but I didn't think it that important at the time.

Then Jake phoned me to arrange a meeting. I thought it might be to discuss the captaincy or possibly my role as a senior player. Very excited, I drove to Johannesburg. We met at a hotel in Sandton. Jake jumped right in, and this is what he said: 'This is an important meeting. I want you to know that you're included in my plans. But,' he added, 'if you want to be part of this team, you have to get a haircut and change your attitude.'

What did I just hear? There I was, thinking that he wanted to discuss my role in the team or his plans for the Boks, but instead he complains about my hair! I couldn't believe my ears, and I asked him to explain.

'It's obvious to me that you are always in the "right place" when there are photographs to be taken and that your image is important to you.' Also, he said, it was ridiculous that we trained in vests – he was probably referring to me and Jaco van der Westhuyzen wearing vests while training hard in the sweltering heat of Pretoria.

'Have you ever seen an international forward with long hair?' Jake asked me.

I thought, well, no one immediately springs to mind, but I am willing to be the first one. And besides, what did the length of my hair have to do with the way I played rugby?

Jake complained that he didn't like long hair and that I came across as someone who played for the spectators … a show pony.

We talked for a while longer and then I got into my car and drove home. I phoned Monja to hear a sympathetic voice. There was no way I was going to have a haircut.

In fact, Schalk Burger was another player who had long hair. Yes, Schalk said when I phoned him, Jake had confronted him about his hair, but he hadn't spoken to him as seriously as he did to me. Schalk was also not going to make an appointment with his hairdresser.

He and I were, however, in the starting line-up for the first Test against Ireland, notwithstanding our long hair. I had my hair trimmed before the first training camp in Bloemfontein, but on arrival Jake wanted to know why it was still so long.

'But coach, I *did* get a haircut,' I protested. And I added that if he didn't want to pick me because of my hair, he was welcome to leave me out.

Shortly after our little altercation, Jake and our team manager, Arthrob Petersen, called me and Jacques Cronjé to a meeting. Now what was this all about? I wondered.

This time, Jake complained about our sideburns. I had impressive mutton-chop whiskers, but Jake and 'Mr P' didn't like it one bit. Jacques and I were told that we couldn't play for the Boks looking the way we did. I thought the whole issue was ridiculous, but in order to keep the peace, I shaved off the mutton chops. So that's how my relationship with Jake started. Over the next four years, there would be plenty of scraps.

All the guys in the squad were excited about the changes in the Bok structure after what had happened in 2003. Jake had picked the right players and it felt like we were moving in the right direction. His assistants, Gert Smal and Allister Coetzee, shared his vision. We were coached well and the necessary structures were put in place. We soon realised that the coaching staff had worked hard behind the scenes and that everyone was well prepared for whatever 2004 had in store for us.

On the first day in Bloemfontein, the entire squad got together and discussed the team rules and plans for the season. There were quite a few similarities with the way Heyneke had approached his job at the Bulls. Jake initially wanted to impose strict rules about player conduct (probably because he had primarily coached under-21s before then), but John Smit, the new Springbok captain, and I, along with some of the other senior players, wouldn't hear of it.

We'd been treated like children in 2003, and we all knew how that had ended. Besides turning us into robots, it didn't have the desired effect. We accepted certain guidelines and regulations, but in later years – having grown as a team and having matured – we would have fewer rules. Fortunately, Jake was well aware of how important it was for players to stay in touch with their loved ones, which he allowed.

But Jake's major accomplishment was once again getting all the players to focus on the significance of the Bok jersey. Of course we still cared about wearing the green and gold, but a lot of players were disillusioned after 2003. It was important that we were reminded of the meaning of Springbok rugby. Jake headhunted two Bok legends who were in the rugby wilderness and got them on board: Os du Randt, who had retired five years earlier, and Percy Montgomery, who was playing club rugby in Wales.

Henning Gericke, our team psychologist, had us sit in a circle, and each player had to describe what the Bok jersey meant to him. When it was Os's turn, he just went quiet. Then we saw the tears streaming down his face. The legendary Bok prop, who had been a member of the 1995 World Cup–winning team, had missed the Bok jersey so much in his 'retirement' years that he couldn't control his emotions when he once again held it in his hands. After all the 'sideshows' of 2003, it suddenly struck us what it was all about. Along with John and Os, Jake and Henning made us feel deeply proud to be Springboks again.

Another key attribute of Jake's was his thoroughness. He worked out the training sessions precisely and knew what he wanted to achieve. The game plan he wanted to import was based on that of the Australians, specifically the Brumbies, which Jake believed was the best-coached team in Super 12 rugby at the time. 'If we can play with that type of structure, we'll be successful,' he often said.

The message was: you did reasonably well with Rudolf as coach and *no* game plan, so imagine how good you could be if you actually had a plan!

Jake also picked a strong support team. Allister Coetzee and Gert Smal, the assistant coaches, had also been part of the Springbok set-up in 2003, and I had an excellent relationship with both of them. As mentioned, Henning was our sports psychologist who helped us to become fit and remain so, while Dr Derik Coetzee was responsible for our conditioning.

Derik was a no-nonsense guy. If he thought that you were gaining weight, he'd monitor you until you reached your ideal mass. His approach was very scientific, and he regularly measured, weighed and tested all of us so that we would know whether our conditioning was up to standard.

Jake didn't hesitate to pick younger players, some of whom he'd worked with at under-21 level. Fourie du Preez, Jacques Cronjé, Ashwin Willemse, Jean de Villiers, Juan Smith, Pedrie Wannenburg and Schalk Burger had all been part of his squad that had won the 2002 IRB Under-21 Rugby World Cup.

The team spirit was light years ahead of what Rudolf had established, and in this, John and Jake both played a massive role. John wanted to make absolutely sure that we didn't experience the same catastrophe as before. In 2003, I'd got wind that some players in the Bok team were earning much better salaries than the rest of us – guys who had probably looked after their own interests at the expense of other team members. John would never have done that. From the word go, he never accepted anything that was to his advantage if it meant disadvantaging the other guys. What one got, everyone had to get.

John was also an important middleman between Jake and the Bulls players in the squad. As good mates who had formed a tight unit, we were perceived as a potential threat. But John convinced Jake that he could trust us and that we would play a pivotal role in the success of the team. Jake couldn't understand why the Bulls players often wanted to do things together, in a group, and he didn't like it. We ate lunch together, we went out on the town together and we shared rooms with one another. For us, this was natural behaviour – as a team, we had a unique dynamic.

'That's how they are,' John told the coach. 'Don't worry about it. When the time comes, they'll give it their all.'

A strong Irish touring side was on its way to South Africa, but for the first time in years we had a decent game plan and were well prepared. With the ghosts of 2003 still lurking in the back of our minds, we were nevertheless excited about our prospects. We had a four-year plan and were on a mission: we were going to win the World Cup in France in 2007. Jake knew that lots of things could happen in the meantime, but his mission was to start building the team that would bring home the Webb Ellis Cup.

We played well against Ireland, and then Wales, winning all three home Tests comfortably: 31-17 and 26-17 against the Irish in Bloemfontein and Cape Town respectively, and 53-18 against the Welsh in

Pretoria. In the last Test, against the Red Dragons at Loftus, and with the Tri Nations series looming, I hurt my right knee. However, I was included in the touring side and was ready for the match against a combined South Sea Islands team in Sydney.

But before long, Jake and I were at each other again.

One of the reasons was that I had brought a claim against SA Rugby, which Jake didn't like at all. He took me on. In 2002, Rudolf Straeuli had promised me, Christo Bezuidenhout and Richard Bands national contracts, which had never materialised, as he'd resigned. Our argument was that the Bok coach had made us a promise and we wanted SA Rugby to honour it.

Before the Test against Wales, Jake called me aside and told me to drop the claim, as one shouldn't take one's employer to court. I was the only claimant who was still playing for the Boks, and I refused to let it slide. In any case, the matter had nothing to do with Jake or my commitment to the Boks. Eventually we lost the case on appeal and I never got the contract I was promised. In 2004, nobody in the Bok squad had a contract. You received a 'squad assembly fee' if you were part of the training group.

Henning realised that something was amiss before the game against the South Sea Islands, and to clear the air he arranged a meeting between Jake and me. It was a good opportunity to be brutally honest with each other, and I got a lot off my mind: Jake's claim that my image was important to me, my long hair (which I wore long because Monja and I liked it that way), Jake calling me a show pony, which I wasn't, and his making Os vice-captain against Wales when I had held the position during training.

Jake wasn't very happy with what I said. He told me that as long as he was the coach, with my long hair, I would never be a Bok captain. We didn't agree on much, but we discussed the issues as best we could.

At the next training session, the pot boiled over again. I took a tackle on the injured knee and was in a lot of pain. I'd injured the knee before, so I knew that it would be okay soon enough. The next day I was running flat out on the treadmill and was ready to play. Our team doctor, Yusuf Hassan, didn't agree with me. Jake took his advice and decided to send me home.

There was a lot of speculation, particularly in the media, on why I was being sent back to South Africa. Some of my teammates claimed that Jake's decision had nothing to do with my knee. I was put on an aeroplane and was back in Pretoria soon enough, where I immediately joined the Blue Bulls for that weekend's game against the Lions in Joburg. I wanted to prove a point to Jake, and I suppose he wanted to find out whether they could get along without me.

Even if I have to say so myself, without me, the Boks struggled in the line-outs. But it was also true that my head was not in the right place. I had a mediocre performance against the Lions, who beat us 36-33, and on the same day the Boks lost 21-23 to the All Blacks in Christchurch.

That Monday, Heyneke called me into his office and told me to take the week off to clear my head. Monja and I went to Pilanesberg to get away from rugby and all the rumours that were doing the rounds. But it was impossible for me to escape rugby completely, and Monja understood. That Saturday we made a bed in front of the TV and watched four games: the Boks against the Wallabies, and three Currie Cup encounters.

I was very down in the dumps. I could handle the problems with Jake, but when I thought that Heyneke was also dropping me, it hurt a lot. All in all, I was not a happy chap.

Although the Boks lost narrowly to the Wallabies (26-30), they played good rugby. Their line-outs, however, were a fiasco, which gave me a glimmer of hope that Jake might give me another chance. Heyneke decided to intervene. With the Boks back in South Africa and before the Wallabies and All Blacks arrived, he set up a meeting between the three of us.

Jake repeated his complaints about my hair and my attitude. I explained my side of the story: that he didn't really know or understand me. Then it was Heyneke's turn. He told Jake that my work ethic was above reproach and that I put in more effort than any other player he knew. I was quite proud of the way he took Jake on.

But then he turned to me and said, 'Jake's view about you isn't completely wrong, Victor. You drive the newest and smartest model car, you dress differently from the other guys in the team and you do like being in the spotlight.'

I was taken aback, but it was a moment of truth. For the first time in my life, I realised that what Heyneke was saying was true – I did like the attention. All the signs were there. I drove a canary-yellow Nissan 350Z sports car, had posed without a shirt in magazine ads, and always tried to act differently from the rest. It suddenly dawned on me that I should eat humble pie and take it down a notch. The meeting changed me; it taught me to adapt to the situation rather than wilfully follow my own lead.

After our meeting, Jake picked me for the home leg of the Tri Nations, which made me very happy. We could now start preparing in all seriousness for the Test against the All Blacks at Ellis Park. Most of the players in the Bok team had never enjoyed a victory over the Kiwis, but after nearly beating them in Christchurch a few weeks earlier, we were up for the challenge.

Shortly before the Test, another issue surfaced. With the new South Africa now 10 years old, rugby had had to adapt to the changing political climate. Transformation and quotas had been on everyone's lips since the 1990s, even though SARU denied their existence. We knew that this wasn't true.

On the Tuesday before the Test, Fourie du Preez was still in the team, but a couple of days later, out of the blue, he was replaced by Bolla Conradie. We knew that this was a race card being played, especially as it was a home Test.

Of course Fourie was both disappointed and unhappy, but as South African rugby players we realised that this was part of the game. If you're not personally affected, it's not so tough, but for a young player who has not had many opportunities to play for the Boks, it must be heartbreaking to find out – just days before the Test – that you're not playing any more. To add insult to injury, it had nothing to do with Fourie's abilities as a player; it was just the reality of the system.

Gary Botha was in the same boat. He played in the same position as Bok captain John Smit, but Jake picked Hanyani Shimange as John's replacement instead. Gary was playing brilliant rugby at the time and we suspected that Hanyani was included to make up the 'numbers'.

It's also not always fair towards the player who is picked under these circumstances, as the expectations are very high and often hard to live up to. Having said that, one should not generalise, as over the years there have been many black Springbok players who performed above and beyond expectations.

So Fourie was relegated to the bench against New Zealand, but later on in the match he was given some game time. It turned into one of the best Springbok Tests I'd ever played in up until that stage in my career. Mils Muliaina scored an early try, but after that there was only one team on the field. Marius Joubert scored three tries that day, and we trounced New Zealand 40-26. It was a fantastic feeling to beat them.

You don't just pitch up and beat the All Blacks. I had to swallow seven defeats against them from 2001 onwards. We also struggled against teams from New Zealand in the Super 12 competition. After this match, the only thing standing between the Tri Nations crown and us were the Wallabies.

In the Durban game, I scored my fifth Test try. Rugby writers later voted that five-pointer shortly after half-time as the best try of 2004. I was extremely proud of scoring it, even though I had just added the finishing touches to the move.

It happened when Breyton Paulse launched an up-and-under and managed to tap the ball back before the Wallaby fullback, Chris Latham, could field it. The ball bounced perfectly for me, and I just had to grab it and sprint to the try line. Nobody thinks of awards when a try-scoring opportunity comes along. You just want to get back in position for the kick-off and think about the team's next try, which was exactly what happened when Joe van Niekerk barged over in the corner a few minutes later.

We destroyed the Aussies in the line-outs too, winning 23-19 in the end and thus securing our second (and my first) Tri Nations trophy. And this was just about a month after I had felt that my whole life was slipping away from me. Now, it couldn't get any better.

**

After the euphoria of the Tri Nations victory, Bakkies Botha, Jacques Cronjé, Fourie du Preez and I went straight back to the Blue Bulls. We couldn't wait to join the Currie Cup campaign, although I'd at least had one game, against the Lions. As consecutive champions, we were under a lot of pressure to lift the trophy for a third time in succession.

I'll always remember the semis and the final from the 2004 season. We played the Lions at Loftus in the semi-final and coasted to victory, even though the final score (40-33) suggested that it had been a tougher match. The Free State upset Western Province at Newlands in the other semi-final (17-11) and had to travel to Loftus for the decider.

The Blue Bulls were unstoppable in the final, and I once again scored a try! Ettienne Botha was one of the stars. He scored twice and had the Free State defence at sixes and sevens with his sidestepping. I was happy for my old room-mate's sake and ecstatic when we won 42-33. To this day, I regard that match as one of our best performances in a final.

We didn't know it then, but it was Ettienne's last final. It was also Rassie Erasmus's last game as Cheetahs player and captain.

For those of us who had missed the Blue Bulls Currie Cup victory in 2003 because of the World Cup, it was unbelievable to be part of the family again. Heyneke's plans had borne fruit and we were enjoying our rugby. That was the most important part: enjoying it. And at the same time we revived our bond with the Loftus faithful; our supporters now packed the same stands that were standing empty at the turn of the millennium.

***

A big challenge awaited the Boks at the end of 2004: a Grand Slam tour of Wales, Ireland, England and Scotland and, to end it all, a Test against Argentina in Buenos Aires. It was a long tour, but we were up for it after winning the Tri Nations title a few months earlier.

Jake made a few changes here and there and picked some new players for the tour, one of them a young winger named Bryan Habana, who had already signed a contract with the Bulls for 2005.

November tours aren't easy. You have about a week to recover after the Currie Cup knockout stages, and most of the players in the touring side usually play in those games. The big challenge is to prepare mentally for such a tour, but thanks to our Tri Nations success, this didn't prove to be difficult.

South African players will always have a special place in their hearts for the Currie Cup competition. To follow this with a visit to the cold, wet British Isles isn't easy. Still, I was looking forward to the tour, as it would be my first since 2001, and it seemed as if Jake and I were finally getting along.

Our first game was against Wales in Cardiff, and we had to dig deep to beat them 38-36. It wasn't a performance worthy of the Tri Nations champions, but a victory is a victory nonetheless, and we could now focus on Ireland.

The Irish were peeved that we'd beaten them twice in South Africa earlier that season. In the week leading up to the Test, Irish journalists set a cunning trap for Jake, and he stepped right into it. They asked him how many current Irish players would make the Bok squad if he had the opportunity to pick them.

'Maybe a lock and a centre,' Jake said.

It was the wrong answer. He'd just given the Irish more ammunition and indirectly insulted me, because the lock he'd alluded to was Paul O'Connell, my direct opponent. It made me think that I was still not good enough for Jake.

The game against Ireland was a weird experience. At one stage, referee Paul Honiss from New Zealand penalised us close to our try line and told John to have a word with the team (about repeated infringements). We huddled together … but Honiss allowed the Irish to continue play. Flyhalf Ronan O'Gara took a quick tap and sailed across the try line with not one Springbok defender laying a hand on him.

We lost 12-17, and we were angry, disappointed and confused. How could Honiss have allowed the try? As a team we'd come a long way, but we weren't nearly wide awake or shrewd enough.

In the game against England, we learnt another lesson, and I hoped Jake did too. It was our first visit to Twickenham since the Boks' embarrassing defeat in 2002. Jake's plan was to play a high-paced game and give the ball air – Super 12 rugby, in other words. He didn't want us to commit too many forwards to the breakdown.

But it was cold and wet. England pulverised us, especially up front, where we couldn't match the numbers they committed to the breakdowns. In wet conditions it's important to deploy one or two extra players at the breakdown, because the ball emerges slowly. The English had no trouble beating us 32-16 in a pretty one-sided match.

And what did Jake tell the media afterwards? 'It was like boys playing against men.'

So how did these 'boys' manage to beat the All Blacks earlier in the year? The fact was that Jake had picked the wrong game plan for the playing conditions, and that was our undoing. The easy way out was to blame the players.

The last game in Britain was against Scotland, who had beaten us in 2002, but usually didn't pose a major threat. As we'd failed to achieve the Grand Slam, we weren't very motivated for the Test, but Jaco van der Westhuyzen had a great game and contributed a try and three drop goals towards our victory (45-10).

Before we travelled to Buenos Aires to play Argentina (we won 39-7), we dominated the IRB's awards ceremony. The Springboks won Team of the Year, Schalk Burger was Player of the Year and Jake won Coach of the Year.

It also led to a minor altercation. Fourie du Preez, never shy to speak his mind, asked Jake with a straight face, 'Have you thanked Victor yet?'

Jake wanted to know why he should thank me.

'Well, if you didn't recall him for the last two Tri Nations games, you would never have won Coach of the Year,' Fourie teased.

It was a joke, with a little nudge in there as well, but Jake didn't appreciate it. He turned around and walked away.

From a Bok perspective, though, 2004 could not be compared to the previous year. The team spirit was much improved, we were treated like adults, there was structure to our game, and Jake and his management team knew what they were doing.

Also, team selections were consistent. Whereas Rudolf had picked a new team almost every week, Jake knew which players he wanted and how to establish balance in the group. He believed in the players he selected and hardly ever made changes. In one year, Rudolf picked no fewer than 48 players to represent South Africa, whereas Jake stuck to a group of more or less 23 players. In total, he picked 41 Bok players, of whom 10 were involved only in the end-of-year tour.

Jake knew that the only way South Africa could win the World Cup in 2007 was to take an experienced team to France. He started building that team in 2004.

7

The start of a dream

A year before it would have expired, Rudy Joubert's contract as Bulls coach was terminated. So in 2005, Heyneke Meyer got his third chance to coach the Bulls in the toughest rugby series in the southern hemisphere.

It would also be the last Super 12. In 2006 the competition would be expanded into the Super 14, incorporating the Lions and the Cheetahs (previously combined as the Cats), and a new Australian franchise, the Western Force.

As players, we weren't involved in the negotiations regarding Rudy's replacement, but rumour had it that the Blue Bulls Rugby Union, a senior partner in the Bulls franchise, wanted more consistency in the coaching structure. Heyneke's success at Currie Cup level counted in his favour.

One of Heyneke's first, and major, decisions when he started coaching the Super 12 Bulls was to appoint Anton Leonard as captain. I wasn't bothered, even though I had led the team the previous year. At that stage of my career, the captaincy was a bonus, not a necessity.

I also knew that Heyneke and Anton had formed a solid relationship from their days at South Western Districts, and the relationship between coach and captain was an important ingredient in a successful team. It was similar to the bond Jake White and John Smit shared in the Springbok squad. Heyneke and I were still getting to know each other.

Besides the change in captaincy – Anton was also the Blue Bulls Currie Cup skipper – our team was pretty set, with very few player changes. The most important addition to our arsenal in 2005 was Bryan

Habana. He was a youngster, but it was obvious that he was a very special player. In Heyneke's attempt to build a world-class team around the World Cup players, Bryan was an important link. Heyneke just knew that he was going to make a big difference.

We told ourselves that sixth on the log wasn't good enough any more. We'd won the Currie Cup three times in a row and just *had* to reach the semi-finals of the Super 12. It wasn't negotiable. The pressure from outside had started escalating, with the media seeing us as South Africa's torchbearer, even though we had finished last just three years earlier.

But we couldn't have had a worse start to the season. We lost our first three games: against the Cats in Johannesburg (17-23), the Brumbies in Canberra (19-21) and the Highlanders in Dunedin (0-23). We failed to score a single point at the House of Pain against one of New Zealand's weaker teams in the Super 12. It was humiliating.

Fortunately, I had some pleasant time off during the competition. After our defeat against the Cats, I travelled to London to play in the so-called 'Tsunami Match' for a southern hemisphere XV against a northern hemisphere XV, so I missed the game against the Brumbies. Each Super 12 team had to sacrifice a player for the tsunami game, and big names like Tana Umaga (Hurricanes), Andrew Mehrtens (Crusaders), George Gregan (Brumbies), Brian Lima (Samoa), Jaque Fourie (Cats), Schalk Burger (Stormers) and John Smit (Sharks) played with me in the team.

It was a very special occasion. The proceeds were donated to the victims of the massive tsunami that had destroyed large parts of South-East Asia a few months earlier. It was a great experience to team up with regular opponents and also to get to know them better.

Previously I'd been invited twice to play for the Barbarians, but something always prevented me from participating, despite everyone telling me what an incredible experience it was.

Our southern hemisphere team notched up an easy victory, even though they literally had to sweep and scoop the snow from the pitch the day before the game for our training session. It was something to behold when Samoa's Brian Lima – who was playing club rugby in Japan at that stage – unleashed his crash-tackling abilities on our opponents. You couldn't help grinning each time he swooped onto an unsuspecting player from the north. Although the final score wasn't important, we won 54-19 – my first victory at Twickenham!

But there was also a bigger picture to this experience: not everything in the world revolved around rugby. Countless people had suffered in the tsunami, and we had the opportunity to help them in their time of need, which made us feel useful. This type of experience distinguishes rugby from other sporting codes: opponents get together, become firm friends and try to make a difference to the lives of people they don't even know. I later heard we'd collected close to R25 million.

Shortly after the game in London, I took a flight via Singapore, Sydney and Auckland to Dunedin to rejoin the Bulls. It had been difficult for them to let me go in the first place, as we had big plans for the season and I was one of the senior players. Heyneke decided to pick the young Pierre Spies in his Super 12 debut – on the wing. The experiment failed, and we struggled against the Highlanders. They were simply better than us physically. After the game some people joked that we had been lucky to get zero points to the Highlanders' 23.

Early the next week, Heyneke was in a foul mood at our team talk. 'Who of you are afraid of the Highlanders?' he wanted to know.

A couple of guys probably considered putting up their hands, because the Otago men had really hurt us, but then decided against it. Not Pierre. He was still young, innocent and way too honest. At that stage it wasn't funny, but to this day we still take the mickey out of Pierre for raising his hand in Wellington. In later years he would develop into one of our most feared players.

If we were brutally honest, Heyneke said, many more players would've put up their hands. 'I know my team on the field, but I didn't know you.'

According to him, some of the forwards had been hiding in the loose scrums. It was also the first time that we didn't want to attack with the ball in hand. The reason was simple: the Highlanders tackled us to pieces on the day. Unfortunately, Pierre was injured in that game, and that was his last Super 12 appearance for the season.

Operation Shape-Up was needed urgently, especially for the remaining two games on tour. Fortunately, we could build on our performance against the Hurricanes in 2003. We beat them again in Wellington (21-12), but a week later the Waratahs were much too strong, and we lost 12-42.

Back in Pretoria, some former Northern Transvaal players who often criticised the team and the coach demanded that Heyneke be sacked immediately. They were angry and disillusioned, but we knew where we were and what we still had to accomplish. There was only one option: win all the remaining games. A solid victory over the Sharks in Durban (23-17) set the ball rolling. In our last group game, against the Stormers at Loftus Versfeld, we needed five log points to reach the semi-finals, which meant that we had to score four tries. We went on to score nine! Even our props, Wessel Roux and Richard Bands, went over for tries. It was the first time in many years that we beat the Stormers, a team that was also loaded with Bok players. The final score was 75-14.

Early on in the game, the whistle went with Joe van Niekerk in possession of the ball. Bakkies Botha shoved him aside with contempt. Joe wasn't someone who tolerated that sort of treatment, but on this day he just stared at Bakkies, turned around and jogged off. It sent a clear message that we weren't going to stand back for anyone.

For the first time since Northern Transvaal in 1996, the Bulls – three seasons earlier still the 'easy targets' of Super 12 rugby – were in the semi-finals. It was almost unbelievable, and we were ecstatic. We still had to travel to Sydney for a tough encounter with the Waratahs, but we'd reached the top four, which had been our goal.

The Waratahs played better rugby on the day and won 23-13 after we'd squandered two or three chances in the first half. At one stage all Bryan Habana had to do was fall on the ball for a try, but the ball bounced from his grasp. It was one of those days.

Even though we lost, we gained a lot of experience in terms of what was needed to win a knockout game. In those years, this knowledge was of great value. Back then we didn't think it possible for a South African side to win the Super 12 competition. The adverse effects of the long flights and playing top-notch Aussie and Kiwi teams on their home turf often proved too much of a challenge. To finish third on the log was, therefore, an achievement in itself.

The key factor in our Super 12 campaign had been the performance of the tight five – one of the best units with whom I'd ever played. Our props were the Namibian Kees Lensing and Richard Bands, with Wessel Roux on the bench. Gary Botha and Danie Coetzee were the hookers, and my lock partners were Bakkies and Danie Rossouw. We really hurt our opponents and created the platform that would secure us many victories up front.

***

After one of my best ever Super 12 seasons, I couldn't wait to wear the green and gold for the 2005 Test season.

However, in the game against the Waratahs I'd received a heavy blow to my right buttock, and the pain started setting in on the flight home. Initially we thought that I would be out of action for a week – maybe two – but in the end it took me four weeks to recover. To make matters worse, I slipped and landed right on the injured side during the Boks' annual hunting excursion.

As a result I missed the first Test of the season, against Uruguay in East London. Jake made a few experimental changes for this game, but the Boks were still way too strong and murdered the hapless South Americans 134-3. It was our biggest Test victory ever. Following that massacre, we drew with the French in the first Test, in Durban (30-all), and beat them in the second, in Port Elizabeth (27-13).

Our current team was not used to starting the Tri Nations series as the defending champions. Only Percy Montgomery had achieved this honour before. Because the British & Irish Lions were on tour in New Zealand at the time, we had to play two additional Tests – one in Sydney and one at Ellis Park – against Australia for the Nelson Mandela Challenge trophy.

We lost the game in Sydney 12-30, our biggest defeat since Jake had taken over as coach. We defended like amateurs. And to travel that distance for just one game, as in the Super 12 season, was tough. Your internal clock goes haywire and there's no time to recover or adapt. The effects of flying in that direction are much worse than flying westwards, towards South Africa. But at Ellis Park we turned the tables. Nelson Mandela attended the game, and he gave us a simple but effective message in the tunnel: Do your best for South Africa.

This inspired us to such an extent that we managed to rattle the Wallabies even before the game started. They passed us on the way to the changing room after the warm-up and we saw the fear in their eyes. The fact that a world icon was giving us a pep talk before a Test match was just too much for them.

With a team consisting of eight or nine players of colour, we cut them down to size and won 33-20. The Wallabies scored two tries late in the game, which made it look like a tighter match than it was. We knew we were ready for the Tri Nations.

Australia stayed on for the first Tri Nations Test, at Loftus, but after what had happened at Ellis Park, they didn't have a chance. Although it was a tougher contest, we managed to start the series with a victory (22-16).

At last Jake had given Gary Botha a chance, and he made his Bok debut in front of his home crowd in Pretoria. Later in the series, after the last Test in Dunedin, he was initiated as a full-on Springbok. The sequel to the ceremony almost landed me in boiling water. We had given Gary a pink G-string to wear during the initiation, which of course was hilarious, as the garment hardly fit him. Later that evening, I picked up the G-string – which was looking a bit worse for wear – and without thinking, stuffed it into my blazer pocket. I completely forgot about it until a couple of days later, when our domestic worker found it. Of course, she asked Monja whether it belonged to her!

I had to explain very carefully where it had come from. Luckily, I could produce photos of the initiation as evidence. Most men would have been in the dog box for days, but Monja just had a good laugh.

A week after we had beaten the Wallabies, the All Blacks arrived in Cape Town for the Test at Newlands, their favourite hunting ground in South Africa. The final score was – hard to believe as it is – 22-16 again. With this win, we notched up our second victory in a row against the All Blacks. It seemed as if slowly but surely the Kiwis were losing their tight hold on us. We could finally start believing that we could beat New Zealand in South Africa, and that a victory had nothing to do with luck. It was a great feeling.

Early on in the game at Newlands, I made a massive tackle on the New Zealand scrumhalf, Byron Kelleher, partly with my heavily band-aged forearm. He was very groggy afterwards and had to leave the field.

As a result, I was cited for a dangerous tackle. Fortunately, however, I was found not guilty and could join the squad on our tour to Australia.

But it wasn't the last I'd hear about that tackle. Kevin Putt, a Kiwi who was sacked as the Sharks coach earlier that season, said on New Zealand television that I had a steel plate strapped to my arm, which was why Kelleher got hurt. This was complete nonsense. I couldn't believe that Putt had said something so ridiculous, and I was furious. Referees have often inspected my arm guard – before that particular Test and since – and have never once found anything that contravened the laws of the game.

We travelled to Perth for our third Test of the year against Australia. Perth to us is what Cape Town is to the All Blacks. South African supporters pack the stadium, and we usually achieve good results there. It was much the same on this day, although it was a narrow victory (22-19). We scraped by largely because of Bryan Habana's brace of tries from movements that had started close to our try line. This was where his career as a world-class winger started in all earnest.

There were high expectations for our second Test against the All Blacks. If we could beat them in Dunedin, we wouldn't only have successfully defended our Tri Nations crown, but also secured the number-one position in the world rankings – something to which Jake aspired.

But a late try by the hooker Keven Mealamu saw the All Blacks beat us narrowly, by 31-27. Afterwards, a lot of people said that we could have won that game if only Fourie du Preez had been sent on as replacement scrumhalf. But that didn't happen. Jake kept the inexperienced Ricky Januarie behind the pack. How to go on to win a game in the dying minutes when you're leading on the scoreboard was another important lesson we had to learn.

Although we'd performed better in the tournament than we had in 2004, winning three of our four Tri Nations matches, New Zealand would be crowned the new champions if they beat the Wallabies in Auckland – which they did.

Relinquishing the Tri Nations crown left a bitter taste in the mouth, but the fact that our game had shown great improvement softened the blow ... a little.

***

The big question in Pretoria at the start of the 2005 Currie Cup competition was whether the Blue Bulls could make it four titles in a row.

Since Heyneke took over, the Blue Bulls had improved to such an extent that we were now the best provincial team in South Africa by far. As a result, we were the team everyone targeted: a victory over the Blue Bulls was the highlight of the season for many opposing teams.

However, another title would not be so easy to accomplish in 2005, and although we completely dominated the Currie Cup competition, we had two early slip-ups when the Boks were not available, losing against the Sharks in Pretoria (14-18) and the Lions in Johannesburg (17-46). However, we won the rest of our games, in Pretoria, Brakpan, George, Cape Town, Bloemfontein, Kimberley and Potchefstroom.

Behind the scenes, Jake didn't want the Boks to play in the Currie Cup competition. National players from other provinces probably welcomed a bit of a breather, but the Blue Bulls Boks had a title to defend. Jake was angry when we opposed his plans, but because the Bulls union paid our salaries, we thought we owed it to them to be available.

Jake wanted all the Boks to adhere to a strict conditioning programme, which I didn't like. As a tight forward, I preferred to keep in shape by playing rugby. Besides, I was extremely disciplined about my fitness regime and always ate healthily, so additional conditioning was quite superfluous. Heyneke was also peeved, as shortly after the end of the Tri Nations season, all the contracted Boks had to undergo intensive fitness tests, during which I injured a hamstring muscle.

In the meantime, a tragedy awaited us.

On a Tuesday evening in September, a few of us had a social get-together at the News Cafe in Menlyn, and later that evening I went home, while Ettienne Botha, Wynand Olivier and Bryan Habana headed off to a club in Centurion. Earlier that week, Heyneke had decided to give Wynand game time at centre against Griquas in Kimberley, leaving Ettienne on the bench. Ettienne wasn't impressed.

The next morning at around 4 a.m., a phone call from Richard Bands woke me up. He had terrible news: Ettienne had died in a car crash. Apparently he had lost control of his car on the N1 driving from Centurion to Pretoria. I was shattered. All the Bulls were shattered. Ettienne was one of my closest friends. On tour we were often room-mates.

I was left with the terrible task of informing his parents and his girlfriend, Elizma Vorster, of his death. It was extremely difficult for me. Where do you find the words to convey such a message?

Later a group of us went to Ettienne's house in Moraleta Park, where we sat in silence, completely gutted. We didn't know what to say. Heyneke had been at the scene of the accident and later told us that Ettienne had opened his eyes for a moment, and then he was gone. It was the second time in less than two years that a teammate had died in a tragic accident. Early in 2004, François Swart had also perished in a collision.

In the weeks that followed, all of us were very emotional. We saw ourselves as tough rugby players on the park, but we weren't prepared for this loss. The tears flowed. We didn't want to believe what had happened, as it felt so unreal.

It wasn't easy to start training that week, and not a lot was achieved during the sessions. But in a strange way, Ettienne's death motivated us. Our first game after the accident was against Griquas in Kimberley, and we beat them 49-30.

The funeral was held the following week, and I was asked to pay tribute to my old teammate. It was one of the most difficult tasks I've ever had to perform. Ettienne and I had been room-mates for a few years and were good buddies. Suddenly he wasn't there any more. I was forced to say goodbye to him for the last time.

After the memorial service, we formed a circle and reminded each other that we had to live our lives to the fullest and use every opportunity that came our way, as you never knew when your life could be taken away.

That weekend we had to play against Province at Loftus. We wanted to say farewell in a fitting way, in front of Ettienne's supporters. After we had massacred the Stormers in the Super 12 and defeated them at Newlands in a Currie Cup encounter earlier in the season, the Capetonians wanted revenge. But they didn't take into account the raw emotion unleashed by the death of our teammate.

We played as if it were our last game ever, and wiped them off the field: 39-3. For a Province team not to score a single try against the Blue

Bulls was a bitter pill for them to swallow. For us, it was the best way we could honour Ettienne and the contribution he had made to the team. He should've been a Springbok, but according to the selectors, he was too small. However, he had the heart of a lion. He still holds many records at the Bulls and scored tries most other players can only dream of.

This tragedy set the tone for the rest of the season – we were unstoppable. We took revenge on the Lions, who'd beaten us earlier in the season. They travelled to Pretoria for the semi-final, where we knocked them out, winning 31-23.

The last hurdle was the final, our fourth in as many years. Again it was against the Cheetahs, who for a second year running had stopped Western Province at Newlands, winning 16-11. It was the first year that Rassie Erasmus, a guy for whom I have the utmost respect, coached the Cheetahs. We were the overwhelming favourites.

In the week leading up to the final, the Free State prop Ollie le Roux tried to unsettle us with some offhand remarks. They were planning to make us 'suffer' in the scrums, and they arrived in Pretoria with a full front row on the bench. And according to newspaper articles, we were 'arrogant bullies'.

It was a weird final. We were in control, but we just couldn't put the Cheetahs away. Bryan received a yellow card for a dangerous tackle, and Os du Randt and I also had to spend 10 minutes in the sin bin. We were good mates in the Springbok camp, but on this day we had a bit of an altercation on the field when I barged into him at a loose scrum. Perhaps I used my forearm a little excessively … Os didn't appreciate the gesture and landed on top of me, from where he took a swing. He missed, which was a blessing, or I would've left the field on a stretcher.

With 10 minutes to go we were leading 25-15, but then things quickly turned pear-shaped. First Bevin Fortuin crossed our line for a converted try, which shrunk our lead to just three points, and then the unthinkable happened. The Cheetahs scrumhalf, Falie Oelschig, launched an up-and-under towards two of our safest players under the high ball, Fourie du Preez and Johan Roets. In a moment of madness they ran into each other, the ball bounced straight into the hands of

Cheetahs reserve centre, Meyer Bosman, and he sprinted through untouched for the winning try. An easy conversion was the last nail in our coffin, and the Cheetahs won 29-25.

For the first time since 1976, the Cheetahs had won the Currie Cup by beating us – at Loftus, to boot. We were gutted. For me – and I believe for many of my teammates – it was the worst day of our careers.

We should never have lost that final, but you don't always win the ones you should. And sometimes, we found out later, you win finals you should've lost.

***

Things went from bad to worse after the match. We tried to hold our heads high, but when we saw Ollie le Roux prancing around on the field with a celebratory cigar in his mouth, we were extremely offended. He seemed to go out of his way to rub salt in our wounds. We thought his behaviour was inappropriate. Later, at their victory parade in Bloemfontein, a pair of bullhorns was dragged behind the Cheetahs' team bus.

As senior Bulls players, we promised each other that we would never lose against Free State again. Following this, I was never again in a Bulls team that lost against the Cheetahs, either in Super Rugby or in the Currie Cup.

We had to report for a Springbok training camp in Johannesburg a day after the final, but we weren't very keen. We asked permission to arrive a day later, but Jake didn't want to hear about it – the Bulls and Cheetahs had to report as instructed.

As is the custom after a final, we had a team braai the next day, but this time round we had nothing to celebrate. And we had to leave for the training camp later that afternoon. But then we heard that the Cheetahs were having a massive party in Bloemfontein and wouldn't arrive in Johannesburg on time, so we decided there and then that we'd also report to Bok headquarters only the next day.

When we arrived, we were given a proper tongue-lashing by Jake and 'Mr P', our team manager. The five Cheetahs in the Bok camp also arrived late, but we were the only ones who had to face a dressing-down.

After the training camp we travelled to Argentina, where we beat the

Pumas 34-23 in Buenos Aires. The following week we had time to relax, and Jake took us to Bariloche in the south of the country, where we spent time at a ski resort. Our goal was team building, so we relaxed, rested and didn't train too much. The situation between Jake and me had also improved, and I became what one might call his confidant – a complete turnaround from the previous year.

Across the road from the cabin where we stayed was an old Irish pub, which soon became our 'gang' hangout. Os du Randt, Schalk Burger, Jean de Villiers, Gary Botha, Bryan Habana, Jacques Cronjé and I often had a few beers there. It was the perfect way to unwind after a long season and before the last two Tests of the year.

After this breather we travelled to Cardiff, where we beat the Welsh 33-16. Then it was off to Paris, where the French turned the tables by beating us 26-20. That evening we were a bit down in the dumps as we sat in our changing room at the Stade de France.

Jake talked some sense into us. 'Boys, we need to learn a lesson from this defeat, because in two years' time we'll be sitting here again. But then the World Cup will be on the floor in front of you.'

The previous year he'd already started instilling in us what our goal was: World Cup glory. At that stage we were well on our way after a good season: 12 Tests, 8 victories, 3 defeats and 1 draw.

Later that evening in Paris, I got Os back for that failed punch in the Currie Cup final. We decided to end the year properly, and I took a whole lot of beers up to the room that I shared with Bakkies. At one stage Os tackled me just for fun, but later he made a vital mistake by standing too close to the window. I launched myself at him to return the compliment he'd paid me earlier. As he fell, his face hit the window sill and blood started pouring from a gaping wound. Even though Os had to be stitched up, we had a good laugh.

When the rest of the team returned to South Africa, Bryan and I stayed behind, as we had been nominated for the IRB World Player of the Year award. It was a great honour, but the Kiwi flyhalf Dan Carter won in a year when the All Blacks had beaten the British & Irish Lions and scooped the Tri Nations trophy, so I didn't really expect to receive an award.

Nevertheless, it was a wonderful way to end the year. The Boks were at the halfway mark in our four-year plan and we felt that our goal was within reach. We'd lost a Test here and there, but we now knew that we had the ability to beat any team in the world.

8

Sweet and sour

Early in 2006, Monja and I made newspaper headlines for reasons other than rugby.

We welcomed our firstborn, a baby girl named Jaime, at Kloof Hospital on New Year's Day. To hold her was more wonderful than I could ever have imagined. Our lives would never be the same. In my (even) younger days – I became a dad at 28 – I would have been at some party on New Year's Eve, but on the last day of 2005, Monja and I were relaxing at home, preparing ourselves for the big occasion.

At 5 a.m. the next morning, we were off to the hospital. On the way, we passed a number of people making their way home after a New Year's Eve bash. A few hours later, Monja had a Caesarean section and Jaime came into our lives.

I always wanted children. With the arrival of Jaime – Monja chose the beautiful name after former model and actress Jaime King – my wildest expectations were exceeded. The pleasure this little bundle of joy has brought us is unsurpassed. Yes, there have been difficult times, but no matter what, you love your child unconditionally.

From the word go I fulfilled my fatherly duties without hesitation, even changing dirty nappies! I cherished those first months and years I could spend with Jaime, and we really bonded. Later Monja and I would be blessed with another baby girl, Giselle, but I will get to her a little later.

With the birth of Jaime, I realised yet again what an important role my wife played in my life and career. Monja is a star. She is my rock. She had to raise our two daughters almost single-handedly, as I was often away on tour. If things were not going well on the rugby field, she was the one I talked to and with whom I shared my frustrations and disappointments.

Also, if your home life is not solid, it can negatively influence your game. For that reason I was – and still am – forever indebted to Monja. She's a strong woman with her own dreams and goals. It would've bothered me had she just been Mrs Victor Matfield. Now I can say I am 'Mr Dr Monja Bekker', as Monja is a qualified dentist with her own practice, although she's scaled it down since the birth of our children.

Unfortunately, in those first few weeks after Jaime's birth, I couldn't spend a lot of time at home, as we were preparing for the new Super 14 competition. As mentioned, the Cheetahs and Lions had split into two separate teams after the Cats were disbanded, and the Western Force, based in Perth, was added as the fourth Australian team in the extended competition.

Anton Leonard retired, and Heyneke appointed me as Bulls captain. I felt very honoured. It was my second season as skipper but my first with Heyneke as coach. He regarded the captain as an important link in the chain and – unlike the situation in 2003 – it was wonderful to have the support of the entire team.

Our preparations went well, but in a pre-season warm-up against the Lions, I hurt my right knee – the same one I had problems with before – and was forced to miss the opening game of the season. Then Fourie du Preez, who took over as captain, hurt *his* knee ligaments during training. So Gary Botha was appointed captain number three. But in the last warm-up match against the Sharks at Sun City, he, too, hurt his knee! Luckily, Fourie recovered in time and he took over the reins for the first three games of the season.

In 2006, Loftus wasn't yet the strong ally it would become in the ensuing Super 14 seasons. After we beat the Cheetahs 30-18 in the opening game of the season in Bloemfontein, the Brumbies beat us 27-21 at Loftus. Home victories over the Waratahs (26-17) and Highlanders (23-16) – my first game of the season – followed. But then we stumbled against the Hurricanes (23-26) and, a few games later, the Crusaders also beat us at Loftus (35-17). Nevertheless, we remained in the top six on the log throughout the series. To qualify for the semi-finals we had to win our last game, against the Stormers in Cape Town, by at least 33 points.

It was almost unbelievable how favourably the results panned out for us in the last weekend's games. The Sharks, who, against all odds, had had a very good season, and the Brumbies left the back door open for us ever so slightly.

In order to qualify for the play-offs, the Brumbies had to get only a single point against the Crusaders, but instead they lost 3-33 and returned to Canberra empty-handed. On the Friday evening, the Sharks beat the Western Force 41-25, but late in the game they leaked two tries, which was bad for them but counted in our favour.

The Sharks nevertheless started packing their bags for the flight Down Under, where they would play in the one semi-final, as they didn't think we would tally up enough points against the Stormers to end fourth on the log.

Nobody had given the Sharks a chance at the start of the season, but they'd surprised the lot of us. It was Dick Muir's first full season as coach of the team, and they had given us a hard time as the top South African team in the competition.

For the Bulls, a team that had never before won a Super Rugby match at Newlands, the prospect of beating the Stormers by 33 points was an almost insurmountable challenge. Still, we were upbeat after the Sharks' let-off. The door had just opened a bit wider.

The evening before the match, during our team meeting in Cape Town, Heyneke wrote the number 33 on a whiteboard and circled it. That was it. No team talk. He just said, 'That's what we need tomorrow.'

The Stormers scored shortly after kick-off, but we never gave up, and we soon had the scoreboard ticking over. Although the Stormers had no chance of reaching the semi-finals, they tried their best to keep us from reaching the top four. Whenever they were given a penalty, instead of opting for a kick to set up a line-out, they went for the posts. They didn't want us to reach the required points difference, which is why we couldn't afford to give away a penalty in the dying minutes of the game.

With 20 minutes to go, Bryan Habana scored our fourth try after fielding a crafty grubber I had kicked. The final score: 43-10. We'd

I was crazy about rugby from a young age. In the bottom picture, I am seated next to my dad, Fai, who coached our under-11 A team at Noordskool

LAERSKOOL
PIETERSBURG-NOORD
o - 11 A
1988

My jersey got really dirty when I played for the Transvaal Unions team in 1995

Lizhel Swan was my date for the matric dance at Pietersburg High School

Imke Henning

Celebrating the Boks' World Cup victory in 1995

Imke Henning

My first taste of Super 12 rugby, in 1999 with the Cats

I became a Springbok for the first time in 2000

In 1999 and 2000, I played for Griquas, and enjoyed two unforgettable years in Kimberley

My first Test try, against Italy in Genoa, 17 November 2001

On tour – a little coffee goes a long way in warding off the European winter chill. I am with Lukas van Biljon in France

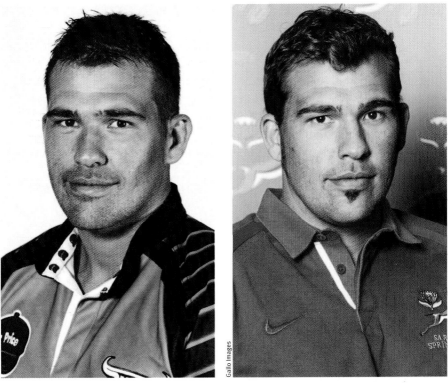

From short-back-and-sides to my longer locks, from 2001 to 2003

Signing autographs at Perth International Airport during the 2003 Rugby World Cup

England were our strongest opponents in the group stage of the 2003 World Cup. They beat us 25-6 in Perth

We were knocked out by the All Blacks in the quarter-finals in Melbourne. Here I am, tackling Keven Mealamu, with John Smit next to me

Joost van der Westhuizen's last Test for the Springboks, 8 November 2003, against the All Blacks in Melbourne

Bakkies Botha and I thank the supporters in Durban after winning the Tri Nations in 2004

Back with the Blue Bulls: Bakkies and I celebrate our win against the Cheetahs in the 2004 Currie Cup final at Loftus Versfeld

Relaxing in the jacuzzi after training in East London in 2005 with Eddie Andrews (left) and De Wet Barry. On the left of the picture, Gary Botha is braving an ice bath

Singing the national anthem prior to the Test against France in Port Elizabeth in 2005

With Jake White, who coached the Boks from 2004 to 2007. This picture was taken prior to my 50th Test for South Africa on 22 July 2006 against the All Blacks in Wellington

Sharing a lighter moment with Os du Randt off the pitch after beating the Wallabies 24-16 on 9 September 2006 at Ellis Park

Enjoying a swim in the sea with Bakkies Botha in Durban

We've got it! In 2007, the Bulls became the first South African team to win the Super 14. Here I am joined on the pitch by Pierre Spies, Wynand Olivier and Bryan Habana after the game in Durban

A Bok practice session at the 2007 Rugby World Cup in France

Singing the national anthem ahead of
the World Cup match against the USA
in Montpellier on 30 September 2007

With Fourie du Preez and Schalk Burger at our
captain's run the day before our semi-final against
Argentina in the Stade de France in Paris

A maul during our semi-final against the Pumas in Paris

We've won another line-out, with England's Martin Corry who just can't reach the ball during the final in Paris

President Thabo Mbeki and John Smit with the Webb Ellis Cup

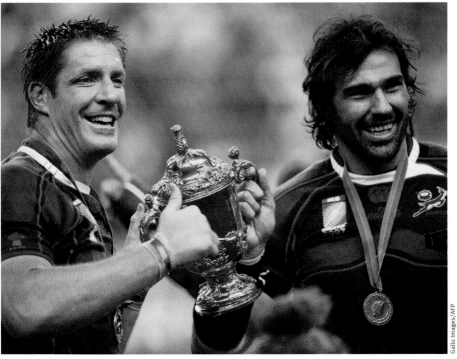

My 'combo buddy' Bakkies Botha and I with the Webb Ellis Cup shortly after beating England 15-6 in Paris

Springbok supporters came to wish us bon voyage at our hotel in Paris before our return home

The official photograph of me holding the Webb Ellis Cup

It was very special bringing the World Cup back to South Africa

Gallo Images

Former president Nelson
Mandela has always been
a huge inspiration to the
Springboks and to me
personally, and I was fortunate
enough to meet him on more
than one occasion

Carl Fourie

Gallo Images

With a few of my international Toulon teammates in 2008. From left to right are Andrew Mehrtens, George Gregan, Mafi Kefu (in front), me, Anton Oliver and Phil Fitzgerald

Potjiekos in Toulon in the south of France with a few homesick South African teammates – from left are Lorne Ward, François van Schouwenburg, Nico Breedt and me

Sightseeing in Cannes with Jaime

The Matfield family at Giselle's christening in 2009

done it! We'd shown tremendous discipline to win by 33 points, just like Heyneke had asked of us.

With our place in the semi-finals booked, we were on our way to Christchurch to take on the Crusaders.

Bakkies said that although reaching the semis was fantastic, what he enjoyed the most was AJ Venter having to unpack his bags back in Durban. The two of them didn't get on, to put it mildly; probably because both were such physical players.

Oddly enough, Bakkies had been on the bench for the Stormers game. Earlier in the season, Heyneke, always true to his word, had promised François van Schouwenburg a place in the team for the Newlands game. In an effort to get Bakkies back into the starting line-up, I suggested that Heyneke pick me as flank, but he didn't want to hear of it.

Travelling all the way from Cape Town to Christchurch for one game – further even than the previous year, when we had to go to Sydney – was no joke. And on top of that, the Crusaders were in top form.

To make matters even worse, on the day of the match, Bakkies slipped while running onto the field and seriously injured a tendon in his heel. I couldn't believe it! He managed to play for a while, but I could tell that the big fellow was suffering, and eventually he had to be replaced – in his 50th game for the Bulls to boot!

The Crusaders were in a different class and easily beat us (35-15). The next weekend they won the first Super 14 title when they beat the Hurricanes 19-12 in thick fog at Christchurch.

For us, two semi-final berths in as many years was the start of greater things. The foundation Rudy Joubert had laid in 2003 and 2004 certainly played a role in our success. But we knew that it would always be tough to win the Super 14 crown if you had to play the semi-final away.

***

Although I was satisfied with my performance in the Super 14, Bok coach Jake White was less impressed. At the training camp in Bloemfontein, he called me aside and told me that although my line-out work was satisfactory, statistics showed that my contribution in other departments wasn't up to scratch.

I was disappointed, because I'd thought that our relationship had improved from the previous year, and I was also quite satisfied with the way I was playing. I had been a contender for the IRB World Player of the Year in 2005 and had had a good Super 14 season with the Bulls. However, Jake said that guys like Johann Muller and Albert van den Berg had a higher work rate than mine on the field. He intended to pick me for the first Test against Scotland, but then he wanted me to sit out for two weeks to give Johann and Albert a chance at Test level.

A large Springbok squad was picked for the 2006 Test season. By then SA Rugby had already decided that the Boks wouldn't be involved in the Currie Cup competition, as there was little more than a year left before the World Cup kicked off. They took this decision after consulting with all the provinces, and although the players accepted it, it wasn't pleasant sitting on the sidelines.

In the end, I played in both Tests against Scotland. Even though we won, we were not convincing. The scores were 36-16 in Durban and 29-15 in Port Elizabeth. In PE, we suffered an enormous setback when Schalk Burger was seriously injured during the game; rumours were even doing the rounds that he wouldn't be able to play rugby again. Schalk was one of our key players. His fearless physical approach and solid defence were important to our game plan.

'It's like losing three players at once,' Jake said. We were all hoping Schalk would recover soon, but he didn't play again in 2006.

The next Test was against France at Newlands, and I did play after Jake abandoned his plan to rest me. But the big problems we would face in the year before the World Cup started during that Test in Cape Town. France beat us 36-26, and it was the beginning of the end for players like Jaco van der Westhuyzen, De Wet Barry and Marius Joubert.

Following the defeat, we embarked on an extended Tri Nations tour of the Antipodes. With the establishment of the Super 14 competition, SANZAR (the controlling body for rugby in South Africa, Australia and New Zealand) had decided to extend the Tri Nations so that each team would play three Tests (instead of two) against each opponent. In 2006, the Boks would play two Tests against the Wallabies and the All Blacks in South Africa, and one Test each in Australia and New Zealand.

The tour started in the worst possible way. The Wallabies slaughtered us 49-0 in Brisbane (in my 49th Test). Damn, that hurt! It was without a doubt my biggest defeat in a Bok jersey and the first time since 1999 (when we lost 0-28 to the All Blacks in Dunedin) that we couldn't score a single point. I really felt for Akona Ndungane and Pierre Spies, who made their Bok debuts against Australia that day.

It was one of those games in which the floodgates opened right after the kick-off and we simply couldn't stem the tide. The previous year we had won three of our four Tri Nations encounters, but now we'd started by haemorrhaging almost 50 points.

Interestingly enough, Jake was very calm in the week leading up to the next Test, against the All Blacks in Wellington. His advice was that it didn't help to get worked up; stay calm and just do what you usually do. His belief in us never wavered. And if it did, he never showed it.

The Test started on a positive note, with Fourie du Preez going over for a try in the first minute. But we couldn't maintain the pressure, and the Kiwis beat us 35-17. It was my 50th Test in the green and gold, but that evening there was nothing to celebrate.

A week later we almost got our revenge against the Wallabies in Sydney, but a converted try in the last minutes of the game swung the result in their favour (20-18). And a few weeks later the All Blacks taught us another lesson, winning 45-26 in Pretoria – another massive defeat, our fifth in a row.

The pressure on Jake started escalating. Many people wanted to get rid of him, which surely wasn't an option in the middle of a Tri Nations series. We just continued to work hard and remained focused on the first Test we'd play at the Royal Bafokeng Sports Palace in Phokeng, outside Rustenburg.

Rumours were doing the rounds that the All Blacks had had a week-long holiday at Sun City before the Test and weren't really serious about the upcoming match, but I didn't believe that at all. No Test between South Africa and New Zealand would ever be a relaxed affair.

And anyway, we couldn't afford to slack off, as we'd not yet hit our stride. Because of injuries, Pierre Spies was called up to form an unlikely loose trio with Pedrie Wannenburg and AJ Venter. After that nightmare against the Wallabies, Pierre was unsure of his future as an international player, but as it turned out, he was the star against the All Blacks and was picked as Man of the Match.

André Pretorius slotted a late and difficult penalty to hand us victory by a single point: 21-20. Although Jake was still under pressure, at least it had dissipated somewhat, particularly when we beat the Wallabies 24-16 at Ellis Park a week later.

That was also my last game of the season. As agreed, the Boks didn't play in the Currie Cup competition, and Jake also decided to take a group of young players on the end-of-year tour of Ireland and England, while the core of the Bok team would stay behind in South Africa for conditioning and a well-deserved rest. Eventually, however, Jake included a couple of senior players in the touring squad.

By that stage, all of the Boks had already decided that we would do anything to achieve success in Paris 11 months later. So we focused on getting bigger and stronger, while also having a proper rest, before the start of the very important international season. We got together at a training camp in Johannesburg for a month and worked hard on our conditioning, concentrating on strength and speed work.

The Blue Bulls were having another good Currie Cup season, and I helped out with the training. For the fifth year in a row, the Blue Bulls made the final, this time against the Cheetahs in Bloemfontein. I attended the game with Fourie du Preez and a few friends. The City of Roses was decked out in orange, and of course almost everyone seemed to support the home side.

Before kick-off we had a braai with friends and experienced what it was like on the other side of the fence, something we hardly ever had the pleasure of doing. I even bought myself a pair of Blue Bull *velskoene* (rawhide shoes) – not quite my style as far as footwear was concerned, but at least Jake would have approved!

Where the Blue Bulls had been the resounding favourites the previous year, this time the roles were reversed. The final was a real nail-biter, and with the score drawn at 25-all after the full-time whistle, 20 minutes of extra time had to be played. The tension became unbearable after Morné Steyn and Meyer Bosman both slotted penalties (28-all). Then the Bulls were awarded another penalty in the dying seconds, but it was just too far to go for posts, so the ball was hoofed over the sideline and the cup was shared.

Morné, who had replaced Derick Hougaard early in the match, had at that stage succeeded with all his place-kicks, and I reckon the Bulls should have taken the risk and kicked for posts to secure the winning points. Fourie, as captain, had made the call to kick for touch – and I never fully agreed with his decision. After the game we teased Fourie about not having had enough confidence in his kicker, even though he always believed that nothing was impossible.

Heyneke argued that a missed kick could've led to a counter-attack by the Cheeaths, and after 100 minutes of rugby everyone was exhausted, making it more difficult to defend than to attack. If Morné had missed the kick, the Bulls would have had their backs to the wall. A valid argument, you have to admit. But if I had captained the Bulls that day, my command would have been: Go for posts!

Back in the day when Anton Leonard was captaining a very young Bulls side, Heyneke, using a two-way radio, would relay messages to the field from the coach's box via our fitness trainer, Basil Carzis, who sat on the sideline, and Basil would then communicate the message to the players on the field.

After I took over the reins as captain, Heyneke allowed me more freedom to make on-field decisions, as he soon realised that I wasn't too keen on receiving a whole lot of instructions from the sideline. Sometimes a captain has a better understanding of the situation on the field than the coach, and Heyneke trusted me to make the right calls. Of course, we always discussed the game plan in detail before a match and I always operated within its framework.

Meanwhile, the somewhat inexperienced and young Bok side lost the first Test, against Ireland, by 15-32. To add insult to injury, this Test marked the 100-year anniversary of Springbok rugby. A week later, they stumbled against England in London, the score 21-23.

Before this Test, the head honchos of SA Rugby had summoned Jake to an emergency meeting in South Africa, where he had to account for the loss against Ireland and explain why we'd lost seven Tests in 2006.

In fact, Jake's head was on the chopping block. If he was sacked, I thought Heyneke might be given the opportunity to coach the Boks. But I also considered it foolish to get rid of Jake after he had worked for three years to shape a World Cup side and with less than a year before the tournament kicked off in France.

Perhaps Jake's dire situation inspired the Boks. There comes a time in the life of every team when it decides: Today we play for the coach. As a result, the Boks beat England 25-14 in the second Test – South Africa's first victory on that hallowed ground since 1997.

I must confess, I was a bit jealous. The Boks winning at Twickenham for the first time in so many years and I had had no part in it! At that stage I had never played in a winning side against England, and here Jake and his relatively young side had achieved exactly that.

Eventually, Jake retained his job as coach, which I thought was the right decision, even though 2006 had been a nightmare from an international perspective. We'd won only five of our 12 Tests, two of which had been against Scotland. On the other side of the coin, we did notch up meaningful victories over New Zealand, Australia and England.

And, most significantly, a few guys who would turn out to be key players in the World Cup had made their Bok debuts – Johann Muller, BJ Botha, Ruan Pienaar, Pierre Spies and Frans Steyn. They were important investments that would deliver good dividends in the months to come.

9

Super success!

The best year of my rugby career started with a great round of golf in Pretoria. Who could have guessed it would end on a sour note in the clubhouse of a golf course in George? But more about that later ...

I am passionate about golf. I try to play at least one round a week, and because I'm very competitive, a fair amount of money is usually wagered on a game. Pedrie Wannenburg usually partners with me, or Schalk Burger when the Boks have a game, and I always play against Fourie du Preez and Danie Rossouw.

Fourie is an exemplary sportsman and has played golf off a scratch handicap. Our rivalry on the course is legendary, as we are always pretty even. This brilliant scrumhalf was the cornerstone of an incredible year for the Bulls and the Boks. He's a rugby genius and a pleasure to have as a teammate. If there had ever been any doubts about his abilities, in 2007 he proved that he was one of the best players in world rugby.

Fourie and I were part of a group of senior players that were given a rest at the end of 2006 and did not go on the end-of-year tour. As mentioned, we also didn't compete in the Currie Cup, instead using the opportunity to work on our conditioning, focusing mainly on strength and speed work.

In November 2006, we joined the Bulls' Super 14 squad. On the first day, Heyneke made us pull heavy iron rods in short sprints, similar to what we used to do in rugby practice at school with tyres tied to a rope secured to a harness around your waist. It was a murderous exercise. The previous month with the Boks, we had done no fitness training, just strength and speed exercises. Halfway through the Bulls practice session, I was on my back with severe calf and thigh cramps. Heyneke told me to take a breather, as this was only the first session of many, but I decided to continue.

After a week of extremely tough sessions in the sweltering November sun in Pretoria, we travelled to George for the annual Bulls training camp. For the first time in quite a while, all the Boks in the squad could join their Bulls teammates for the entire two weeks.

The George camp usually starts with a planning session in which we set out our goals for the coming season. Nothing less than second spot on the log would do if we wanted to win the Super 14 trophy in 2007. To travel overseas to play a semi-final was just too tough, and after consecutive semi-final games in third and fourth spot on the log, we just had to aim higher.

We knew it wouldn't be an easy task, but we felt that we could do it. The team had gained considerable experience since the days when we had to start each new season with new players and in different jerseys. Heyneke believed that in order to win the competition, a team should consist of at least five or six players who had 50 or more Super Rugby games under their belts, and four or five players who would be obvious choices for a World XV. We were almost in that position.

Pundits described the Bulls' 2007 draw as 'tough', because we would have to play five games in Australia and New Zealand: against the Brumbies (two-time champions), Waratahs (runners-up in 2005), Crusaders (six-time champions), Highlanders and Hurricanes (runners-up in 2006). The advantage of a tough tour is that the home games are easier, which is where a team can pile up the log points. Add to that one or two victories on tour, and the team should finish in the top four.

Team building was another important component of the George training camp. One evening in December, after a round of golf at the Oubaai Golf Course, we camped on the empty plot I'd bought in the resort town and enjoyed some beers. We started talking about winning the Super 14, and the conversation continued till late that evening.

The next morning we were 'treated' to a heavy scrum session and practised endless line-outs and kick-offs. In the windy conditions, a lot of balls were knocked on. Heyneke wasn't amused. Team building was one thing, he said, but our timing was inappropriate, as we were in George to work, not to fool around. Fourie and I were given a tongue-lashing. We were the senior players and had to set an example, Heyneke said. We felt terrible.

The whole squad knuckled down after the talking-to, and in the end the training camp turned out to be a massive success, possibly our best ever. Basil Carzis, our conditioning coach, had an ingenious plan and introduced the 'Strongman Competition', which made the fitness sessions competitive and far more enjoyable. When we said our good-byes after two weeks, we were in peak physical condition and excited to start the competition.

But not everything worked out quite as we'd hoped it would. We lost our first two games, one of them against the Sharks in Durban (3-17). To play them in the Shark Tank in February, in extremely warm and humid conditions, was a tough ask. I was so tired that I struggled to remember our line-out calls. We couldn't even settle down against the Western Force at Loftus, and lost 27-30. The Force was a rather mediocre side, plus it was only their second year in the competition!

In between these two defeats, we managed to beat the Cheetahs 24-20 in a humdinger at Loftus. But then, when we stumbled against the Force, it felt as if we were struggling for survival as we had in the bad old days. Our supporters weren't happy, and we knew why. I was too embarrassed to even show my face in public and sent Monja to the shop to buy groceries. A week later, against the Chiefs, we had our backs to the wall yet again. We had to dig really deep and put the ball through many phases before Bryan Habana scored in injury time. We scraped through 30-27. Despite all the planning and our high confidence levels, the season had started on a very shaky note. We knew that if we wanted to achieve our goal of a home semi-final, we simply had to improve our game on the overseas leg.

We kicked off the most difficult part of the tournament on a positive note when we beat the Brumbies 19-7 in Canberra, and then the Waratahs 23-19 in Sydney. We couldn't have asked for a better start to the tour.

Our victory in Sydney almost meant more to our backline coach, the Australian Todd Louden, than it did to us. The Waratahs had declined his services as coach before the start of the season, and he saw our victory as just revenge. He really motivated us before the game and was thrilled with the result. It had not been easy for Heyneke to appoint Todd, as the former Bok centre Mike Bayly had been his assistant for years. But Heyneke wanted an outsider with fresh ideas, and who could take the backline to a higher level.

Unfortunately for us, one of Heyneke's beliefs was that the team had to be brought back to earth after a series of victories. The Monday before our next game, against the Crusaders, he suddenly decided that we should do the 'bleep test'. This exercise really saps your energy, as you have to sprint between two points, increasing your pace at each turn. And Heyneke also expected us to improve on our previous bleep-test results. On the way to the training ground, some of us started complaining about the exercise that lay ahead.

'Is it really that bad?' Heyneke wanted to know.

'Well, have you done the bleep test at level 13?' I asked. (Level 13 was my personal best.) I shouldn't have said that. Heyneke completely lost it. 'Get my whistle,' he barked at Basil. 'I'll show you lot how hectic a training session can really get!'

Luckily, Basil managed to calm him down, and in the end we just did the bleep test. We'd had quite a scare and completed the exercise without so much as a whisper of complaint escaping our mouths.

The Sharks had done us no favours by beating the Crusaders two weeks earlier in Durban (27-26). As defending champions, the 'Saders had been the strongest team in the Super 14 till then, and we knew they would want revenge.

Before the start of the tour, Heyneke had decided to start me from the bench for this game in order to give me more time to rest, and Bryan Habana and Gary Botha, two of our sharpest players in the competition, were nursing injuries. Both, however, were in the starting line-up. To top it all, JP Nel had been suspended after a dangerous tackle in the game against the Waratahs. The Crusaders, therefore, had no trouble beating us. The final score – 32-10 – was a wake-up call after a very good start to the tour.

The only way to overcome a terrible weekend was to have a team-building session, so the week before the game against the Highlanders, we stayed in Queenstown, a pleasant holiday destination on New Zealand's South Island, where we could just relax. By the fourth week, a tour usually starts taking its toll, and this was the ideal opportunity to clear our minds.

During our stay, we found a small, quiet pub in town on the Sunday evening, and for about three hours Jaco van der Westhuyzen told one hilarious joke after another and had us in stitches. It turned into one of the best times I've ever had with the Bulls.

But of course Heyneke suspected what we'd been up to, and that Monday at practice, he decided that a few scrum sessions and driving mauls from line-outs were just the medicine to 'cure' us of our hangovers. But this session was different from the one we'd had in George – this time we managed to concentrate and were razor-sharp. It was one of our toughest training sessions of the season, but the guys – headaches and all – were fully committed and worked very hard.

That weekend we made history by beating the Highlanders 22-13 in Dunedin, the first time we'd won at Carisbrook, the infamous House of Pain. Later it was said among the team that we'd already won the game on the Sunday in that pub in Queenstown. And maybe – as with so many jokes – there was an element of truth to it.

In our last game on tour, we lost 9-17 to the Highlanders, but we still returned to Loftus with 13 league points in the bag. The Bulls were the only South African team to win three games on tour, which was a big confidence-booster in our aim for a home semi-final. But our chances seemed slim nevertheless.

In order to achieve our goal, we would have to win our remaining games *and* secure a handful of bonus points in the process. Above all, we would have to rely on favourable results in other games to finish as one of the top two on the log.

We went on to beat the Stormers 49-12, the Lions 31-7 and the Blues 40-19, and in the process accumulated the bonus points before our last league encounter, against the Reds. Then, like the year before, unbelievable coincidences started working in our favour.

On the Friday, the Crusaders unexpectedly lost against the Chiefs (24-30) to finish on 42 points on the log. The next day the Blues easily beat the Force in Perth (33-6) and also moved up to 42 points. They had been so certain that they would finish second or third that they had already travelled to Sydney for the flight back to Auckland.

I worked out that we had to beat the Reds without a bonus point to finish fourth on the log and travel to Durban, rather than taking on the Crusaders in New Zealand. The Sharks had had a super season with Dick Muir at the helm and would finish first if they beat the Stormers. The Capetonians were struggling and chances were slim that they'd get the better of the Sharks.

As the Reds were last on the log, we were the overwhelming favourites; however, how does one plan a win without scoring a bonus point? Heyneke had an altogether different idea.

'Victor,' he said, 'I think we can pass the Blues and Crusaders on the log. All we have to do is beat the Reds by 76 points.'

Did he say 'all' we have to do?

That was a helluva lot of points in Super 14, even against the worst team of the season. At first I thought Heyneke was joking, but he was the coach and he made the decisions.

The Friday before the game, Heyneke walked into the team room and, like so many times before, started telling us a story. One day, Heyneke said, hundreds of people gathered together to pray for rain. A little boy in the crowd wanted to know from his father what was going on, and his dad explained that they were praying for rain.

'Dad, do you believe it's going to rain if we pray?' the boy asked.

'Yes,' his dad replied.

'But, Dad,' said the little boy, 'why did you not bring along an umbrella then?'

In other words, if you believed that you could achieve your goal, you also had to act as if you believed it. Heyneke wrote '76' on the whiteboard without saying a word. We got the message.

On the way home, I phoned my dad and told him about our plan. He was very worried and asked whether it wasn't better to focus on securing a victory instead of chasing all those points. I said, 'To win this competition, we have to play in a home semi-final, and for that to happen, we have to win by 76 points.' As I heard myself saying the words, I really started believing that it was possible.

During the week preceding the game, the Reds coach, Eddie Jones, was quoted in the press as saying that his team 'knew' how to play the Bulls, but we didn't take any notice of his banter.

In the match, the Reds scored the first points with a penalty kick, but we responded with a try shortly afterwards. As we turned around at the try line and started jogging back to the halfway line, I knew we had brought the proverbial umbrella along to Loftus.

Eighty minutes later, we left the field after one of the most unbelievable games of rugby in which I'd ever played. The Bulls had won 92-3, the biggest winning margin in Super 14 history … and 13 points more than we'd been aiming for. I was one of only a handful of Bulls who *didn't* score a try! We finished second on the log – for the first time there would be a Super 14 semi-final at Loftus.

Supporters were already queuing for tickets when we left the stadium later that evening. Earlier that season I had avoided being seen in public, but now I couldn't venture out without someone stopping me for a chat or asking me to sign an autograph. With the World Cup just a few months away, the excitement over rugby had reached a new high. Two South African teams had finished top of the log in the Super 14 competition and both semi-finals were being played locally.

The Blues had to make a U-turn in Sydney and head off to Durban to take on the Sharks, and the Crusaders were on their way to Pretoria. For the first time in Super Rugby history, teams from New Zealand could experience what it was like to travel so far for the play-offs. They didn't arrive as the favourites.

The first semi-final was played in Durban; the Sharks were impressive, beating the Blues 34-18. Then it was our turn, against the Crusaders. Before the match, we'd decided to adapt our game plan, as bonus points were no longer a factor. Even without the injured Fourie du Preez, we played well. His replacement, Heini Adams, had a brilliant game. Both teams defended as if their lives depended on it, and no tries were scored. Derick Hougaard kicked us into the final with eight penalty goals and a drop kick. The final score: 27-12.

In the meantime I had turned 30, and that Sunday after the semi-final we had a big party at my business partner Willem Britz's house. We roasted a sheep on the spit and tons of people attended. One could argue that we should rather have focused on the final, but it turned out to be a good team-building exercise, with everyone having a great time.

At Monday practice, quite a few of the guys turned up with blood-shot eyes, and I wondered, how the hell did *we* reach the finals? Here it was the most important week in our Blue Bulls careers and we have guys pitching up for practice with hangovers! But I also knew that it was a good sign, because every time we had a bit of a party, we went on to give a good performance on the field.

A big advantage of playing such an important game at your home ground is the way supporters start firing up long before kick-off. On some Sunday evenings during the tournament we'd drive past Loftus just to see how people were queuing for tickets. Without them realising it, they really motivated us. We knew they couldn't wait to see us play in the final the next weekend, and that they were backing us all the way.

Heyneke insisted that we chat with our supporters and thank them whenever the opportunity presented itself. He wanted us to experience the atmosphere and the gravity of the occasion. It was always pleasant to talk to supporters and sign autographs in the shade of the Loftus grandstand. The fans told us how some Bulls supporters had left the stadium 15 minutes before the final whistle had gone in the Crusaders game so that they could immediately drive down to Durban to buy tickets for the final.

Our supporters firmly believed that we would win, but we knew that a final wouldn't be easy. The Sharks were at the top of the log and had beaten us convincingly earlier that season. And the Shark Tank was not our favourite venue, as it was usually extremely hot and humid.

Fourie was in a race against time to be fit for the final after he'd torn ligaments in his shoulder. I'd had a similar injury – the pain as you tried to pass the ball was unbearable. On average, it takes about six weeks to recover from such an injury, and even then it still hurts when you move your arms. But Fourie's never-say-die attitude prevailed when he declared himself fit for the final after just two weeks' recovery time.

A day before kick-off, Heyneke had another story to share with us. In this allegory, a guy had a perfect heart; the tissue and arteries were absolute perfection. However, another man from the same town claimed that his heart was even better, when in fact it was in rather bad shape, having been patched up several times.

'How can you claim that your heart is stronger than mine?' the guy with the healthy heart wanted to know.

'Well,' said the man with the patched-up heart, 'over the years, when-ever my friends were in need, I gave them little pieces of my heart. And every time I was sad, they gave me bits of theirs. That's why my heart is so strong.'

Heyneke was saying that although life isn't always easy, if you always support your friends and loved ones and in turn are supported by them, your heart grows stronger as a result. And that sentiment would be illustrated in the final. A week after some light training sessions, we left for Durban.

It wasn't an easy game. We didn't play well, and the Sharks did. They never allowed us to build up any momentum; it was a real see-saw affair. Pierre Spies burst through for our first try, but JP Pietersen later inter-cepted to score for the Sharks. At half-time the home side led 14-10.

The second half was evenly poised until Albert van den Berg scored for the Sharks with two minutes to go. They were leading 19-13 and the game was nearly over. While we were waiting for the conversion to take place, I called the guys together. 'If they miss the kick, we have to secure the restart. It's our last chance.'

I was surprised to see the young but talented Frans Steyn place the ball for the conversion kick. It was also odd that, with 15 minutes to go, Dick Muir had replaced his captain, John Smit, and recognised place-kicker, Percy Montgomery. I had expected Ruan Pienaar or Butch James to take over the kicking duties. Maybe Frans was rushing a bit, but he missed the conversion. We were still in with a chance.

The last two minutes were marked by a nervous frenzy. We restarted the game, but they secured the ball. Butch kicked it downfield, but he couldn't find touch. We launched an attack, but then Gary Botha kicked away possession. Under tremendous pressure, Frans had to kick the ball out, but he missed touch. Yet *again* we lost possession.

Then came the 'highlight' of flanker Derick Kuün's career. On the ground, right in front of the referee, he used his hands in the ruck to steal the ball. I waited for the whistle and the Sharks to be given the penalty. But referee Steve Walsh apparently hadn't seen the infringement!

Play continued at a frenetic pace. Akona Ndungane made some valuable metres, and little Heini Adams (who had replaced Fourie in the last minutes) ducked under a few Sharks players before the ball was passed back to Bryan Habana. He stepped inside, and suddenly a gaping hole appeared in front of him. He pinned back his ears, sidestepped once and scored a magnificent try.

The Bulls were ecstatic, but we knew it wasn't over yet. With the score now 18-19, Derick Hougaard still had to convert the try. And he had to do so at almost exactly the same angle as Frans had, when he'd missed a short while before. I went down on my knees about five steps behind Derick. I was dog-tired. Derick was still stepping back to take the kick when the Sharks players stormed him. There was no chance for him to settle down and concentrate. He had to rush the kick, but the ball cleared the crossbar: 20-19. The Bulls were the Super 14 champions!

The next moment the entire Bulls team swamped me. I remember that Jaco van der Westhuyzen had said before the game that he would climb up onto one of the crossbars if we won. When I finally freed myself from the group hug, I saw Jaco balancing on the crossbar in the Shark Tank. It was the best feeling of my entire rugby career.

After receiving the trophy, we stayed on the field. Nobody wanted to leave – the moment was too special. Our girlfriends and wives joined us, and we probably stayed there for an hour before going to the changing rooms. For a long time we just sat there, reliving the game. It was a unique, calm feeling of joy I'd never experienced before.

Nobody had ever thought a South African team would win the Super 14. The travelling involved was just too big a factor, but we had overcome it. For the *Bulls* to achieve this victory was an even greater feat. Just five years earlier, we couldn't win a single game in the competition – played 11, lost 11.

Heyneke had slowly but surely built the team's confidence. When we won the Currie Cup, we steadily started working our way to the top of the Super Rugby log. Very few of the Bulls players in this final had been around during the dark days of 2001 and 2002 – most of them didn't know what we'd had to endure to reach this pinnacle.

In rugby, the little things often play a huge role. If there's a gap, you have to take it. The Sharks must've been gutted to lose in the final. Their supporters had started popping the champagne corks after Albert's try, but we never stopped believing in ourselves and kept on fighting.

Later that evening I saw the disappointment on John Smit's face. I really felt bad for his sake, but I was in seventh heaven.

Sometimes you lose a game you should never have lost. And sometimes you win games you should never have won: the Super 14 final in 2007 was one of them.

10

Glory in Paris

In South African rugby, the Springboks are the number-one priority, but on Sunday 20 May 2007, the Boks had to make way for a Bulls tradition.

Usually after winning a final the whole team got together for a braai and a little celebration. But it was also the World Cup year, and we had to prepare ourselves mentally for the international season. Jake had already gathered a group of players at a training camp in Bloemfontein, and he wanted the Bulls and Sharks players that had made the squad to join him the day after the final. But we had decided beforehand: win or lose, that wasn't going to happen.

We left Durban for Pretoria early in the morning and then planned on catching a flight to Bloemfontein around lunch time. But somebody at Tuks had organised a braai to celebrate our Super 14 victory, so we decided to pop in. Of course, it turned out to be a most enjoyable get-together, and all the Boks in the team decided that there was no way we could leave for Bloemfontein immediately.

Luckily, Jake understood, and we left later that afternoon on a chartered flight from Pretoria: Gurthrö Steenkamp, Gary Botha, Bakkies Botha, Danie Rossouw, Wikus van Heerden, Pierre Spies, Fourie du Preez, Wynand Olivier, Bryan Habana, Akona Ndungane and me.

Because John Smit and the other Sharks in the Bok group would be at the training camp, we didn't want to walk around with big, victorious grins on our faces. They were shattered and we were ecstatic. But we didn't want to stop celebrating either, so we had to kind of do so under the radar. That Sunday evening we all gathered in Fourie's room, where we listened to music and relived every moment of the final.

The next day we were back on the practice field and the Super 14 euphoria had come and gone. England, the toughest opposition in our World Cup group, were on their way to South Africa for two Tests, and we had to face Samoa too.

That's the nature of rugby. For five years you work like a dog towards a common goal, but when you finally achieve it, the glory is short-lived. You have to shift your focus onto the next big thing. A victory is quickly forgotten after the smallest defeat. Nothing really lasts longer than a week.

Jake was, of course, very happy that two South African teams had dominated the Super 14 competition. At the camp, he handled the situation very professionally and congratulated everyone who had been involved in the final. He also made a point of stressing that we were now one team with a common goal.

We were ready for England. I'd never been in a team that won against them, so it was a massive Test series for me, even though people were claiming that England would send only their third-best side. But that was their decision – all we wanted was to beat them good and proper. The Bulls and Sharks players wanted the confidence we'd gained in the Super 14 competition to carry over to the Bok squad.

For two successive weeks, we scored more than 50 points against England: 58-10 in Bloemfontein and 55-22 in Pretoria. We played solid rugby. So what if it wasn't their first-choice players? We had landed the first blows before the World Cup.

The Test in Bloemfontein was special because Bakkies and I made our 26th appearance as the starting lock combination – a new South African record. Although we didn't play against Samoa, we were back for the home leg of the Tri Nations series, and we beat Australia 22-19 in Cape Town thanks to Frans Steyn's two brilliant drop kicks, which certainly made up for those missed opportunities in the Super 14 final.

John was injured in this Test and would be out of action for quite some time. Despite our differences over the years, Jake made me captain for the Tri Nations Test against the All Blacks in Durban. It was a great honour to be the 52nd Springbok skipper, even though I knew it was only temporary. In any case, it wasn't a game I would remember fondly. We were outclassed and lost 21-26.

Jake and the rest of the Boks then set off for Christchurch and the away leg of the Tri Nations without the core of the squad he'd built for the World Cup tournament. The idea was to rest the senior players for a couple of weeks and let them prepare at home, while the guys who were knocking on the World Cup door would be given a chance to stake their claim.

So we gathered at a training camp in the Cape, where Rassie Erasmus was our technical adviser. We trained hard every morning and had detailed planning sessions in the evenings. We discussed aspects like game plans, movements from set pieces, defence patterns and tactical kicking until we had assimilated all the information.

It was great to work with Rassie again. In my days with the Cats I'd realised that technical analysis was his forte. Jake and his assistants relayed their input from New Zealand and Australia, and by the time they returned, we had the complete blueprint. I believe we did our most important preparation for the World Cup during that time in Cape Town.

But then a big setback hit the team: Pierre Spies, our best forward in the Tests against England, had to withdraw from the Bok squad. Pierre was destructive on attack, and with his speed and power, he would've been a key player for us in France. When he started coughing up blood at a training session one day, we knew it was serious. He was diagnosed with a rare lung disease, and in the end he couldn't join us in France. He would have been our X-factor at the World Cup.

There were rumours about why Pierre had withdrawn, with some people alleging that he had tested positive for drugs. Absolute nonsense. He was really sick and we all felt very sorry for him.

The Boks may have lost both away games in the Tri Nations (17-25 against the Wallabies in Sydney and 6-33 against the All Blacks in Christchurch), but having the team compete without the senior players was very informative. As a young team, they had by no means been overpowered. It was a very positive sign.

**

Jake's willingness to bring in help from outside the squad made a huge difference. Initially he'd brought Rassie in as technical adviser, but Rassie accepted a job at Western Province and could no longer join us in France.

So Jake contacted former Wallaby coach Eddie Jones. At first it was weird to have an Australian as part of our team. None of us knew Eddie all that well, so we didn't know what to expect from him. Over the years, Eddie had built a reputation as someone who spoke his mind – raising that one eyebrow of his slightly higher than the other – but we quickly learnt that he was a passionate rugby pundit who shared our love for the game.

In fact, his energy and passion were contagious. He had an incredible knowledge of rugby and found an immediate confidant in Fourie, who also liked to analyse the game. Eddie didn't try to reinvent the wheel. Instead, he provided input into our game plan and suggested small changes here and there. With his previous experience of a World Cup, he helped keep Jake calm. He had a massive influence on the team, and Jake deserves all the credit for involving Eddie in our plans.

As players, we now had far more experience than we'd had in the 2003 World Cup, when most of the players had only been involved in a few Super 12 seasons. We were young and unprepared then. In 2007, most of us had 30, 40 or more Tests to our names. As a team, we'd been together for four years. Whereas in 2003 I had sat in the front row in the team photograph with only 20 Tests under my belt, there were now guys who had played 30 or 40 Tests (such as Schalk Burger, Juan Smith, Bakkies Botha, Jaque Fourie and Fourie du Preez) who had to stand when we had our team picture taken.

This time there were no controversial issues like the supposed racial tension or Kamp Staaldraad; the team made the headlines for the right reasons. We were considered serious contenders for the trophy, even though we weren't the outright favourites. We couldn't wait to get to France.

But before we could depart, we also had to be in peak mental condition. John Smit, Henning Gericke, our team psychologist, and Annelee Murray, part of our management team, came up with an ingenious plan. All the players (no management) gathered at the Selborne Golf Club, south of Durban, for a long walk along the beach. Every few kilometres we would stop at a 'station' that had been set up, each one representing a World Cup from 1995 to 2003, where the players had the opportunity to talk about their previous World Cup experiences.

Os did all the talking at the first station, which represented the 1995 RWC. At the next station, Percy told us about the 1999 RWC. When we reached the third station, a few of us talked about 2003 – what had worked and what had not. It was wonderful taking a relaxed stroll along the beach and listening to what one's teammates had to say – the words were like provisions we could take along on our journey to France.

The only way we could apply the lessons learnt in 2003 was to do exactly the opposite of what we'd done then. That walk on the beach was the polar opposite of the humiliation we had had to endure sitting naked in a black pit at Kamp Staaldraad.

We decided that the sacrifice we'd make this time was to work even harder at our game. If that meant my line-out analysis needed work, I would pay extra attention to it. In order for our place-kickers to improve their accuracy, they would have to put in additional hours of practice. If our scrums needed fine-tuning, we'd have to knuckle down and work harder at them.

Everything we did in future had to have the team's best interests at heart. This experience, as well as our daily circumstances, was aimed at getting all the players in the right frame of mind for the biggest rugby tournament on earth. For that reason, it was decided that our loved ones could join us in France, and we would also stay in the best hotels. The tournament had to be a memorable experience for everyone involved.

The walk on the beach concluded at John's holiday house in Pennington, where another surprise awaited us: all the players' mentors – fathers or others who had played a significant role in our rugby careers – were waiting for us there. Lions coach Loffie Eloff and Bulls coach Heyneke Meyer, among others, were there. We had a braai, listened to music and enjoyed a few cold beers. It was the first time my dad had seen me getting a bit tipsy – something I was teased about for quite some time afterwards.

The message was the polar opposite of the one we had received at Kamp Staaldraad in 2003: this was the best time of our lives, and we should enjoy it as much as possible. After being together for four years, we knew each other well. The young and inexperienced team of 2003 had grown into a balanced side with experienced guys in almost all positions by 2007.

Experienced indeed, but not prim and proper; later that night we went down to the beach to continue partying. Jean de Villiers caught Os off guard and floored him with a massive tackle. We thought, that's it … Os is injured. But the Capetonian centre was too much of a light-weight to prevent the massive Free Sate farmer from stamping his authority on rugby's biggest showcase!

About two weeks before the tournament, I was almost in the same boat as Os. I was playing a round of golf with some friends and busi-ness partners at Silver Lakes, east of Pretoria. After teeing off, I wanted to get into the golf cart, but Patrick Goddard, an associate of mine in a restaurant venture in Pretoria, suddenly pulled away. My foot got stuck in a rope cordoning off the tee-off, and I was pulled from the cart.

Patrick carried on driving, and I could feel the ligaments in my weak right knee pulling alarmingly. I fell to the ground and thought, that's it – you can forget about the World Cup. Poor Patrick was close to tears when he realised what had happened. Luckily, it wasn't that serious, but I got a helluva fright. Perhaps I had escaped without injury because there were no more decent ligaments to tear!

Our first warm-up game for the World Cup was against Namibia, who travelled to Cape Town for the match. It was a one-sided affair that we won 105-13, my first victory as Bok captain, since John was not yet fit enough to play.

After this massacre we travelled to Ireland and Scotland for two more warm-ups against the Irish province Connacht and the Scottish touring side. Connacht is one of the lesser-known provinces in Ireland, but they gave the youngsters in the Bok side a fight for their money. Then we were off to Edinburgh on a trip that should have taken four hours, but ended up being almost eight hours long because the arrange-ments had gone a bit haywire, and we weren't very happy when we eventually arrived in the Scottish capital.

For this reason, Fourie and Bakkies decided to liven up our next practice session, and they each took half a sleeping tablet before we started. Of course they soon realised that it wasn't the brightest idea. It was hilarious to watch them. They were so scared that the pill would take effect that they concentrated doubly hard to stay awake. It turned out to be one of their best practices ever! Jake was none the wiser, but their precarious situation lifted our spirits and we soon forgot about the unnecessarily long journey.

The Scots were making a big fuss about their preparations for the World Cup. Their conditioning was apparently top-notch, and their big, strong pack of forwards was ready to take us on. But we were just as prepared for them. Early in the game they tried to start a driving maul, but Bakkies, CJ van der Linde and Gary Botha soon had them on the back foot with a massive counter-drive. It was clear to everyone that our pack wasn't going to be dominated that easily. Although we didn't run up a huge score (27-3), the Bok forwards got a tremendous boost from the game, having annihilated the 'bigger and stronger' Scottish pack.

We were still not the favourites to win the World Cup – New Zealand and France shared that honour – but it didn't bother us. We believed we could do it. We were packing our umbrellas for France.

In Paris we were mildly irritated when John had to attend a function in honour of the team captains and all of them were transported to the venue by bus … except for Richie McCaw, the All Black captain, who arrived in a private vehicle, escorted by the police. It was annoying to see them making such a fuss over him and the All Blacks. After all, they were not the only team, nor was 'Sir Richie' the only rugby captain, at the tournament. But the incident just motivated us to play even better.

We decided to make ourselves at home in Paris, the location of our first two games. In the previous World Cup, our first two games took place in Perth while most of the action was happening thousands of kilometres away in Sydney. This time we were right in the thick of things, and the heady atmosphere put us in the right frame of mind.

SA Rugby really looked after us. A couple of South African channels were available on the TV sets in our team room and we were accommodated in single rooms, so no problems with room-mates. And Monja and Jaime could stay with me for the first two weeks.

During the official opening ceremony, the Eiffel Tower was lit up. The plan had been for the lights to be blue, in support of the home side, but when they were switched on, they were green and gold! To this day we still don't know whether the French electricians had their wires crossed or whether SA Rugby had pulled off a very clever marketing strategy. Either way, we saw it as a good omen.

Jake decided that we needed to get into the spirit of the tournament as soon as possible and managed to arrange seats for us in a private suite for the opening game between France and Argentina. As far as I know, we were the only team attending the game as spectators. Although it was great to watch the game, it was at times difficult to keep one's eyes from wandering. A group of Argentine supporters were seated a couple of rows in front of us, and there were some really beautiful girls among them. The more points the Pumas scored, the more pieces of clothing the girls removed. In the end, they were basically dressed in just their undergarments and pom-poms!

The Pumas shocked the host nation by winning the thrilling encounter and confirmed what we'd told each other: in this competition, anything is possible.

As in 2003, England and Samoa were in our group. This time we would face the tough island men in our opening game, at the historical Parc des Princes, which had been France's premier Test field before the Stade de France was built in the late 1990s.

The Samoans are difficult customers. They are massive, strong and aggressive. The Samoan 'sidestep' is, after all, someone running right over you! Everyone was talking about their humongous eighthman, Henry Tuilagi. I was curious to see for myself how big he really was, so when we lined up in the tunnel before kick-off, I quickly scanned the bulk of muscle standing next to me. He was quite impressive.

Then he took a few steps forward and I noticed the number 11 on his back. This wasn't Henry but Alesana, his younger brother – the *wing*. I turned round and saw the *real* Henry – he was a *giant*. After the first line-out, Danie Rossouw and Schalk Burger were flat on their backs after Henry had run right over them. *Mean*!

As was always the case against Samoa, it was a tough game, but they couldn't contain us and we won 59-7. Unfortunately, Jean de Villiers, one of our leaders and a key player in the backline, suffered a serious injury early on in the game. It was a massive setback to lose a second stalwart before the tournament was even properly underway. In 2003, Jean was injured in a warm-up game, and now he'd barely played one half before his tournament came to an end.

But one player's disappointment is another's opportunity. Frans Steyn seemed comfortable at inside centre and had delivered some impressive performances for the Sharks in that position. His unpredictability in the backline and his ability to punt the ball a long way would add a new dimension to our game plan.

Then, as if the injury to Jean wasn't a big enough blow, Schalk was cited and banned for four weeks for tackling a Samoan player in mid-air. Schalk was known as a hard, uncompromising player, and I think in this case his history counted against him. The South African business-man Johann Rupert made his private jet available for a lawyer to be flown in from London to defend Schalk's case, but in the end he arrived on a commercial flight. On appeal, Schalk's sentence was reduced to two weeks.

Jean and Schalk had been part of the team for four years and their absence left a huge hole. Jake, however, had the utmost faith in every squad member. Frans and Wikus van Heerden stepped up, and both would excel.

The group match against England was probably one of the best games I'd played since making my debut seven years earlier. We were all very eager to go up against the English, and Fourie was simply untouch-able on the day. It was the closest we came to the perfect execution of our game plan. The final score: 36-0. Although we still had two group games, against Tonga and the USA, the first place on the group log was within our reach.

After the resounding victory, a couple of the Bulls players in the squad decided to experience some French culture, and a day after beating England, we had lunch at Café George V, a top restaurant on the famous Champs-Élysées. Fourie, Danie, Wynand, Gary and I were joined by our wives, children and two of my friends, Willem Britz and Daan van Rensburg. We had a few cold ones and superb French cuisine in a very relaxing atmosphere. Before we knew it, the sun was setting! We were utterly enjoying the Paris vibe and becoming part of the World Cup experience in France.

The team was brimming with confidence by the time we travelled to Lens for our encounter against Tonga. Jake wanted to rest some of the senior players for this game, but his decision almost backfired on the field, as the Boks were in trouble shortly after half-time. Bob Skinstad was captaining the team, and John Smit, Juan Smith, Bryan Habana, Frans Steyn, Percy Montgomery and I were on the bench. When the Tongans extended their lead to 10-7, we were sent on to help save the day.

In the two movements that followed, we scored two tries. I handled the ball in both and, although I didn't score, it felt good to contribute as a substitute player. At the death we were leading by five points, and I was just thinking that we'd scraped through when the Tongans kicked the ball cross-field and one of their players set off in pursuit. Fortunately, it bounced just out of the guy's reach, as it would have been an easy try had he gathered the ball. So we pulled this one off 30-25 – albeit with a lot of luck on our side.

After this game, the former Springbok prop Balie Swart, who helped us with our scrumming technique, managed to find a case of Beyers-kloof Pinotage. Dr Derik Coetzee, our conditioning coach, was very strict about our alcohol intake and he didn't want to know anything about the Beyerskloof. As usual, we took his 'advice' with a pinch of salt and decided to treat ourselves anyway. The French make excellent red wine, but enjoying some of our own fantastic wine in Paris was very special.

That evening, while sipping the excellent pinotage, Fourie du Preez, Eddie Jones and I talked rugby for about two hours. We exchanged ideas, shared our rugby philosophies and worked out strategies for the games ahead. Perhaps this was the moment that Fourie started thinking about continuing his rugby career in Japan, at Eddie's club, after the 2011 World Cup.

Our next game was against the USA, and Schalk was back. We smashed the Yanks 64-15, but the game will probably be remembered for one of their moves, when the Zimbabwean-born Takudzwa Ngwenya ran circles around Bryan Habana to score a magnificent try. We didn't think anyone could get away from Bryan, and we made sure that he heard the story about the unknown Zimbabwean who had caught him flat-footed over and over again! This victory secured us our first goal: a place in the quarter-finals.

The evening after beating the USA, we had a get-together in our team room. Jake was a bit reluctant for us to venture into the city 'after hours' in case we made headlines for the wrong reasons, but most of the senior players weren't into nightclubs and bars any more anyway. A couple of the youngsters might have gone out, but the older guys preferred to stay in.

Two of these senior players were Os du Randt and Percy Montgomery, who set an example for everyone. Even though Os had helped win the World Cup in 1995, he was more excited than most of us to be part of the 2007 campaign. He told us in no uncertain terms that we should enjoy the experience, as you never knew when your career could come to an end.

In the meantime, I had a personal item on my agenda that I needed to tend to. Before the World Cup, French second-league club Toulon had approached me to play for them. Toulon is a wealthy club and they made me an offer that no other player had been offered before. The remuneration, however, was not the only consideration. Even before the tournament it had become clear that Jake had little chance of staying on as Bok coach after the World Cup, and rumours were also doing the rounds about major changes that were planned for Springbok rugby, allegedly with politics playing a bigger role in the near future. I, on the other hand, was keen to try something new and to explore a different direction in my career.

Being in France for the tournament offered me the ideal opportunity to visit Toulon. On our day off in the week before the quarter-final game against Fiji, a sports agent picked me up in his car and drove me to Toulon, about an hour's drive from Marseilles, where the Springbok squad was staying at the time. I expected to meet the club's management and to inspect the club's facilities, but I didn't yet know Mourad Boudjellal, the billionaire owner of Toulon. He did things on a *much* bigger scale.

What was supposed to have been a quick, quiet visit turned into a major event: first a press conference was held, and the level of media interest was something we seldom see in South Africa. Journalists, radio reporters and TV cameras crowded the reception hall as if a soccer super-star were present. They'd even organised an interpreter for the event.

My face and that of the Aussie George Gregan were displayed on dozens of banners and posters around town. It was weird that people I'd never seen or met before were making such a fuss over me!

I even had to pick the house we would stay in. Earlier the club had emailed Monja and me pictures and specs of a few houses for us to look at before I would make a final decision on this visit.

After spending a few hours in Toulon, I returned to the Bok team in Marseilles, where we were preparing for the game against Fiji. They had surprised everyone by beating Wales 38-34 to finish second in Group B.

Then it was the weekend of the quarter-finals.

The game between Australia and England, also taking place in Marseilles, was played first. We followed the match on TV in our hotel rooms, not far from the Stade Vélodrome, and watched as the Wallabies lost 10-12. I don't know whether Eddie Jones enjoyed it, but we were celebrating as if we were already in the final. It was a huge relief to see one of our biggest rivals knocked out of the competition.

Then New Zealand faced France in Cardiff. I was so tense during this unbelievable game that my shirt was soaked with sweat. When the final whistle blew, France had succeeded in achieving a feat no one had thought possible: they had beaten the mighty All Blacks. Afterwards some people complained about a forward pass that had led to a French try, but the scoreboard had the last say: 20-18.

Now we were celebrating as if *we'd* just won the World Cup, but I think Eddie Jones joined us on this occasion. If we didn't have to play Fiji the next day, we would've opened a few bottles of champagne.

We couldn't believe that two of the favourites, the Wallabies and the All Blacks, were on their way home. But their defeats also served as a warning to us, because what had happened to them could just as easily happen to us. The fact that we were so emotional after those two results perhaps accounted for us struggling against Fiji the next day.

We were leading to start with, but then Fiji replied with two tries that were scored against the run of play, and suddenly the score was 20-all. JP Pietersen managed to save another certain try in the corner with a superb tackle. If Fiji had scored then, it would've been tickets for us.

John called us together and told us to calm down and stick to our game plan. The biggest mistake a team can make under pressure is to start playing too loosely. We pulled ourselves together and played magnificent rugby in the last 15 minutes, slowing down the pace of the game and concentrating on what we do well: driving mauls from line-outs, scrums and rucks. The end result: South Africa 37, Fiji 20.

Later that evening, Schalk and I joined Os in his room. We sat on the balcony and talked for hours. People always said there was provincialism in the Bok camp, but at that stage it had disappeared off the radar. We were all friends; even the smaller splinter groups had all united as one. The conversation kept coming back to the matters at hand: the Boks against Argentina in the one semi-final, and England against France in the other.

Although the French were the host nation and the Six Nations champions, they had lost against the Pumas in the opening game of the tournament. England had a terrible season behind them, and we had beaten them three times. And Argentina had always been one of the smaller Test nations in world rugby, and had to cope with many behind-the-scenes problems, which hampered their development. And the Boks? We had finished last in the Tri Nations series and had lost five Tests in a row the previous year.

But the four teams in the semi-finals had one thing in common: the best packs of forwards in the tournament. That in itself was an indication of how important the basic aspects of rugby were.

Because the Boks had never lost against the Pumas, they could have been seen as an easy opponent, but anything can happen in a World Cup semi-final. Most of the Pumas were contracted by French clubs and were, therefore, familiar with the playing conditions. They also enjoyed a lot of crowd support.

Part of our game plan was to test them under the high ball, which they weren't used to. With Fourie and Butch James's kicks spot on, the tactic worked like a charm.

Many people compared Butch with Henry Honiball, who also preferred to stand close to the breakdown and tackle like a man possessed, but during the World Cup Butch played more like Joel Stransky did in the 1995 World Cup. His tactical kicking was superb, and he knew when to boot the ball and when to pass it. It wasn't the 'old' Butch – the one who had gained a reputation for his involvement in off-the-ball scuffles – but still the Butch feared by those opponents who dared hang on to the ball for too long.

In the end we outplayed the Pumas, overpowering them 37-13 to reach the final. Bryan scored two tries in the match, pushing his 2007 World Cup tally to eight, thus equalling Jonah Lomu's record set in 1995.

Over the years a lot has been said and written about Argentina's *bajada* scrum technique, but early in the tournament they didn't really achieve much with it. We, therefore, probably underestimated its impact, and as a result we struggled against them in the scrums. It was a good wake-up call for us, though, before taking on England – who'd had an upset victory over France (14-9) in the other semi – in the final. A power-ful scrum was one of England's mightiest weapons – they had basically scrummed the Wallabies out of the tournament in their quarter-final. We knew it was going to be a massive challenge in the final.

The atmosphere in Paris was most peculiar in the week leading up to the match. Even though all the tickets for the game were sold out, it didn't feel as if a major international sporting event was about to take place. Obviously, the fact that France had been bundled out of the tournament had something to do with it. Fortunately, the atmosphere began to improve on the Friday, when more and more South African supporters started arriving in Paris.

Earlier that week our team psychologist, Henning Gericke, had decided to focus our attention on the sheer size of the occasion. He showed us video footage of how South Africans at home were experiencing the World Cup: thousands of people were getting together in Bok Towns across South Africa, and supporters were wearing the green and gold in schools, bars and offices. World Cup fever had gripped South Africa. The images gave us a tremendous boost.

Henning's role in the World Cup should not be underestimated. Throughout the tournament he knew exactly how to motivate us before a big match, be it with an inspirational DVD or stirring music on the bus en route to the stadium. He was the one who started playing the

Robbie Wessels and Bok van Blerk song 'Ons vir jou, Suid-Afrika'. In 2011, we were still listening to this song before big games. Personally, the song motivated me a lot. Sometimes I'd sing the other verses on my own, even after I'd got off the bus!

Although some drama or other always occurred during a World Cup tournament, nothing too serious happened in 2007. But it nearly did ... Fourie du Preez, Danie Rossouw, Schalk Burger and I usually enjoyed a round of golf on our day off, no matter where we were. But this time Jake wasn't keen on the idea and told us on the Thursday before the final that we couldn't go. However, we decided not to break with tradition and secretly planned to 'escape' for a round at the Disneyland Paris course.

Of course it wasn't so easy to slip away unnoticed, especially dressed in one's golfing gear, but there we were, walking down the passage to the elevator. The door opens and who walks out? Jake, of course!

Schalla, Danna and I had time to hide around the corner, but Fourie wasn't so lucky. Obviously, Jake could tell that Fourie was on his way to the golf course, but he said nothing. He probably didn't want to create unnecessary friction by making an issue out of it. For some of us, a round of golf was an important part of preparing for a big game. It was an opportunity to get away from the pressures of training, and it helped calm the nerves.

Our loved ones were returning to France for the final, and I decided to invite my parents, Fai and Hettie, as well. They had supported me throughout my rugby career, from my days as a barefoot tyke in school rugby right up to the World Cup final in Paris. It meant a lot to me to thank them in this way, but it's nothing compared to the hours they spent and the distances they travelled to see me play in Kimberley, Durban, Bloemfontein, Johannesburg and even Cape Town.

That Friday, Paris was literally teeming with people dressed in Springbok jerseys. Former Bok coach Harry Viljoen had brought over a large group of supporters – he had even hired a bus. He loaded some South African supporters onto that bus, among them our wives and girlfriends, and drove them to the final at the Stade de France. On the morning before kick-off, President Thabo Mbeki and a few ministers visited our hotel to wish us well.

I'm not very superstitious – though Monja and my parents won't agree – but it had become my custom to go for a cup of coffee prior to a game. Before our group match against England, I had coffee in our hotel with my friends and business partners, Willem and Daan – and we all know how well that game had turned out for us. So the morning of the final, Monja, Willem, Daan and my parents joined me for a cup at a Starbucks not far from the hotel.

I'm not a very emotional person and approached the game like any other, even with the World Cup at stake. I wanted do the same things I usually did before a game, like enjoying a round of golf and a cup of coffee. I prefer to stick to my routine instead of emotionally exhausting myself.

Before I could think twice, we were on the bus on our way to the stadium. 'Ons vir jou, Suid-Afrika' was blaring from the speakers, and although I tried to stay calm, I couldn't help realise that this wasn't just another game of rugby. It was time to prepare myself for the biggest and most important match of my life. As the song says, 'It's not about us, but about the whole of South Africa'. It was the *World Cup* final.

After dropping off our kit in the changing room, we walked out onto the field to soak up the atmosphere. I carried a stress ball in my right hand. There, on that pitch in the Stade de France, I knew that the big moment had arrived.

A while later, Irish referee Alain Rolland blew his whistle for the kick-off, and the final began … In the first minute we gave the English a little hint of our intentions when Bakkies stole their line-out ball. Two minutes later, I, too, nicked one of England's throw-ins, and from that moment on they were never sure what to expect. Competing for the opponents' line-out throws was one of the strongest weapons in our arsenal, and on this day we were more successful than usual. In the end we stole about seven of their balls and basically annihilated any chance they had of attacking from that platform.

The match itself was a typical final in which risk taking is limited and possible points from penalty kicks are taken immediately. The result was a totally different game plan to the one we had employed in our group encounter against England.

Percy opened our tally with a penalty in the seventh minute, but four minutes later, Jonny Wilkinson made it 3-all. In the 14th minute,

Percy added three more points after Lewis Moody had tried to trip Butch James.

Our best opportunity for a try came in the 35th minute after we'd won another line-out ball on England's throw. Frans Steyn gained a good few yards, a couple of phases followed, and John Smit was stopped inches from the try line. Unfortunately, Fourie knocked the ball on and England escaped, but not for long. Two minutes later, Percy made it 9-3 with a third penalty, which was the score at half-time.

Shortly after the break it became 9-6 when Jonny slotted a second penalty. Then the centre Mathew Tait crashed through our defence, gaining a whole lot of metres. Percy was waiting when Tait sidestepped past him and I tackled him two metres short of the try line. But England managed to keep the ball alive and fed Mark Cueto, who crossed the line in the corner. After a referral, the television referee, Stuart Dickinson from Australia, judged that Cueto's foot had touched the touchline in a desperate tackle from Danie Rossouw.

Later, England fans claimed that the game would have swung their way had the 'try' been awarded, but we disagreed. If it had been a try, we would simply have stepped up a gear.

Before the final, a lot was said about how England would demolish us in the scrums. But although we didn't overpower them in this facet, our scrum was solid, which was all we needed. We were also disciplined and conceded few penalties, whereas England's infringements slowly but surely kept the scoreboard ticking over in our favour. Percy kicked like a champion. With 30 minutes to go, he made it 12-6.

We were in control of the game and could sense England's increasing desperation. In the 61st minute, Frans slotted a massive penalty kick from the halfway line to extend our lead to 15-6. The last 19 minutes passed by in a flash. Before we could check the stadium clock, Alain blew the final whistle. The Springboks were the world champions – again!

Besides my line-out work, my personal highlight was stopping Tait two metres short of our try line. And the cherry on top was when I was named Man of the Match – a massive honour in such an important game.

Holding the trophy and celebrating our victory in Paris are moments I'll remember forever. Afterwards we spent hours in the changing room, drinking beer and champagne from the Webb Ellis Cup. Some of the players were relaxing in a massive Roman bathtub, chatting and singing away. We were all very calm, actually. It was more a case of inner bliss than exuberant joy.

Later that evening, at our hotel, it was a completely different story. Whereas only the squad usually gathered in the team room, hundreds of people were now present. Some of us decided to escape the chaos to do our own thing. Monja, Daan, Willem and I had a few drinks at a club in the city, but surprisingly enough I didn't get to bed late.

The big festivities only started the next day. First we joined hundreds of South Africans at a hospitality tent under the Eiffel Tower, and that evening the IRB hosted its awards ceremony, where we could enjoy the celebrations as a team. On the way to the event, we sang South African songs as the knowledge that we were the world champions slowly sank in.

To crown a spectacular 24 hours, Jake won the Coach of the Year award, Bryan was voted Player of the Year and the Boks walked off with the Team of the Year award. The following day, we headed back to South Africa.

Nothing could prepare us for the euphoria and celebrations that were awaiting us at home. Thousands of people had gathered at OR Tambo International Airport, a vast improvement on the hundred or so who had welcomed us back four years earlier. The nation was ecstatic, and we were extremely proud to have contributed something towards national unity.

In 1995, when the Boks won the World Cup against the All Blacks at Ellis Park, I was a supporter who celebrated the victory with my mates. To experience as a player what the victory means to the nation is something you can't put into words.

Our victory parade across South Africa started in Pretoria at the Union Buildings, where President Mbeki waited to greet us. We would go on to parade through the streets of Johannesburg, Soweto, Port Elizabeth, Durban and Cape Town. Everywhere thousands of people cheered us on, waving banners and flags and running behind the bus that transported us.

The final party took place on Johann Rupert's farm L'Ormarins, near Franschhoek. The rock musician Arno Carstens provided the entertainment and it was, as we would say, a biggie. The last bus back to Cape Town only left at 5 a.m. that morning, but by then I was already fast asleep in my hotel bedroom. Those were the last few hours of an unbelievable two months.

Jake's contract with SA Rugby was not renewed, but before he said his final goodbyes, the Springboks still had to undertake a short tour of Wales and England. By then I'd signed my contract with Toulon, but Monja and I still had many arrangements to make. For one, we had to move out of our house to make way for our new tenants. But there was also the possibility of remaining in Pretoria if Heyneke was appointed as the new Bok coach.

I wasn't available for the tour of Wales and England. Besides personal business that needed my attention, the tour would have been an anticlimax after winning the World Cup. So I informed Jake that I was withdrawing from the squad for personal reasons, but then I received a letter from SA Rugby stating that I wouldn't be excused from touring. There was even talk of a summons.

I suggested joining the Boks on the Wednesday before the Test against Wales, but I was turned down. Eventually nothing came of the summons. I stayed at home and sorted out my affairs.

It wasn't the last time that Jake and I would clash. In December 2007, Fourie du Preez, Schalk Burger, Jake White and I were invited to play in the Ernie Els Golf Tournament at Fancourt near George.

A function was held on the first evening, after which we went to the clubhouse, which was reserved for members only. At around 1 a.m., a few of us, including Jake and Ernie's caddy, Ricky Roberts, were still there. We were discussing the World Cup and how much it meant to each of us to win it.

Then the conversation turned to who would be the next Bok coach. Jake supported Allister Coetzee, his assistant Bok coach for four years. Although I thought Allister was a good candidate for the job, I said Heyneke would be the best appointment.

Jake knew that Heyneke and I had a good relationship, but he still said that he thought Heyneke wouldn't be able to coach the Boks successfully.

'Jake, you had success with the Boks. I've been coached by both of you, and Heyneke is the best coach I've played under,' I said. It was probably not the right time to make such a statement.

Jake was furious. He reached across the table and grabbed my collar. How could I say such a thing only weeks after he'd won the World Cup? he wanted to know. Ricky had to calm him down; he was hopping mad. 'You and Fourie think you can dominate everyone around you, but I won't allow it,' were his parting words.

It was an unpleasant incident. The next day, Jake apologised, and I admitted that I should have chosen my words more carefully. We made peace. I did see him a few more times afterwards and we would greet each other, but by then I had realised we would never be best buddies. He would surprise me again later in my career, but for a completely different reason.

With that little scrap at Fancourt and the prospect of moving to France, the biggest year in my career ended on a very interesting note.

What a year it had been!

11

An odd interlude in France

After visiting Toulon during the World Cup tournament, I was looking forward to living in France. However, I made it clear to the club that I would return to South Africa if Heyneke Meyer was appointed Bok coach, and that this escape clause should be included in my contract.

Before the World Cup had even started, rumours were doing the rounds that Jake White would be replaced as coach and that transformation in South African rugby would be a priority. Of course, this led to a lot of uncertainty among the white players, with many of them signing contracts with overseas clubs.

I had signed a contract with Toulon for three years, with the option of deciding whether I wanted to stay on or not after the first season. Although I'd signed the agreement before the World Cup, I secretly hoped Heyneke would get the Springbok coaching job. Toulon, quite honestly, was Plan B if things in South Africa didn't work out.

A rugby player's career doesn't last forever, and I had to figure out how I would provide for my family the day I stopped playing. Toulon offered me five times more than I could've earned in South Africa – the club would ensure my financial security … and peace of mind.

December 2007 was tough, as I still had no idea who SARU was going to appoint as the next Bok coach. Everyone had expected an announcement in November, which would have given me time to finalise my arrangements with Toulon, while the Bulls management could also have put plans in place to appoint a new coach in Heyneke's place. But nothing happened.

Heyneke, Ian Schwartz, the commercial manager of the Bulls, Barend van Graan, the union's executive chief, and I tried hard to get an answer from SARU, without any success.

Because of what was happening behind the scenes, the Bulls couldn't start executing their plans at their annual training camp in George, and practice sessions were, therefore, less intense than usual; this despite the fact that Frans Ludeke, whose name was being mentioned as Heyneke's possible successor, was at the camp. To add an extra twist to the convoluted tale, Toulon had offered Heyneke a job! Things were a bit messy.

In the end, I couldn't postpone my departure any longer. The afternoon before I was to fly to France, I drove to Johannesburg to fetch our visas from the French consulate in Rosebank. Monja and Jaime's passports and visas were in order, but my passport was too full to add another stamp. Now what?

The only solution was to apply for a new passport at the Department of Home Affairs in the centre of Joburg. The next morning I reluctantly travelled into the heart of the concrete jungle without even knowing how to get to Home Affairs. My sister, Trudie Horn, had lent me her Kombi, and in my rush I was involved in a fender-bender.

There were long queues at Home Affairs, and I simply couldn't wait that long. Luckily, someone from the department recognised me and quickly sorted out my problem. Then I had to rush to the French consulate. With only an hour to spare before we had to leave for the airport, I got my visa.

Monja, Jaime, our au pair, Bernice Bates, and I arrived in Toulon on New Year's Eve. We were dropped off outside our new three-storey home with its views of the Mediterranean Sea. Fortunately, Monja loved the house I'd chosen. We were invited to a New Year's Eve party at the house of Nico Breedt, a former Sharks and Cheetahs lock. François van Schouwenburg, my former Blue Bulls teammate, was also in Toulon, and he showed us around the first few days.

It immediately struck me that our house was much bigger than those of the other players. I realised later that it was just me, former Wallaby captain George Gregan and former All Black captain Tana Umaga who had 'special' houses. The club had even offered us the services of a chauffeur and a cook, but we didn't take them up on those.

Living in Toulon was a very pleasant and exciting time for Monja, as I was home more often and could spend quality time with her and Jaime. Monja also has a knack for languages and wanted to learn to speak French.

SARU eventually announced the new Bok coach in mid-January: Peter de Villiers. It was like a punch in the stomach. Personally, I had nothing against Peter, but it meant that Plan B was now the only option available to me and I would not be playing for the Boks for a long time.

I didn't know Peter all that well. I was only concerned with playing rugby, but one couldn't compare what he had achieved as a coach with Heyneke's successes – that much I told him. Heyneke had won the Vodacom Cup, the Currie Cup and the Super 14 title, while Peter's success was limited to what he'd achieved with junior teams. I thought Heyneke would have been a better option as Springbok coach.

If Heyneke had got the job, he would have appointed me as captain. He had a world of respect for John Smit, but Heyneke and I had a very good relationship. However, nothing would now come of those plans.

There wasn't a lot of time to ponder the situation, because by then Toulon had lost the plot. I thought I was going to play a bit of stress-free, second-league club rugby in the south of France, but the club had other ideas. They had apparently decided that I was their biggest asset – so much so that I was even introduced to the mayor, who gave me the keys to the city!

My face also appeared on billboards, and all the locals wanted to meet me and shake my hand. And the only French I knew was *merci* and *au pair*! At my first practice session with the club, the stadium was packed with spectators who wanted to see me in the Toulon jersey – even though it was just training gear.

My first game for Toulon was against La Rochelle, for which I was on the bench. As we exited the tunnel to take to the field, we passed through a large shredded banner with my face on it. *Everyone* had to go through the banner to get to the field. All the fuss they were making made me feel very uncomfortable.

I was sent on in the second half after having had only one practice session with the team. Nevertheless, the first time I touched the ball, I almost scored a try. My career at Toulon could have started with a bang, but unfortunately I was tackled inches before the try line. At least we beat La Rochelle easily: 36-0.

Toulon's home ground is the Stade Félix Mayol. With seating for only about 25 000 spectators, it isn't a very big stadium, but it was packed for every game, and the atmosphere was amazing … *if* you played for Toulon. The supporters were fanatical – even more fanatical than the Bulls faithful!

With all this attention showered on me, I felt more like the world-famous soccer star David Beckham. Even though I wasn't the shy boy from Pietersburg any more, it was still hard for me to understand why everyone was making such a big fuss over me.

The standard of rugby, however, was not what I was used to. Toulon was a second-league team and the tempo was rather slow. I soon realised that I would have to do more if I didn't want to fall behind the guys in South Africa, so on Fridays before games and on Sundays I practised on my own.

I soon formed a close bond with a few South Africans in that part of the world – François, Nico, Chris Rossouw and Wessel Roux. We missed South Africa and often had a braai or made potjiekos (a traditional stew made in a cast-iron pot). I also befriended George Gregan, the New Zealanders Anton Oliver and Andrew Mehrtens, and England's Dan Luger. Because of the language barrier, it was hard to make friends with the French players.

One night Anton, Andrew and I had a braai at George's house. I had lots of plans to elevate Toulon to its rightful place as a top club in the first league, the French version of the Super 14 competition. I was excited and also full of confidence about the prospect, as it would give us a goal to aim for. It was better than having to try to dodge punches in the second league every weekend.

The other guys just looked at me as if I were crazy. 'You'll see. Just pull back,' George advised me. I soon realised that strict discipline and hard work were not really the French way of doing things. They also weren't too keen to try out anything new, because why fix what had worked the previous year and the one before that?

After about two weeks, I understood exactly what George meant. I learnt to take it easier during practice sessions, but I still didn't slack off completely. The fact that the French didn't understand my work ethic or my self-discipline didn't bother me.

Mourad Boudjellal, Toulon's wealthy owner, wanted to appoint Heyneke to coach the club, especially when we lost a game and he was in an emotional state. It was rumoured that a whole lot of players would come with Heyneke if he became the coach, such as Fourie du Preez, Jaque Fourie and Danie Rossouw. But in the end, nothing came of it.

By that stage, after a month in France, I had already started making plans to return to South Africa, despite Heyneke not coaching the Boks. But then a communication glitch between Tana (the Toulon coach), Peter de Villiers and Andy Marinos, SARU's manager of national teams, almost cost me my Springbok career. Peter and Andy were travelling to Europe to meet with John Smit at Clermont and Percy Montgomery at Perpignan. I got a call from South Africa saying that Peter wanted to see me too, and I was very excited.

However, he and Andy never arrived in Toulon. I kept phoning but couldn't get hold of anyone. I later learnt that they had phoned the club and Tana had apparently told them that I wasn't available. In turn, Tana told me that Peter and Andy would no longer be meeting with me. It was a big (and calculated?) misunderstanding, and I was both angry and disappointed.

While I found the quality of rugby in the French second league frustrating, things were rosy on the personal front. Because we didn't practise that often or that hard, I had plenty of time to spend at home or to take Monja and Jaime on outings.

We lived in a beautiful house in Carqueiranne, at the top of a mountain overlooking the harbour. We often took Jaime, who was then two years old, to the beach, and I also enjoyed socialising with guys like George and Anton.

However, I was getting increasingly anxious because I simply couldn't get hold of Peter. Some people were saying that I didn't want to work with Peter because I preferred Heyneke to him as a coach. I was desperate to talk to Peter so that I could assure him of my commitment.

Eventually I arranged a meeting with Peter via his assistant, Neil de Beer. Neil informed me that Peter would be able see me for an hour on a Saturday in late March 2008 at George Airport. Fortunately, I was injured at the time and out of action for three weeks – again the ligaments in my right knee – and I decided to fly to South Africa. I told the club that I was going to see my knee specialist, which they accepted, but I had to pay my own way there and back.

The flights were fully booked, and the only seat I could get – thanks to a contact at Air France – was in business class. It cost me €3 000 – R35 000 in those days – but I paid it. I would have paid anything to get back to South Africa.

I had another problem when I arrived at Paris's Charles de Gaulle Airport. All of a sudden, my credit card wouldn't work. I knew a lack of funds could not be the issue, but with my limited French, I didn't know what the problem was. Eventually, with the help of an interpreter, I managed to pay for the ticket and could board the flight. Ten minutes later, and I would've been stranded in Paris.

On the Friday morning I saw the knee specialist in Pretoria, and he booked me off for another three weeks. I was going to fly to George the next morning, but then the flight was delayed. What was going on? Did the gods not want me to play for the Boks any more? A few anxious calls and SMSes later and I eventually got to George and met Peter at the airport. I was ready for any questions about my long hair, my public image or whatever else he wanted to discuss with me.

But Peter caught me off guard: 'Victor, are you a racist?'

That's how I got to know Peter from the start – an honest, straightforward guy who pulls no punches. Apparently he had been told that I had gone overseas because I was a racist and didn't want to play for the Springboks while he was coaching them.

It was utter nonsense, and I told Peter as much. He was satisfied and took me at my word.

On rugby and the part that I would play in his plans, he said: 'I can't pick you on reputation alone. You will have to prove yourself.'

This I understood and accepted, as I didn't expect any favours. Andries Bekker was having a super season for the Stormers in the Super 14, and Peter wanted to try him out as the No. 5 lock – my position. Peter explained what he wanted to achieve with the Boks and said that he wanted me back in South Africa. John Smit was going to be his captain, which gave me a lot of hope for the future of Bok rugby.

I went back to Toulon with a song in my heart. My biggest challenge now wasn't getting out of my contract with Toulon, but convincing Monja to move back to South Africa.

And of course, it wouldn't be all that easy to just return to the Bulls. I had received offers from Toulouse, one of the strongest clubs in France, as well as Northampton in England. But of course I wanted to go back to the Bulls – if they could make me a good offer. Although the Toulouse offer wasn't as enticing as Toulon's had been, it was still more than acceptable. Northampton, however, offered me a very good deal, which I knew the Bulls would find difficult to match.

My agent, Jason Smith, was pressurising me to accept the Northampton offer, so I met with them. Jason thought I was crazy to even consider the Bulls, as Heyneke had left, Frans Ludeke was the new coach and the team was struggling in the Super 14 competition. I knew Frans from the 2000 Bok tour, and of course from his days as head boy of HTS Tom Naudé in Polokwane.

But the Bulls' results in the Super 14 didn't really concern me. I just wanted to go home. Jason wasn't interested in helping me with this, so I phoned Barend van Graan, the Blue Bulls chief executive, and told him that I wanted to return to Pretoria. By that stage, the contract with Northampton had already been drawn up. I told Barend that the Bulls would have to guarantee me a certain amount of money or returning to Pretoria would not be financially viable for me. The amount I wanted was substantial in South African terms, but it was only a third of what Toulon was paying me.

Barend tried his best to come up with the money and approached other parties for help, but it was difficult. Eventually I was at my wits' end, but with Fourie's help I got hold of businessman Brand de Villiers, the chief executive of SAIL, who had a 50 per cent interest in the Blue Bulls Company. I gave the Bulls until the coming weekend to make a decision.

Monja, Jaime and I were planning on joining some friends in Nice that weekend, as Toulon had a bye. If the Bulls had not made me an offer by then, I would fly from Nice to London on the Saturday to sign the contract with Northampton.

By the end of the week I'd still heard nothing from Pretoria, and I was getting very tense. Late that Friday evening, Ian Schwartz, the guy who handled the Bulls' contracts, phoned me with the news: 'Victor, we can offer you the contract you want.'

I was over the moon. It was one of the best days of my life. It was almost a better feeling than when we'd won the World Cup a few months earlier. I would be returning to my family and my country.

I immediately phoned Jason to cancel my appointment with Northampton. He was livid, as he would lose a lot of money on the commission, but that didn't bother me. It was the beginning of the end of my professional relationship with Jason. He wanted to make me as much money as possible, but I had different dreams and aspirations.

After my meeting with Peter, I knew that Springbok rugby would not, as many people believed, change for the worse overnight, and when the Bulls offered me what I wanted, the millions in Europe simply weren't an option any more.

That turned out to be the easy part. Monja was not pleased with my decision to return to South Africa so soon, and as a result we had quite a few arguments. She couldn't understand why I wanted to leave behind the good life in the south of France, where we spent more time together as a family than ever before, to go back to Pretoria. Also, after three years in Europe, we would have been financially well off. But now I wanted to go back to South Africa for less money, more pressure and less family time!

But I was unhappy at Toulon. I wanted to be with my rugby family at Loftus. In Pretoria I was part of a tight-knit group in which everyone had a say and made a contribution, but at Toulon I was just another international star. There, for the first time in my life, rugby had become a job. Nothing motivated me and I had no personal goals.

In Toulon, I usually walked around with a sour face, resembling a spoilt child or a moody teenager. I spent most of my time surfing the Net in order to catch up on what was happening at the Bulls, and I frequented KuduClub, an internet channel that featured South African TV programmes like *7de Laan* and broadcast rugby matches.

I used to help Monja around the house, but now I turned into a couch potato. I didn't even make myself a cup of coffee. It was tough on Monja, but I wanted to show her how bad things could be in Toulon. After all, she was the one who wanted to live there.

Afterwards I realised how ridiculous my behaviour was. It also didn't have the desired effect, so I stopped acting like a brat. After three weeks, Monja concurred and said that she understood why I wanted to go back. It would also be good for Jaime to see her grandparents more often, and for us to be with our friends in Pretoria.

We had had good times in France, but I missed South Africa more than I ever realised. Before we returned home, the South Africans at the club – Wessel Roux, François van Schouwenburg, Chris Rossouw, Nico Breedt and I – decided to make a proper South African potjie. Finding a cast-iron pot in the south of France wasn't easy, but Chris knew someone who'd played rugby in Toulon years ago and apparently he had a potjie.

So we picked up a flat metal sheet, bought some wood, and when Chris arrived with the cast-iron pot, we had a traditional South African day at my house. The women made the side dishes: salads, bread and rice. The guys were outside, carefully nurturing the potjie.

Later on, it started to rain. Some of us stayed outside, beer in hand, and talked about South Africa. We missed our country very much and reminisced about all the good and bad times, the rugby games, the music of Robbie Wessels, biltong, pap and gravy … everything we missed. I'd had a good deal at Toulon, as I had been given loads of game time, but Chris, Wessel, François and Nico weren't so lucky, which contributed to their growing frustration.

Despite feeling homesick for much of the time, Monja and I did get a chance to enjoy Europe. We took Jaime to Disneyland Paris, and we went on weekend breaks to St Tropez, Monte Carlo and the ski resorts of Italy and France.

The Monte Carlo weekend was breathtaking. The club paid for our stay in a top-notch hotel so that we could explore the town and also gamble a little. Toulon really looked after us in all respects. Besides the big house, I also had a four-wheel-drive vehicle at my disposal. At the club, I was quite something in my fancy VW Touareg, but stuffed with our toddler's toys and our beach gear, we were a far cry from Monte Carlo's Rolls-Royces, Ferraris and Porsches. When we pulled up in front of the hotel, the bellboys were all over us to offer assistance. I wanted to stop them, but when they opened the boot, there was nothing but toys and spades and buckets for building sand castles as far as the eye could see.

A French breakfast usually consists of a slice of bread, strong coffee and a cigarette – no bacon and eggs. By now Monja and I were used to having only croissants, but Jaime wanted scrambled eggs, which would be for our own account. But how expensive could eggs be, right? Well, how does €12 sound? Almost R150 at the time! It was a different life-style to the one we knew, I realised.

Back in Toulon, I spoke to Mourad about my plans to return to South Africa. Initially he tried to persuade me to stay on, but eventually he could see how determined I was to play for the Springboks again. He understood. At least we had achieved our goal: Toulon finished top of the log for the season and was promoted to the first league.

Mourad was passionate about rugby and Toulon. He was the son of a North African Arab, not exactly the most popular people in the south of France. Rugby was his means of addressing the socio-economic problems of the town, and he also wanted to prove to the French that an Arab could make a difference.

His strategy was to use his fortune to entice big rugby stars to the town. He had little knowledge of the game and didn't know the difference between a tighthead and a loosehead prop, but if a newspaper article mentioned a top player elsewhere, he wanted the guy to play in Toulon's black-and-red jersey. International players in France were his prime targets.

Although the club looked after our interests off the field, during a game there was no one to protect you. I'd never been punched so many times on a rugby field as I was there. You wouldn't even be close to the ball and someone would take a swing at you from behind. I had my balls grabbed, I was headbutted, I was stomped and trampled on – you name it and I endured it. And you didn't even dream of retaliating, as the incident would then escalate into a group fight. Everyone would join in with feet, fists, knees, elbows and heads. I remember one game in which a big scuffle broke out within sight of a TV cameraman. A member of our management team sprung into action and tackled the guy with the camera. The reason? So that there would be no video evidence were there to be a disciplinary hearing. Unbelievable!

George and I always stood to one side when the fists were flying. I wasn't really a fighter, and the last thing I wanted was a broken jawbone or having to have stitches. George also wasn't very keen on contact sessions during training. If a situation got too heated, he would pack up his things and head for the gym.

For years George had been one of my fiercest competitors when he played for the Brumbies and the Wallabies, but as a teammate at Toulon I realised what a wonderful person he was. This may sound crazy to those South Africans who saw him as a cocky little firebrand, but I got to know George well. We immediately clicked and became good friends. On many Friday nights we would sit and chat, and not just about rugby. You had to win George's trust before he would discuss his private life.

Anton Oliver, too, was an interesting guy who had a broad general knowledge. We could chat for hours about everything under the sun. Anton was the intellectual type and he didn't stay in a big house like the rest of us. He wanted to live in the town, close to the other players. He didn't even have a cellphone. While most of us eventually returned to top-level rugby, Anton decided to play for Oxford University, where he also furthered his studies.

Andrew Mehrtens was everybody's mate. Because he was so casual, he was the only one who managed to narrow the gap between the French and the foreign players. And as casual as he was off the field, so he was on the pitch as well – not much of a tackler or a defender. But he was a brilliant flyhalf and, like Naas Botha in his heyday for Northern Transvaal, he got away with his 'lazy defence'.

In the six months I spent in France, I played a total of 15 games for Toulon. Because the games were played at a much slower pace, I could run with the ball more often. I even played at flank for a few games, which I enjoyed. I also enjoyed experiencing the French passion for the game. Before the start of one of our matches, two Toulon teammates went so over the top that one had to be stitched up!

One passion I didn't really care for though was the French custom of greeting a person with a kiss. George embraced the custom wholeheartedly and later even greeted Andrew Mehrtens with a peck on the cheek. We just laughed. At Toulon, the kissing action was more like a little headbutt from the side. Although greeting someone with a kiss was also a way of showing respect, I always held out my hand if I had to greet someone. Before my second-last game, old 'Le Banque', the legendary Toulon prop David Banquet, slapped away my outstretched hand and greeted me the French way.

To me, this was a sign that I'd become an accepted part of their rugby family, even if I was on my way back to my true rugby family in Pretoria.

12

Back with my people

It was a wonderful feeling to walk through customs at OR Tambo International in June 2008 after six months in France. But unfortunately, not everything went smoothly after our return. The renovations we wanted done to the house we had bought in Pretoria weren't finished yet, and we had to stay in a small two-bedroom townhouse in Silver Lakes for a few weeks. It was a world apart from the villa we had grown used to in Toulon, but at least we were home, with our friends – and Loftus was just around the corner.

Peter de Villiers invited me to the first Bok training camp, in Cape Town – the first time in years it wasn't held in Bloemfontein. We stayed in the Lord Charles Hotel in Somerset West and had practice sessions in Stellenbosch in preparation for our first Test of the year, against Wales.

John Smit was back from France and retained the captaincy, while Peter also roped in most of the stalwarts, as well as a few exciting young players. At our team meeting on the first evening, I realised that things were going to be done differently from the previous four years under Jake White.

Peter and Dick Muir, one of his assistants, wanted drastic changes to the way the Boks played. We had to attack the gaps, pass the ball in contact situations and generally play more instinctively. John and I looked at each other, both knowing that this wasn't going to work.

At our first field session I was in the so-called B-side, as I wouldn't be in the starting line-up against Wales. The B-side had to defend while the A-side tried out Peter's new game plan. But it just didn't want to work. The ball was dropped again and again.

Later we switched around so that the B-side could attack. As a senior player in the squad, I told the guys that it was impossible for us to play the way that Peter envisaged. Some of my Blue Bulls teammates were in my side and we decided to target the defenders and secure possession on the ground. This worked well, as it was so simple. Peter came to me afterwards and told me that he really liked the way we'd played.

Because they haven't coached at the highest level, some coaches make all kinds of clever plans that seem like a winning formula in theory, but in practice – on the field – they fail completely. John and I spoke to Peter about our concerns and implored him not to discard the basic principles of Bok rugby.

During the camp, Peter and I got to know each other better and I started to appreciate him as a coach and people manager. Our relationship as player and coach started on a positive note and just grew from there. Some so-called rugby pundits reckon Peter isn't the best coach around. I agree. I've been coached by people with a better technical knowledge of the game, but Peter knows how to work with people, which is a major asset. He is not afraid to listen to other people's opinions and appreciates their input. He has no ego, and he makes all his decisions with the team's best interests in mind, even if it's something he doesn't entirely agree with.

After a line-out session during our first field practice, where I competed well for the ball, Peter started talking about picking me for the starting line-up in the second Test against Wales. He'd already decided that Andries Bekker would start in the first Test, in Bloemfontein, and he picked his team accordingly. But I'd be included in the starting XV for the second Test, in Pretoria.

While sitting on the bench during that first Test against Wales, I realised that I'd never been so nervous about going on the field before. For six months in France I'd played second-league rugby, which can be compared to the Vodacom Cup competition, and although I had done additional training on my own to stay in shape, I was now one of the 'older men' and no longer sure whether I could handle the pace.

My fears weren't unfounded. In the 46th minute I replaced Andries, and by the end of the match I was dog-tired. The tempo was so much faster than what I'd grown accustomed to in Toulon. Fortunately, the Boks won easily, 43-17.

We also won the second Test, in Pretoria (37-21), and beat Italy 26-0 in Cape Town. John had to return to France to represent Clermont in the Top 14 semi-final, and thus missed our game at a drenched Newlands. Peter appointed me captain – a big honour. After three back-to-back victories, in which we'd played average to good rugby, we left for Wellington for our first Tri Nations encounter against the All Blacks.

It was a game I try not to remember (the All Blacks won 19-8), but one incident stuck in my mind: the terrible spear-tackle Brad Thorn made on John Smit early in the match. Brad was the Kiwi version of Bakkies Botha, but apparently he was judged by a different set of rules. We were shocked when he was suspended for only a week, for a 'dangerous tackle after the whistle had gone'. John had to leave the field shortly before half-time with a groin injury, probably sustained in the tackle. As a result, we would be without our captain for the remainder of the Tri Nations series.

As if this weren't bad enough, we had to face the All Blacks again a week later, in Dunedin. No Springbok team had won at Carisbrook since 1921. And our star player of 2007, Fourie du Preez, was also still injured.

As captain, I tried my best to keep the guys focused. The weather was horrendous and we were far from home, but we played for the Springboks, and our pride and honour were at stake. We weren't afraid of the All Blacks, and on the day we played really well. Shortly before the end of the match, with the Kiwis leading 25-23, I was sent to the sin bin. It was only the fourth yellow card of my career, in my 72nd Test, but I felt terrible. My team was trailing and I couldn't take part in the rest of the match. Talk about a captain abandoning a sinking ship. To add insult to injury, Dan Carter slotted a penalty to stretch the lead to five points.

But then Ricky Januarie had a moment of sheer brilliance. He got the ball in the All Blacks' 25, chipped it over the defenders' heads, fielded his own kick and scored the equaliser. We can win this, I thought on the sidelines, if Frans Steyn can stay calm and convert the five points into seven. Many rugby fans probably had a flashback to the Super 14 final in 2007, but this time Frans banged the ball over to give us the lead.

A couple of minutes later, the ref blew the final whistle. Against all odds, we'd won. The score: 30-28. And at Dunedin's House of Pain, of all places! It was a historic moment. We almost couldn't believe it, because for the first time since Nick Mallett's team in 1998, the Boks had won a Test in New Zealand. Percy Montgomery was the only remaining member of Mallett's winning team.

At the press conference after the game, the South African rugby writers shared our joy, but the Kiwis were sour. They refused to refer to us as the world champions and wrote that we had won the World Cup in 2007 only because France had an upset victory over the All Blacks. What absolute nonsense!

Jean de Villiers, who took over the captaincy after I was sin-binned, told everyone with a broad smile on his face that he was the first Springbok captain to have won a Test in Dunedin. Jean has a good sense of humour and we had a good laugh at his 'opportunism'. But the fact remained that in six Tests since 2001, I couldn't help the Boks win in New Zealand. Of course, we thoroughly celebrated our victory, as Dunedin is a student town with many watering holes.

The self-belief that South African Super 14 teams had started developing in 2007 played a major role in our success. The Bulls, Sharks and Stormers now won fairly often in New Zealand, and that inspired us. And, of course, the Boks were the defending world champions, which further boosted our confidence.

Ricky Januarie, too, had come to the party. For the past few seasons, he had hardly been given an opportunity in the starting line-up for the Boks, but he was a gutsy little terrier who could deliver moments of brilliance when his conditioning and fitness levels were top-notch. He had more heart than most guys and was a much better player than people wanted to admit.

From Dunedin we travelled to Perth, but we had a bad week in Western Australia. I suppose we were still thinking about our victory in Dunedin. Initially it felt as if we were in control of the game against the Wallabies, but then we simply started making too many mistakes and didn't use our opportunities. We lost 9-16.

On our return to South Africa, our first game was in Cape Town against the All Blacks. It was Percy Montgomery's 100th Test for the Boks, the first player to achieve this milestone. Unfortunately, we were outplayed on the day and lost 0-19. I was disappointed that we couldn't make it a special occasion for Monty, as he's a very special guy. He was always fully committed to the team – in fact, he was one of the best team players I knew and always went out of his way to support his teammates.

Very few people know that Percy was born in Walvis Bay, Namibia, and that his dad is Afrikaans. As a result he speaks the language very well, and in the squad he spent a lot of time with the Afrikaans guys. If a hunting expedition was being organised, Percy was the first to sign up. Not quite the image people have of him as a 'pretty boy' from Cape Town!

Monty had joined the Welsh club Newport/Gwent Dragons in 2002, where he worked very hard and almost completely redesigned his playing style. As a result, he returned to South African rugby as a superb place-kicker, and as a senior player he set a brilliant example with his work ethic and maturity. He and John Smit were the heartbeat of the team after Percy returned to the Bok fold in 2004.

Despite the victory in Dunedin, it was clear that all was not well within the Bok camp. The problem, as far as I was concerned, was the presence of the No. 6 flanker from Western Province, Luke Watson. My first experience of Luke was on the tour to Australia, during which he was very distant, preferring to do his own thing. Or he hung out with the guys from Western Province or the black players in the squad. He didn't mingle with the rest of the team.

Before the Tri Nations Test in Durban against the Wallabies, I decided to do something about the negative atmosphere that pervaded the camp. I called the players to a meeting on the Monday to find out what the matter was, as I thought it was important to get everyone's feedback. I also wanted to gauge whether the guys who hadn't been part of the World Cup squad felt marginalised.

I tried to include Luke in the discussion, because I knew he was a strong leader, but he ignored my efforts. When I asked him whether he had anything to say, he said, 'No thanks, I'll just sit here and listen.'

On the Saturday we lost against the Wallabies in South Africa for the first time since 2000 (15-27). Peter and I were booed after the game during the post-match interviews on the field. It was a low point in my career.

Later that evening, at our kontiki, Percy informed the team of his plans to retire after the last Tri Nations Test of 2008, which would take place that coming weekend against the Wallabies in Johannesburg. Percy and John were very emotional, but Luke was standing to one side, talking on his cellphone. He didn't look very interested in what was being discussed, and many of the guys decided right there and then that they'd had enough of him.

Although he was still injured, John travelled to Johannesburg with the rest of the squad, and before we left the hotel for Coca-Cola Park (also known as Ellis Park), he asked if he could say a few words. He asked Peter and the rest of the management team to leave the room.

Then he stood up and said that there was one member of the squad who had no interest in being part of the group, and that this person wanted to destroy everything we'd carefully crafted over the past four years, after the terrible days of 2003. John was very worked up and even shattered a glass against the wall. I'd never seen him so angry or emotional before. He talked about what Springbok rugby meant to him and many of the other players, and said that one guy was screwing it up for everyone else. We all knew that he was talking about Luke.

To make matters worse, it was as if John's words made no impression on Luke. I was left with the feeling that he was not interested in what we wanted to achieve as a team. Later it was revealed that Luke had made a speech in which he'd said that he felt like vomiting on the Springbok jersey. But despite his strong personality, his negative behaviour couldn't divide the team.

Instead, John's words motivated the rest of us tremendously. We felt that the honour of the Springbok jersey was at stake, and we pulverised the Wallabies 53-8. Jongi Nokwe, one of the fastest rugby players I've ever seen, scored four tries on the day.

In that Test, the last Luke would play for his country, he came on twice as a replacement. The next year he joined the English club team Bath and never played for the Boks again.

This episode made me realise what it meant to John to play for the Springboks. I was the captain at that stage, but I never saw myself as the official skipper while he still held that position. Captaincy encompasses far more than just leading the players onto the field.

At the press conference after the Test, the journalists sensed that something was brewing when Percy joined Peter, Jongi and me to answer their questions. Then Monty dropped the retirement bombshell. We were going to miss him a lot. It was a sad goodbye later that evening. Percy had represented South Africa in 102 Tests from 1997 to 2008; he is a true Springbok legend and one of my best rugby buddies.

***

My contract with the Blue Bulls Company was now signed and all the Bulls in the Bok group could return to Loftus for the remaining games in the Currie Cup competition.

After a mediocre Super 14 in 2008, the Bulls were in the process of rebuilding. We won a few important games and then had to play in the semi-finals against the Cheetahs in Pretoria. We won that match 31-19, and I even scored a try!

Then it was off to Durban for yet another final against the Sharks. This time round the Sharks stayed calm and played well, while we squandered one or two chances to score tries. Unfortunately for us, they used all their opportunities and beat us 14-9.

We didn't find Durban a pleasant place to play rugby, despite having won the Super 14 final there in 2007, as it was always so hot and humid. We often used to tease the Sharks players about their changing room at the Shark Tank having air conditioning while we had to make do with a useless portable fan.

It was the first time since 2000 that Frans Ludeke and I had worked together again, and we developed a strong relationship while planning to build on the successes achieved while Heyneke Meyer had coached the team. But the most important part of my return to Currie Cup rugby in 2008 was that I was back with my Bulls family. I was the old Victor again. Monja immediately saw the change in me.

***

The 2008 Springbok end-of-year tour was extremely important, as the British & Irish Lions were due to visit South Africa the following year. During our tour, we would come up against three of the four Home Unions: Wales, Scotland and England.

We knew Ireland would be a key factor in the structuring of the Lions side, but in the meantime we could create some doubt in the minds of the players who'd make the squad. Wales had played exceptional rugby in 2008, winning the Six Nations trophy. Playing them in Cardiff would be a tough task. Wales had only ever beaten South Africa once in Test history: in the inaugural game of the Millennium Stadium in 1999. Since that slip-up we had been too good for the Red Dragons time and time again, even though they always talked a good game before kick-off.

In previous years the Scots had been the worst team of the four Home Unions, but they had certain key players and would test our abilities in a different way. And then England always posed a challenge at Twickenham. We'd beaten them in our previous five encounters, but for them the Test was a way of avenging the World Cup final, and they also wanted to prove to their critics that they were a better team than was commonly perceived.

Peter de Villiers didn't bring many changes to the team that had played in the Tri Nations, and most of the guys who had tasted sweet victory on that unforgettable day in Dunedin were back in the squad. I was very excited about the tour and looking forward to the last Test, against England, in particular, as I'd never been in a winning Bok team at Twickenham. I believed we had a good chance of beating England this time. Our preparations went off well and we left for Cardiff.

To play in cold, wet conditions while your friends back home are enjoying the summer weather isn't pleasant, but it's a challenge professional rugby players have had to get used to. It's always a privilege to wear the green and gold, despite the sacrifices that you have to make.

As always, the Welsh were full of bravado before the Test, but they were no match for us on the day, even if we did look a bit out of sorts. We scored two tries and won 20-15. With that result, we'd beaten them in all three Tests in 2008. And they couldn't score a single try against us, which was a bitter pill for them to swallow. Unfortunately, Fourie du Preez was injured in Cardiff, and that was the end of his tour.

We then had a really bad game against Scotland – one of our worst performances of the season, even though we won 14-0. When the Scots are given no chance of winning, they can come up with a performance that will surprise any team, as the Wallabies would discover at the end of 2009 and the Boks in 2010.

After two average performances, it was no surprise that the media had written us off for the Twickenham Test. However, we always enjoyed playing against England. On the day of the match, John Smit approached his team talk a little differently. Shortly before kick-off he asked the management team and reserves to leave the changing room. Then he addressed each player individually. John's team talks are legendary, but on this day he was in a different league altogether. When he came to me, he said that my presence in the team was always reassuring to him and that it gave him more confidence when I was playing. As with his team talk before the Test against the Wallabies in Johannesburg, John pushed all the right buttons that day.

The Boks were unstoppable, and the Roses wilted under the onslaught. We beat them 42-6 – England's biggest hiding at Twickenham since this hallowed ground's inauguration in 1910. It was also the most points England had ever conceded at their home ground.

After a few big Springbok losses at Twickenham, this was one Test I'd cherish forever. To beat England on their home turf for the first time – and with such a big score – was more than special to me. We would build on this performance in 2009 and show the critics – especially those who always gave us a hard time – that they would have to think twice before writing us off again.

It had been a see-saw season that had started in cold, wet weather in France and ended amid the same conditions in London. There was, however, a big difference in my state of mind, as 2009 lay ahead, and I knew it was going to be a big year … perhaps even bigger than 2007?

In rugby, nothing is impossible!

13

Frans at the helm

A year is a long time in rugby. Whereas the Bulls' annual training camp in George had been in disarray in 2007, the situation was completely different in December 2008. This camp would play a pivotal role in our planning of and preparation for the upcoming Super 14 competition.

The Bulls had struggled in that year's Super 14 and were written off as one-hit wonders who had won the competition in 2007 simply by fluke. But we knew that this wasn't true. Although there were new players on the scene and our coach, Frans Ludeke, was also new, all the structures were in place and a second title was not a mere pipe dream.

After initially struggling to find his feet with 'Heyneke's team', Frans slowly started to leave his mark in 2008. He didn't have an easy start with the Bulls. First, there was Bakkies Botha's court case, and later John McFarland, our brilliant defence coach, left under a cloud of uncertainty to join Heyneke at Leicester.

Both the Sharks and Toulon had made Bakkies big offers, and his agent, Bernie Habana (Bryan's dad), wanted him to sign up with one of them. The media speculated that Bakkies had already signed an agreement with Toulon but that the Bulls had refused to let him go. The dispute ended up in court, but fortunately Bakkies remained with the Bulls. This sort of thing just adds to the pressure on the player, the coach and the union when, in fact, it's unnecessary.

John was one of the best defence coaches in the world and we wanted him to return to the Bulls, but many of the players believed he had turned his back on Bulls rugby by defecting. From his side, John felt he owed Heyneke a great deal and wanted to help him settle in at

Leicester. But it didn't work out for him there, and he returned to Pretoria. There were some problems with his Bulls contract, but once these were sorted out, he apologised to the players and explained why he had left. Unfortunately, an apology wasn't good enough – he had to regain our trust on the practice field.

I tried to keep the players calm and focused despite all the off-the-field dramas, as I knew there were two sides to every story. One of the reasons the Bulls were such a strong unit was that we were a tight family. We shared the same goals and we all wanted to play a part in achieving them. If you didn't want to be there, you could pack your bags and go.

With all the problems now behind us, we could look forward to 2009. Frans gave the Boks in the Bulls squad some time to rest and we were excused from the tough sessions at the training camp in George. But at least we were there and could help with planning our campaign.

As many teams do, the Bulls used the off-season for conditioning work, but we also spent valuable hours working on our structure and game plan, because there's so little time available during the season to fine-tune these aspects.

In the morning, we would start with tactical sessions – line-outs, scrums, attacking lines and defence. Then we'd sweat it out in the gym, followed by a big on-field practice in the afternoon and, to end the day, a tough fitness session. Heyneke used to call these exhausting exercises the 'blue-blood sessions'.

During the camp, an article in the *Pretoria News* claimed that some of the black players in the squad were complaining because the white guys were receiving preferential treatment. We were quite shocked, as this was simply not true.

Management had arranged accommodation for us in a school hostel in George, where almost all the players stayed. However, this was not ideal for some of the senior men, whose families had joined them. A few of us, therefore, rented holiday homes in the George area, which we paid for ourselves. We also didn't have every meal with the rest of the squad, purely for practical reasons. It was each player's prerogative where he wanted to stay and eat his meals, as long as he attended every practice.

However, I realised that there was a degree of racial tension in the group and I knew the issue had to be resolved. Fourie du Preez and I spoke to John Mametsa, one of our wingers, who had apparently been responsible for leaking the story to the newspaper. John told us that the standard of accommodation in the hostel wasn't of the best, and because the senior players were quite comfortable in their rented homes, he'd thought that they couldn't care less about the comfort of the rest of the team. And so a whole race issue had developed. Fortunately, our talk cleared the air. I am sure some of the other players were probably just as dissatisfied with the accommodation.

And then, to further complicate matters, Bernie Habana, who acted as his son Bryan's agent, as well as being Bakkies and Wynand Olivier's agent, was upset because his clients had to be at the training camp when he wanted them to rest. But we insisted that the entire Bulls squad had to be in George for us to benefit from the camp. Frans and his team managed us efficiently and we had plenty of time to rest. There was no danger of burnout or working ourselves to a standstill. Later on, the team would vote on whether or not the next training camp should be held in George again. About 90 per cent were in favour of returning to the Garden Route.

These two issues caused a lot of dissension when we got together again in January in Pretoria. Frans decided he had to step in. He'd been with the Bulls for a year by then, and firm action was needed. Frans is a soft-spoken, relaxed kind of guy who wants the best for everybody. He very seldom gets upset and he treats people with great caution. The risk with such an approach – especially if you work with people who may think they're quite 'important' – is that they could easily walk right over you.

But by then, Frans had had enough. He called us all together and made it clear that he would no longer tolerate any distractions. 'This team has certain principles and values according to which we must behave and act,' he said. 'You must decide as individuals whether you want to be a part of the team. If you don't want to be a part of the team, take your things and leave. We can't afford to make a big deal about every little issue that comes up.'

It was the first time Frans had given us such a serious and straight talk. The players quickly realised that they couldn't just do what suited them.

We went on to lose both our warm-up games, against the Lions and the Cheetahs. We just didn't play with any urgency, which further irritated Frans. The Wednesday before our first game of the Super 14 series, against the Reds, Frans was very emotional in the changing room. He told us that he was giving himself one last game as coach. If we didn't start the competition with a good performance, he would resign and move on. 'We have the right team to perform well,' he said, 'but if I can't coach you to start winning, I'll step down and let someone else try.' It was just the message we needed.

As a team we decided that we had to pull up our socks, and we started the series well, with bonus-point victories over the Reds (33-20) and the Blues (59-26) at Loftus, and then we beat the Lions 16-9 in Johannesburg.

I was injured in the game against the Reds and missed the next two games, but I was on the bench for our next encounter, against the Stormers. It was a very emotional game. A few months earlier, Luke Watson had made his infamous 'I wanted to vomit when I wore the Bok jersey' speech, and according to reports, he'd also had some unsavoury things to say about Afrikaners. Of course, this didn't go down well in Pretoria.

Luke was playing for the Stormers, and he enjoyed a 'warm' reception at Loftus, where the crowd booed him and waved banners addressed to him. Some were quite funny, like the one that said, 'LUKE, WE ALSO WANT TO VOMIT WHEN WE SEE YOU!' When Luke got involved in a bit of a scuffle with the young Bulls winger Gerhard van den Heever, the crowd went ballistic. Luke cupped his hand behind his ear, as if he wanted the crowd to speak up, but by taunting the supporters, he just made them angrier.

I replaced Danie Rossouw shortly after half-time and was then injured again, this time so badly that I would miss the first two matches of our overseas tour. Fortunately for us, we won this tough yet 'interesting' fixture 14-10.

Many teams focus primarily on defence, but we approached the game a little differently, although we knew full well how important a good defence was. In our view, gaining bonus points was just as important in Super 14 rugby. We always tried to score tries, so we usually kicked for touch when we were given a penalty instead of going for posts.

I was often criticised when I decided to kick for position late in the game while trailing on points. In fact, it was a rather easy decision to make. If you go for posts and you draw the game, you get two log points. If you lose the game, you only get one point. But if you kick for touch, win the line-out ball, drive it up and score a try, you can earn four, or even five, log points. In other words, your team can earn more log points by taking a risk than by drawing or losing by a few points.

As captain, I had to take into account the team's frame of mind at the time. If the players were positive and fired up, I'd opt for a kick for touch because I knew they'd be ready to score that try. But if the guys were out on their feet and their heads were hanging, I'd give the ball to our place-kicker to aim for posts.

The Bulls always tried to keep opponents under pressure and play in their half of the field. We trusted our game plan and knew that we could score a try when it was necessary.

We started the New Zealand/Australia leg of the tournament on a high note when we beat the Hurricanes 19-14 in Wellington, with Bakkies Botha and Danie Rossouw leading from the front. But a week later, with a terrible wind blowing across Palmerston North's unprotected stadium, the Bulls' wheels came off badly against the Highlanders and we lost 12-36. The defeat happened in the notorious second week on the road – always the toughest period of the tour, when the jet lag hits you the hardest.

Winning the toss is important on a windy day, but the luck went their way and the team from Otago had the wind behind their back for the first 40 minutes. Had I won the toss, I would've chosen the same option. By half-time they were leading 21-5.

Even with the wind behind our backs in the second half, we couldn't make up that many points. We were forced to play catch-up rugby, where scoring tries was the only option, instead of being patient and keeping the pressure on our opponents.

I was back in the team for our next game, against the Crusaders, and we really wanted to beat them, as we'd never tasted victory in Christchurch before. But they scraped in just ahead of us, winning 16-13.

Fortunately, we were back on track against the Waratahs in Sydney and won 20-6.

After that game I flew back to South Africa for the birth of my second little angel, Giselle.

As captain, it was difficult for me to leave the team. We'd lost two games on tour before the superb victory in Sydney and only one challenge remained: the Brumbies in Canberra. Fourie du Preez took over the reins, as he had done earlier in the season when I was injured. It was comforting to know that the team was in capable hands, but I still felt I was letting the guys down. However, it was also extremely important that I support Monja. Fortunately, all the Bulls players were close to their families and thus understood that I had to go home. Although it is special to win cups and trophies with your team, the privilege to be present on the day that your child is born and to hold her for the first time is incomparable.

From the start, Giselle didn't resemble her older sister. Jaime is her dad's child – she has darker hair, a darker complexion and beautiful, round cheeks. Zellie, as we nicknamed her, resembles her mother, with Monja's strong features and fair skin.

As it was at Jaime's birth a few years earlier, it was a wonderful moment to be present when Giselle was born. Children are an immense blessing, and Monja and I are overjoyed to have two such beautiful daughters. Their existence puts life in perspective and makes you realise how often you are far too concerned about trivial matters.

Monja and Giselle were still in hospital by the time the Bulls played the next game on tour. Bossie, my old buddy from university, dropped by our house and he and I had a braai and watched the game on TV.

The team knew that the game against the Brumbies in Canberra was going to be a real challenge because, during the week before the match, one of the Brumbies players, Shawn Mackay, had died tragically after being hit by a car in Durban. We knew we would be playing against a highly charged side, as four years earlier, after the death of Ettienne Botha, we had been in the same situation.

The Brumbies were leading at half-time, but a try by Pierre Spies and another by Wynand Olivier after the turn put us in the lead. However, the home side didn't give up, and they scored in the last minute to clinch the match by one point: 32-31. The Brumbies had wanted to honour their late friend's memory, and that was exactly what they did.

And so we won only two games on tour. Once again we had to win all our home games if we wanted to host the semi-final at Loftus in May. This time, we beat the Chiefs (33-27), Western Force (32-29) and Cheetahs (29-20) at Loftus before we travelled to Durban for our match against the Sharks. The two teams found themselves in the same situation as in the Currie Cup competition a few months earlier. The Sharks had to win with a bonus point to make it to the semis, and we would finish top of the log if we beat them.

In the changing room, I told the guys that only *we* could determine our future. If we beat the Sharks, we stood a good chance of winning the competition; but if we lost, we'd have to fly to Australia to play in the semi. And then we could forget about winning the trophy.

The saying goes 'don't put all your eggs in one basket', but before the game I decided that that was exactly what we had to do against the Sharks. We had to give *everything*. Home-ground advantage in the semi-finals was non-negotiable if we wanted to win the Super 14. I found it hard to deliver that message, as you don't want to talk about losing, but I had to tell the guys that we could kiss a semi-final victory goodbye if we stumbled against the Sharks.

It was a roller-coaster ride, with the Sharks using all the weapons in their arsenal, but we managed to stay ahead the whole time. Later in the game, with about 10 minutes to go, we were leading by a single point when we were awarded a penalty right in front of their posts. The Sharks, who had to score four tries *and* beat us to reach the semis, had already scored three. If we slotted the penalty and extended our lead to four points, it still wouldn't safeguard us against them. They could throw all caution to the wind in an attempt to score, get that fourth try and beat us.

I looked at Fourie, and he confirmed what I was thinking: kick for the corner. Moments later, having secured the line-out ball, Danie Rossouw burst over for a try that Morné Steyn converted, stretching our lead to eight points. The Sharks then also managed to score a converted try, but when the final whistle blew, we had won by one point: 27-26.

And so we moved into the top spot on the log. When we took on the Crusaders at Loftus a week later, we were very aware of the fact that a home final was at stake. It was our third semi-final against the men from Canterbury, and even though they had narrowly beaten us in New Zealand, we knew that we could even the score.

In 2007, when we'd won the Super 14, New Zealand rugby bosses had withdrawn the All Black players for the first half of that year's Super Rugby series to rest them for the forthcoming World Cup. Many of our critics now reminded us of this fact and that we may not have such an 'easy' task this time round. Nevertheless, stars like Dan, Richie and Mils had been available for the Crusaders for the whole of 2009, but *we* were top of the log. It felt good.

However, Wynand Olivier was injured and would miss the semi-final, and JP Nel was suspended, so we had a crisis at centre. Jaco Pretorius had to move to inside centre, and Marius Delport was thrown in at the deep end as outside centre. To lose both first-choice centres before a big game is a real problem, but as our structures were good, we had confidence in all the players in the squad. However, it's of no use when everything else is in place but the players you call on are out of form, and for that reason we were quite comfortable having Jaco and Marius in midfield. As it turned out, they didn't let us down.

The game against the Crusaders couldn't have had a worse start. They set off at a frenetic pace, scored two early tries and led by 20-7 after 25 minutes. Interestingly enough, and despite popular perception, many New Zealand teams enjoy playing at Loftus. Over the years, the All Blacks have fared well in Pretoria, and in the dark years they always won at Loftus.

We were trailing badly. However, as always, our attitude was not to panic or change our game plan. Even if we had been leading comfortably, we would have stuck to our guns. As soon as you start taking chances, you start making mistakes, and that's when the opponent strikes. We knew we'd score in the last 30 minutes at Loftus, because that's when playing at altitude starts affecting the visitors.

Slowly but surely, we started chipping away at their lead, with Pierre Spies and Akona Ndungane scoring excellent tries in the process. Morné Steyn kicked four drop goals, proving that he was a certainty for the Springbok team. In the end, those drop kicks broke the Crusaders, and we won 36-23. They could score only three points in the final 55 minutes.

We would not normally have attempted drop kicks in Super Rugby, as we always wanted to score tries, but they were the right option in this game. Seeing the scoreboard ticking over sustained our momentum and gave us renewed energy.

The Loftus faithful were once again unbelievable. Besides the altitude factor, the crowd was our biggest ally in a big game such as this one. Reaching the Super 14 final was not only hugely satisfying for us as a team, but also a great way of thanking our fans for backing us.

It had taken a long time to regain their support. Between 2000 and 2002, when we were struggling badly and everyone wanted to get rid of Heyneke, we decided to play for ourselves, because at that stage we had such fair-weather supporters. The Bulls have a proud tradition and our fans have high expectations, but it was still disappointing to see fewer and fewer people pitching up for games the more we lost.

At Toulon, the fans supported their team through thick and thin. The stands were always packed whether the club was winning or losing. It would have been nice if the Loftus fans were a little more loyal and accommodating too. The Blue Bulls and Super 14 Bulls want to play before a packed stadium every weekend, but the minute things start going pear-shaped on the field or we play against a lesser opponent, thousands of people simply stay away. This is quite a sad sight for any player.

Support for both the Bulls and Free State had noticeably increased over the years – I suspect because the teams were successful on the field and had managed to win some trophies. The Sharks had always enjoyed support throughout South Africa, but there were now also many Bulls fans outside of Pretoria, which made the away games far more pleasant.

It was wonderful to see people already lining up after the game against the Crusaders to buy tickets for the final. We would face the Chiefs in the final (they had beaten the Hurricanes in heavy fog), but they would have to travel all the way from Hamilton to Pretoria. We took a little pleasure in the fact that the roles were reversed for a change. I wouldn't have minded if the Hurricanes had won, actually, as the Chiefs were a dangerous side that could score tries from anywhere on the field.

When we arrived for training on the Monday, the ticket queue was a few hundred metres long, stretching right up to the practice field next to the stadium. Vendors were selling hot dogs, and radio stations and newspapers were covering the ticket frenzy ... If you weren't previously aware that something big was going down at Loftus, you would've realised it then.

As in the semi-finals against the 'Saders, we started the final off with a bit of a wobble. After we launched a poor kick downfield, Lelia Masaga scored a try, but that was the last time the Chiefs really had any say in the game. From then on, until the final whistle, there was only one team on the field.

We thumped the Chiefs good and proper. Everything went our way and we scored one try after the other. Even I got an opportunity! After I scored, Kurt Darren's hit, 'Kaptein, span die seile', resounded around the stadium at full blast. I could have burst with pride. For me, it was the best moment of the entire season's Super 14 action. Usually you can't hear what the crowd noise is about, but almost the entire stadium was singing along to 'Kaptein' as I jogged back to join the team. I had goosebumps, and Kurt later told me that so had he at that moment.

The worst incident was Jaco Pretorius's almost-try. At that stage he'd never scored a Super 14 try, and against the Chiefs he had managed to cross the line, but lost the ball. Werner Kruger, our loosehead prop, was on his shoulder and scored instead, but unfortunately Jaco was still without his Super 14 try.

Jaco is a fantastic guy, and in his first year on the team wanted to make a positive contribution to show the Bulls board that it had made a good investment by offering him a contract. For most of the year he had been in JP Nel's shadow at outside centre, but he'd shown his worth when he had to play at inside centre in the semi-finals against the Crusaders.

We delivered an almost flawless performance against the Chiefs. Later, when we wanted to look at an example of how we should be doing things, we used this game as a reference. In the end, we won easily: 61-17. It was not exactly the kind of score one should see in a final, and I couldn't help feeling a little sorry for the Chiefs. Frans,

Ian Schwartz, our media manager, and I decided to present 10 players at the press conference after the game. It turned into a mini-festival with our South African friends in the media.

Frans, of course, was over the moon. It was the first trophy he'd won in years. His track record with the Lions and Bulls had been pretty average in 2008. After those harsh words from him early in the season, it was a pleasure to see how much he was enjoying our victory.

Frans is a very modest guy. He never wanted to accept credit for any of our achievements but always praised everyone else for their successes. He even kept his distance when we received the trophy; I had to go and fetch him for the team photographs. After all, it was his trophy as much as it was ours.

We celebrated in the changing room right through the night. The music blared, the champagne flowed and the cigars being handed out added to the festive atmosphere. When the sun came up between the east and north stands the next morning, we were still there!

A few of the diehards joined me in the middle of the field to wait for the sun to light up Pretoria. We couldn't stop wondering whether it was all a dream. Could it be true that we had won the Super 14 final by beating the Chiefs 61-17?

While I was sitting there taking pictures, I knew why I had missed Pretoria and wanted to return to South Africa – to rejoin my Blue Bulls family, and, of course, for the chance to play against the British & Irish Lions.

Everyone was talking about avenging the Lions' 1997 series victory over the Boks. Even though South Africa had scored more tries than the Lions, we'd lost the first two Tests. Nothing but pride was at stake in the third Test, which the Boks won convincingly.

Could we improve on their performance in 2009?

14

Riding high

While the Bulls were witnessing the sunrise over Loftus after winning the Super 14 competition, the British & Irish Lions were already settling in in South Africa.

In fact, the day before the final, they'd played their first game on tour in Phokeng, outside Rustenburg, against the Royal XV, an invitational team consisting of players from the Leopards, Griquas and Pumas. We were disappointed that the Blue Bulls wouldn't get the chance to play against the touring Lions, but there was simply no time for us in their packed schedule.

For the Springboks, as world champions, the series against the British & Irish Lions was of great importance. Peter de Villiers had picked a strong team and we had a few weeks to prepare, unlike previous seasons, when we would have played our first Test a week or two after the Super 14 final.

Not every rugby player is given the opportunity to play against the British & Irish Lions. You could easily play in two or three World Cup tournaments and in numerous Tri Nations series, but the Lions come to South Africa only every 12 years. Those of us who were in the 2007 World Cup squad started talking about playing against the Lions immediately after our victory. It was the opportunity of a lifetime.

The Lions were different from any other Test opponent we'd ever played. Of course we were familiar with the Australians and New Zealanders thanks to the Tri Nations and Super Rugby tournaments, but the British were a different kettle of fish. They loved talking big in the media and were perceived as somewhat loud and arrogant, in particular their skinhead defence coach, Shaun Edwards. I suppose one couldn't really blame them, as they had a good team and had beaten the Springboks in the 1997 series. They were full of confidence when they arrived on our shores.

However, for a team who talked up their game, the Lions' record was pretty average, as they had lost against Australia in 2001 and New Zealand in 2005, and their concept of sportsmanship differed significantly from ours. When they played in the series against Australia and New Zealand, the players shouted and swore excessively in the changing room in order to motivate themselves, which was not the way we approached games.

It was Peter's second season as Bok coach, and even though we had ended 2008 on a positive note with a win against England, we also had a problem. Dick Muir, one of Peter's assistant coaches, wanted us to play attacking rugby and spread the ball wide against the Lions. But some of the senior players in the squad – John Smit, Schalk Burger, Fourie du Preez, Jean de Villiers and I – disagreed with this game plan, as we believed we could win the series playing conservative and more traditional Springbok rugby.

Peter decided that our training camp would take place in Durban, where the first Test was to be played. We trained as hard as always, doing some valuable work that would also stand us in good stead for the rest of the season. As in 2007, when we'd enjoyed that walk on the beach before the World Cup, we had another very positive team-building session. This time we went shark diving. Some of the guys were pretty scared, but we were assured that the sharks weren't dangerous. We actually swam among them, and it was an unbelievable experience in the end.

Back on dry land we played a few games on the beach, and that evening at the team braai, we were entertained by singer Robbie Wessels. Later we went back to the beach, where we spent the night. There was a fire going and some guitar music, and we relaxed and chatted away. It reminded me of the time at John Smit's house in Pennington. Many of the same faces that had been around in 2007 – Danie Rossouw, Fourie, Schalk, Jean, John and I – were present again, and we enjoyed ourselves like there was no tomorrow. After so many years as Springboks, a very special bond existed between us.

If the team-building experience was wonderful, the next day's fitness session wasn't quite as enjoyable. Afterwards, we all went to watch the Lions play the Sharks in the Shark Tank, where the visitors were impressive. Ian McGeechan, their coach, had picked a team consisting of almost all the players who would be in the Test side. We realised that we would be dealing with a very well-organised team. I even found a remarkable similarity between the Lions' attacking play and that of the Bulls. The visitors played clinical rugby and beat the Sharks convincingly, 39-3.

Paul O'Connell, the Irish lock and my direct opponent, was the captain of the Lions. In an interview, a former Lions player had said that Paul would make an ass out of me, but Bakkies Botha was quick to respond. 'Nobody has ever made an ass out of Victor,' he said. 'So why would Paul O'Connell suddenly be able to do it?'

We showed them what we were capable of early in the first Test, in the Shark Tank, when John scored our first try after we'd executed a planned move. As we all know, it's always difficult to stop a big guy who gets quick possession at full speed. Ruan Pienaar slotted four penalties, and at half-time we led 19-7. Shortly after the break, Heinrich Brüssow also scored a try, and with the score at 26-7, it looked as if we had the game in the bag.

The British pundits had believed that the Lions would have the upper hand in the scrums, but we gave them a hard time up front too. The general perception was that teams from the northern hemisphere were strong at scrumming, whereas it was considered a weak point in the Bok game. In this Test, however, they were on the back foot as soon as the referee called 'crouch, touch, pause, engage'.

We had them in reverse gear at every scrum, and the crowd in the Shark Tank roared their approval: 'Beeeeeeeeeeeeeast!' The supporters' enthusiasm was amazing, and it motivated us tremendously. But then, apparently for no specific reason and at the wrong time, on came the Springbok replacements, and the Lions started fighting back. Peter and his assistants even replaced John with Deon Carstens, although John was brought back into action a little later on. As a result of all the changes, we lost our momentum and our game went pear-shaped very quickly.

In the end we hung on for dear life and won 26-21, but in all fairness, we should've buried them after half-time. Of course, the British media had their say: The Boks were lucky to win this one! It was a very frustrating situation. The Bulls had dominated the season, and the Sharks had also had a good run, but here were the Boks struggling to beat the Lions in the first Test. Everyone except me seemed to be chuffed with the victory afterwards.

I still believe that it was insane to replace players like John and Fourie, who was replaced by Ricky Januarie. For many of us, this was our most important Test in two years. We *had* to win it. I suppose in the end I was just relieved that we'd managed to hold on and scrape through. Peter and his management team admitted afterwards that they had been too hasty with the replacements.

In this Test, I found it particularly weird to run onto the field at one of our home grounds, in front of our own people, to find almost half the stadium filled with the opponent's red-clad supporters. It happened during the second Test in Pretoria too. It was quite a shock for us Bulls players to see Loftus swathed in red, as we were so used to always being greeted by a sea of blue shirts, flags and banners. But it helped in the sense that it motivated us to clinch the series then and there, as it was like waving the proverbial red rag at a raging bull!

We had the worst possible start to the match when, within the first minute, Schalk Burger – playing in his 50th Test – was sent to the sin bin. He was lucky not to have received a red card, as recommended by the assistant referee. The French referee, Christophe Berdos, had not understood him.

With Schalk in the sin bin, the Lions stepped on the gas. We trailed early in the game and were wobbling under the pressure – quite the opposite to what had happened in the first Test in Durban. At half-time, with the visitors leading 16-8, Peter addressed us in the changing room. He trusted us with his whole being, he said, but then we repaid him by playing poor rugby. John also shared some strong words with us, and we determined to do better in the second half.

We knew that the high altitude would not affect the Lions too much, as they had played three games at high altitude already while we had been at sea level for three weeks.

Fortunately, the replacements that came on this time seemed to make more sense. Morné Steyn took over from Ruan Pienaar, who had missed a few opportunities at goal, and Jaque Fourie replaced Jean de Villiers and scored an unbelievable try that got us back in the game. It happened in the 74th minute, with Jaque on the right wing. He managed to side-step a few Lions defenders before squeezing through the tiniest of gaps to crash over in the corner. With this try, Mossie, as his friends call him, proved that he was a class player. It was one of the best individual tries – at the most pivotal moment in a game – I'd ever seen.

The last few seconds of the match were extremely nerve-wracking, with an unbelievable twist. Ronan O'Gara, the Lions' flyhalf who had come on to replace Jamie Roberts, caught the ball after we'd launched a long kick downfield. All he had to do was kick for touch and the game would have ended in a draw (25-all). But instead he hoisted an up-and-under. Fourie jumped high in the air to gather the ball, but before his feet could touch the ground, O'Gara brought him down. Penalty to South Africa.

O'Gara had hoisted the ball for the same reason the Bulls kick for touch when awarded a penalty under similar circumstances. If the Test ended in a draw, the Lions could no longer win the series. But by keeping the ball in play, he might have created an opportunity for the Lions to launch a counter-attack, from where they could score a winning try or be awarded a kick to posts, thus keeping their series hopes alive.

The penalty was a long way from the Lions' goalposts; if we con-verted it, we would win the match and, of course, the series. Frans Steyn stepped up, as he usually took the long ones, but I told John to give the ball to the other Steyn – Morné. I had no doubt that he would slot it over – we were at Loftus, after all, and he'd had a great season kicking for the Bulls. This was well within his range.

Morné placed the ball in the middle of the field, about 55 metres from goal. It was as quiet as a graveyard at Loftus, and many spectators probably couldn't even watch as Morné stood over the ball. But he struck it perfectly and it sailed over the crossbar.

We had won the Test 28-25 and clinched the series. We were ecstatic, and the crowd roared with joy.

I was extremely pleased for Morné's sake. In only his second Test, he had contributed a vital kick after spending many years at the Bulls in the shadow of Derick Hougaard. Also, the Bok selectors time and again hadn't picked him for the national side.

After the victory, the British press were at it again: Schalk should've received a red card, the Boks didn't deserve to win and the Lions had played much better than the home side. What happened to being gracious in defeat? I wondered. The truth was that we'd shown tremendous character to claw our way back into the game. Worse teams would've crumbled under the pressure, but the Boks prevailed.

It was our first series victory over the British & Irish Lions in 29 years. We had last beaten them in 1980, when most of the players in our team hadn't even been born yet. This victory, the glory of the World Cup and the two Super 14 titles were the best moments of my entire rugby career.

The kontiki after the Loftus Test was something to behold. The cigars came out and the guys celebrated like crazy. The only pause in the festivities occurred when we received news that Schalk and Bakkies had been cited for inadmissible play, but even that couldn't dampen our spirits. Later our wives and girlfriends joined us, and the party continued for hours after the final whistle.

Some newspapers said afterwards that we were dirty players, mentioning in particular the incident in which Schalk Burger had allegedly eye-gouged Luke Fitzgerald. The press also criticised Peter for his response to the incident, when he said that rugby wasn't ballet and that South Africans went to the bush if they wanted to poke their fingers in a lion's eye.

The Lions' management team was very crafty in the way they drew attention away from their two defeats by pointing fingers at our transgressions. But they'd nevertheless lost the series. Subsequently, Bakkies and Schalk were found guilty and suspended. We knew Schalk could be in trouble for 'making contact with Luke Fitzgerald's face', but Bakkies was given a raw deal. He had 'cleaned out' Adam Jones at a ruck well within the rules of the game. As far as we were concerned, he had done nothing wrong, but Jones had hurt his shoulder during the charge and Bakkies was cited for having used 'unwarranted' force.

Bakkies plays a hard game of rugby. That's how he likes it, and it suits us too: every team needs an enforcer. But many players barge into rucks during games, which was why we were so sure that Bakkies would be found innocent. Instead he was suspended for two weeks.

As a team, we decided that something had to be done, and we chose to display our dissatisfaction with Bakkies's suspension by wearing white armbands in the last Test. We discussed our intention with Peter de Villiers, who gave us his blessing, and also informed the SARU president, Oregan Hoskins, and the manager of national teams, Andy Marinos, of our plan. They both supported us. We wrote the word 'Justice' on the armbands, and a few of the guys, me included, also added the figure '4' – the number on Bakkies's jersey. I wrote 'Justice' on my scrum cap too. After all, Bakkies was my lock partner, or 'combo buddy', as we sometimes referred to each other.

Unfortunately, these off-the-field events distracted the players' attention from our preparations for the third Test. And Peter also decided to make some changes to the team to give other players exposure at this level. We eventually lost the final Test 9-28.

Afterwards the IRB lodged a complaint against SA Rugby and the Springboks for wearing the armbands, but because we had notified SA Rugby about our 'protest' in advance, it was up to them to explain why they had allowed us to go ahead.

All the drama resulted in a rather unpleasant end to the tour. The winning trophy was handed to us after the conclusion of the last Test, in rather disappointing circumstances. I think it would've been more fitting if they'd held the presentation ceremony after we'd clinched the series at Loftus.

The tour was wrapped up at a formal function in Sandton. Usually a sociable atmosphere prevails among players at these occasions, but it was not the case here. Paul O'Connell, it has to be said, was a true gentleman. He held his head high after losing the series and only had positive things to say to us.

Probably because he's such a hard-working lock!

***

In 2001, Australia had tamed the British & Irish Lions, and later that year won the Tri Nations trophy. New Zealand repeated the feat four years later. Was it our turn to be crowned as kings of the southern hemisphere in 2009?

Before we could tackle the Tri Nations series, we needed to establish whether all the players were on the same wavelength regarding what we wanted to achieve and how we were going to go about it. We had to take care of a few little niggles.

John and I, as captain and vice-captain, called a meeting with the coaching staff: Peter de Villiers, Dick Muir and Gary Gold. Andy Marinos was also present.

Initially, Peter's game plan had been to spread the ball wide and score tries, but at Test level, where teams have well-organised defensive patterns, this didn't always work. Later, he basically discarded this plan.

Dick propagated 'play the situation as it occurs on the field', but we wanted a more structured game plan. Not everyone shared the same ideas, but if we wanted to be successful, we had to agree on the game we would play.

There are many ways to approach a game, and one person is not necessarily right and another wrong. You have to know what your team's strong points are and shape your game plan around those. Most importantly, each team member has to accept and own this plan. If they don't, the young, inexperienced guys won't know what to do in certain match situations.

Our style of play can probably be considered conservative, but it's all about making the right decisions at the right time on the field: you don't take chances in your own half; if an opportunity arises to counter-attack, go for it. (That's how Bryan scored his two tries against the Wallabies in Perth in 2005 – both started from counter-attacks deep inside our half. They were the right option to take.)

One of our sayings was: Instead of committing only 50 per cent and doing the right thing, give 100 per cent, even if you make mistakes. Before the start of the Tri Nations, we had a hard but straight talk, and in the end we all agreed on a game plan. We might have differed from each other on a personal level, but as a team we had to be united as one.

During the meeting, I once again realised what value John brought to the Boks. The only thing he cared about was the team – everything we did had to be for the team's benefit. He would confront anyone, including the coach or the chief executive, if it was in the best interest of the team.

With the air cleared, we all got together in Bloemfontein for the first

Tri Nations encounter with the All Blacks. The capital of the Free State is home to one of our favourite grounds. Besides the fact that the whole province supports the Boks, we usually get the chance to do a bit of hunting – usually on one of Os du Randt's neighbouring farms outside Theunissen. The region's farmers and their wives are very hospitable, and we were treated to tasty snacks every time we went there.

Percy Montgomery was usually the most excited about the hunting expedition and couldn't wait to fire off a few rounds. He would lead from the front when aim was taken at a buck, although he usually had to fire several bullets before actually hitting anything!

Those who shot their first buck on these hunting trips naturally had to be initiated into the hunting fraternity. I still laugh today when I remember the expressions on Chiliboy Ralepelle and JP Pietersen's faces when they realised that they had to eat the testicles of the first buck they'd shot.

Then it was back to Bloemfontein.

Three New Zealand teams had qualified for the Super 14 semi-finals, an indication of the standard of their game. We knew that the Kiwis would pose a massive challenge, but we'd won the tough series against the British & Irish Lions and were well prepared.

The 2009 changes to the rules of the game also benefited us, perhaps more than other teams. Referees often penalised attacking teams, and because we played low-risk rugby, focusing on tactical kicking, we thought we might have a slight advantage. The All Blacks liked to carry the ball, but Heinrich Brüssow was a master at stealing possession at the breakdown and we knew he could secure the ball for us.

That was exactly what happened. Mossie and Ruan both scored tries, and in the end we beat the All Blacks 28-19. It was a solid performance as we continued building on the momentum we had gained from beating the Lions.

A week later, in Durban, Morné single-handedly beat the All Blacks. He scored all our points and we won 31-19. To beat the All Blacks twice in a row was fantastic. Suddenly they weren't as invincible as we'd always thought them to be. Maybe we had shown them *too* much respect over the years?

The Wallabies never really had a chance to beat us in the Cape

Town match. We may not have been as sharp as we'd been against the All Blacks, but we still managed to win 29-17. And I scored a try again, which I really enjoyed. It happened after a superb little grubber from John, and with his left boot as well! My last try for the Boks had been in 2004, incidentally also against the Wallabies at Newlands. I had played a total of 57 Tests between my fourth and fifth Test try – apparently a rather unique achievement!

With five victories from six outings, we had started the 2009 Test season with a bang. Sometimes everything works in your favour, as was the case that year. As a team we had the necessary experience, and we also believed that we could achieve our goals.

Three games remained in the Tri Nations series: two in Australia and one in New Zealand.

Just a few days before the first match against Australia, we travelled to Perth. It worked out well, as we only experienced the nasty effects of jet lag after the Test. We beat the Wallabies easily (32-15) and scored four tries. It was Fourie du Preez's 50th Test.

We had asked John Mitchell, a former All Black coach, to hand out the team jerseys the Friday before the Test, which we were later criticised for. The players didn't have any problems with Mitchell performing this task. Peter had discussed his choice with me and John, and we were happy with John Mitchell because we respected him as a coach. When he coached the All Blacks, his success rate was more than 80 per cent, but he was fired after the 2003 World Cup because his team didn't reach the final.

Brisbane – not one of our favourite places – was our next destination. This time we couldn't score a single try. The Wallabies were bent on revenge and beat us 21-6. It was a poor performance by the Boks. It was also disappointing, as we'd played good rugby up till then. After the defeat, we spent a few days on the Australian Gold Coast to unwind.

Our next match was in Hamilton, and although we had visited the town quite often in the Super 14 series, we'd never before played the All Blacks there. We knew we'd have to beat them to secure the Tri Nations trophy, but this didn't stop us from teasing John relentlessly. He'd missed our historical victory in Dunedin in 2008 because of a groin injury and was one of a few players in the team who'd never beaten the Kiwis on their home turf. It was, therefore, very important to him that we win the Test in Hamilton. The senior guys at the back of the bus pulled his leg mercilessly: we said that beating the All Blacks wasn't as great as one would imagine – it was nothing to write home about, anyway. We said we'd rather aim for bonus points than a win in the game.

John was getting a bit hot under the collar, but we pretended not to notice. But of course we were serious about winning the Test – we wanted to finish the competition on a high note.

The referee made a few interesting decisions against us in the Hamilton game, but nothing could stop us on the day. Frans Steyn slotted two monstrous penalty kicks, which proved to be decisive. When the final whistle blew, we had beaten the All Blacks in New Zealand again, for the second year in a row. The score was 32-29.

Later, Johann van Graan, the Bulls forward coach, showed us that one of Frans's long-range penalties had never crossed the bar! When you study the video recording frame by frame, you can see that the ball had passed millimetres *under* the bar. The assistant referees had simply missed it. Sometimes luck *is* on your side!

We had won in New Zealand in 2008, the first time we had done so in a decade; the following year we beat them three times on the trot. We were the proud receivers of the Tri Nations trophy as well as the Freedom Cup, an additional award that South Africa and New Zealand rugby have lately competed for.

A big celebration followed in the team room in Hamilton. The funniest moment of the evening, and a highlight of the festivities, was Jean de Villiers's rendition of the *haka*. We partied till late, singing and cheering and celebrating an unbelievable season for the Springboks.

***

The Test season went on for quite some time, and the Springboks, therefore, did not play Currie Cup rugby for their provincial teams. This offered younger players the opportunity to stake their claim. At the Bulls, a whole range of new players was making an impression on the pundits. Thanks to the good contracting system, players like François Hougaard, Flip van der Merwe and Dewald Potgieter were quickly becoming part of the Bulls family.

After our return from overseas, one of my first games for the Blue Bulls was on a Friday evening against the Leopards. I heard through the grapevine that a few of the younger players had partied till late at a Brooklyn club the night before the game. Although they apparently hadn't drunk much, it simply wasn't a Bulls custom to go out the evening before a game.

Perhaps it was just a coincidence, but we struggled against the Leopards, at half-time leading by only 21-17. Some of the spectators were making nasty comments because we weren't on form against a lesser team, which pushed my frustrations beyond the limit. I asked Frans Ludeke to leave the changing room during the break and barked some choice words at the team. Some of the players thought that because we'd won the Super 14, the Bulls Boks were back and we were playing an 'easier' opponent, they could just pitch up and we'd win.

But it was totally against our team culture to be ill prepared for a game, no matter who our opponent was. We normally didn't want to lay down the law at the Bulls, as we were all adults and professional players who could distinguish between right and wrong. But even if you only had a glass of water in a bar the night before a game, it could send out the wrong message. You are in the public eye and people are quick to point fingers.

My tough words helped, and we upped our game to beat the Leopards 61-24 to finish third on the Currie Cup log.

At the end of the season, the Bulls did well to beat Griquas at Loftus, but then had to travel to Cape Town for a semi-final clash against Western Province. We were third on the log and Province second. Still, the Cape Town press saw us as favourites to win at Newlands, probably because we had built good momentum and had more experience in play-off matches than the Capetonians, who had surprisingly lost 25-27 against the Lions in Johannesburg in their last game.

Province, however, had shown a general upward curve in their results since Rassie Erasmus had become part of the coaching staff.

The semi-final started on a negative note. Before kick-off, it appeared as if I didn't want to shake hands with the Province captain, Luke Watson, after the toss. I was honestly not being malicious. My thoughts were somewhere else. I simply walked away without wishing Luke and his team the best for the game, as I normally did. When I realised my mistake, I turned around and shook his hand.

Nevertheless, we started well, and despite Bakkies receiving a yellow card, we were leading 12-0 after 20 minutes. Province fought back, however, and even though it felt as if we were in control, the pressure was on us in the second half when the lead shrank to 12-6.

With a few minutes remaining, we were suddenly trailing 18-19. But we stuck to our plan, didn't panic and continued to play our usual game.

Shortly before the final whistle, the Province winger Sireli Naqelevuki was penalised for a high tackle on Jaco Pretorius. It wasn't an easy kick; it was certainly more difficult than the one Morné Steyn had to kick to clinch the series for the Boks against the Lions a couple of months earlier. The kick was close to the sideline and almost on the halfway line, there was a strong wind to factor in and we were at sea level. But I was convinced that Morné would not miss, as he had had an excellent year with the boot. Our match winner was spot on again: 21-19, and we were in the final.

Because the Sharks had lost against the Cheetahs earlier that day in Durban, the final would be played at Loftus. We knew nothing of this beforehand, as we didn't want that result to distract our attention from the task at hand. Although many people are under the impression that the Cheetahs are our bogey team, this is simply not true. Besides the final in 2005, they hadn't won a game against a full-strength Bulls team in seven years. Yet before every game against the Cheetahs, we'd read in the newspapers or hear on the radio how they were the one team who knew how to beat us!

If we did have a bogey team, it had to be the Sharks in Durban – but certainly not the Cheetahs. In fact, we actually enjoyed playing against the Free Staters. One of our stars against the Cheetahs in that final was Bryan Habana, who had recently announced that he would be moving to Cape Town to play for the Stormers the next season. The final would be his last game for the Blue Bulls.

It was a big loss for us, as he had been one of our key players for five seasons and had also become a good friend. Bryan wanted to be one of the leaders in the team, but with Fourie du Preez and Wynand Olivier controlling things in the backline, he felt he couldn't reach his full potential with the Bulls.

The Bulls had a strong start to the final and were soon in control of the game. The Cheetahs fought back hard at the end, but it was too little, too late. Bryan said goodbye to the Bulls with two tries, and François Hougaard (a scrumhalf we often deployed at wing) showcased his versatility by scoring our third try.

The Cheetahs scored three tries as well, but yet again Morné's boot made all the difference. He slotted three conversions, four penalties and a drop kick for a personal tally of 21 points in our 36-24 victory.

On provincial level, the Super 14 was a much tougher competition than the Currie Cup, as you had to compete against superstars week after week. But for South African players, the Currie Cup has always been special. That's where all the emotion is – it has such a long history of healthy interprovincial competition attached to it. It's always a wonderful experience for a team to win the golden cup.

Frans Ludeke could also look back on a year that had had a difficult start but in the end delivered two trophies; it had, in fact, turned out to be one of the most successful for the Bulls and for Frans as coach. To help such a good, down-to-earth guy achieve a double success made us players very happy. We hoped that Frans would receive the acknowledgement that he deserved, as he bluntly refused to take any credit for our success. To lead a team to three big titles in two years more than proved his value as coach.

And in two unbelievable years, I was part of a group of players who won every worthwhile trophy, starting with the World Cup in France. Then the Bulls won the Super 14 title for a second time, the Boks beat the British & Irish Lions and tasted Tri Nations glory, and it was capped off with a Blue Bulls victory in the Currie Cup. I'm eternally grateful for and very proud of these achievements.

South Africa was once again the centre of world rugby and the Bulls were the reigning kings of the local scene. Nobody could argue with that.

The day after the Currie Cup final everyone gathered at my house and we discussed the fantastic season we'd just experienced. Again, the celebrations were short-lived, as the Boks were already preparing for the end-of-year tour to France, Italy and Ireland. And everyone wanted a piece of us, especially the Irish.

***

Exhaustion is a favourite topic whenever there is a discussion about rugby players and their standard of playing. This is understandable because, in the course of a year, professional players are involved in many games.

Since 2004, I've played in 28 games every year on average. The most matches I played was in 2008, when I participated in 34 games for Toulon, the Springboks and the Blue Bulls. The least I played was in 2006, when I was involved in just 20 games, as I was part of the conditioning plan for the World Cup tournament in 2007.

I spent, on average, about 35 active hours a week on rugby. This included games, field training, gym sessions, conditioning, video sessions, team talks and other engagements. At an average of 28 games a year, it meant that I spent more or less 840 hours on rugby, including pre-season preparations. But it was still much less than the hours an average office worker clocks. However, I would like to think that I sweated more than the average office worker, but then 40 hours a week sitting behind a computer sounds like hard work to me!

In terms of travelling, I spent, on average, six to eight weeks twice a year in Australia and New Zealand for Super Rugby and the Tri Nations series, as well as undertaking the month-long tour of Europe every year. Add to this the odd tour of Argentina and the US ...

I've covered vast distances over the years. As the crow flies, Pretoria is 11 000 kilometres from Dunedin, the farthest destination in New Zealand we have had to play. Dublin and Edinburgh in the northern hemisphere are 9 300 and 9 500 kilometres from Pretoria, respectively.

With stopovers and detours that included Auckland, Hamilton, Wellington, Christchurch, Brisbane, Sydney, Perth, London, Cardiff and Paris – cities we often visited – I spent an average of 70 000 kilometres a year on aeroplanes. And those were just the international flights.

There were also local flights to Cape Town, George, Durban, Bloemfontein and Kimberley, and we often travelled by bus to destinations like Pretoria, Potchefstroom, Witbank and Johannesburg. All added up, I've travelled around the world in many different forms of transport!

My favourite way to kill time when waiting to board a plane was trying to win my teammates' money with a game of poker. A few of us would usually find a table in the business-class lounge, grab a cup of coffee and deal the cards. On long flights I tried to sleep, but I usually had my laptop switched on to do some work (like on this book, for instance).

This much travelling and playing sounds exhausting, but for me fatigue was more psychological than physical. It's tough trying to get yourself in the right mindset for a rugby game every week. There isn't a lot of time to relax during a season, so often your mind takes a bigger knock than your body.

The Bok tour at the end of 2009 wasn't easy, as we had two week-day games every week and the touring group was fairly big. It somehow reminded me of my first Springbok tour in 2000, when we were basic-ally two teams that almost never interacted with each other. We hardly got to know one another.

Half of the touring side in 2009 first travelled to London to play Leicester, while the rest of us travelled to France for the first Test in Toulouse. Training together was complicated by the fact that there were either too few players or too many at any given time. It was difficult to form a tight unit, even though we were all Springboks. On my first tour, I'd been on the other side of the fence, in the so-called weekday team, which was not a pleasant experience. You almost felt like excess baggage.

In the first game, against Leicester, we lost 17-22. Then, in the first Test against France, in Toulouse, we lost 13-20. I can't remember much from that Test. Early in the game one of their forwards tackled me so hard at a loose scrum, I lost consciousness. Afterwards, after about 10 minutes of trying to play rugby, I left the field to get stitches above my eye. I still felt groggy on my return. I was so out of sorts that I even got our line-out calls wrong a couple of times.

This Test will always be remembered for Ras Dumisani's pathetic rendition of the South African national anthem. As usual, I was stand-ing between Bakkies Botha and Schalk Burger to sing the anthems. The three of us always sang 'Nkosi Sikelel' iAfrika' at the top of our lungs, but on this day in Toulouse, it wasn't possible.

When Dumisani started 'singing', at first I thought that his voice had gone. But the longer he continued, constantly changing the rhythm, the sooner I realised that something was amiss. The man didn't know what he was doing. It was hard not to burst out laughing. Schalk and I looked at each other in total disbelief.

To this day, nobody has accepted responsibility for that fiasco. It was a special moment every time we sang the national anthem, as it served to remind us what an honour it was to represent our country on the rugby field. For that reason, the person who commissioned Ras Dumisani to lead in the singing of 'Nkosi Sikelel' iAfrika' owes all South Africans an apology.

Although Dumisani's rendition was unacceptable, it had nothing to do with our defeat in the Test. We faced a very motivated French team who overpowered us physically in every facet of the match. Maybe we underestimated them somewhat. At this level you can't afford to lose even 5 per cent of your concentration, otherwise you're staring down the barrel of defeat.

After losing to the French, we had to travel to London to support the weekday team in their second game, against Saracens (we lost 23-24), before flying back to Italy for the second Test. It was a logistical nightmare.

Peter picked me on the bench against Italy and we played much better. I had about 30 minutes' game time, and we won 32-10. François Hougaard made his debut for the Boks after Fourie du Preez was injured late in the game.

After John had played at tighthead prop for the last part of 2008 and the whole of 2009, it was decided to move him to hooker for this tour. He was criticised for his performance at prop, but I thought we scrummed well and were a solid unit with him at tighthead.

We focused on the scrums in our game against Italy. Their tighthead, Martin Castrogiovanni, had given us a hard time in the game against Leicester (where he played club rugby), but we survived the first half against the Azzurri with John at tighthead. In the second half he moved to hooker, with BJ Botha at tighthead and Tendai 'Beast' Mtawarira at loosehead.

Suddenly the Italians were murdering us in the scrums, and John was moved back to tighthead.

Bismarck du Plessis is also a good hooker and an asset to the team, but at that stage we had no destructive force at tighthead. CJ van der Linde and BJ Botha were both playing for overseas clubs, while Jannie du Plessis didn't have a good tour with the Boks.

John is more at ease as a hooker and he worked hard at his conditioning to move to prop. I didn't see him as the weak link in the front row, but it's not easy for a player if week after week the media criticises you for your poor performance.

As for the tour, it was a nice change to visit places we'd never played before. In France we usually played in Paris, so Toulouse was something quite different. With my limited knowledge of French, I also enjoyed my stay there more than before.

In Italy we stayed over in Udine. Monja and Jaime joined me for that week, and they had the opportunity to visit Venice with Peter's wife, Theresa, and their daughter. Jaime thought the bidet in the bathroom was the weirdest thing on earth. She persistently wanted to take a bath in it!

Our game against Ireland took place at Croke Park, another venue we hadn't played before, and 85 000 fanatical Irish fans pitched up. I'd never won a Test in Ireland and nothing would change this time round, largely due to my poor performance in the line-outs in what was probably my worst game ever for South Africa.

Gert Smal, South African assistant coach between 2003 and 2007, was Ireland's assistant coach at that stage. Because we'd worked together before, he knew exactly which strategy I followed in the line-outs. The weather before the Test was terrible. We tried to get a game of golf in, but with a wind howling at 60 knots, we simply packed it in and left. We had to practise our line-outs on an indoor netball court.

I knew Gert understood our line-out signals, so we tried to disguise them. We also hoped the use of Afrikaans would baffle the Irish. But when I called the first line-out and their jumpers moved straight to where we were to receive the ball, I knew we had a big problem.

Gert was one of the best forward coaches I've ever worked with. He was a hard worker and spent hours behind the scenes analysing things. He'd done his homework thoroughly, because the Irish taught us a lesson that day.

The Boks scored the only try of the game when Schalk Burger crashed over, but Ireland came out on top and won 15-10.

It was the first time in my entire Bok career that I was outsmarted at the line-outs. Statistics showed we had lost four of our throw-ins and stolen three of theirs, but it was terrible to lose so much possession in a set piece.

Criticism poured in after we ended a fantastic season on such a low point. The Boks had won only one out of five Tests during the November tour, and everyone said that we were fatigued and had played too much rugby.

The Springboks were nevertheless appointed as the IRB's Team of the Year, but it was disappointing that Fourie du Preez didn't receive the Player of the Year award. This honour was bestowed on Richie McCaw, a brilliant player in his own right, but in our hearts we knew that Fourie was the world's best rugby player in 2009.

Suddenly I wasn't looking forward to playing for the Barbarians a week later at Twickenham against the All Blacks, but Fourie, a few other Boks and I had already agreed that we would. I just wasn't in the mood. Monja and our daughters would've joined me in London, but in the end decided against it.

Danie Rossouw withdrew from the squad, and I wished I could have joined him on the flight back home. But it would be my first outing for the Baabaas, and I decided to bite the bullet. In the end it was a fantastic week shared with many new faces.

When we arrived in London, I told Fourie I just hoped that Nick Mallett, the Barbarians coach, wouldn't appoint me as captain. And what happened? As we walked into the hotel foyer, Nick greeted me and said 'congratulations', as I was his choice for skipper. It was my first experience of a Barbarians week, and to top it all I had to lead a group of guys I hardly knew.

Yes, I had by then met most of them, but we hadn't shared much time together and I didn't know what to expect from them. Luckily, Bryan Habana had played for the Barbarians before, so he helped me to get to know the guys better. As a shy Afrikaans guy from Polokwane who didn't easily mingle with other people, I had no choice. My English was a bit suspect, but it was great to chat to and get to know Wallabies like George Smith and Rocky Elsom.

That Sunday evening we kicked things off with a function, some drinks and a speech by the president of the Barbarians. Afterwards, Fourie and I stayed in the hotel while the other guys hit the streets of London. We thought we had a training session the next morning, so we stayed put and carried on chatting to Nick Mallett and Barbarians president Micky Steele-Bodger.

When I saw the guys the next morning, it looked like a hay-fever epidemic had spread among them. They were dog-tired and had blood-shot eyes from little sleep. Halfway to the practice field the rain came down in buckets and we decided to turn back to our hotel.

That evening there was a team dinner with an abundance of beer and wine. The Baabaas apparently had no rules – written or unwritten – about this kind of behaviour, and I realised I wouldn't be able to give them my Leopards speech. It was obviously not the best way to prepare for a game against the All Blacks.

The dinner was in an Italian restaurant, and the chef provided us with a feast. It certainly built team spirit and a lot of jokes were told. The owners of the eatery sang a few opera arias and our Italian prop, Salvatore 'Toto' Perugini, who looks a bit like Luciano Pavarotti, also sang a song.

Fourie and I were sitting next to the Cheetahs prop WP Nel. He was the only member of the group not to have played Test rugby and was very shy. He didn't say a word for the first two days, but that night we made sure he had a couple of glasses of wine, and soon enough he had everyone crying with laughter telling typically South African jokes.

Afterwards, most of the players carried on to another pub, but Fourie, Toto, Nick, our assistant coach, Alan Solomons, and I stayed behind and talked some more. I didn't know Nick that well, but after a week with the Barbarians, I understood why he was so highly rated as a coach.

At our team meeting the next day, we decided to keep the game as simple as possible and planned only three moves. We had a short practice session on the Wednesday afternoon – just two line-outs, to be precise – and passed the ball around a bit, as the guys weren't really interested in training all that hard.

Nick can be a real rogue. He decided that WP, the youngest member of the team, had to get rid of all the wine he had had the previous night by way of a light fitness session. The rest of us had a good laugh, as the youngster couldn't really protest, even though he was nursing a hangover.

That Wednesday evening I decided if you can't beat them, join them. So I had as much fun at the functions as the other guys. I even went out for dinner with a group of friends the Friday evening before the game … against the mighty All Blacks!

It was a wonderful feeling to run onto the field that Saturday as part of a team consisting of some of the most talented players in world rugby. It was unique to have regular opponents like Jamie Roberts, George Smith, Drew Mitchell, Matt Giteau, Stephen Moore, Rocky Elsom and Andy Powell suddenly playing alongside you.

We started the game at a slow pace and hardly had any possession. My legs felt like lead, and I thought I was going to pass out from all the tackles I made. I was convinced that we were in for a massive hiding, but slowly we started clawing our way back. Bryan Habana scored three tries for us, a very special moment in his career. Not many players get to score a hat-trick against the All Blacks.

I still don't know how we did it, but we beat the All Blacks 25-18 – only the second time New Zealand had lost against the Barbarians.

I learnt from that experience that we often make the game too complicated. Rugby is really simple if you understand the basics and execute them properly. There was probably also a lesson to be learnt from the week's jollifications, but I was too scared to make any assumptions on how well wine and rugby go together!

I will never forget 2009. In many instances, it was even more remarkable than 2007. Although the Boks had had a poor November tour, I had been a member of three different teams that had swept across rugby fields like a tsunami.

To win the Super 14, the series against the British & Irish Lions and the Currie Cup, as well as beat the All Blacks four times, was simply unbelievable.

15

From Dublin to Soweto

On Sunday you are sipping champagne from a trophy, but on Monday you are back to drinking black coffee from a mug. Even though you want to savour your success, it's not long before the next challenge is knocking on your door – such is the life of a professional rugby player.

This was also true early in 2010. Although my season had ended with another victory over the All Blacks – albeit in the black-and-white colours of the Barbarians – I couldn't forget the terrible defeats at the hands of the French in Toulouse and Ireland in Dublin.

As usual, the Bulls gathered in George for the annual pre-season training camp, but the Boks in the squad who had played for the Barbarians in November 2009 were given a breather.

Somehow, after the Blue Bulls' wonderful season, it seemed easier to prepare for the new one. We always aimed to improve ourselves, and with the Super 14 and Currie Cup titles now ours, we could improve on those successes only by winning the trophies again in 2010.

We thought that we were now a force to be reckoned with in world rugby. Many of the Springboks who had been involved in the series win against the British & Irish Lions and had captured the Tri Nations title were Bulls players. Also, Fourie du Preez and Morné Steyn were in the Barbarians team with me, and we had helped to outsmart the All Blacks at Twickenham. Who wouldn't have had loads of confidence after such stellar results?

People probably thought us arrogant when we said that we planned to win the Super 14 trophy again, but they were missing the point. We simply believed in ourselves; we believed in the way we played and how we approached any challenge.

The interpretation of the rules at the breakdown required our biggest mind shift that year. In 2008 we had resisted some changes to the rules, which had clipped our wings. We didn't want to make the same mistake again. Before the start of the 2010 season, referees were instructed to once again focus on certain aspects of the rules. A few of the senior players – me, Fourie, Wynand Olivier, Derick Kuün and Pierre Spies – along with the coaching staff, gathered at former Springbok Braam van Straaten's guesthouse in Glentana and thoroughly studied the rules and their interpretation. Most important to understand were the rules regarding the breakdown, where all the players had to stay on their feet and the attacking team had more time to secure possession.

We decided to embrace the new rules, as they might even work in our favour, although many of our opponents probably thought that we were going to struggle to adapt. But if you adopt a positive attitude towards change, it always benefits you more than a negative approach.

The Bulls were often regarded as a team that could only kick the ball, but we actually just didn't like taking unnecessary risks. Instead of trying to keep the ball alive with precarious pop-up passes and off-loads during a tackle, we preferred to go to ground, force a ruck and make sure that we retained possession.

However, we did change certain aspects of our game. Our plan was to counter-attack more often by running the ball rather than kicking it back to our opponents. We had realised during Heyneke's early days as coach that more tries are scored from counter-attacks, and that became our blueprint for 2010. In fact, in the 2009 Super 14 competition we had scored many of our tries from the opposition's kicks that had been launched at our back triangle.

When there isn't a lot to pick between two teams, the little things can make the difference between winning and losing. Those were the small details we identified in Glentana that evening.

Kicking had always been an important weapon for the Bulls and the Blue Bulls, but that evening we analysed our strategy in depth. We looked at *how* and *why* we kicked the ball. You can't kick the ball just for the sake of it. First, there had to be a good reason for kicking the ball and, second, the kick had to be executed perfectly, or it could work against you.

We decided not to follow a predetermined kicking pattern, but to pick the right time to kick the ball and aim it at the perfect spot on the field. Fourie was a master in this regard, and Morné Steyn and Zane Kirchner were also excellent kickers. The point is, after kicking the ball you have to be in a better field position than you were before the kick.

We would also try to kick in such a way that we had a good chance of winning back possession, be it with an up-and-under, which we could contest in the air, or by isolating an opponent and putting him under pressure so that we could win back the ball in his territory.

Another myth regarding our style of rugby was that we had a massive but 'slow' pack of forwards, but it actually counted in our favour, as many teams thought that if they passed the ball around a bit, our forwards would get tired and they could run all over us. Of course, this never happened, as their assumption was based on a misconception.

Our forwards were a lot more mobile than people thought. I was pretty agile for a big guy, and so were Gary Botha, Chiliboy Ralepelle and Gurthrö Steenkamp. Danie Rossouw, as lock, could easily have played at flank or eighthman. Dewald Potgieter and Deon Stegmann were two agile loosies, and Pierre Spies at eighthman was as quick as lightning.

At Loftus especially, where the altitude counted in our favour, we realised that our opponents tired quickly if they regularly had to turn around to chase after our clever kicks. As soon as they tired it became easier for us to retain possession, and all we had to do then was be patient, as the tries would come eventually.

In our first four games of 2010, our strategies worked like a charm. We scored 50 points in three of those matches (51-34 against the Cheetahs in Bloemfontein, 50-32 against the Brumbies at Loftus and 50-35 against the Highlanders, also in Pretoria), and we beat the Waratahs 48-38. That's 199 points in four games, including 24 tries.

We took very few kicks at goal, preferring to kick for touch, from where we could attack. Yes, the other teams also scored points against us, but that was fine, as bonus points against you in the Super 14 don't mean all that much; it is the bonus points that *your* team accumulates that are of greater importance. To win 48-38 is always much better than to win 12-10.

In the end, the new interpretation of the rules suited our game, as our strategy was relatively simple: conservative, attacking rugby played in our opponents' 22-metre area would eventually lead to tries. On attack, phase play, ball retention and patience were our three focus points, and we scored many tries that way.

Of course you can't neglect your defence, but in Super 14 rugby, defensive play only really becomes important as the competition draws to a close. Events in 2010 illustrate this point perfectly. When the last of the fixtures was played, we were level with the Stormers on games won, but thanks to the bonus points we'd scored, they couldn't overtake us on the log any more.

Our game against the Waratahs further underlined the value of our game plan. As the Waratahs were obtaining better field positions than us and retaining possession of the ball, we were in trouble virtually from the beginning of the game. Shortly before half-time, they led 26-10 and we were defending as if our lives depended on it. Although they camped on our goal line the entire time, we managed to keep them at bay, which boosted our confidence for the second half.

In the final 30 minutes of the match, we were forced to kick for position in order to score tries to wipe out the deficit. We did exactly that, and in the end we beat them. We scored four of our six tries in the second half.

Before we'd embark on our tour of Australasia, another tough game awaited us, against the Hurricanes. It was raining cats and dogs in Pretoria, which made it difficult to hold onto the ball, but the 'Canes were used to playing in wet conditions. It was Steve Walsh's first game as referee after a long leave of absence due to personal problems. He was extremely strict on our defensive line, while the Hurricanes seemed to get away with murder. On many occasions when we were on the attack, they brought down our rolling mauls without being penalised. Matters improved a bit in the second half, though.

I'd always enjoyed Steve as a referee, but in that game he didn't interpret or execute the new rules as well as other referees that season. However, we managed to scrape through in the end, winning 19-18, which meant that we left for the Antipodes with five consecutive victories to our credit.

Our first game on tour was against the Western Force in Perth. We started brilliantly and played good rugby in the first 20 minutes, but for some reason we couldn't seem to score any points. It wasn't an easy game, but nevertheless we won 28-15. The fact that we had flown to Australia just two days before playing our first game worked in our favour, as the energy levels of the players were still high.

At the halfway mark of the competition we were at the top of the log, which was just what we'd wanted. Just as impressive was the fact that we had done this without the help of Bakkies Botha, who would miss almost the entire Super 14 season with an injury. Luckily, Danie Rossouw could fill his shoes.

A few years earlier, Heyneke had started rotating Danie and Bakkies, especially against teams who preferred playing the ball wide, like the Crusaders. The more mobile Danie brought another dimension to our Super 14 strategy, where the game was played at a faster pace. Bakkies, on the other hand, was cut out for tough Test rugby. His boots-and-all attitude was invaluable at Test level, where you often had to work harder to get your hands on the ball. It was therefore a blessing to have both men in our side. If Danie hadn't had to compete with Bakkies for a place in the national starting line-up, he would surely have notched up close to a hundred Tests for the Boks by now.

This again brings me to the misconception that the Bulls pack was big, heavy and slow. In the past few years, the Sharks and Stormers have probably had heavier packs than the Bulls. But make no mistake – although we were mobile, we were still pretty intimidating.

It's quite interesting to listen to other people's perceptions about our playing style. They reckon that the Bulls play 10-man rugby, with a heavy pack and a kicking flyhalf. Still, for the past few seasons we were among the top try-scoring teams in the Super 14. In fact, we scored more tries than any other South African team. Not too shabby for a bunch of conservative rugby minds from Pretoria!

We won a lot of games in 2010 because of the brilliant rugby played by our backline. I was very impressed with Wynand Olivier's contribution and felt he deserved to be named Super 14 Player of the Year in 2010. Stormers lock Andries Bekker walked away with the title instead.

But the other teams' preconceived ideas about Bulls rugby suited us just fine. They didn't see our backline as a threat, but it was. They thought our forwards were slow and would tire quickly, but they didn't.

I actually find the many misconceptions that exist about different teams quite odd. Take the Stormers and Western Province, for instance. The common view is that they have a brilliant backline and the forwards are basically there to supply the backs with possession. This assessment of their game originated in the 1980s, when Province had ample flair in the backline and won many games with their backline play. But this is no longer the case; you ignore the Capetonians' forward force at your own peril.

Unfortunately, we couldn't continue our good performances from earlier in the season in our next match, against the Blues. If only we had tackled as well as the Stormers in that game! We were still undefeated at that point, while the Blues had had a mediocre season. However, playing in Auckland was never easy, no matter how inconsistent the Blues were. Up until that stage I'd never played in a winning team at Eden Park, neither as a Springbok nor as a Bull. Auckland was a bit like Brisbane – not a nice place to visit.

Jet lag had also caught up with us. Because we had left South Africa shortly before our first game on tour, the jet lag only kicked in the week before our game against the Blues. We certainly experienced the symptoms during training – you felt like you just wanted to go to sleep. Your mind and body simply weren't in the same place.

The Blues had magnificent game-breakers in their team; in fact, they've always had some of the most exciting players in the Super Rugby series. For some reason, however, they struggle to play to their full potential week after week. I think if they played more conservative and structured rugby, they would be a tough team to beat. Their forwards were strong and physical, but it was as if they had carte blanche to do just what they wanted ... which was when the mistakes started creeping in. In 2009, at Loftus, we'd scored eight tries against them, almost all from turnover possession. It was like they were playing without considering the consequences of the mistakes they were making.

They were always willing to take risks and never shied away from trying something new. If everything worked on the day – with all their talent to back it up – they could wreak havoc. Unfortunately, 3 April

2010 was one of those days. They ran from all over the field and every pass went to hand. To add insult to injury, we were totally out of sorts. At the start of the second half we were still in with a chance, but at the restart a hoisted ball slipped through my hands, and they secured possession and scored. That was the turning point – we lost 17-32. It was a poor performance by the Bulls and one we wanted to forget as soon as possible.

Before our next game, against the Chiefs, we stayed at Lake Taupo for the week, which was a bus ride away from Auckland. On the bus, I realised yet again what the Bulls spirit was all about. Despite having lost the game, the team remained upbeat. On this occasion, someone had discovered an old Meatloaf CD, which blared from the speakers and prompted Jaco van der Westhuyzen to give a hilarious and unforgettable karaoke performance.

We prepared thoroughly for the Chiefs game, but without exerting ourselves too much. There was even an opportunity for two rounds of golf, one at the beautiful Kinloch links course. On the way back to where we were staying, our team manager, Wynie Strydom, very thoughtfully produced a few chilled six-packs for us to enjoy.

We left for Hamilton on the Friday, and when we got there, the local media were claiming that the Chiefs would take revenge on us for having overpowered them in the Super 14 final in 2009. I wasn't unsettled by that sort of propaganda, as I considered it a given that the Chiefs would pull out all the stops at home. After all, they had had mixed results until that point. So it was a great feeling when we beat them again (33-19), *and* we secured a bonus point with our fourth try. That defeat seemed to signal the end of the Chiefs' season, as they did not win a single Super 14 game again in 2010 (lost five, drew one).

After years of struggling in New Zealand, South African teams had started realising that even though it was never easy to play there, it wasn't impossible to win either. We had started notching up victories, and the triumph against the Chiefs went down particularly well. Self-confidence and self-belief are crucial elements in rugby, and over the past five years we'd learnt that we could beat any team, anywhere.

We were ecstatic with the two victories from three games, and even an upcoming visit to Brisbane wasn't going to dampen our spirits. When we arrived in Queensland, the Reds – from the outset of Super Rugby the worst of all the Aussie teams – were on fire, and suddenly a semi-final spot seemed within their reach. They'd just returned from South Africa, where they'd beaten the Cheetahs and the Lions, and narrowly lost to the Sharks. Everyone was talking about the newly revitalised Reds, and we knew we were in for a tough battle, especially in Brisbane. Nevertheless, we lost the game narrowly, 12-19, just unable to score that last try.

And so we'd won half of our games on tour, which was not too bad, but we knew that a few challenging weeks lay ahead in South Africa if we wanted to finish top of the log.

While we were on tour, a sensational event occurred back home. The leader of the ultra-right-wing Afrikaner Weerstandsbeweging (AWB), Eugène Terre'Blanche, was murdered on his farm in North West – just a few months before the start of the FIFA World Cup in South Africa. Racial tension in the country escalated.

A few of the Bulls players had formed a Bible-study group, and we got together once a week on tour. At one of the sessions we discussed what role we, as rugby players, could play in South Africa. Our lives were blessed in many respects and we wanted to pass on those blessings to try to make a difference in other people's lives. We decided that when we got back to Pretoria, we'd do something for people less fortunate than us. So on our return we visited Danville, a less privileged neighbourhood in Pretoria West, and later a few of us spent time in Mabopane, a black neighbourhood in Pretoria, where we played rugby with the kids.

Although we enjoyed giving something back to the community, we still felt we could do more, perhaps something similar to what François Pienaar and his Springbok team had accomplished when they won the World Cup in 1995 and united South Africa. It was just 15 years later, but it seemed as if things in the country were starting to fall apart. But we just couldn't find anything that would have a big enough impact.

Back in Pretoria, we first defeated the Lions before taking on the Sharks. I would play against the Durban boys at Loftus for the first time since 2006, and all the guys were keen to have a go at them with a full-strength team. Although the Sharks had started the season with a wobble, they were ready for action when they arrived at Loftus, having secured five victories on the trot. And they came complete with their Springbok front row of Tendai 'Beast' Mtawarira, John Smit and Jannie du Plessis.

Although the Sharks pack was the toughest to play against, our rolling mauls went according to plan and our scrums were solid, despite those who'd said we wouldn't be able to take the pressure for the entire season. Although the Sharks and the Cheetahs both had strong scrum units, our pack had improved a lot, thanks mainly to the return of Gary Botha, who'd played for Harlequins in England for a few seasons.

As I'd realised during my stint at Toulon, the northern hemisphere teams have a different approach to the scrum. Whereas in the southern hemisphere we basically see the scrum as a way to restart the game, they use it to put the opponent under pressure and get a psychological grip on the game. And so we devised a new strategy for the scrum, in which Gary played a key role. Werner Kruger also improved tremendously, while Gurthrö Steenkamp had a lot to prove after struggling on the 2009 end-of-year Bok tour. We realised we could use the scrum as an attacking platform and experimented with the 'double shove', where the first shove is followed by a second in order to catch your opponents off guard. Exerting this kind of pressure usually led to penalties in our favour.

Therefore, our scrum became a weapon, and we started using it to great effect, even in the first game of the season, against the Cheetahs. In that game, the referee, Jonathan Kaplan, awarded a penalty try against the Free State late in the game after we'd demolished their scrum.

But back to the game at Loftus: it's difficult to say whether our good scrumming performance alone nailed the Sharks, but it certainly played a major role in our 27-19 victory. Now, with two games left to play before the semi-finals, we were well on our way to the top position on the log.

In the meantime, the Crusaders had arrived in Pretoria. They were always difficult opponents, whether you played them in Pretoria or Christchurch, and they enjoyed taking on the Bulls. This time, a home semi-final was at stake – a lot to play for, in other words. But the game ended on a controversial note when Marius Jonker, on recommendation from the assistant referee, Jaco Peyper, ruled after several replays that François Hougaard had indeed scored the try that secured our victory

(40-35). Richie McCaw and his team complained bitterly, but it was the right decision. In the replays it was obvious that one of the Crusaders had knocked the ball backwards after Bandise Maku had passed it.

It was a wonderful victory, as it meant that the Crusaders had to fly all the way back to Christchurch to play the Brumbies in their last group match and then fly back to South Africa to face us in the semi-final.

Our last group match was against the Stormers at Newlands, but after beating the Crusaders we were assured of the top spot on the log and had the luxury of resting some key players. It proved invaluable for the big guns to enjoy a breather a week before the semi-final. Tickets for the Newlands encounter were sold out weeks in advance, and although we wanted to give our supporters in the Cape something to brag about, it was more important to win the Super 14. I'm sure even our staunchest Cape fans were happy with this decision a couple of weeks later.

The so-called B-side of the Bulls was strengthened with the return of Bakkies Botha – who would captain the side – after injury, and the inclusion of the former Stormers centre De Wet Barry, who'd returned to South Africa as part of the EP Kings squad after playing club rugby in England. De Wet had vast experience at Super Rugby level, whereas our second-choice centres, Stefan Watermeyer and Stephan Dippenaar, had lots of talent but lacked experience.

Perhaps our youngish team got too worked up before the game, as they wanted to show the Capetonians a thing or two, but they certainly lacked composure. They basically played on emotion, as we had during our dark struggle years. But in time we'd learnt to control our feelings so that we could focus on what was happening on the field.

There is a very fine line between too much and too little emotion on the pitch. Teams with fewer talented players sometimes win a game or two on sheer emotion, as they will do anything to win. They will play negative rugby and bend the rules by holding onto the ball a little longer, thus preventing the opposing team from getting quick possession. Depending on how the referee interprets their actions, such a team can totally unsettle their opponents and even win games.

A more experienced side concentrates less on emotion and focuses instead on their winning game plan. Also, an experienced player concentrates on his own role in the team instead of looking for ways in which to unsettle his opponents. You can't afford to get heavily psyched up week after week in a lengthy competition like the Super 14, as it will drain you emotionally. More important is not to lose your hunger for success, because that's when other teams can catch you off guard with their passion and emotion. The art is to balance the passion and emotion with sound judgement.

Although the Stormers won easily (38-10) – their first victory over the Bulls since 2003 – it didn't help them much, as they knew a different Bulls team would be waiting for them in the final.

The Stormers surprised everyone in 2010. We thought the Sharks would be South Africa's other torchbearer, but it was the boys from the Cape who, almost against expectations, made it the furthest. For years the Stormers were underachievers, the team with the big names and an abundance of talent that never played to its potential. A number of factors contributed to their renaissance: in 2010 their pack of forwards upped their game and delivered the same quality of play as the backline. The pack's success was largely attributed to their new forward coach, Matthew Proudfoot, a former Scotland hooker who had made his mark as club coach for the Pukke of North West University.

The Stormers' defence also improved greatly; in fact, it was the cornerstone of their revival. Then Rassie Erasmus, with his knowledge of the game, also had an obvious influence. And one of our former stars, Bryan Habana, had moved to Cape Town at the end of 2009. He immediately settled down at the Stormers and showed his worth with good performances in the Super 14. He was an immediate hero at Newlands. We really missed Bryan early on in the series, but later, when the young wingers Gerhard van den Heever and François Hougaard started getting used to our structures, Bryan's absence was no longer a problem. Although replacing someone with Bryan's talent is never easy, Gerhard and François eventually had a fantastic 2010 season. François scored seven tries, the same number as Bryan, and Gerhard scored eight. Pretty ironic, I thought.

When it was announced that our beloved Loftus would be one of the forthcoming FIFA World Cup venues, we knew that it would not be available for the Super 14 play-off rounds. The Blue Bulls administration even had to evacuate their offices in the main stand. So, when it became apparent that we would finish first or second on the log, we had to look for an alternative venue, and SuperSport Park in Centurion and Wanderers in Johannesburg were mentioned. Both are cricket stadiums. Later, Orlando Stadium in Soweto became an option.

As proud South Africans we were swept away by soccer fever, knowing how much this tournament meant for our country. If I remember correctly, we were the first rugby team to show our support for Bafana Bafana by wearing the national soccer side's yellow jerseys when we left on our overseas tour.

One day Fourie and I were chatting about the FIFA World Cup. He mentioned that he'd heard that black South Africans did not think white people were showing enough support for the tournament. Of course there were people who were negative about it, but we decided to show the country how *we* felt, and wore our Bafana jerseys with pride. I would like to believe we made a difference to some people's attitude.

In the meantime, the head honchos of rugby were still trying to decide on a suitable venue for the Super 14 semi-finals. Eventually the Blue Bulls Company, SA Rugby and SANZAR chose Soweto. And then it dawned on me that this could be the conciliatory gesture we'd been looking for a few weeks earlier.

The players discussed the new venue and we all agreed that although the stands and the changing rooms would be a little different, our two big allies – the Highveld altitude and our fanatical supporters – would still be there. And so we welcomed the decision to play in Soweto with enthusiasm. Because most of us had never been to this well-known township south-west of Johannesburg, it was a big adventure for us and one that we looked forward to experiencing.

On the Wednesday before the game, we drove to Orlando Stadium for our first training session in Soweto, and residents came out of their houses and cheered us on, while photographers and journalists swarmed all over the place. We didn't know quite what to expect, but it actually looked just like any other lower-income neighbourhood. Although one could see that the people here did not lead a life of luxury, the neighbourhood was neat and well maintained, unlike many other parts of Johannesburg. The stadium itself was magnificent and the facilities just as good as at Loftus. We took photographs and felt like tourists in our own country. It was a new experience for us, and we started looking forward to playing in Orlando.

The team itself was relaxed and focused – nothing would stop us from reaching our third Super 14 final in four seasons. Although it was sad not to see hundreds of people queuing at Loftus to buy tickets, the excitement of the new experience made up for it. However, we weren't even sure whether our supporters would pitch up, but on our return to Soweto on the Saturday of the match, we were astounded. Thousands of Bulls supporters had arrived to support us. People had braais going next to the road, and blue flags could be seen everywhere. White and black people were drinking beer together in the shebeens. Just as in 1995, strangers were embracing each other as fellow South Africans.

Once again I realised that only sport can unite people in this way. We had wanted to do something big for South Africa the whole year, and this is how it had come about – without any real effort, just by being positive about playing in Soweto.

Monja and the other wives and girlfriends had left for Soweto on the Saturday morning to soak up the atmosphere. They visited former president Nelson Mandela's home and had lunch at a shebeen, and they sent us photos they'd taken with their cellphones. Everyone was happy, including us, because when we saw the astonishing scenes, our energy levels shot sky-high. I knew then that we wouldn't lose the game.

However, there was a bit of drama behind the scenes. Because of a huge traffic jam outside the stadium, the referee, Stuart Dickinson, almost missed the kick-off. Just before the toss, Jonathan Kaplan approached me and said that he would probably have to referee the match, as Dickinson hadn't arrived yet. Kaplan took charge of the toss, but shortly afterwards Dickinson showed up.

And he was not the only one affected by the traffic. Thousands of supporters arrived late, thus missing the opening minutes of the game. It was weird running onto the field and seeing a half-empty stadium, especially having witnessed the party atmosphere on the streets.

We were ready for the Crusaders. Two weeks earlier, at Loftus, we had learnt a lot about their playing style. They had caught us off guard in that game by spreading the ball wide from the first phase, but we would not let that happen again. This semi-final was also my 100th Super Rugby game for the Bulls, and it was a huge honour to celebrate the achievement in a special venue such as Orlando Stadium.

In the third minute, a try by Pierre Spies set the wheels in motion for us. Then Zane Kirchner also scored. Our kicking game was top-notch, the forwards were playing well and we managed to limit our mistakes. At half-time we led 23-10.

The second half was over in a flash. Fourie du Preez scored a brilliant individual try with a sniping blindside run. In the end we beat the Crusaders easily, with the final score 39-24. It was our third semi-final victory in a row over the Crusaders in South Africa. For years they had determined the pace while we had struggled to catch up. Our win record against them clearly underlined one vital fact: any team travelling across time zones to play in a knockout game would struggle to compete.

Later that day the Stormers beat the Waratahs 25-6 at Newlands to set up a dream final: north against south, South Africa's two traditional rugby powers pitted against each other to determine who was the best provincial team in the southern hemisphere.

Although the Stormers were playing good rugby, I found it quite strange how many pundits did not give us a chance, branding us rank outsiders for the final. Since Western Province had last won the Currie Cup in 2001 – also the last time they'd won any significant trophy – the Bulls had won the Super 14 series twice, the Vodacom Cup three times and the Currie Cup five times (shared once).

Nevertheless, the Cape Town media couldn't praise their team highly enough. Every time Province or the Stormers played well, they were the 'champions'. I think the press did the team a great disservice by writing them up to such an extent the week before an important game. Accordinging to the press, the rugby power was shifting to the south and the Bulls were past their best. We read that the Stormers had 'momentum on their side', that their defence was so much better than ours and that they would give us a hard time up front.

But I knew that our experience was worth more than any nonsense a journalist could conjure up. Even the most experienced Stormers players had little knowledge of competing in a Super Rugby final. Only Bryan Habana, who in his five years with the Bulls had played in four big finals, had experienced this type of challenge. Later I heard that Monja had bumped into John Smit and his wife Roxy before the game, and John told her that the Stormers' lack of experience in finals would count in the Bulls' favour. He was spot on.

After the Wednesday practice session, Pieter Rossouw – the former Springbok and Stormers wing who was now our backline coach – was concerned that the Bulls were a bit restless and not completely focused. I reassured him by telling him that we always approached games in this way. Most of the guys just wanted to get the practice session over and done with because all they were thinking about was Saturday's final. They just wanted to play. The week before a big game almost every effort is devoted to mental preparation. At that stage it is too late to try something new on the field anyway.

As usual, we had the Thursday off, when the players preferred to get as far away from rugby as possible. You didn't want to think about the game too much, as it could drain you emotionally. As was my custom, I had golf on my agenda that Thursday, and I enjoyed a round at Blair Atholl, south-west of Pretoria. There was some superstition attached to this course, because we never lost a rugby game after playing a round there.

Our preparation for the match was methodical and without frills. While we'd heard that the Stormers were training behind closed doors, away from the media and public, anyone could attend our sessions. We were an open book: with a Bulls game, what you saw was what you got. Our approach was simple: if we followed our game plan and executed it properly, we would be unstoppable.

I never got worked up and emotional before a game, but on this occasion, my team talk was quite fiery. Earlier we'd been in a pretty relaxed mood, but when we walked into the changing room, the atmosphere changed markedly. I gathered the guys together and said: 'As a team, we have been building for six, seven years to get to where we are today. We don't just buy three rugby stars, make it to the final and think that we are now another team who can compete at this level.'

Everyone agreed and reacted perfectly. We ran onto the field as men ready to play for and with each other for 80 minutes. To put it differently, we had brought our umbrellas along.

In the first 20 minutes, we completely dominated the Stormers. As so many other teams did that season, they fell into the trap of thinking that they could pass the ball around while waiting for us to tire. And for some reason they did not launch any of the rolling mauls they had used to such great effect throughout the season. We'd even devised a strategy to combat their mauls, but we never needed to use it.

The Stormers were at their most dangerous if they ran directly at their opponents, but by playing all their possession quick and wide in the final, they actually played to our advantage. Because they sent the ball wide every time, we were never put under any pressure. They also didn't vary their game plan. At every kick-off, their forwards divided into two groups so that we wouldn't know which side they were going to kick to. But then every time they kicked the ball to the side where Bryan Habana was standing, so that he could chase after the ball. Werner Kruger and I simply stood guard on Bryan's side of the field and the ball came straight to me every time.

When François Hougaard scored a try halfway through the first half to stretch our lead to 16-0, many people believed it was all over, but we knew a lot of hard work was still required. Yes, we knew we were in control of the game, but the Stormers were a good team and could never be written off. We didn't dare stop concentrating.

In the second half, Bryan scored an intercept try to narrow our lead to 16-10, but the Stormers never really pressurised us. We overpowered them in the scrums and were awarded a few penalties, which Morné calmly slotted over. With eight minutes to go, we were 25-10 ahead, and then we knew it was too late for them to catch us, even after Pieter Louw scored another Stormers try late in the game.

Besides the wrong tactical approach, I also thought that Andries Bekker's injury early in the game had cost the Stormers dearly. Without him, their tight five struggled. He was one of the leaders in the pack and an important source of possession in the line-outs.

Nonetheless, I was relieved when the final whistle went. We had dictated things on the field, but it was not easy to communicate with the constant noise of thousands of vuvuzelas hooting the whole time. It was almost impossible to make or hear the line-out calls. Even if we stood close to each other, we could not hear what was being said. I had to walk up to each forward and tell him what the play in the line-out was. The vuvuzela may be great for soccer, but communication on a rugby field is important and with such a racket it was almost impossible. It sounded as if all 40 000 people in Orlando Stadium were blowing one. Even little Jaime, a mere four years old, had one!

After the game, it was a different story. Some of the Bulls got hold of their own vuvuzelas and joined in the celebrations. We did a lap of honour, thoroughly enjoying out third title.

Winnie Madikizela-Mandela even visited our changing room afterwards. She and some of her children and grandchildren came to congratulate us and thank us for playing in Soweto. She even invited us to a braai at her house. Unfortunately, we already had other plans.

Because Loftus was being prepared for the FIFA World Cup, we did not head back to our headquarters for the after-party, but instead got together at the Pretoria Country Club, where we could listen to some music and enjoy a few cold beverages. Paul Anthony, one of our junior coaches, and his band provided the entertainment. It was not long before Dewald Potgieter also got hold of a guitar and started playing a few tunes. It was a wonderful evening, but with a funny twist in the tail.

The Super 14 trophy consists of a rugby ball held in position by a thin piece of metal that is attached to a framework. I don't know how it happened, but during the festivities – while our prop Bees Roux had it in his hands – the trophy broke. It wasn't the end of the world. After all, we had won the trophy three out of five times and basically considered this piece of silverware our property!

The last two weeks of the Super 14 series in 2010 made me realise that we live in a very special country with very special people. Our foray into Soweto had proved to me how people of different cultures can come together and share the same joy. Again, it was sport, and in this case, rugby, that had made it possible.

I will remember the day *before* the semi-final – when we were driving through the streets of Soweto observing white and black people drinking beer and braaiing together – longer than the day we lifted the trophy.

16

A roller-coaster ride

The Springboks had to play Wales in Cardiff just a week after the Super 14 final in Soweto. It was simply asking too much. SARU were heavily criticised for subjecting their national players to such bad scheduling after they had just come out of one of the world's most demanding rugby tournaments, but there was an agreement in place and the Boks had to fall in.

I wasn't too bothered at first, as I would not have been part of the touring squad, but when Andries Bekker was injured in the Super 14 final, Peter asked me to stand by. When Andries did not recover in time, I got my call-up, but Peter gave me permission to fly to Cardiff on the Wednesday before the match, as he knew I needed some rest. At least I could also spend a couple of days with my family.

Later it was reported that Andries was having marital problems after a local gossip magazine published sneak photos of him with another woman in a Cape Town park. I couldn't believe it. It was not the Andries I knew. Andries was the quiet bloke in the team and a very hard worker. I felt really sorry for him.

This incident reinforces what I said earlier: when players – especially the younger ones – start achieving some success on the field, they also gain prominence in the public eye. All of a sudden they attract a lot of attention, especially from the fairer sex, and can easily fall into a trap. Maybe it was a blessing in disguise that I did not get married early on in my career.

But there wasn't a lot of time to mull over this incident, as I had to prepare for a Test match.

Peter had picked a young Bok side for the Test against Wales, and the energy and excitement among debutants like Gio Aplon, Bjorn Basson, Juan de Jongh, Dewald Potgieter, François Louw and Alistair Hargreaves was palpable and heartening to see. And this after most of them had played in a tough final only a few days earlier! Super 14 rugby is a good barometer for Test rugby, as a player who performs well at that level will most probably be able to take the step up to international rugby.

So the young guns were raring to go, but our team would be without the services of Fourie du Preez for the rest of 2010. Fourie had been South Africa's Player of the Year in 2009 and was one of the most vital links in our chain. He'd informed me two weeks before the final that he would have to undergo shoulder surgery and would miss the rest of the season. Actually his timing was perfect, as we would have preferred to do without him in 2010 than the following year, when the Boks would defend their World Cup title in New Zealand.

Jean de Villiers, our other leader in the backline, was also not available to play against Wales, as he had club-rugby commitments in Ireland. So our new backline, consisting of Frans Steyn, Gio Aplon, Jaque Fourie, Juan de Jongh, Odwa Ndungane, Ruan Pienaar and Ricky Januarie, had little experience among them. However, we overcame that challenge and won a tough encounter 34-31.

The most important Test we would play at home before the start of the Tri Nations was against France, a team we last beat in 2005. Peter intended to pick his strongest side for this game, but then rest some of the senior players against Italy in the next Test. We really wanted to prove ourselves against Les Bleus, as we had a very average record against them, partly because we mostly played them in France. Anyone who's ever played club rugby in that country will tell you how important it is for the French to win in front of their home crowd, be it in a lower-league club game or a Test.

Since making my debut for the Boks, I had played in eight Tests against France, of which only three had been contested in South Africa. The defeat we'd suffered in the Toulouse Test in 2009 was a blot on our record, and we wanted to expunge it. This time round, the players were confident and relaxed – especially the Bulls and Stormers players, who had performed well in the Super 14 competition.

In the meantime, the biggest sporting event in South African history kicked off on the Friday before the Test: the FIFA World Cup. In the week leading up to the game, you could feel the excitement in the air, and a party spirit permeated the Mother City. Peter was a bit worried about the distractions and suggested that we train in Paarl, far from the hustle and bustle, but by then we'd caught the World Cup fever and were enjoying all the noise from the vuvuzelas and the festive atmosphere.

In the opening game on 11 June, Bafana Bafana played against Mexico in Soweto, and our guys acquitted themselves really well. The final score was 1-1. In the evening, France and Uruguay played in the brand-new Cape Town Stadium, which was just down the road from our hotel. France put up a lacklustre performance against an equally boring Uruguay, with no goals scored during the game.

And the next day, the French rugby side was thrashed 42-17 by a very motivated Bok team that delivered a magnificent performance. This resounding victory significantly buoyed our expectations for the Tri Nations. The forthcoming Tests against Italy, in Witbank and East London, would allow the new guys the opportunity to adapt to our way of playing and serve as good preparation for the rest of the team.

When John Smit was injured in the Test against France, my Bulls teammate Chiliboy Ralepelle replaced him in the second half. The media often implied that Chili was in the Bok squad only because he was black. I thought their insinuations were both unnecessary and unjust, and they hurt Chili tremendously.

I'd had a long conversation with Chili about two years earlier, when he told me how fed up he was to always be on the bench. No matter which team he played for – be it for the Bulls or the Boks – he never got enough game time. And although he believed in his own abilities, he was still made to feel like a political pawn.

Chili is a brilliant hooker and one of the toughest guys I've ever encountered. Unfortunately, he plays in the same era as guys like John Smit, Bismarck du Plessis and Gary Botha, three Springboks with vast experience. But Chili is the youngest of the four, and I believe that he will still get his chance. Tight forwards can be competitive into their 30s, and Chili was only born in 1986.

Chili also had to overcome quite a few injuries, and never really got the opportunity to cement his spot in the team. In 2010, however, after recovering from a serious injury, he and the Bulls' brain trust came up with a plan to get his career back on track. Even though he was ready for Super 14 action, it was decided to use him in the Vodacom Cup competition instead.

Many uninformed people disapproved when he was picked for the Boks, but the fact that he played most of his rugby in the Vodacom series was not a reflection of his true abilities. As a replacement player for the Bulls, he had had limited game time, but he played in almost five full matches for the Vodacom Cup side in 2010, which helped him to be on form, fit, injury-free and brimming with confidence when he joined the Boks. As a result, he gave a brilliant performance when he came on as replacement for John against the French. I've always considered Chili to be a fantastic player, a strong leader and a great guy, and I believe he will be very successful as a professional player.

With John injured, Peter asked me to captain the Boks against Italy at the Puma Stadium in Witbank. I would miss the second Test, in East London, when John would return as skipper. In South Africa, the Springboks play almost all their Tests at the home grounds of the Super 14 franchises: Pretoria, Johannesburg, Bloemfontein, Durban and Cape Town. Every now and then we would play in Port Elizabeth or other, smaller venues, and although it was a treat for the locals, it was sometimes tough for us as players. The atmosphere in big stadiums is infectious, but at the Puma Stadium, for instance, it's difficult to motivate yourself because it somehow doesn't feel like a Test when you play there, no matter who your opponents are.

Of course, we knew how important Test matches in smaller places were to the supporters. During our training sessions at these venues, thousands of people would gather to watch us, more even than in the big cities, and people would pitch up at our hotel in their droves to wish us well, ask for our autographs or to pose for photos.

In the week leading up to the Test against Italy, we all went to Loftus – not for a practice session, but to watch Bafana Bafana play Uruguay. We sat in the notorious East Stand, where all the hardened and most fanatical Bulls fans normally congregate, sang 'Shosholoza' with our fellow South Africans and blew our vuvuzelas. We enjoyed every minute of the experience. It was the first time since the Currie Cup final in 1998 that I was at Loftus as a spectator.

In our game against the Azzurri, our plans didn't quite come off on the pitch. Although we beat them 29-13, we gave a terrible performance. We could only score four tries (by Bryan Habana, François Louw, Morné Steyn and Zane Kirchner), whereas before we had never really struggled to cross Italy's goal line in home Tests. Butch James, who was playing at inside centre, was sin-binned midway through the second half for a dangerous high tackle, which slowed down our momentum, and our ball retention was poor. But all credit to the Italians – they played really well on the day, and their captain, Sergio Parisse, was the well-deserved Man of the Match.

Bakkies had missed the Tests against Wales and France after being suspended for unlawful play for four weeks after the last Super 14 group game of the season against the Stormers in Cape Town, in which he captained the side. Fortunately, he was back for the Tests against Italy and he was ready for big rugby. He was also available for our Tri Nations tour of three Tests against New Zealand and Australia.

Although Bakkies was a very important member of the Bok squad, he was often the target of provocation on the field. Opponents knew he had a short fuse, so they would pester and harass him to see if they could provoke him enough to take a swing at them, which was basically what scrumhalf Jimmy Cowan did early in our first Test against New Zealand, in Auckland. Cowan got hold of Bakkies's jersey as he was chasing a loose ball, and the big guy lost it. I didn't see it happen, but during a break in play, the New Zealanders made sure everyone knew what he'd done to Cowan by replaying the incident on the big screen in the stadium. After tackling the scrumhalf, Bakkies had headbutted him from behind.

Having beaten the All Blacks in our previous three Tests, we were full of confidence before the start of the game. But when the headbutt happened, our hearts just sank. We knew another suspension was unavoidable – it was just a question of how long it would be this time. To add insult to injury, a few minutes later Bakkies was sent to the sin bin for an infringement at a loose scrum on our try line.

To play the All Blacks with 14 men is almost impossible. With one less defender, they can build momentum quite easily, making it increasingly difficult to stop them. By the time Bakkies returned, they had already established a sizeable lead and we were unable to catch up.

It was more of the same the next week. This time Danie Rossouw received a yellow card. To beat the All Blacks, you have to put them under pressure from the kick-off and you can't let up for the duration of the game. It's just not possible to do this with 14 men. The scores were 32-12 at Eden Park in Auckland and 31-17 at the Westpac Stadium in Wellington.

These two defeats set the tone for the rest of the Tri Nations series. The year before, the power in world rugby had shifted to the Springboks, but since then the All Blacks had worked hard to purge their game of the mistakes that had cost them so dearly. In the line-outs, where we usually had their number, they tried different tactics to secure possession: quick throw-ins, short throws to the prop at the front of the line-out, long balls over the top ...

Although they played good rugby and managed to keep us on the back foot, things might have turned out differently had it not been for those two yellow cards.

Despite losing the Test in Auckland, I thought I had given one of my best performances in a Bok jersey in New Zealand. Os du Randt, our scrum coach at the time, said afterwards that he had never seen me play so hard before. Even though I broke my nose in that Test and was very disappointed that we'd lost, at least Os's words were some comfort.

Bakkies learnt an important lesson in the Auckland Test. After the headbutting incident, he was a different player, with a different attitude towards rugby. He even started training harder, as he wanted to show everybody that he was not the bully he was perceived to be. And in other matches, as well as in the end-of-year tour in 2010, he showed his worth.

Earlier that year, however, he'd been a frustrated man. First an injury had kept him out of action for the whole of the Super 14 series, and then he was suspended after the Stormers game, with talented players like Andries Bekker and Danie Rossouw breathing down his neck. He wanted to prove himself, but he wasn't as fit as he should have been and as a result probably took some unnecessary short cuts on the field.

Unfortunately, he had also done a few stupid things in close succession, which was what people remembered. One of the rugby jokes doing the rounds at the time went as follows: 'Why does Bakkies, after running onto the field, always go down on one knee to pray before a game? Because he's asking for forgiveness for what he is about to do in the next 80 minutes.'

Bakkies's Christianity is very important to him, which contributed to his feelings of guilt after the headbutt. Religion plays an important role in many of the Bok and Bulls players' lives. We always try to set a good example and live according to the right principles. I attended Bible-study groups at both teams, and every Friday before a game we would spend an hour in the presence of the Lord. Of course, this was not a prayer session in which we asked the Lord to let us win the game, but an opportunity for the guys in the team who wanted to spend time together on a spiritual level.

We always tried to lift the spiritual bond between us and supported each other during tough times, and as a result we formed a tight unit. As life was not always that easy, it helped tremendously to know you could count on the support and understanding of friends and loved ones.

***

As if a double defeat against New Zealand weren't bad enough, a young and exciting Wallaby team awaited us in Australia ... and in Brisbane, of all places. The Boks always struggled in this city in Queensland, where I, personally, had never beaten the Wallabies. This time they thumped us 30-13.

We simply could not maintain the momentum, and suddenly everyone was questioning our game plan. The molehills were starting to look like mountains. As usual, Peter de Villiers endured a lot of criticism, but he stood his ground. One could easily give in to panic under these circumstances and make 15 changes to the team, but Peter believed in and supported his players.

Various disruptions didn't help our cause. Two of our best players of 2009, Fourie du Preez and Heinrich Brüssow, were injured, and Bakkies was serving out his suspension. Juan Smith's dad had passed away, so he stayed behind in South Africa (an act of kindness from Peter, reaffirming the empathy he had with his players). Then John Smit was moved from prop back to hooker when Bismarck du Plessis was injured.

John and I met with Peter, and we confirmed that we believed in our approach, no matter what doubt people cast on our team selections and game plans. But we also knew that we had to find players who could slow down the opponent's possession on the ground, as our pack was quite big and not everyone could get to the loose scrums in time. Every good pack consists of a few workers who hit the loose scrums hard and drive back the opponents, those who turn over possession or slow down the ball on the ground, and two or three strong ball carriers. It is, therefore, always a tough and often controversial decision when the coach is forced (usually because of injuries) to leave a brilliant player out of the team in order to obtain the right balance among the forwards.

After playing against the British & Irish Lions in 2009, my next goal was to represent South Africa in 100 Tests, a massive milestone in any rugby player's career. Once I had achieved that, I would decide whether or not I wanted to go on playing until the World Cup in 2011. Then, suddenly, it was 2010, and I had 98 Tests to my name. I thought about whether I should continue for another season, but it was not a difficult decision to make, as I was physically and mentally ready for the next challenge. At that stage, John had already played in 99 Tests and he had to make a similar decision. If all went well, he would play against the All Blacks in his 100th Test for the Springboks. My 100th Test would be a week later, against the Wallabies at my home ground, Loftus Versfeld.

In the meantime, there were more urgent matters on the agenda. The Tri Nations tour had been a failure and required proper reflection. Back in South Africa, Peter, John, Fourie, Andy Marinos, SARU's manager of national teams, and I held a meeting in Stellenbosch. Gary Gold, the Boks' forward coach, was also present for a little while. We had all got together in the Cape for Jean de Villiers's wedding that weekend, but again our women had to accept that 'rugby issues' had priority. The opportunity to defend our Tri Nations title had come and gone. With the World Cup in mind, hard decisions had to be made:

What type of players would we need?

How did we want to play?

Did we still believe in our game plan?

How could we improve the execution of our game plan?

The meeting was of crucial importance, in particular deciding whether or not we would stick to our game plan. The big problems, however, were the execution of our game plan and the team's bad decision-making, which had hampered our whole season.

We also tried to understand why the referees had penalised us so heavily on tour, and we concluded that we had to change our body language on the field. Whenever a referee penalised us from then on, even if we did not agree with his call, we would immediately fall back 10 metres and react to what our opponents – and not the ref – were going to do next. We wanted to cultivate a positive attitude towards referees and hoped that they, in turn, would respond positively towards us.

Fourie's injury was also a huge setback, and although many people blamed Ricky Januarie for our backline's woes, it wasn't his fault. Ricky was talented in his own way, but his game differed from Fourie's. Fourie would often fall back and control play from deep in our own half, whereas Ricky preferred to get involved with the action up front. Ruan Pienaar played more like Fourie, but he was also injured, so we decided to start the Soweto Test with François Hougaard at scrumhalf. Hougie also had his own style. Sometimes he played like Ricky, but in recent years he had learnt a lot from Fourie. François usually played at wing for the Bulls and had experienced a great season in 2010, and he brought a new confidence to the Bok team.

In the meantime, the rugby bosses had decided that the first Test against the All Blacks would be played at the FNB Stadium in Soweto – a brilliant decision. Although the match had originally been allocated to the Golden Lions Union, the FNB Stadium, with its more than 90 000 seats, would generate much more revenue. Although we always enjoyed playing at Coca-Cola Park in Joburg, it was wonderful to be given another opportunity to play in front of our 'home crowd' in Soweto. The FNB Stadium is one of the World Cup's greatest legacies. This unbelievable stadium, with its impressive 360-degree construction, has the most modern changing rooms and facilities, and a fantastic playing field.

And it would be John's 100th Test. The players hugely respected John, especially those of us who played with him regularly, and we knew that it was a massive occasion for him. As a team, we wanted to make it up to him for the 'bad' Tri Nations tour. John didn't want a big fuss made about his milestone Test – beating the All Blacks was all that mattered to him. But we could see that he was nervous before the match.

John had invited his two former school coaches, Paul Anthony and Jannie Biddulph, to hand out our Bok jerseys the day before the Test, and it turned into a very emotional occasion. When John thanked us for the roles we had played in his career, he had tears in his eyes, and I wished I could have wiped them away. I have to admit that I was feeling quite emotional too!

Although we played well in the Test, we just couldn't get the better of the Kiwis, despite the fact that we controlled large parts of the game. While we'd played with great confidence against the All Blacks the year before, they managed to turn the tables this time.

With the score locked at 22-all we thought they'd settle for a draw, but we assumed wrongly, because they never gave up. In hindsight, we should have kicked deep to pin them back in their own half for the last couple of minutes of the game, when the scores were level. However, we opted for a short restart and, even though we secured the ball, we lost possession shortly afterwards and gave them a chance to score the winning try.

Not only was the try a mortal blow, but the move also had an unfortunate start. I was trapped under a loose scrum and didn't see the incident, but the replay on the big screen showed John missing a tackle on Ma'a Nonu, which subsequently led to the try. Final score: New Zealand 29, South Africa 22.

It was terrible seeing John down on his knees. It must have been a heartbreaking moment for him. We knew we should've won that game, but we'd thrown it away. John was not to blame. However, he blamed himself, and I tried to console him. Although we had lost in his 100th Test, we had to remember that he'd played in 99 other Tests too. In 10 years, he'd made a massive contribution to South African rugby.

And then it was my turn.

The big week had arrived at last, and I resolved to enjoy every moment of it. Never in my wildest dreams did I think I would play in 100 Tests for the Springboks! My first Test, in 2001, when I came on as a replacement, was special, but reaching 100 Tests was almost unimaginable back then. I'd played my 50th Test in 2006, against the All Blacks, and regardless of the fact that we lost, that match remains one of the highlights of my career.

I woke up on Monday morning, 23 August 2010, in Pretoria at the beginning of my 100th Test week with my emotions running wild. Although I would probably thank the most important people in my life at a later stage, for the entire week I just wanted to tell my family how grateful I was for their support over the years.

First, I wanted to thank my fantastic wife, Monja, and our two beautiful daughters, Jaime and Giselle, who each in their own way had supported me with so much love. If I did not have such a wonderful wife, I would never have reached that milestone. Rugby 'widows' have to make many sacrifices. They often have to take a back seat to their husbands' careers and have to share them with thousands of fans. They basically raise the children on their own, and they have to have broad shoulders when things go pear-shaped on the rugby field and the men need sympathy.

I am also forever grateful to my mom and dad, Hettie and Fai. I've been privileged to have parents who always supported and encouraged me, who followed me to sporting events around the country over thousands of kilometres and who – through victory and defeat – were always there for me, loving me no matter what.

But I had to keep my emotions in check for the extraordinary week that lay ahead. And it didn't even start that well. On the Monday, the media were mercilessly critical of our performance in the Soweto Test. The knives were out. The Boks were down in the dumps and under tremendous pressure after four losses in a row in the Tri Nations series.

Things improved a bit as the week progressed, but then terrible news reached us just one day before the Test. That Friday morning, as we were about to attend a press conference, we learnt that one of our Blue Bulls props, Bees Roux, had been involved in an incident the night before in which a Metro police officer from Pretoria had died. Bees was under arrest for murder after he'd had an altercation with the officer, who allegedly wanted to charge him for driving under the influence of alcohol. Rumour had it that certain Metro cops were extorting money from motorists by forcing them to pay a bribe or face the consequences of a drink-driving charge.

It was shocking news. Bees was a teammate, one of the most soft-spoken and pleasant guys I knew. The terrible news also badly affected the Bulls, who would play the Pumas in Nelspruit that evening. They subsequently lost the game.

We wanted to help Bees, but how? We had to concentrate on the next day's Test. Although we wanted to discuss the incident, it would have been unfair to involve the rest of the Bok team. What I knew for sure was that Bees would never have planned such a terrible deed. Accidents happen, but this was almost surreal. A few months earlier, we'd been talking about how the Bulls could make a difference in South Africa, but shortly after the Bees incident it was tragic to see members of the Metro police tossing a Bulls jersey into the road outside the court building and trampling on it. It broke my heart.

Fortunately, there was also a moment of light relief amidst all the doom and gloom. We conducted that Friday's press conference next to the swimming pool of the Southern Sun Hotel in Beatrix Street, where we were staying. The journalists were firing questions at us and the cameras were rolling when, all of a sudden, a bird in a tree above us 'relieved' itself on my head. Of course, everyone thought it was extremely funny. A few superstitious journalists even said it was a good omen. Well, in that case the bird can have another go, I thought!

Something else that amused everyone were the 30 000 masks, with my face superimposed on them, that SARU had ordered before the Test. Photos were taken of my teammates and supporters wearing the masks, and I was the brunt of many jokes.

As I could choose who would hand out our jerseys, I picked Hey-neke Meyer and George Gregan. I had hoped that George would be in the country for the Test, but unfortunately he couldn't make it. Although some people found it odd that I'd asked one of my fiercest opponents to participate in this ritual, George and I had been good friends since our days at Toulon and I had a lot of respect for the man. Until 2011, nobody had played in more Tests than George (139), and I also knew that he respected Springbok rugby and he respected me.

Outsiders probably found some of our choices to hand out our jerseys odd, but we always enjoyed this little ritual on the Friday before a match.

During our Tri Nations tour in 2010 we'd asked the former South African netball captain Irene van Dyk to do the honours. Although our first choice was usually a former Springbok rugby player, that wasn't always possible. Some of our other esteemed guests included former All Black coach John Mitchell, whose talk I enjoyed very much, the former Proteas cricket player Gary Kirsten, Archbishop Emeritus Desmond Tutu, Raymond Ackerman, the founder of Pick n Pay, and Kurt Darren, the pop star. Anyone was welcome, as long as they had achieved success in their field and had an inspiring story to share with us.

Two visits in particular stand out: that of former Springbok captain and 1995 World Cup team manager, Morné du Plessis, and Steve Atherton, a Sharks lock who had played in only eight Tests. Steve's talk was short and to the point: he might have played in only eight Tests, but nobody could take away the memories he had of playing in them. You had to cherish every moment you got to play in the green and gold as if it were your last. We could tell that Steve meant every word he said, even though none of us had ever had him as a teammate. His talk put my situation in perspective for me – I felt very humble, and also grateful, to be on the brink of my 100th Test.

Morné addressed us prior to the All Black Test at Newlands, and his message was simple: 'Do whatever is needed to win the Test. If more than your best is required to win, you will have to produce something extra, because you represent South Africa. Your best is never good enough if you lose.' Everyone respects Morné. In my 11 years as a Springbok, I never heard a bad word said about him, nor did he ever have anything negative to say about the Boks or any other players.

Not all the former Boks' talks were as well received as Morné's. The players were sometimes disappointed by what the person had to say, as was the case with Bok legend Frik du Preez. He told us how different things had been in the days of amateur rugby and that the game was no longer played in the same spirit. He seemed to insinuate that we were not as committed to the game or the Springbok jersey as he had been in his day, perhaps because we got paid to play. I wondered whether he was referring to 2002 and 2003, when the Boks went through a particularly bad patch. At the time, we were young players and our results were often poor. Our commitment, however, was never in question.

It hurt to hear these accusations, especially as they came from someone we held in such high regard. Frik will always be one of the stars of Springbok and world rugby, but I think on that day he could have picked his words with more care. I don't hold it against him, however, and Bakkies and I still felt honoured to be photographed with this legendary lock. However, I can assure Frik, and all former Boks, that the green-and-gold jersey was as important to us as it had been to them, and that we did not lack the passion and commitment to play for South Africa.

And so I chose Heyneke to hand out our jerseys on the occasion of my 100th Test. He was an easy pick, because he was one of my mentors and the man who had helped turn things around at the Bulls. I couldn't believe it, but he was actually quite nervous before the occasion. However, as I'd expected, his stories were inspirational. This time, they centred on coffee beans and charcoal!

'If you put a banana in boiling water,' Heyneke said, 'the banana turns soft. And if you put an egg in boiling water, the egg becomes hard. But if you boil coffee beans in water, the beans produce a tasty cup of coffee.' According to Heyneke, the boiling water was the pressure we often had to face on the rugby field. If we folded under the pressure, we would either become soft (like the banana) or hard (like the egg), neither of which was good. 'You must be like the coffee beans, which use the boiling water to produce a tasty cup of coffee. In other words, if you can handle the pressure, you can mould it to benefit you.'

The second story was about charcoal, which turns into diamonds under tremendous pressure. 'You are diamonds already,' Heyneke said, 'because you've handled extreme pressure before. You will know what to do if you are under that kind of pressure again.' Afterwards John Smit came to me and said: 'Now I understand why the Bulls are always so motivated before a game.'

Then the big day was upon me. Although it started like any other day, the butterflies were flitting around in my stomach by the time we arrived at Loftus. Reaching this milestone at my home ground, against a team I always enjoyed playing, was unbelievable. Jaime and Giselle joined me on the field for the national anthems. Jaime had seen John's two kids with him on the field the week before, and she immediately wanted to know when it would be her turn. It was a very special moment to have my two little princesses with me. They were astounded by the thousands of 'Victors' in the stands. What an unbelievable experience!

But we started the Test poorly, and after 10 minutes the Wallabies were leading 21-7, and then 28-17. Despite being behind the posts again, waiting for the conversion to be taken, we weren't panicking. As a matter of fact, we knew just what to do: stick to the game plan. Shortly before half-time, Pierre Spies scored a try to shrink the deficit to 24-28.

In the second half we played clinical rugby, and in the end we won easily (44-31). The victory was a tremendous relief, and it was also fantastic to win my 100th Test at my home ground. After the game, my emotions got the better of me. I did a lap of honour on my own to thank the crowd for all their years of support. To play in 100 Tests had been my goal, and now I had achieved it. To play in just one Test for your country is reward enough, but I had experienced a hundred rewards …

That evening, a function was held for the players and their families, and it gave me great pleasure to have my mom and dad there as well. I was given the chance to say a few words, and I thanked everyone who had been involved in my career. I also singled out the Wallaby lock Nathan Sharpe, as he and I had competed since our days as under-21 players, and it was fitting to have him as an opponent in my 100th Test.

Later, almost the entire team and most of my friends attended a party thrown by my business partners, Daan van Rensburg and Willem Britz, at Willem's house in Pretoria to celebrate the big occasion. It carried on till the early hours of the morning as we simultaneously celebrated our first Tri Nations victory of 2010 and my 100th Test.

Daan and Willem have meant a lot to me over the years. Initially they sponsored my car, but later on we became firm friends as well as business partners. Many rugby players are concerned about what will happen to them after they retire, but thanks to Daan and Willem and my third partner at Pharmacy Direct, Antoine van Buuren, my future is secure. Another partner, Patrick Goddard, who has shares with us in a few restaurants, was also present. He made sure there was no shortage of food or drinks! Even my older sister, Trudie, attended the party. She is very shy and reserved and hardly ever attends this sort of function, and it was therefore very special to have her there. It was a wonderful celebration of something that happens only once, and in very few players' lives.

A day later, it was back to the drawing board. The fact that we'd lost five out of six Tri Nations Tests was something the rugby writers were not going to let us forget soon. Quite a few players – me included – were criticised for our 'poor performance'. Yet I thought the Test in Auckland had been one of my best performances. Statistics showed that my work rate at the loose scrums, the tackles I had made and my general play were above suspicion. Nevertheless, the media criticised me as much as they did one of the other senior players who was not on top form at the time. However, I was happy with my performance and thought I had reason enough to feel satisfied.

The Tri Nations tournament was drawing to a close and we wanted to finish the series on a high note against the Wallabies in Bloemfontein. It felt like our ship was on course again and we were ready for the Australians, but yet again we had a pathetic start. After just 25 minutes, we were trailing 6-31. How the hell did that happen?

We fought back – a short, hanging kick that I'd punted led to a try by Jaque Fourie – and for about 20 minutes in the second half we played our best rugby of the entire season. During this time we scored three great tries and had the Aussie defence at sixes and sevens. But this time they didn't fold under the pressure. Whereas in previous years we would have won it from there, luck was not on our side in 2010. With half a minute to go before the final whistle, and with us in the lead, Flip van der Merwe was penalised and Kurtley Beale converted a difficult kick to clinch a Wallaby victory.

Afterwards, when we analysed the game, we noticed the similarities to our Tri Nations campaign of 2006, which gave us a bit of hope for the 2011 season. As had been the case with Jake in 2006, rumours were circulating that Peter de Villiers was going to be sacked as coach. Heyneke's name was mentioned as a possible replacement, and even though the players obviously had no say in who would be appointed as the new coach, I had sleepless nights about it. On the one hand, I liked Peter a lot and believed that we were on the right track with him as coach. But on the other hand, I couldn't help wonder whether someone like Heyneke, with his firm belief in structured play, wouldn't achieve better results. I had a great deal of respect for both coaches.

Heyneke spoke to me and Fourie about taking over from Peter. He had last coached the Bulls three years previously, and I would lie if I said we didn't think it would be great to work with him again. He could be credited with many of the Bulls' successes over the years and knew most of the players well. But Peter, with his human and empathetic touch, was also good for the team. He had created a relaxed atmosphere in the squad, which was wonderful.

Of course, coaching a Springbok team is vastly different from training a provincial side. At the Boks, you have the best players at your disposal, whereas at provincial level you often train young, inexperienced guys. For instance, not many coaches can teach Jean de Villiers and Jaque Fourie anything about playing in the centre position, and I was in charge of organising the line-outs.

Peter excelled at managing his players – he had unfaltering faith in us and listened to what we had to say. And when things went wrong, he often took the blame to protect his players. He would step forward and take up the cudgels for the team on even the smallest of issues. When Schalk was cited for the eye-gouging incident, for example, Peter came to his defence, even when the media accused him of being stupid and arrogant. That is just the way Peter is, and the players respected him tremendously for it.

But, like Jake in 2006, Peter was not sacked. In any case, at that stage Peter was hardly the team's biggest problem. The real challenge lay in getting all the coaches and players to agree on the Springboks' style of playing. Dick Muir's ideas on how we should play differed from Peter's, and although a fine line exists between what's right and what's wrong, we were being given contradictory messages. It is confusing for the team and detrimental to its success when it receives contrasting instructions on how to play the game.

Each week started with a meeting between the coaches and the players. We often disagreed and argued with each other, which was fine, as long as we ultimately carried the same message back to the team. Unfortunately, this did not always happen. The backline players often complained that what they did on the practice field was not what had been decided in the team meeting. This situation usually occurred with the younger players, as senior guys like Fourie, Jean and Jaque normally ensured that the plans were executed as discussed. But in 2010, a lot of younger players were given the chance to play.

We'd experienced similar problems in 2009 during our preparations for the British & Irish Lions, and Peter made it clear at the time that players who didn't want to buy into his plans could pack their bags and leave. Thereafter, we played to a specific structure and went on to win the Tri Nations.

But now the same problems were re-emerging, and although there were rumours to that effect, none of the coaching staff was fired after our poor performance in the 2010 Tri Nations.

17

How must we play?

After not playing for six weeks and training on our own, my fellow Bok teammates and I could once again don the light-blue jersey in September 2010. While we'd enjoyed our time off, we also had to watch the Blue Bulls struggle to get their Currie Cup campaign on course, and it wasn't easy being only an observer.

Although we had some talented players, most of the senior guys and, hence, the decision-makers, were not available to play for the Blue Bulls. But even so, for a young team to finish fourth on the log – with the same league points as the Cheetahs, but with a worse points-difference – was not bad at all. This young team had beaten both Western Province and the Sharks at Loftus.

Gurthrö Steenkamp (who was injured in his first game just after recovering from an injury), Danie Rossouw, Bakkies Botha, Pierre Spies, Morné Steyn, Wynand Olivier and I joined the team late in the season, and we were a bit rusty after our long break. It always takes a while to get back into your stride. The semi-final against the Sharks in Durban was only the second Currie Cup game of the season for most of the Boks returning to the squad.

Besides the fact that Kings Park is not one of our favourite grounds, on this occasion we had additional drama when a massive swarm of bees invaded the field shortly before kick-off. We had to seek cover in the changing room. We were ready to tackle Sharks, not a swarm of bees! As a result, the game started almost 45 minutes late. Keegan Daniel scored an early try for the home side, after which neither team gave an inch. Late in the game, we almost had the opportunity to clinch the match – some people believed we should have been given a penalty when the Sharks interfered with our rolling maul – but it did not work out the way we wanted, and we lost 12-16.

Afterwards, I was again criticised because I did not always opt to kick for goal when we were given a penalty. Although I usually have a good reason why I opt for a kick to touch, I did make some mistakes that day. Earlier in the game we were given a penalty when we were trailing by just four points, but I told Morné to set up the line-out. Later on, when we got another penalty, there was not enough time left to score a try, and a kick for goal would not have given us enough points to erase the deficit.

I take the blame for those decisions.

Another mistake was the selection of Wynand Olivier, who had hurt himself during the captain's session the day before. Although his injury didn't look too serious, in hindsight we should have played Stefan Watermeyer at inside centre, as he'd had a very good season. It's always a risk to play someone who is injured, as you never know whether the injury will get worse during the game or have a psychological effect on the player. That day in Durban, it cost us dearly.

The Currie Cup is very important to the Bulls, and we were very sad when we had to relinquish our title. It would also have been my last chance to hold the golden trophy, as I had already decided to retire at the end of 2011, and the key Bok players would not take part in that year's Currie Cup competition because they would be rested for the World Cup tournament.

Nevertheless, I think we gave the Sharks a better run for their money than Western Province did in the final a week later. Province learnt the hard way that it's not that easy to win in Durban. The Sharks' massive pack was on top form, and guys like Beast Mtawarira, Bismarck and Jannie du Plessis, Willem Alberts and Ryan Kankowski were brilliant on the day.

***

It was nearly time for the Springboks' end-of-year tour, and this one would offer plenty of challenges. Tests were scheduled against Ireland, Wales, Scotland and England, and a game against the Barbarians. The intention was to leave some of the senior Boks at home, for two reasons: to give them a chance to recharge their batteries and to expose the younger players to international rugby before the 2011 World Cup.

However, a few of the seniors, me included, decided that we wanted to go on tour, even if we played in only a couple of Tests. After all, we'd already had a good six weeks' rest and were feeling fit. As fate would have it, some of the warhorses were nursing injuries and couldn't go on tour: John Smit, Gurthrö Steenkamp, Danie Rossouw, Schalk Burger, Jaque Fourie, Wynand Olivier, JP Pietersen and the exciting young centre Juan de Jongh would all have to stay at home. Besides that, Andries Bekker, Heinrich Brüssow and Fourie du Preez had not yet fully recovered and, once on tour, Bryan Habana had to return home after an early injury.

Despite John being injured, as his second in command, I still had the option of not going on tour. But I decided to accept the challenge of captaining a young Bok team that was basically being written off before even boarding the aircraft for London. I found it an exciting prospect to be tour captain, as I would be more involved with decision-making off the field as well. On a tour, your role as captain also involves managing the players. And I would be the captain for the entire tour for the first time in my Springbok career. It had previously been said that I struggled with my game when I captained the Boks, but I knew I now had the opportunity to prove my critics wrong. In some respects, it wasn't that difficult to be the leader of a team at this level, as our plans were always well formulated and everybody knew what was expected of them.

But it soon proved to be a rather complicated task. After a tough season, a young Bok team would play in four challenging Tests. Over the past two years, Ireland had developed into a strong side, and not one of us in the squad had ever won a Test in Dublin. Wales had it in for us, and we would be in the same World Cup group as them at the 2011 RWC, which lent extra importance to the Test. And England at Twickenham was always a massive challenge, despite the fact that we had not lost against them since 2006. The only 'easy' game, according to the media, was against Scotland. We disagreed, as we'd had to dig deep to beat them in our last encounter in Edinburgh.

Gallo Images

I've always loved cricket. This picture was taken when the Bulls played against the Titans in 2008

My golf fourball: Danie Rossouw, Fourie du Preez and Pierre Spies, in November 2008

Gallo Images/ Beeld/Nardus Engelbrecht

A few lengths in the pool warm up the muscles

Dad Fai, Mom Hettie and my sister, Trudie Horn, celebrate the Bulls' second Super 14 title in 2009

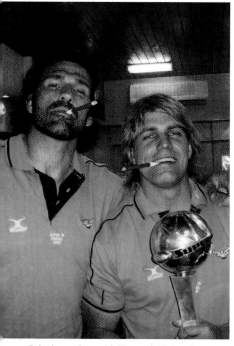

Enjoying a cigar with Wynand Olivier after we massacred the Chiefs in the Super 14 final in 2009 at Loftus Versfeld

With Monja, Kurt Darren and Dewald Potgieter (at back) at the Super 14 victory party at our house in 2009

Sharing the Super 14 trophy with Frans Ludeke and Heyneke Meyer. These two coaches played huge roles in my rugby career

Gallo Images/AFP

Lifting the Tri Nations Cup and Freedom Cup with John after we beat the All Blacks in Hamilton in 2009

Maria Ramos from ABSA presents Fourie du Preez and me with the 2009 Currie Cup trophy

Paul O'Connell, captain of the 2009 British & Irish Lions, was one of my strongest opponents over the years. This picture was taken after the third and last Test at Coca-Cola Park

At the end of 2009 I was appointed captain of the Barbarians, and we beat the All Blacks at Twickenham

I scored a try against the Wallabies at Newlands in 2009 after a well-placed grubber by none other than John Smit

I scored my seventh – and last – Test try on 13 November 2010 against Wales in Cardiff

The Super 14 final of 2010, against the Stormers at Orlando Stadium in Soweto, will always remain one of the highlights of my rugby career

Carl Fourie

The 'Orlando Bulls' win their third Super 14 title, in Soweto in 2010. In the picture below, our wives, girlfriends and children share in our joy

Carl Fourie

My 100th Test for the Boks, against the Wallabies at Loftus Versfeld on 28 August 2010, was a very special day

Jaime and Giselle were with me on the field when we sang the national anthem

Monja congratulating me on my 100th Test for South Africa. My Bulls teammate, Flip van der Merwe, is on the right

A relaxed day with the family at Sun City in 2010

This is what a dad looks like when his daughter decides to play with her mom's make-up

Having fun at home for Halloween 2010 with Giselle (in my arms), Jaime (in the golf cart) and my sister's children, Vian, Armand and Carla Horn. Far right is my mom, Hettie

With Springbok coach Peter de Villiers

Training hard

Jean Deysel and CJ van der Linde try to stop me during a Bok practice prior to my last Test in South Africa, against the All Blacks in Port Elizabeth

Gallo Images

Gallo Images/AFP

Line-outs were in my blood

Gallo Images

As part of the Blood Brothers programme, Bakkies and I visited the Red Cross Children's Hospital in Cape Town in 2011. I realised again how fortunate we are

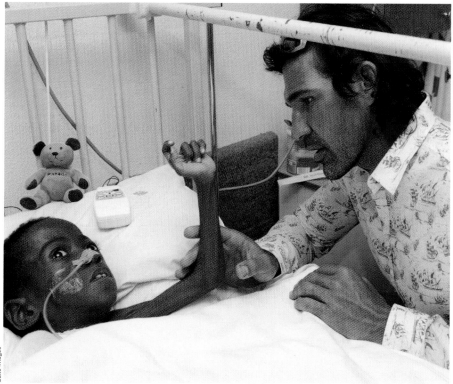

Our 'road trip' during the 2011 Rugby World Cup in New Zealand was a lot of fun. In the top picture I am with Danie Rossouw, John Smit, Jean de Villiers, Butch James and Fourie du Preez, and in the bottom picture I'm with Willem Alberts, Jean, Schalk Burger and a couple of Kiwi cops

Our first game at the 2011 Rugby World Cup was against Wales in Wellington, and we won a closely contested battle 17-16

Passing the ball in our game against Samoa, which I captained. We won 13-5

Our line-out functioned very well against Australia in the quarter-final, but it wasn't enough for us to win the game

Competing with James O'Connor for the high ball in the quarter-final. Australia won 11-9, shattering our World Cup dream

Shaking hands with New Zealand referee Bryce Lawrence after we'd lost against the Wallabies

My last farewell in the Bok jersey – 9 October 2011, Wellington, New Zealand

Yet I was full of confidence when we left South Africa. The selectors had picked a strong side, even though the usual complaints were lodged about certain inclusions in the team. Peter and I had discussed the team selections at length, and we also relied heavily on Jean de Villiers's opinion. Guys like Coenie Oosthuizen, Willem Alberts, Keegan Daniel, Patrick Lambie, Elton Jantjies and Lwazi Mvovo were rewarded for top performances during the Currie Cup season, while Deon Stegmann and Zane Kirchner were late replacements for the injured Juan de Jongh and Schalk Burger, respectively.

When Peter and I had spoken before the Currie Cup final, Zane and Deon were still being considered for selection, but when the squad was announced, their names were not read out. I assumed the selectors had not agreed with Peter's choices, and I left it there. But before the first Test against Ireland, the options at outside centre suddenly became an issue because of all the injuries. We tried to get Waylon Murray to join the squad, but he had problems with his passport, and Frans Steyn was unavailable due to club commitments in France. However, we were quite satisfied with the fact that Jean and Adi Jacobs would be ready to man the midfield. With Gio Aplon as our only fullback on tour, the decision was eventually made to include Zane as a replacement to maintain the balance in the side.

But then, during a practice session, we realised that Adi's fitness levels were not quite up to standard. He had only just returned from injury and was not 100 per cent ready for Test rugby. Our options were to play either Zane or Bryan Habana at outside centre, and in the end Zane got the nod because of his solid tackling abilities. Bryan was picked at left wing and Adi was on the bench.

Jean was nursing a groin injury, but it was not that serious and he could play. I was quite relieved, because I relied on him to help with the decision-making on the field, as I did in 2008 against the All Blacks in Dunedin. Nobody gave us half a chance against Ireland. It was a week after the Currie Cup final and the first Test that would be played in the new Aviva Stadium (the former Lansdowne Road). And Gert Smal was still part of Ireland's coaching team.

The Friday before the Test I called everyone together and gave those who wanted to say a few words the opportunity to speak. Bakkies Botha,

Juan Smith and Jean de Villiers basically said the same thing: 'It matters not who we play – we are the Springboks. A year before, we ruled rugby, so we know we have the ability, and now we have an opportunity to silence the critics and sceptics once and for all.'

The players were quite peeved at the time, as the media in Ireland were claiming that the Boks wouldn't be a match for the home side. But we were there as Springboks, despite our side being severely depleted because of injuries. Although it was unacceptable that the Boks were being shown so little respect, it did ignite the fire in our bellies.

So it was a very motivated Bok team that took on Ireland, albeit in awful weather. We played clinical rugby on a drenched field and executed our game plan just as we'd foreseen. Our tactical kicking and mauls were almost textbook-perfect, and our line-outs were much better than in 2009 – although it must be said Ireland were without the services of Paul O'Connell. We'd also changed our line-out calls to confound Gert Smal's charges, a ploy that worked.

But then we were once again subjected to some very odd substitutions, which gave Ireland the chance to fight back. I was completely astonished when the young Pat Lambie came on for Morné Steyn. As captain, I just couldn't understand why you would want to replace a flyhalf who had not missed in 41 attempts at goal before that Test. And this in wet conditions not conducive to running rugby!

Pat has tremendous talent and I expect he's going to play in many Tests for South Africa, but under adverse conditions in the Aviva Stadium, Morné should have stayed on the field. A few minutes after Pat came on, we were given a penalty, and I gave him the ball. Percy Montgomery, our kicking coach, wanted Ruan Pienaar to take the kick, but seeing that we hadn't decided before the kick-off who would take over the kicking responsibilities if Morné went off, and as the coaches showed so much confidence in Pat, I felt he should shoulder the responsibility. He was, after all, the place-kicker for the Sharks in the Currie Cup. Unfortunately, he missed his first penalty for the Boks, and it hadn't been a very difficult kick.

In the end we hung on and beat Ireland 23-21. For the first time in my life I could enjoy a Guinness as a winner in Dublin. It tasted better than ever. This victory gave me more satisfaction than usual, as our loss against Ireland a year earlier had probably been one of my worst Tests for South Africa. In that game we were punished in the line-outs, so I felt partly responsible for our defeat. I not only wanted to make amends for that Test, but for everything that had gone wrong during our Tri Nations campaign as well. It was, therefore, very satisfying to walk off the field in 2010 as captain of the winning team against Ireland and accept the Man of the Match award.

This was the perfect start to the tour, and it gave me some courage for the speech I had to make at the post-match function. My English might have improved a lot since my days as a country boy in Polokwane, but it was still intimidating to address a large group of people in my second language.

Then we were off to Cardiff for our second Test on tour. The Welsh Rugby Union had closed the roof over the Millennium Stadium, which indicated that the Red Dragons were planning to play attacking rugby, as they wouldn't have to worry about a waterlogged or muddy field. Their decision was not without merit, as shortly after half-time they were leading 20-9. I tried to keep the guys calm and told them, 'Just do what we do well.' There was no lack of motivation. We stuck to our game plan, stepped up the intensity a gear or two and fought back. Our ball retention improved, and this time the use of replacements – especially when Willem Alberts and François Hougaard arrived on the field – was more inspired.

So we found our groove and played much better in the second half. Willem, especially, made a massive difference, and he and I both scored tries in the second half. In the last 10 minutes, though, we had to defend as if our lives depended on it. The final score: South Africa 29, Wales 25.

With two victories in the bag, we travelled to Edinburgh, full of confidence for the Test against Scotland. But it was not to be the best of weeks. First I was criticised for having played too conservatively against Wales, and then Chiliboy Ralepelle and Bjorn Basson were sent home after testing positive for illegal substances, which led to a lot of confusion within the squad. The use of all supplements was stopped immediately. Even a Red Bull before the game was suddenly forbidden. It caught a lot of the players off guard, and I could just as easily have tested positive, as many of us take the same supplements.

I had seriously started considering the advantages of supplements at the end of the 2002 season, when I wanted to get rid of a few kilograms and change my training and eating habits. I then started using quite a lot of supplements, and where I used to have a slice of bread with peanut butter and syrup with my coffee, I now had a protein shake before going to gym. After training I'd have another energy drink, followed by a light lunch. The results were astounding: I lost 10 kilograms and reached my optimum weight, which since then has stayed between 106 and 108 kilograms.

Although the Bulls and Bok players were given supplements, Gary Botha and Gurthrö Steenkamp, for example, had an almost religious belief in their own pills and potions. I preferred to use the supplements we were given. Most players took protein shakes and so-called meal replacements to build muscle and control weight, while others also used carbohydrate and caffeine drinks to boost energy levels.

What you took had a lot to do with your personal preferences (or your superstitions!). Gary would sometimes concoct a potion for Bakkies before a big match, whereas I preferred a watered-down Red Bull and Juan Smith had a can of Coca-Cola. Nobody was ever forced to use supplements, but we had learnt that a game could be very taxing and punishing on the body, so it made sense to utilise any legal way there was to protect yourself.

Everything we were given underwent strict tests by our medical team to ensure that it was within the laws, and the suppliers of the supplements also had to indicate whether any illegal substances were contained in their products. Nobody wanted to take any chances. Therefore, it came as a complete shock when Chili and Bjorn tested positive. When Chili said his goodbyes, I could see that he was gutted. I couldn't imagine what he and Bjorn were going through. They had done nothing wrong, yet the possibility existed that they could be handed a two-year ban. However, we were pretty sure that they had taken the illegal substance for which they had tested positive – methylhexaneamine – unknowingly.

Two months later, a judicial committee found that there had been 'no fault' on the part of the players for testing positive for a banned stimulant, and they were allowed to play rugby again, but in the meantime all this drama happened in the week before our Test against Scotland at Murrayfield. The weather was also terrible – probably the worst conditions in which I'd ever played. It didn't rain during the week leading up to the Test, though it was bitterly cold. But of course, when we ran onto the field on the Saturday, the rain came down in buckets.

We got off to a decent start and were leading by 6-0, but then the referee, Stuart Dickinson, started penalising us. Oddly enough, the Bulls always enjoyed playing with Dickinson in charge, but it was often a different story with the Boks. In Edinburgh, he showed no mercy for us. We were penalised 13 times against the 9 penalties Scotland conceded.

I had never before thought that a ref was cheating us, but I have to admit that, on this occasion, the thought crossed my mind. I struggled to keep my emotions in check on the field. It was a sad day for me when we lost 17-21 to Scotland. Big defeats against the All Blacks and Wallabies hurt, but the Springboks should never surrender to the Scots.

For the third time in three weeks, Morné Steyn had been replaced early on in the game. Again, it made no sense. The rain was pouring down and running rugby was out of the question. We needed to keep possession and use tactical kicking, but instead our best kicker was replaced!

It was eerily quiet on the aircraft to London the next day. We were all devastated. In the meantime, the International Rugby Board had announced their candidates for the Player of the Year award, and my name was on the list. I did not expect this honour at all, especially since the Boks had had such a poor season. The other candidates were All Blacks Richie McCaw and Mils Muliaina, Wallabies David Pocock and Kurtley Beale, and France's Imanol Harinordoquy. McCaw got the award in the end.

It was a massive honour to be nominated for a second time, and the fact that McCaw won the award did not bother me at all, because I didn't really play for awards. It wasn't the right time to celebrate my nomination either, as we had just lost a Test and were preparing to take on England at Twickenham.

On our arrival in London, the media informed us that the home side would completely overpower us. Naturally. After all, they had notched up a magnificent victory over the Wallabies the previous weekend while we had lost against Scotland. As had happened so many times in the previous few years, a heated debate ensued at our Monday team meeting. Present were Peter de Villiers, his assistants, Dick Muir and Gary Gold, Os du Randt, our scrumming coach, and Bismarck du Plessis, Juan Smith, Pierre Spies, Ruan Pienaar, Morné Steyn, Jean de Villiers and me.

This Bok group had been together for almost three years, but we still had to hear how some members of the management team described our game plan as 'too conservative'. This really upset me. After almost three full seasons, we *still* could not agree on the best game plan for the Boks.

We discussed the matter at length, but failed to reach an agreement. As soon as Gary suggested one strategy, Dick suggested another. Eventually I got up, walked to the front and said: 'We have to decide now what we must do and how we are going to play. The past three seasons we've been playing direct rugby from good field positions. If it seems like a good option to play the ball wide, then we'll do it, even in our own 22-metre area. But we never take unnecessary chances. We do *not* play high-risk rugby. That is not how we, the Springboks, play.'

As nobody disagreed with me, we finally managed to reach a consensus: we don't play like the All Blacks. We don't play like the Wallabies. We play Springbok rugby. Peter, too, was adamant: there was only one way we could beat the English, and that was by playing direct rugby without frills and flourishes. We needed to take England on physically. I believe this meeting made a huge difference to the final result.

We were in it boots-and-all after the kick-off and tackled England into oblivion. We knew what our strong points were, and we stuck to them. The plan was to break them down up front, which was exactly what we did. I broke three ribs early on in the game when their young wing sensation, Chris Ashton, tried to bring me down, but he was the one who had to leave the field. Despite the pain, I carried on. I wouldn't miss this Test for anything in the world, I said to myself.

I couldn't help grin every time the Boks floored the England players. Early in the game, Juan Smith – with Bakkies on his back – crash-tackled the England captain, Lewis Moody, into the ground. England's scrum was considered to be one of their most dangerous weapons, but Beast, Bismarck and Jannie taught them a lesson in the front row.

England might have overpowered Australia, but on that day at Twickenham, the Boks defeated them 21-11 thanks to solid Springbok rugby. It was by far our best performance of 2010. We were good against France, but against England we were brilliant. I just hoped that with this performance, we would finally lay to rest any doubts about how we were going to defend the Webb Ellis Cup in New Zealand in 2011.

After the match, Pierre Spies and I were excused from the Boks' last game on tour, against the Barbarians, and returned to South Africa. The injured Zane Kirchner joined us. More withdrawals followed: the Du Plessis brothers, Jannie and Bismarck, were both injured. Peter eventually had to send for replacements from South Africa. A very young Bok team, therefore, took on a tough Barbarians side, and although they lost 20-26, the team did well under the circumstances.

Back in South Africa, the consensus was that I had finally proved that I was ready to take over the reins as Bok captain, and that John Smit should retire. Although it had been a big honour to captain the team, I arrived home convinced that John was the man who should lead us in New Zealand – if he was fit and on form. Of course, the same criteria of fitness and form applied to every other player who wanted to go to the World Cup.

Someone I really sympathised with on our tour was Morné Steyn. He had apparently cemented his place as Bok flyhalf in 2009 and had played good rugby in 2010. His accurate place-kicking was indispensable, but week in and week out the media were harping on about how Pat Lambie deserved to be picked above him. Peter, however, assured Morné that he had faith in him and that he would not leave him out of the team.

Pat is very talented and has a bright future. On the tour, he was one of the youngsters who staked his claim. Others who seized the opportunity were Lwazi Mvovo, Elton Jantjies and Willem Alberts. Earlier in the season, players like Gio Aplon, Juan de Jongh, François Hougaard and Flip van der Merwe also showed their Springbok mettle.

But the youngster who had impressed me the most was 'Vic'. No, not Matfield, but Willem Alberts – 'Vic' being the burly loose forward's nickname. Every time he came on as a replacement, he played magnificently. He always gave it all he had, whether with the ball in hand or in making a tackle, and was often rewarded with tries. For this reason, some rugby writers criticised the team selections, saying that Willem, rather than Deon Stegmann, should have been in the starting line-up.

However, right from the outset of the tour we had decided to start every Test match with a recognised ball-chaser. The balance in the starting line-up would not have been right with both Willem and Juan Smith as flank forwards.

To win the World Cup, you need 30 good players, and many of the guys mentioned here showed that they would not let the team down, ever. With so many talented players in South Africa, we could look forward to the following year's World Cup, even if we didn't have the best season in the lead-up to the competition.

Despite our defeat against Scotland, I enjoyed the tour tremendously. Nobody thought we'd do well, but we did well nevertheless. And the tour had been a great success in terms of developing new talent: many youngsters had grabbed the opportunity to play for the Boks with both hands.

18

Not so 'super'

It surprised me like a thief in the night. In my earlier days as a player, the older guys always told us how quickly one's career is over, before one even realises it. At the time, I used to think that they were a bit sentimental, but then I was suddenly faced with the 2011 season: the 'beginning of the end' for me.

If I got a rand each time someone asked me what I still wanted to achieve in my rugby career, it wouldn't have been necessary for me to take my golf buddies' money when we played! I had helped the Boks win the World Cup, I had experienced a series victory over the British & Irish Lions, I had drunk champagne (and beer) from the Tri Nations cup, lifted the Super 14 trophy three times and taken the Currie Cup home to Loftus Versfeld as many times.

By the start of 2011, I'd played in 105 Tests for South Africa, 101 Super Rugby games for the Bulls and 52 matches for the Blue Bulls. What *else* could I possibly achieve?

Well, it would've been nice to be crowned Super Rugby kings for a fourth time … And another Tri Nations title would also have been welcome … And no team has ever defended the World Cup successfully.

'Victor, don't you dream of leading the Boks at the Rugby World Cup?' I am often asked. On the eve of my last season, leading the Boks in the Rugby World Cup was by no means my biggest goal. All I wanted to do in my final season as a professional rugby player was to give my best for the Bulls one more time and help them win the new Super Rugby series (two changes were made in 2011, with the Melbourne

Rebels being added as the 15th team, and the format of the competition now consisting of 'conferences'). I also wanted to play a part in the Springboks' campaign to retain the William Webb Ellis Cup.

But before I could entertain that dream, the Super 15 series was upon us. It was my 12th Super Rugby season and I wanted to ensure that it ended on a high note. Since 1999, I'd only ever missed the 2008 series, when I played for Toulon. Our preparation was, as ever, excellent. The guys had worked hard at the pre-season training camp in George in December and we continued putting in the hard graft in Pretoria in January.

To assess whether we didn't overindulge and relax too much over the festive season, we started 2011 by doing the so-called bleep test, as well as a test in which we had to jump up and down repeatedly. I wanted to be the fittest lock in the group, and doing well in these tests would prove it. No lock, no matter how young he was, would beat me. If you want to be the best, you have to work the hardest. Champions train when the others rest.

I had trained hard during the December break and had even run a few kilometres on Christmas Day – something I'd become used to doing. At 33, I was the oldest in the team, but I was certainly no has-been. I beat all the other locks in the jump test and ran further than any player in the squad in the bleep test. I was ready for the season.

But despite being so fit, I had a problem. I made no physical contact at all during training sessions, and most of my teammates thought it was because of the broken ribs I had suffered a few months earlier in the Test against England at Twickenham. But it had nothing to do with that injury.

No, I had a hairline fracture on one of my cervical vertebrae. During the November tour my neck had bothered me constantly during games, and in the end I even struggled during my workouts in the gym, as my left arm had grown weak and was hurting like hell. Before the first Test against England I underwent a scan, but they couldn't find anything amiss.

In January I made an appointment with Dr Mark Velleman, a radiologist, and he spotted the hairline fracture in my neck. He estimated that the rest period between the England Test and the Bulls' first Super

15 game would be enough time for the injury to heal, but a week before our first warm-up game, against the Mpumalanga Pumas, a scan revealed that the fracture was still there. However, I was told that it would not pose a threat if I played.

Injuries were nothing new to me. Since 2006 I'd played without a posterior cruciate ligament in my right knee, just for starters. But you don't take any chances with a neck injury. I was really worried and had trouble sleeping. If I was told that I had to stop playing, I would've done so immediately, as my well-being and that of my family was more important than rugby. But damn it, I was looking forward to the season!

After examining me again, Dr Velleman could also not hide his concern. He'd expected the fracture to have healed by that stage, so he decided to consult his colleagues on the matter. Some days later, when I had my follow-up examination, he looked more confident. A few of the specialists had suggested that I retire from rugby, but others had concluded that it was probably an old injury and not too serious. I had another scan, which showed that things were looking a lot better. Dr Velleman gave me the go-ahead to play again, but it was decided that I would not play in the warm-up game. My first Super 15 match of the season, against the Lions, was just around the corner anyway.

For the game against the Pumas, I joined the coaching team in their box at the stunning new Mbombela Stadium in Nelspruit. What an experience! I'd always dreamt of coaching after retiring. Frans Ludeke was attending his brother-in-law's wedding that weekend, so I watched the game with Pieter Rossouw and John McFarland. I found it interesting to see how the coaches followed the game, hear the messages they relayed to the field and pick up what aspects of play they were assessing.

I'd already started talking to the Bulls and to Frans about coaching in 2012, and they suggested that I help coach the Vodacom Blue Bulls team to start with before moving on to coaching at Currie Cup level. With me involved, Frans could focus on coaching the Super Rugby team, plus he would guide me and show me the ropes at the same time. Our discussions progressed to the point where the board of directors only had to approve my salary.

But back to Super Rugby. Before the start of the season, the media made a big commotion about the 'new, improved' Lions. The Golden Lions had struggled for years, but in 2010 they had been a considerable force in the Currie Cup competition. Two investors had bought a 49.9 per cent share in the union and rumours abounded about large amounts of money being spent on contracting top players. They had also appointed John Mitchell, former All Black coach, as the new Lions coach. He would have a huge impact.

The big to-do the press was making about the Lions inspired us to start the season with a bang. We kicked off the game on the same note we had ended the 2010 season on, and were leading 24-5 at half-time. The second half, however, was a different story. We simply couldn't get our hands on the ball, with the Lions retaining all the possession. It was a brave fightback by them, but in the end we had just enough left in the tank to win 24-20.

Our second game was against the Cheetahs in Bloemfontein. I hadn't been in a Bulls team that lost against the Free Staters since the Currie Cup final in 2005, and I was not going to relinquish that record now. But we started the match as we'd finished against the Lions. We had feet like lead, made far too many mistakes and gave away loads of possession. With 20 minutes to go, we were trailing 8-23.

Most of our fans must have thought that it was tickets for us, but I never stopped believing in my team and told the guys that we could still fight back. The Bulls can draw on their resources when in desperate need, which was exactly what happened that night in Bloemfontein. Danie Rossouw and Fourie du Preez both scored, and we eventually won 25-23. It was one of those very special team efforts that only this group of players could achieve.

But even though we had won the first two games, something was wrong. Somehow, we couldn't dominate our opponents. In the past we would have won games like these quite easily *and* would have picked up bonus points for four tries, but now we had to fight to the last just to squeeze a victory out of the game. I was concerned for my team. I felt that we were not our usual selves. At our customary Bible-study session before the captain's run on the Friday, we decided that we had to stay positive. I also spoke to each player individually to find out where he thought the Bulls were going wrong.

According to Pierre Spies, we were on track and there was nothing amiss, whereas Dewald Potgieter felt that we put ourselves under too much pressure. Fourie du Preez and Derick Kuün agreed that we weren't playing to our abilities, but said that we had to believe in what we were doing and simply try harder.

Instead of reprimanding the team for their rather lacklustre performances in the first two games, I told them to forget about the pressure, play to the standard they knew they could play and to just enjoy their rugby. Unfortunately, this advice turned out not to be very useful.

In the meantime, the Highlanders had arrived in Pretoria. In the past few seasons they had been New Zealand's worst Super Rugby team, but after two convincing victories over the Hurricanes and Chiefs, it was clear that their new coach, Jamie Joseph, was turning things around.

The day after my team talk, we lost in front of our home supporters for the first time since April 2008. For me, it had been even longer – my first home defeat since February 2007, when the Western Force beat us. We had won 20 consecutive home games, including the two play-off matches in Soweto in 2010 – the second-to-best home record in Super Rugby history.

We were beaten by a team that was more desperate than us for victory. They killed us at the breakdowns, and we missed too many tackles and were unable to build any momentum. It didn't help that Stuart Dickinson was the referee either. For the second time in three months I felt that he had it in for us, as had been the case when the Boks lost to Scotland in Edinburgh in November 2010. The Highlanders eventually won 35-28.

It was heart-rending to walk into the changing room as the losing team. Afterwards, I couldn't sleep for two nights. Time and again I woke up and replayed the game in my head. What could we have done differently? How could we have avoided the defeat?

On the Monday, Frans gave everyone the chance to speak. Many of the junior players expressed their concern about the future – what was going to happen in 2012, when most of the experienced players wouldn't be there any more? But a few of the senior guys were perhaps too worried about what was going to happen the next year. At least 20 of the players were still negotiating their contracts with the Bulls, a process that can be stressful. As some of them were unable to reach an agreement with the union, it created a great deal of frustration.

After everyone had said their bit, we decided that we simply had to knuckle down and focus on the next game. Although it would be tough to raise our game against a good team like the Stormers, we had no alternative. And as usual when South Africa's rugby giants from the north and south take each other on, Loftus was packed to the brim.

On 19 March 2011, I felt for the first time the pain of a team completely losing faith in itself. We made mistakes we'd never made before and conceded way too many penalties. In the end, we lost 13-23 – the first time since 2005 that I'd played in a Bulls side that lost against the Stormers or Western Province. The team was gutted. How on earth were we going to set this ship on the right course again? And besides that, the Lions were on their way to Loftus. They were by no means as easy to beat as in previous seasons, plus our confidence had taken a huge blow.

The Monday evening after practice, Monja, Jaime, Giselle and I had a picnic next to the dam in Silver Lakes, where we stay. Then Frans phoned. He and Johann van Graan, our forward coach, felt that we should take a break from practice the next day and have a team-building exercise instead to lift the spirit of the squad. I agreed. A training session wouldn't help us much. The problem was largely in our heads.

The next day everyone duly arrived at practice, but instead of tackle bags, cooler boxes and a bus awaited them. Wynie Strydom herded everyone onto the bus and off we went to Leriba Lodge in Centurion, where we had a braai and a bit of a party, and where we reconnected as Bulls, teammates and friends. This team-building exercise was just like in the old days and desperately needed. After the get-together, the rest of the week went much better, and we were sharp and focused in our training sessions.

The Friday morning before the Lions game, Pierre Spies, Morné Steyn and I had a photo session for Canterbury, posing in the new Bok jersey as well as in the one we'd be wearing during the World Cup. Up until then a lot had been said and written about the new jerseys, especially about the Springbok emblem that had been moved to the left sleeve, with only the Protea and the World Cup and Canterbury logos remaining on the chest.

Although we knew that there would be a new design, we were still shocked to see how small the Bok emblem on the sleeve actually was. Ask any player: the Springbok emblem was and always will be very special. It is very close to all our hearts. But at the same time, it's an honour just to wear the jersey. Once you put it on, you are representing South Africa, regardless of whether the springbok is on the chest or the sleeve.

The game against the Lions was as tough as they come. Although we controlled the run of play, they never gave up and fought back relentlessly. Then it happened – every rugby player's biggest nightmare. Late in the first half I started seeing stars in the corner of my eye, which was strange, as I hadn't even had a hard knock or a bump.

During half-time, our team doctor, Org Strauss, held an ice pack to my head, which helped a bit, and I could start the second half. With about 20 minutes to go in the game, I tackled Lions flanker Derick Minnie and got a hard knock against the head. I immediately thought that I had injured my neck again. I was disorientated, had a massive headache and felt nauseous. But I didn't want to leave the field, and I carried on playing.

In the dying moments of the game we received an attacking penalty, and I decided we should go for a line-out. We were leading by seven points and had already scored three tries, so a fourth would result in a bonus point. Taking the line-out was a big risk, because if we lost possession, the Lions would surely launch a counter-attack and could possibly score, which meant that our season would be in serious trouble after just five games.

However, we won the ball, but we just couldn't penetrate their defence. At some stage I decided that enough was enough. Although we were on their try line, I picked up the ball from a loose scrum and kicked it into touch, sealing a 30-23 victory. Had it been the right decision? I still don't know.

Maybe the headache had made the decision for me. Maybe I would have tried to score a try if I could have focused properly. After the game my head and neck were aching so badly that I asked Fourie du Preez to do the post-match TV interview. The pain was almost unbearable, but the only thing that mattered was that we were back on the winning path.

Later Org explained that the pain in my head had been caused by the bump I'd got. He gave me an injection and a handful of pills. The nausea disappeared, but the headache continued for a few days. I avoided physical contact during training, and later in the week the headache was mercifully gone.

With three victories in five games, the tour to New Zealand and Australia loomed like a mountain, even though we were in high spirits after beating the Lions. Funny how just one victory can lift a team's morale! As had become custom, we only departed on tour the Tuesday before the first game. We landed in Auckland, where we had a stopover, shortly before midnight on Wednesday. To alleviate the effects of jet lag, we only got up at 2 p.m. the following afternoon and then departed for Napier, where we would face the Hurricanes.

We had fond memories of Napier. It was, after all, where the Bulls (and I) had first tasted a Super Rugby victory overseas (in 2003, against the selfsame 'Canes, the score 46-34). But, like eight years ago, we knew it would take a momentous effort to beat them at home.

McLean Park, Napier's small stadium, provides seating for more or less 20 000 spectators. The pavilions are set low, which means that the (almost ever-present) wind often plays havoc. Fourie and I shared a little superstition regarding the wind, believing that on away games we should start with the wind at our backs. Luckily, I won the toss, so the decision was made to play with the wind for the first 40 minutes.

Morné and Fourie dictated play with clever tactical kicking, using the wind to our advantage, while the forwards were going in boots and all, just like in the good old days. Fourie had also decided beforehand that it would be vitally important to keep the scoreboard ticking over. Twice he shouted at Morné to take a drop kick. Both times the ball sailed over the crossbar. At half-time, we were leading 15-3.

The second 40, against the wind, was a different story altogether. Defence, defence and more defence – we didn't concentrate on anything else. Although the Hurricanes fought back with the wind from behind, we clinched the deal when Wynand Olivier broke their line and sent François Hougaard over for a try. The final score: 26-14.

It had been a team effort, but one guy stood out above the rest: new loosehead prop Dean Greyling, who had to fill the shoes of our injured

Bok loosehead, Gurthrö Steenkamp. Both Dean and hooker Gary Botha were pretty emotional after the game.

The next morning we were up early to tackle Cape Kidnappers. It's an unusual name for a golf course, but then Cape Kidnappers is no ordinary golf course. It is one of the most spectacular golf courses in the world and certainly one of the most beautiful I've ever played. Situated near Hawke's Bay on the east coast of North Island, it is about a four-hour drive from Wellington.

We only had time for nine holes, which in hindsight was a blessing, seeing that we were still aching from the previous day's game. Fourie and Jaco Pretorius were both nursing shoulder injuries and I had a buttock spasm. I looked like an old man getting in and out of the golf cart and had trouble retrieving the ball from the cup every time I sank a putt. Jaco van der Westhuyzen joked that struggling on the golf course was the price we had to pay for our successes in Super Rugby. After a victory like the one we'd had against the Hurricanes, way down in New Zealand with our backs against the wall, you just took the knocks and bruises and moved on. Oh, and by the way, I also took Fourie's money in the golf!

Our base in Queenstown on South Island for our next game, against the Crusaders, is without a doubt the most beautiful place in New Zealand and heaven on earth for any adventure seeker.

An invitation wasn't necessary to revisit the Red Rock Bar & Café, where we'd had our famous impromptu team-building day in 2007. We even sat in the same corner as before, and we chatted about what we'd achieved up till then and what we could expect from the game against the Crusaders, which had been moved to Timaru, a small town on the east coast of South Island, after a devastating earthquake had hit Christchurch a few weeks earlier.

Nobody among us had ever won a game against the Crusaders in New Zealand, and it was one of our big goals to beat them on tour. We worked hard that week, and on the Wednesday Johann van Graan showed us a video recording of the 2010 Super 14 semi-final, when we'd beaten the 'Saders in Soweto. I would've liked for the guys to run onto the field to smash the Crusaders right after watching the recording, but unfortunately we had to wait a few more days.

We had the Thursday free, and the golfers among us enjoyed a round while the hunters took aim at some red stags. The biggest excitement, however, was generated by the opportunity to go parachuting. Unfortunately, it meant that a few guys had to keep their diet under control, as the maximum weight for prospective jumpers is 105 kilograms. Pierre Spies was very concerned about his food intake, as he was bordering on 105 kilograms, and it was quite funny to see him so worried. I think he even cut down on his meat-eating so that he could jump!

Eventually the wind had the final say – no parachuting on the day. Only Frans Ludeke seemed pleased. He didn't want to deny the guys a fun day out, but as a coach he probably didn't consider parachuting a guaranteed injury-free activity.

Bakkies Botha, Deon Stegmann and Dean Greyling went hunting and came back smiling from ear to ear that evening. Bakkies had shot a 15-pointer, and Wors (our nickname for Dean) a 20-pointer. (The number refers to the 'points' on the horns of the target.)

As far as the golf was concerned, it also allowed for a few surprises, as the Hills, where we played, turned out to be even more beautiful than Cape Kidnappers, and I ran into an old friend, none other than my first Super Rugby coach, Laurie Mains. We had time for a cup of coffee and a good rugby chat. Laurie said that the 2010 Boks reminded him of the 2009 All Blacks – a brilliant team who thought they could just pitch up at the ground and they would win. And Laurie said, 'When you are the top team, your opponents harbour a certain amount of hatred towards you – they want to be where you are.' Their envy actually works to their 'advantage', as it provides the additional emotion they need to dethrone you. According to Laurie …

I enjoyed my chat with him. When I was 22 and he was coaching the Cats, I was really scared of him, but he has always been a rugby man through and through and we share a passion for the oval-shaped ball. Very few people's lives completely revolve around rugby, but Laurie's does.

We travelled to Timaru by bus the day before the game to play at the Alpine Energy Stadium, which could seat only 12 000 spectators. We had to share the bathroom, which had only one toilet, with the Crusaders – an odd situation and not something I'd experienced before. On the field, the situation wasn't any better. We simply didn't gel as a team. Although we managed to turn around possession a few times in the first 10 minutes, we just couldn't get going. Still, it didn't feel as if the Crusaders had us under pressure. Then came the turning point. Sonny Bill Williams received the ball from a scrum on our 10-metre line, cut inside, Wynand Olivier slipped and 'SBW' slipped through the gap to score.

Later we lost a line-out ball when Bakkies got the call wrong, which frustrated me no end, as we were much better than the Crusaders at this facet of the game. Those two mistakes gave the Crusaders the momentum and led to our eventual downfall. At half-time we were trailing 0-14, but I still thought we had a chance.

At the kick-off for the second half I lost the ball in a tackle; they kept possession for a few phases and scored again. The die had been cast. This may sound odd, but I was really proud of the team – the guys didn't give up. The Crusaders were able to score their third try only late in the game and we made mistakes at critical times, which cost us dearly. Their goal-kicker, Matt Berquist, missed three conversions but added four penalties. Morné missed his only shot at goal. The final score: 27-0. You could hear a pin drop in the changing room afterwards.

I had started seeing stars in the corner of my eye again late in the game and felt very odd. My head was aching like hell, and on our way back to the hotel, I asked Fourie to take over the team-talk duties. It's always interesting how outsiders 'analyse' a team's performance. When you win, it's thanks to the senior players and the way you put your opponent under pressure with a tried-and-tested game plan. When you lose, the senior players are too old and the game plan obsolete. You can't win!

In Brisbane the Reds awaited us. As mentioned, our success rate in that city is rather abysmal, to put it mildly. And the Reds were not the team they had been a few seasons ago by a long chalk. They were now the best Australian side in the competition and serious contenders for the Super 15 title – it was hard to believe after we'd beaten them hands down in 2007.

As had become our custom, we stayed on the Gold Coast, and the Monday after the 'Saders game we decided to swap the bump and grind of field practice for a spinning class at the gym ... an interesting experience, seeing how none of the Bulls players was a Lance Armstrong or Miguel Indurain. There were some funny comments made about a few of the players' calf muscles and we had a good laugh while sweating away. The rest of our preparations also went well and I thought that we might be ready to shake off the humiliating defeat we had suffered in Timaru.

But then again, as soon as a team starts losing, doubt starts creeping in. You can fight it tooth and nail, but you can't escape it. I thought I had played really great rugby in 2010, probably the best of my career, but it was said that I was past my prime. It was a different scenario in 2011. Although statistics showed that I was maintaining a good work rate, I wasn't always 100 per cent satisfied with my game. I was making mistakes I didn't make in the past.

To top it all, my body was feeling the strain. By the time we were ready to take on the Reds, I'd been struggling with headaches for a month and also had a stiff buttock muscle that had been bothering me for two weeks. Were the critics right? Was I past my best? And what could we do to get this team back on the victory road again? Were we doing all we could? Those questions kept me awake at night.

At least I could use all the nonsense milling around in my head in my team talk before the game. I hardly ever get emotional and I don't do the *Braveheart* speech before games, but before the kick-off to the Reds match, the situation required more from me. We formed a circle in the centre of the changing room and Frans Ludeke said his piece first, followed by our vice-captain, Wynand Olivier. I then asked the guys to sit down again. A minute before kick-off, our team manager, Wynie Strydom, gave us the call. I walked to the middle of the room. I was very emotional, but I managed to get these words out: 'This week was the first time in my entire professional career that I doubted my own abilities. But worse, it was the first time in four years I doubted this team.' My voice shook. 'This team, which had won seven games on the trot in 2007 and had to beat the Reds by more than 70 points to finish second on the log; this team, which had won the 2009 final with a record score; this team, which last year was given no chance at all but still won the final in Soweto.

'The time for doubt is over. I believe with everything I possess in each one of you sitting in this changing room. But nothing will happen by itself. We have to decide whether we want to change things. If you feel you're ready to make that happen, get up and join me in this circle. If not, stay where you are. I'd rather run onto that field with half a team of dedicated men than with 15 who aren't fully committed.'

Everyone stood up, and Bakkies shouted from the back: 'Ja, let's go!'

Although we were playing a very good Reds team, we were on the attack with 15 minutes to go. Zane Kirchner broke the Reds' line and passed the ball to Bjorn Basson on his inside, but one of the Reds knocked the ball down and kicked it downfield. What was to be a sure try for us turned out to be a try for their winger Digby Ioane and was a turnaround of 14 points. In the end, we lost 30-39.

I felt better about my game afterwards, although I was peeved that I'd missed a tackle on James Horwill that had led to his try. But at least I knew the old Bulls were back. We had played with great dedication and had executed our moves perfectly, which, in my eyes, made us a very special group of players.

After the game I was interviewed for TV, and as I started making my way back into the stadium afterwards, I saw the whole team waiting for me on the field. Usually the guys retreat to the changing room while the captain is being interviewed. My head was aching dreadfully, but this was a very special moment and a gesture I'll never forget.

No one said a word in the changing room. We showered and headed back to the hotel for dinner. There, Frans said a few words, and then I gave Fourie a chance to talk. The previous day, Fourie had read an article in one of the local papers about Scott Prince, a legendary Australian rugby-league player and one of the stars of the Gold Coast Titans. The situation Scott described in the article was similar to ours and occurred when he was playing for the Wests Tigers in 2005. The team was having a terrible season, having won only one out of five games, and they now had to face the mighty Brisbane Broncos. At half-time they were in deep trouble, but their coach, Tim Sheens, said that the time had come to turn the season around. He inspired them to such an extent that they won the game in the end, made the play-offs and were later crowned national champions.

'Let's do what they did,' Fourie said. 'Ja, we lost against the Reds, but we played much better and I believe that we, too, can turn this season around.'

Our next game was against the Western Force in Perth. We still had a chance of winning the South African division of the competition, but only if we beat the Force. I sat on the sideline during training that week, as the headaches and muscle spasm were giving me a hard time. The team doctor suggested that I start the game from the bench, but that was out of the question. I wanted to be part of the effort to turn things around.

I did, however, insist on a head and neck scan, as, back in South Africa, Monja and my parents were getting really worried about the constant headaches. Jaco Pretorius – who'd also been suffering from neck pain – and I both underwent a scan. It's funny how your mind starts playing tricks on you while you're lying there. I thought: What if I have another neck fracture and have to stop playing rugby? Or worse: What if they find a brain tumour, as had happened to Bok flanker Ruben Kruger? Luckily, the scan revealed nothing unusual, except that the old neck fracture had almost completely healed. Although the headaches persisted, at least I felt more reassured.

We scored two tries early in the game against the Force, which was just the start we'd had in mind. Our third try was disallowed because of an alleged forward pass. But then our discipline started letting us down and James O'Connor slotted one penalty after the other. With 20 minutes to go, we were still leading, but only by 18 points to 12.

However, O'Connor soon slotted another two penalties and Cameron Shepherd scored a try. We had lost again: 21-26.

Although we had never been under pressure and had played decent-enough rugby, we still lost. I just couldn't understand it. In the changing room afterwards I looked at the guys around me ... all brilliant players, all still hungry for success, but on the field things just weren't coming together.

Back at the hotel, I invited anyone who wanted to speak to say a few words. Pierre suggested that we work even harder. That's the way he is: he knows no 'bodily boundaries' and will simply train harder and harder, but I didn't think our problem lay there. Gary Botha took a leaf out of Heyneke Meyer's book and said that we should each give something of ourselves if we wanted to turn the ship around, but it had to be something special, more than our usual effort. Gary was one of our most loyal team members – someone who was willing to die for the team.

Quite a few of the guys mentioned how much they had enjoyed the tour, despite it being a failure on the scoreboard. For those of us playing in our last season for the Bulls – Bakkies, Fourie, Danie Rossouw and I – it was a terrible end to our overseas campaign. When it was my turn to speak, I said that even though we had lost the last three games, I wouldn't want to play for any other team than the Bulls. And then my emotions got the better of me. I couldn't say another word.

**

It had been a tough couple of weeks, but I was convinced that we would still undertake one more tour as a team – in the play-off games. Seven games remained and each one would be a 'final', but we could still make it. According to the competition's new structure, we had to win three away games (besides the seven 'finals') if we wanted to win the competition.

It was good to head home, but along with the pleasure of seeing my wife and two beautiful daughters, there was also the pain of having to face the local media and our disgruntled supporters. I knew the first week in Pretoria would be tough. Hard questions would be asked. People would whisper as they walked past us and we would probably all be called a variety of rude names behind our backs. But I was nevertheless proud of my team.

Giving up was not an option. As with a gladiator in the arena, death might be imminent, but the fight had to continue. However, I'd lie if I said that it didn't hurt to hear everyone writing us off and accusing us of not having tried our hardest. Supporters don't realise that failing on the field upsets us even more than it does them. Rugby, after all, is my life.

When I walked through the gates at OR Tambo's international arrivals, Jaime came running towards me, with Giselle following a few steps behind. My heart just crumbled. The pain was gone. Monja, with her beautiful long legs, wasn't far behind our daughters, and I immediately noticed that she had a sexy new hairstyle.

Three losses in four tour matches didn't upset my family; they were behind me all the way, which made me the happiest person in the world. We weren't even on the R21 on our way to Pretoria when my parents phoned to say that they loved and supported me. Yes, rugby might have seemed to be everything to me, but even then, nothing was more important than my family.

Despite the defeats on tour, I still believed we could win the tournament. After all, Frans's motto was 'the best is still to come'. While we were preparing for the game against the Chiefs at Loftus, I reckoned that now was a good time for the 'best' to arrive. No more talking; the only way out of this mess was to set an example. As Pierre had said, 'Push yourself further than ever before'; as Gary had said, 'Contribute something special'; as Fourie had said, 'Keep on believing'.

Fortunately, the headaches were not as bad as before, but somewhere along the line I hurt a sural (calf) muscle. It's probably ironic that I suffered this particular injury, as I wasn't exactly known for my massive calves. After all, my nickname is 'Kiewiet' (the skinny-legged plover). Despite my injury problems, our preparations went according to plan, and it wasn't long before one of the most important Saturdays of my career, 30 April 2011, was upon me. Usually the squad got together at Loftus about four hours before kick-off, when we would do a few stretching exercises and have lunch before some of the guys rested. Then we'd all get together in the changing room for a final team talk about 75 minutes before kick-off. But on this occasion Bjorn Basson was nowhere to be seen.

Bjorn had played excellent rugby for Griquas in 2010, even breaking the old Currie Cup record for scoring the most tries in a season. He fitted perfectly into our game plan and was one of our rising stars. But that afternoon, nobody knew where he was. And after a few unanswered calls to Bjorn's cellphone, Frans – clearly peeved – gave up and started his team talk. We later learnt that Bjorn had been late because he'd left his entrance ticket at home and the security guards at the gate wouldn't let him in without it. He was summarily dropped and Frans told Akona Ndungane to wear the No. 11 jersey. Frans, usually a calm, relaxed man, was shaking with anger.

'There's no more room for mistakes,' he grumbled. 'We've had our chances. Coming late is not an option. It's unacceptable.'

I don't know whether the situation in the changing room had a negative influence on us, but after 20 minutes we were in trouble and trailed 6-20. Most teams would probably have given up there and then and written off the 2011 season, but the Bulls refused to roll over and die. As we stood behind the posts waiting for the Chiefs to convert their second try, I said to the guys that we simply had to score before half-time. A few minutes later, Wynand Olivier crashed over for a five-pointer, and we could take the break with the score at 13-20. The try lifted our spirits, and in the first eight minutes of the second half, we scored three more tries. It was the best rugby we'd played that year. We were on a winning course again (43-27) and it felt as if a massive weight had been lifted from our shoulders.

Although everyone was happy, I was deeply concerned, because my back was killing me. But I didn't have time to worry, as the next day I had to be in Cape Town for a Springbok meeting. During the first session of the meeting, Peter de Villiers called John Smit and me to the front and announced that we would be the Bok captain and vice-captain, respectively, for the World Cup tournament. I didn't expect Peter to make the announcement then, but it didn't come as a complete surprise either, as he'd discussed his plans with us before. And besides that, John and I had been the official captain and vice-captain for the past few seasons, so no surprises there.

The Springbok squad had never come together in the middle of the Super Rugby season before, and it was an interesting experience, as we still had to play against each other for a place in the knockout rounds of the Super 15 and the atmosphere was a little tense at the beginning. But the guys started relaxing soon enough and we ended up enjoying the get-together, especially the 'old hands' like John, Jean de Villiers, Mossie Fourie, Schalk Burger, Fourie, Pierre and me. As friends and teammates, we'd forged a special bond since 2004.

***

As if matters weren't bad enough in Bulls rugby, a whole lot of non-sense was happening off the field as well. The Wednesday after the Bok camp, during our Blood Brothers golf day at Zimbali in Durban, I was told that a Gauteng tabloid was going to break a 'big story' about my alleged affair with Gary Botha's wife, Anrike. At that stage the Bothas were in the middle of a divorce.

My first reaction was to laugh it off, as it was totally ridiculous, but during the course of the day I received three or four phone calls from friends who told me that the tabloid had approached them for comments. I phoned Monja, and she immediately said that it was a laughable allegation. She was good friends with Anrike. Monja was fully behind me.

Still, the newspaper people kept on digging for dirt. That Friday morning, Monja, my sister, Trudie Horn, and I were having breakfast in Pretoria when I received a phone call from my friend, the singer Arno Jordaan. He told me that the tabloid had decided that there was no story and that they'd drop the matter. Trudie suggested that I call our parents, but I didn't want to upset them with unnecessary nonsense.

That afternoon, Monja, my daughters and I went to Jaco Pretorius's farm near Bela Bela for the weekend. On the Sunday morning, Trudie phoned me from Polokwane. She was with my mother and they were both in tears because another story about me had been published in the same paper. This time the article insinuated that Gary and I had a personal feud going, which was the reason behind the Bulls' bad performances. The story also stated that I'd apparently asked for women's phone numbers and that I'd invited them to late-night rendezvous at Trademarx, a bar next to Loftus, even though I've never been inside the place after dark in my life.

My parents were really upset when they read this fabrication on the front page of the newspaper, but Monja never doubted my innocence. Although my parents also didn't believe a word of it, it hurt them, especially my mom, considering that the story had come out on Mother's Day.

The next week the paper kept trying to do a follow-up, but there really was nothing to report and the story eventually vanished without a trace. The whole sordid episode made me realise how important it is to have a supportive wife. If Monja didn't believe in herself and in me, this could have had a major effect on our marriage, our family and the team. Fortunately, all the drama occurred during a weekend with no rugby commitments. The next week I could return to more important business, because we had a Super Rugby campaign to salvage.

The bye had given my aching body ample time to recover and I felt much better, although that Monday Dr Velleman still gave me four cortisone injections for the pain in my back. It's extremely difficult to play rugby with a sore back. I couldn't run properly and whenever I had to bend or turn, my back was on fire.

Our next game was against the Melbourne Rebels, the new team in the competition, so Frans and the medical team decided to give me another week's rest. I didn't want to be too far from the action and sat on the bench. We had no problem beating the Rebels: 47-10. Slowly but surely, we seemed to be building up steam. Because of the changes that the new format had brought to the competition, we had to play four of our last five games against South African teams: twice against the Sharks, a visit to Newlands to take on the Stormers and a game against the Cheetahs at Loftus. The local derbies usually have an extra dimension to them, because besides giving 'bragging rights' to the winning side, they also function as 'national trials' for places in the Springbok team.

We started our preparations for the game in Durban. The Sharks were sixth on the log and we'd move up a place if we beat them on their home turf. Our plan was to contain the Sharks' strong ball carriers, Bismarck du Plessis, Willem Alberts and Jean Deysel, and early on in the game that is exactly what we did. As a result, the Sharks couldn't gain any momentum. Our mauls from the line-outs also worked brilliantly.

Tactically, Morné and Fourie were brilliant, but I thought the Bull who most dominated play was Chiliboy Ralepelle. Chili was sick and tired of being considered a political pawn, so in this game he decided to take on Bissie, the Boks' first-choice hooker for the overseas tour in November 2010, and he played like a man possessed. Chili made countless tackles and seemed to be all over the field. He really gave that 'something special' Gary had talked about.

But in the end it was another great team effort, and we won 32-23. Three up, four to go.

We were enjoying the sweet taste of victory, but then we tasted the sour too. Fourie had torn his medial ligaments in the first half, but he continued playing. How he managed to carry on, nobody knows. I've had this injury before and it's almost impossible to play rugby when you have it. Fourie showed great courage and determination by over-coming the pain and soldiering on.

Fortunately, we could rely on François Hougaard at scrumhalf for the last games of the season, with Dustin Jinka on the bench. They would be our halfbacks against the Cheetahs, who arrived at Loftus full of bravado after four big victories, including one over the mighty Crusaders. They also thought they knew how to beat us. After the Sharks game, however, our confidence was at an all-time high too. We could still qualify for the knockout stages and knew that we could beat the Cheetahs if we stuck to our game plan and executed it to perfection.

But in the match itself, although we controlled the game and played well, the Free Staters refused to buckle under the pressure we were exert-ing. At that stage of the competition, collecting bonus points was of the utmost importance. In the dying minutes of the game, we managed to score three tries. But Deon Stegmann was in the sin bin and we were leading by just 25-21 when we were awarded a penalty in their 22.

Although it was a risk, we took a quick tap and drove the ball towards their line in an attempt at scoring the fourth try. I was actually lucid when I took this decision, although some of our fans probably thought that I was insane. However, a few phases later Hougie crossed the line for the bonus-point try, and I was in seventh heaven. We won 32-21 and were back in the running. For the first time that season, I also completed a game without any aches and pains.

Our last game against an overseas opponent was against the Waratahs. In 2010, they had been one of the best Aussie teams in the competition. Although they'd lost against the Sharks, they were still a dangerous out-fit, with Kurtley Beale providing the magic touch at fullback.

We started the match well and were leading 20-6 shortly after half-time, with our pack dominating things up front. I was already envisaging the bonus point. Then both their props were injured, and all at once we had to make do with uncontested scrums. The rules state that two teams may only contest in scrums if both have a fit front row. In one fell swoop, our big advantage was taken away. Suddenly the Waratahs weren't on the back foot any more and could fight back. Although we still beat them (23-17), we didn't get the longed-for bonus point.

Suddenly the log was looking very different from the one a few weeks earlier. For a change, the Bulls were in the top six. We still had games against the Stormers in Cape Town and the Sharks in Pretoria, but with five victories on the trot since returning from our overseas tour, we'd turned the season around.

The north–south derby at Newlands was the biggest game of the season. The Stormers were second on the log and were playing good rugby. But the line between success and failure is paper-thin. A victory at Newlands would give us the opportunity to finish top of the log in the South African conference, but if we lost, it could mean the end of our efforts to reach the knockout stages. Fourie was still recovering from his injury and Bakkies had to withdraw due to a knee injury.

Nevertheless, Bakkies came along on the Wednesday when I flew to Cape Town for a Blood Brothers golf day at Pearl Valley outside Paarl. With Newlands hosting this massive rugby match, the atmosphere in the city was electric and the tickets had been sold out weeks in advance.

That evening at the golf function, former Springbok prop Toks van der Linde was hilarious as the master of ceremonies. Later on, in his role as auctioneer, he competently auctioned off all the items on the auction list, and even some that did not appear on the list. Toks's wonderful sense of humour helped us collect quite a substantial amount of money for our preferred charities: the Red Cross Children's Hospital and the Walter Sisulu Trust.

Even our former Bulls teammate, Stormers wing Bryan Habana, joined us in Paarl for the event, which again confirmed what a great guy he is. Two days before a pivotal game between the Bulls and the Stormers, and he still went out of his way to support Bakkies and me.

Unfortunately, the same couldn't be said for the Bulls board. As part of our Blood Brothers bonus year, we were planning to play two games against the New Zealand Maoris in November. We wanted to pick a team that would consist primarily of Blue Bulls players, but the morning before the golf day, we were informed that the union would not release any players for the game. I was livid and immediately phoned Frans, who said that he'd given permission for the guys to play. I then phoned Barend van Graan, the union's chief executive, but he was in a meeting. I even phoned the union president, Louis Nel, but even he didn't have any answers.

Finally I contacted Brand de Villiers, the chief executive of SAIL, which had a 49 per cent share in the Blue Bulls. His explanation? It was to the Bulls' advantage not to participate in the match, as it was more important for the players to rest in November ahead of the tough 2012 season. What really annoyed me was that there was never a problem when Bulls players were picked for the Barbarians, but when Bakkies and I asked for a similar concession, we were turned down.

I was very unhappy about the situation, but on the Friday before the Stormers game, I got a new perspective on life. Bakkies and I visited the Red Cross Children's Hospital, not far from Newlands, as part of our Blood Brothers fund-raising campaign. In the first ward were the really sick and frail children, and there I saw how some little kids have to fight for their lives every second of the day. The reality of the situation hit me hard. I was lucky enough to be blessed with two healthy daughters, but I often moaned about trivial matters. I realised again how grateful I should be for what I have, and that my health and my family's was a great blessing.

In the second ward were the children waiting for organ transplants. One of the kids had been in and out of hospital for 12 years and was still waiting for a suitable donor. He'd been fighting against his disease for as long as I'd been a professional rugby player! I couldn't imagine how hard it must be to be sick for so long. Still, the boy was happy and positive. Now that shows true character! Seeing those sick children opened my eyes and got me into the right state of mind for the game against the Stormers.

We had our usual team talk before the match, and Frans took us back through the years, reminding us of how well we'd done on other occasions when we'd been under tremendous pressure. In 2006 we had beaten the Stormers by 33 points to reach the semi-finals. In the last game of 2007, we had to beat the Reds by a massive score to ensure a semi-final at Loftus, which we did. In 2010, when our beloved home ground wasn't available for the semi or the final, we still pulled through and won the tournament. Nothing was impossible for this team.

While the bus slowly crawled past spectators milling around Newlands, it almost felt as if we were about to play in a Test match. Thousands of people, many of them in light-blue jerseys, lined the streets, and as we got off the bus behind the main stadium, I felt quite positive. I dropped my bag in the changing room and headed out to the field through the narrow tunnel under the pavilion. This was probably going to be my last game at Newlands.

The roar of the crowd overwhelmed me as I stepped outside. Quite a few Stormers supporters booed me, of course, but there were plenty of Bulls fans voicing their approval.

The game itself was very tough. As we'd expected, the Stormers defence was almost impenetrable, but our tactics were never to hold onto the ball for too long and to kick every time we lost momentum, which worked well. We also put pressure on their line-out throws, and our only try, scored by François Hougaard, came after the Stormers made a mistake in their line-out close to their try line. I was very pleased with our performance in the line-outs, because their Springbok lock, Andries Bekker, had been my toughest competitor at all levels of rugby over the past few seasons.

In the final minutes of the game, the result was still in the balance. I missed a tackle on Jaque Fourie, and in the last move of the match he passed to Bryan Habana, who raced towards our try line. But Bjorn Basson managed to catch up with him and brought him down. When the final whistle went, we'd won 19-16. Our campaign was still on course!

I was complimented afterwards for having outplayed Andries (which obviously made me very happy), but I thought all the Bulls players deserved credit, as they had all given that something extra when it was needed.

Our last game of the season, against the Sharks, would determine who'd go through to the knockout rounds. A few of us flew to Durban on the Sunday after the Stormers game to attend a Springbok planning session, but on the Tuesday we were back in Pretoria to prepare for the decisive match of our season. Most of us were nursing aches and pains, so training wasn't too hectic. After all, we didn't really need more practice; we needed instead to be mentally sharp for Saturday's big game.

That week, newspapers reported that quite a few of the Bulls would probably be playing their last game at Loftus, while Bakkies was also playing in his 100th Super Rugby game for the Bulls. The media thrives on stories like these, but for us the team's performance was of far more importance than the possible departure of some players. We never even discussed it as a team, because our focus was on the Sharks.

The permutations, however, were not in our favour. If we beat the Sharks, we would finish fifth on the log, which meant a knockout game against the Blues in Auckland. We believed that if we could get to Eden Park, we could win the competition. But things don't always go according to plan. The Sharks were brilliant on the day and beat us 26-23 in an exciting match.

Suddenly, for me, everything I was doing was 'for the last time'. It was the last time I would be interviewed on TV after a match as captain of the Bulls. It was the last time I'd walk into the changing room, take off my scrum cap, remove my strapping and sit down. It was the last time I'd take off that light-blue jersey and navy-blue socks. It was my last game at my beloved Loftus.

I thought I'd be very emotional, but oddly enough, I wasn't. Over the course of 10 years we'd achieved feats at the Bulls that no one would've thought possible at the start of the millennium. And although we had lost in my last game for the Bulls at Loftus, my career stretched over a decade and not just one season.

I had had the best time of my life, and I couldn't help but feel happy and proud.

Our wives and girlfriends came into the changing room carrying a massive banner and presented us with a video about our years as Bulls players. Nobody – besides maybe the women! – had thought that this was going to be our last game for the Bulls. We were going to beat the Sharks and reach the knockout rounds, weren't we?

I can honestly say that the Bulls had given their best in 2011, but it was just one of those years where things didn't go according to plan. The Sharks game basically summed up our whole season. Any moment now, you thought, the big breakthrough would come, but the dam wall never burst.

When my parents and best friends joined Monja and me to reminisce about the good times and I saw all the children playing together on a mattress, I did feel sad for a while. The Bulls guys had formed a very strong bond over the years, both on and off the field. We were like family, and now we didn't know whether this would still be the case in the future.

We all got together at Loftus on the Sunday to bid farewell to the season. It was a very emotional event and the tears were flowing. The end had come too soon for us, as we had truly believed we could make it to the final.

But one highlight of the day was seeing how much respect everyone had for Frans. It could not have been easy for him to take over from Heyneke, as we would have walked through fire for the man. But now, after three years, we would do the same for Frans. A few other members of the management team also deserve mention: Johann van Graan, a young but talented coach; Basil Carzis, who was there from the start and is the best fitness trainer in South Africa, if you ask me; and, of course, our rugby-mad defence coach, John McFarland.

I woke up on the Tuesday morning with an empty feeling in my heart. Never again would I compete for the Super Rugby trophy. I felt really terrible that we had been unable to make it to the knockout stages in 2011. But my natural instinct is to always find the good in a bad situation, and in this case it was the knowledge that I would have an extra three weeks to rest before the start of the international season.

And so I went back to the gym to start preparing for the Test season and the World Cup that lay ahead ... and to get rid of that empty feeling inside me.

With the Bulls campaign now history and with a few weeks to go before the start of the international season, I had plenty of time to contemplate my future. I decided to stick to my plan to retire from rugby at the end of the 2011 season. SuperSport had approached me with an offer to join their commentating team, but coaching was also an option, as Frans was keen for me to get involved in coaching the Blue Bulls.

Then, out of the blue, a third option came up. The Wednesday after the Sharks game, I received an SMS from Jake White, who had just been appointed as the Brumbies' head coach for the 2012 season. To my great surprise, he wanted me to join him in Canberra as a player-cum-coach. According to him, the Brumbies needed a player with experience, and I was the right man for the job. If I wanted to become a coach, I could only benefit from the knowledge I would gain there, as I would be working with him, Eddie Jones, Stephen Larkham and my old friend George Gregan.

Jake's offer really took me by surprise, especially taking into account all the disagreements we'd had between 2004 and 2007. I think it proved that, despite our different characters, we respected each other. In the end I decided not to take Jake up on his offer because Monja, the children and I were happy in Pretoria and I wasn't keen on living overseas again for an extended period of time.

Unfortunately, the Bulls management was not so positive. Although I was offered a full-time coaching job at Loftus, the Bulls board and I couldn't agree on a salary. When they didn't offer me what I wanted, I passed. Of course I was very disappointed that they couldn't make a plan to employ me after all my years with the union, but, having said that, the Blue Bulls will always have a special place in my heart. If the right opportunity arises to get involved, I'll grab it with both hands.

And so my career as a Bulls player – after almost 14 seasons at various levels in the famous light-blue jersey – came to an end. Although I'd had a plan to make the transition from player to coach, it didn't work out the way I'd wanted it to. But the Bulls remain like family to me, and my family and I have always been able to surmount any obstacle.

19

A rocky road
to New Zealand

After the disappointment of my last Super Rugby season with the Bulls, and while the Sharks and Stormers were waving the South African flag in the knockout stages of the competition, I immediately started focusing on the Springboks and our quest to retain the World Cup crown.

The Bok squad had got together on a couple of occasions during the Super Rugby season to exchange ideas and to ensure that we left nothing to chance. We'd already started planning in May how we would approach the World Cup, when we had our first meeting in Cape Town, but thoughts of a second successful World Cup campaign had been on the minds of the core team members long before that meeting.

The most important part of our approach was how we would properly manage the players. We had to be in peak condition, both mentally and physically, when we arrived in New Zealand in September, and we had to do everything within our power to achieve this goal. The management team, therefore, decided that they could not risk playing any of the injured players in the Tri Nations series, and the players involved concurred. Of course, any competition between the Boks, the All Blacks and the Wallabies was important, but in a World Cup year, the Webb Ellis Cup was the Holy Grail – nothing else mattered as much.

Rugby is a physical game. It demands a lot from the players. I know very few of my colleagues older than 25 who are not nursing a chronic injury of some sort due to rugby. But we wanted to 'manage' these niggles by giving the players as much time as possible to recover. We weren't going to take any chances.

At out first training camp after the Super Rugby series (the Sharks lost in the play-offs and the Stormers in the semis), all the Bok players underwent a thorough medical examination. Because Peter didn't want to risk even slightly injured players, the decision was made to withdraw a handful of guys from the matches that were to take place in Sydney and Wellington. This caused quite a stir – especially in Australia – but we didn't care.

Besides being given a decent recovery period for their injuries, it was also important that the first-choice players had time to prepare for the tournament and to rest after a taxing Super Rugby season. By the same token it was important for some players, like John Smit, for instance, to get more game time, so the decision was made that he would go on tour.

While Peter, John and a very young Bok team travelled to Australia, the rest of us joined Rassie Erasmus, the new technical specialist in the Bok squad, in Rustenburg for training. Besides me, guys like Bakkies Botha, Fourie du Preez, Schalk Burger, Frans Steyn, Jaque Fourie, Jean de Villiers, Juan Smith, Willem Alberts, Bismarck and Jannie du Plessis, Andries Bekker, François Louw, Gurthrö Steenkamp, François Hougaard, Butch James, JP Pietersen, Tendai Mtawarira and Bryan Habana were present. Rassie and I had known each other for years and I was very happy that he had joined our set-up.

Dr Derik Coetzee was also part of the squad. Rassie's job was to draw up plans for the World Cup with the input of the senior players; Derik had to ensure that we were fit. Derik was our conditioning coach during Jake White's tenure as Springbok coach and I considered him to be one of the best, but I was nevertheless a little disappointed that Basil Carzis of the Bulls hadn't been appointed instead. Although he had been Peter's first choice, SARU and the Bulls couldn't agree on certain conditions pertaining to his services. In all the years Basil and I worked together at the Bulls, he'd meant a helluva lot to the team, as well as to me personally. I'd never worked with a better conditioning coach, and he played an invaluable role in many of the Bulls' victories.

Another new face in the management team was that of Jacques Nienaber, who'd worked with Rassie at the Cheetahs and later followed him to Cape Town. Jacques's speciality was defence. He was the man behind the Stormers' watertight defensive play in 2010 and 2011, when they conceded the fewest tries in the Super Rugby series, and he was held in high regard by the players from the Cape. Jacques's record was exemplary and I was quite excited to see how he would approach our defence.

Jacques had initially been a physiotherapist with the Cheetahs, but when he joined Rassie at Western Province, he started specialising in defence. With his positive attitude and brilliant ideas, he was a true team player and far more than just another member of the management team.

Although the media criticised the touring side's lack of experience, Peter did include a few old hands. As mentioned, John was back as captain and, because he was given so little game time with the Sharks in 2011, it was decided that he would play in as many of the initial Tri Nations games as possible. And of course his leadership was very important in this relatively young touring side.

My Bulls teammate Danie Rossouw was also picked, as he needed game time too. But the really interesting selection was at flyhalf, with Morné Steyn going on tour and Butch James staying behind. Morné certainly didn't need any match time, as he had played in every Bulls game that season. The only logical explanation was that the selectors weren't 100 per cent convinced whom to pick as their number-one flyhalf. And it was a tough call, as both Butch and Morné were excellent players who each had their strong points. Even I wasn't sure who would be the better option.

Before the World Cup in 2007, our training camp in Cape Town had delivered the desired results, and in 2011 we were hoping for a similar outcome from the Rustenburg camp. Our aim was proper planning and conditioning. Every last detail needed to be planned to perfection and noted down in writing, so that each team member knew exactly what was expected of him.

Unlike in 2007, we didn't have a lot of time to prepare for the 2011 World Cup. Then we'd played in two home Tests against England and one against Samoa, four Tri Nations Tests, a Test against Namibia, a warm-up game against the Irish province Connacht and a Test match against Scotland. In 2011 we only played in four Tri Nations Tests, and because the Super Rugby competition had gone on for so long, we had six weeks less than in 2007 to prepare.

Four years elapse between World Cups, but it is actually hardly enough time to plan your campaign properly. The Boks get together three times a year: for the Tests in June, the Tri Nations series and the end-of-year tour, but there is very little time then to sit down and plot the finer details, as you have to prepare for the games at hand. We also seldom planned more than two weeks ahead, which was why the Rustenburg training camp was so important.

All the players had to understand how we wanted to play and they had to buy into the game plan. Sometimes not everyone grasped the plan in its entirety, and that concerned us most of all. Although we weren't trying to reinvent the wheel, all the players who boarded the aircraft to New Zealand had to know *exactly* what was required of them. We didn't want to deviate from what had worked for us over the past few years, but we did make minor changes. Everyone had to be satisfied with these changes, as well as every detail of our approach to the World Cup tournament.

Our game plan – from the first, second, third and fourth phases, to attacking and broken play, defence and cross-defence – had to become second nature. Like well-trained soldiers who can dismantle and assemble their rifles in pitch-darkness, we also had to know exactly how every nut, bolt and spring of our plan fitted together.

In rugby you're at your most vulnerable when you're tired and under pressure, and that's when you fall back on old habits that have been stored in your subconscious – those that you acquired while playing for your provincial side. But we were not the Bulls, the Stormers or the Cheetahs now – we were the Springboks, and there was no room for 'provincial habits'.

Rugby can be played in many different ways, which is why it's such a wonderful game, but a team has to pull together towards a common goal or things can quickly go pear-shaped. That's exactly what happened in the away Tests against the Wallabies and All Blacks. The team simply didn't have enough time to prepare properly and many of the players lacked experience. When they were put under pressure, everyone suddenly wanted to follow their own lead.

The Boks lost both Tests badly (20-39 against Australia and 7-40 against New Zealand), and unfortunately it damaged a few of the younger players' reputations. The best among them will bounce back and they will still play many Tests for South Africa, but in the short term the tour wasn't good for anyone involved. Maybe it was unfair to expose certain players to such pressure, but our most important consideration was the World Cup and how to retain it.

Not many positives were gained from the tour, but if there was a lesson to be learnt, it was that SARU should consider a central contracting system in which the country's top players only have national contracts and are allocated to the various provinces – the way it's done in New Zealand. In this way, players will be managed efficiently throughout the season and when they have to report for national duty, they will all be fit and ready to go. You will never again have to sacrifice a Test for the sake of recovering players.

Playing for the Boks is the highest honour that can be bestowed on a player. However, it makes no sense if a Springbok can't play in a Test because he has to rest, yet he has to run on weekend after weekend to represent his home union. That's the dilemma we face: the unions fork out more money than SARU for the services of their contracted players and they want their money's worth.

**

In Rustenburg we stayed at the Royal Marang sports complex, a brand-new facility built specially for the England soccer team at the 2010 FIFA World Cup.

'World class' is probably the best way to describe the Royal Marang complex. There are six grass soccer fields, two soccer fields with synthetic cover, an indoor soccer field, a beach soccer field, a rugby field, six netball courts, two tennis courts, an athletics track, a gym with the latest and best equipment, medical and rehabilitation facilities, swimming pools and spa baths … you name it, the Royal Marang has it.

So while John was doing his best to hold a young Bok side together, the rest of us were hard at work with Rassie, Jacques and Percy Montgomery. Rassie has an unbelievable eye for detail. His approach may sometimes be a little too scientific, because there are a lot of variables in rugby, but his was a good way of measuring yourself as a player. Rassie's method tracked where a player was on the field at any given time and measured the contribution he made to the game.

As quite a few of us were nursing niggles or minor injuries, we also focused on our fitness, and Doc Coetzee had no mercy in this regard. However, in order to give the guys time to recover, no contact training was allowed.

Training days were planned to the last detail. After breakfast, game strategies were discussed and then refined during the morning session. Then it was off to the training grounds, where the new plans were put into practice and, if necessary, adapted.

Later we took part in fitness training on the field and in the gym, where we devoted a lot of time to the rehabilitation of specific injuries and whatever other minor niggles some of the players were suffering from. As was always the case with the Boks, our food intake was carefully monitored. As all our meals were carefully pre-planned by a dietician, any hotel we stayed in had to be informed of our dietary requirements beforehand. We were always provided with healthy food that gave our bodies the necessary fuel to sustain a physically taxing training programme.

We even had a video conference with the Boks who were touring in Australasia. During the session we all watched a video recording of the game and everyone gave their input, even though we were thousands of kilometres apart.

When you look at the Royal Marang and its facilities, you quickly realise how huge soccer is and how far rugby still lags behind. One possible reason for the gap is the lasting effect of amateurism. Super-successful businesspeople and billionaires haven't taken over rugby like they have soccer. You only have to look at the power that is still wielded by the elected officials of SARU to know that much. Most of these officials are basically amateurs, even though they manage huge amounts of money. The same can't be said about soccer. The sooner rugby whole-heartedly embraces professionalism, the better it will be for the sport.

While in Rustenburg, we were also impressed with how self-sufficient the Bafokeng nation was. Whereas a sense of entitlement had taken root among the people of South Africa over the past few years, the Bafokeng nation had initiated a master plan that will benefit generations to come. Their king, Kgosi Leruo Molotlegi, joined us for dinner at our hotel one evening. He's the leader of roughly 300 000 people who have maintained their own unique culture and traditional leadership structures.

They've already made plans to ensure their future income, even though their raw-material wealth, mainly platinum, is nearing depletion, despite their having about 1 200 square kilometres of land rich in valuable raw materials. In order to ensure that the Bafokeng people have access to the best education system, healthcare, job opportunities and recreational facilities, they now invest in tourism and sport. At one point we were invited to Bafokeng's own high-performance sports school, where learners enjoy the best facilities.

But back to work: we were in Rustenburg to prepare for a World Cup tournament. One of our big concerns was the serious injuries that afflicted two of our key players – Juan Smith had hurt his Achilles tendon early in the Super Rugby season, and Schalk Burger had broken a bone in his thumb against the Crusaders in the Stormers' last game of the season. The two were training on their own, as their injuries were far more serious than the rest of the team's niggles and bruises.

Whereas we knew that Schalla would be fit for New Zealand, Juan had only a slim chance of recovering in time, although he worked very hard to regain his fitness. Juan was not only passionate about the game of rugby, but also one of the leaders in the squad and a crucial element in our line-outs. And he was – without a doubt – one of the toughest guys I'd ever played with for South Africa, so it was terrible to see him trying so hard to be fit for his third World Cup. Unfortunately, though, injuries are part and parcel of rugby and one cannot always escape them.

Andries Bekker also attended the training camp, despite the serious ankle injury he was nursing. Over the past few years, he'd developed into one of the best young locks in the world, and he had become the ideal candidate to assume some of my workload. But, like Juan, Andries only had a slim chance of making it to the World Cup. In fact, the first bit of bad news we received was about Andries. He had consulted a specialist and, shortly afterwards, SARU announced that he would have to undergo surgery and would not recover in time for the World Cup. Suddenly we had much less depth at lock.

Andries brought valuable balance to the team. He might have been behind me in the line-out, but his excellent play over the past couple of seasons had kept me on my toes. He was also more than just a line-out jumper; he was the type of lock who could replace both me and Bakkies. His withdrawal was a massive blow to the side.

After our training camp, the Wallabies arrived in South Africa. We had only two Tests before the start of the World Cup – the first being against the Aussies in Durban – but because we'd played together as a team for so long, we felt that the two outings would be preparation enough.

We worked hard in Durban and were looking forward to playing again, although some of us were a bit nervous, worrying that we'd be somewhat rusty because of our lack of game time. But it was great to have Fourie du Preez and Heinrich Brüssow back in the Bok team for the first time since 2009. As scrumhalf and ball-fetcher flank forward, these two played a major role in our set-up. However, it was a bit unfair on them to assume that everything would just fall into place with their return to the team.

Still, both Fourie and Heinrich delivered excellent performances against Australia. We played good rugby in the first half, and I felt quite positive, as the little niggles were no longer bothering me and the hard work in Rustenburg was paying some dividends. The Wallabies couldn't break our defensive lines, but we squandered a couple of chances to score tries, possibly because we were, indeed, a bit rusty.

In the second half, they managed to score a try after we kicked the ball downfield. At that moment, Frans Steyn pulled a hamstring and was unable to join the first line of defence. The Wallabies exploited Frans's absence by slipping through the gap he would've been guarding and went over. The try swung the momentum in Australia's favour, and they beat us 14-9. Again it showed how little room for error there was at this level. Although it's natural for you – not to mention the supporters – to start doubting yourself after this sort of defeat, if we'd won that Test, the situation would've been very different.

Afterwards I thought we should have been more patient, especially when we were in their 22, as we had been close to scoring on a few occasions but just couldn't carry it off. We managed to penetrate their defensive line more often than they did ours, and even though the pundits accused us of playing a kicking game, the Wallabies had kicked out of hand far more than we did. Yet the kicking as such was not the problem: our decision-making and execution let us down. In the Super Rugby series, official statistics showed that the Lions, who ended at the bottom of the log, had kicked the ball the least of all the teams, whereas the Reds, who'd won the competition, had kicked the ball the most.

Of course, it was terrible to lose, but for most of the guys it was their first taste of rugby in almost two months and most of us lacked the sharpness needed at Test level. Unfortunately, we also struggled in the scrums later on in the game, and this was singled out as one of the main reasons why we lost. The problem started when Gurthrö Steenkamp and Bismarck du Plessis were sent on as replacements and John Smit was moved to tighthead prop in place of Jannie du Plessis.

Guthie had been out of action for quite a while with an arm injury and had to get some game time, but I thought it was a bit unfair to move John to tighthead. He'd played one of his best matches of the year at hooker shortly before this Test, despite not getting any decent game time at the Sharks. After the match, both the media and the supporters remembered only that the Bok scrum had struggled, especially before John had left the field with an injury. Then, when Jannie took over from John, our scrumming seemed to improve.

More bad news followed soon afterwards when Juan Smith was forced to withdraw from the World Cup squad. He wanted to continue, but in the end he made the right decision. I believe he still has a lot to offer South African rugby if he completely recovers from his foot injury.

There was no time to ponder the setback. We were already in Port Elizabeth, preparing for the All Blacks. This would be my and John's last Test in South Africa. He was under tremendous pressure from both the public and the media about his form, and everyone was asking whether he was indeed the right man to lead the Boks in the World Cup.

On the Tuesday before the Test against the Wallabies, the coach and I had had a long chat. Peter told me how important it was for him to win the World Cup, as he believed it would have a positive impact on the coloured community and give them hope for the future. He also talked about the changes he'd planned for the team – he wanted to give Gurthrö and Morné a chance to show their mettle.

Then Peter asked me to captain the Boks the following weekend against the All Blacks. I was surprised, but his reasoning made sense to me. He'd earlier promised Bismarck that he would give him decent game time against the Kiwis, which meant that John had to move to the bench and I would take over the captaincy duties. Peter had a lot of faith in both John and me as leaders; there was no hidden agenda in his decision.

Of course, I felt hugely honoured to lead the team, as it was my last Test on home soil, and against the All Blacks of all teams. To captain the Boks in this game made me feel prouder than I'd ever been.

Initially, John was not aware of Peter's intentions, which I found very odd. The Sunday after the Wallabies Test, we left for Port Elizabeth. That evening, Peter called John aside and told him that Bismarck would play against the All Blacks and that I would captain the team. The next day, I could see that John wasn't happy. On the Tuesday, when we boarded the bus for training, John came to sit next to me. It was clear that he had something on his mind, but I couldn't immediately determine whether he was angry or just upset.

After everyone had left the bus, he asked me, 'Vic, as captain, can I rely on your support?' He'd caught me completely off guard, as I'd never for a moment thought that John would doubt my support. I assured him that I was fully behind him, as had always been the case. Then he asked a much tougher question: 'Do you think I deserve to be picked as first-choice hooker instead of Bismarck?'

Before I could say anything, John told me to think seriously about his question and to answer him at a later stage. It was probably one of the most difficult training sessions of my life. John's question kept popping up in my mind, and I didn't know what the answer was.

Back at the hotel, I immediately confided in Fourie du Preez, my rugby buddy whom I could chat to about anything.

'Vic, it's not your decision to make,' Fourie said. He suggested that I talk to John about the matter as soon as possible. To clear my mind, I phoned Monja. Her advice was basically the same as Fourie's.

After talking to Monja, I went straight to John's room. My heart was racing at the prospect of our conversation. John and I are good friends and I have nothing but the utmost respect for him as a player and a leader. If you ask me, he's the best Springbok captain South Africa's ever had. We'd played our first game together for the Boks 10 years earlier, and it was John who'd convinced Jake White to pick me for the national squad when he'd wanted to leave me out. We were more than just rugby buddies. We'd shared successes and failures, the lighter side of things and serious matters. I could see how one day, old and grey, we would look back together on this decade in our respective careers.

So I responded to his earlier question: 'John, do you believe in yourself? Do *you* believe you have what it takes to start in a Test for the Boks? Because that is the only thing that counts …'

He still believed in himself, John said. But he also said that he felt as if he were in the same situation as a few months before, when he'd sat on the bench for the Sharks for most of the season. It wasn't good for the team, John said. I advised him to discuss the issue with Peter in order to determine exactly what the coach had in mind for him. John was willing to move to the bench or withdraw completely – whatever was best for the Boks.

I didn't think it was a good idea to name a new captain a few weeks before the start of the World Cup, so I suggested that John and Peter devise a plan whereby John would start in some of the games and Bismarck in the others. I also assured John that it was not my ambition to be the Bok captain at the World Cup. I was happy with my role as his vice-captain and would support him wherever I could, as I had over the past few seasons. But I also had no problem should I be asked to lead the team in some of the games.

John was visibly relieved after our talk and we continued to chit-chat for a while. I was convinced that whatever Peter (and John) decided about John's role in the World Cup, it would crucially affect the Boks in the months to follow.

I understood why John felt unhappy and uncertain about his role – he wanted to end his Bok career on a high note. He'd already announced his decision to retire from Test rugby after October 2011, after which he would move to England to play club rugby for Saracens.

As the weekend drew closer, John's mood lifted. We invited former Bok captain Hannes Marais to hand out the jerseys before the All Black Test, and he had a special message for us: 'You are in the same position we were in after our tour of the British Isles in 1969/70, when we lost two Tests and drew two. We had our backs against the wall and the All Blacks were on their way to South Africa.'

We told ourselves exactly what the Boks told themselves 41 years ago: Each player had to believe in himself, because if he didn't, how could his teammates or the nation believe in him? And we had to play for each other.

Well, the 1970 Boks beat the All Blacks 3-1 in that Test series, and that was the last time South Africa had played New Zealand in Port Elizabeth. Until now.

The message was very relevant. I was no longer convinced that the guys truly believed in themselves, and I was relieved that Oom Hannes had raised this point. The senior guys in the squad felt that it was time for the team to pull together, as we'd be leaving for New Zealand in only a few weeks' time. We allowed our players a lot of freedom, but the senior players now decided that we would set the example in order to show the rest of the guys that the team always came first and that it could only perform successfully if we worked as a tight unit.

The bus ride to the stadium on the Saturday was very special to me. I didn't want to make a big thing about it being my final Test in South Africa, but I struggled to keep my emotions in check. It was the last time I would ride in the team bus; we were on our way to play the All Blacks and I was captaining South Africa. We were also under immense pressure, but during the seven-kilometre drive from the hotel to the stadium, I once again realised what the Springboks meant to South Africa.

Everyone we passed (except the couple of All Black supporters, of course) cheered us on – whether they lived in shacks or in mansions. Most people didn't care whether Victor Matfield, John Smit or Bryan Habana was on that coach; they were rooting for the Springbok emblem displayed on the outside. Although the Bok players also had their worries, problems and challenges, they brought hope to the people out there, a fact no Springbok should ever forget.

In South Africa, the national rugby team's mission was always bigger than just being another successful sports team. I felt very strongly about this, as I believed we could contribute something meaningful to our country. Peter, too, had worked towards this goal during his tenure as Bok coach. We wanted to give the team back to the people, and I think we succeeded in doing so.

As a result, the Boks received spectacular support in Port Elizabeth, even though we knew that the All Blacks would have a great many people shouting for them too, mainly because a large number of coloured people had supported the team during the apartheid years.

The Test started at a hectic pace, and early on the All Blacks cut through our defensive line twice, but our cover defence stood strong. After the initial flurry, Morné Steyn kept the scoreboard ticking over with three successive penalty kicks from close to the halfway line, before adding a drop kick. The All Blacks were under pressure. We didn't give them an inch to move, and in the end we won 18-5, with Morné scoring all the points.

We learnt something very important that day: Morné simply had to be our first-choice flyhalf. Before the match it had still been a toss-up between Butch and Morné, but afterwards it was clear that we couldn't start a Test without Morné's kicking abilities.

What a wonderful way to end my Test career in South Africa! Even though I'd pulled a hamstring early on in the second half, I managed to carry on playing till the end of the match, and afterwards I did a lap of honour to thank the fans – not just the faithful packing the Nelson Mandela Bay Stadium, but *everyone* who had supported me over the past 10 years.

My first Test in the starting XV for the Boks had been way back in 2001, also against the All Blacks. To be able to look back as the Springbok with the most Test caps at that stage and the most Tests against New Zealand – and as captain on the day – once again made me so thankful for all the privileges and blessings I'd received.

After that victory, the public support for the Boks started building. We'd won only one Test, and not even against a full-strength All Black side, but now Bok fever was spreading throughout the country.

The World Cup squad was announced a few days after the All Black Test. We spent an enjoyable evening on set at the SuperSport studios in Randburg. In general I thought the selectors had done a good job with the 30 players they'd picked, but I would have liked to see a player like Zane Kirchner included as well. The squad didn't include a specialist fullback, and although we had brilliant players who could fulfil this role, I thought Zane would have added value in New Zealand.

The big talking point, however, was who would play hooker and what Peter's intentions were with John and Bismarck. I was quite relieved that it wasn't up to me to decide how to utilise them! I believed that both players had a major role to play in our World Cup campaign, but I didn't know how one would deploy them while maintaining a happy squad. It was probably the most important decision Peter had to take in his four years as Bok coach.

The issue was about what would happen not only on the playing field but also off the pitch and the effect that it would have on the team. Whatever decision was made, it would have a huge impact at the World Cup. Interestingly enough, neither the players nor team management ever discussed the issue openly among themselves; most likely because everyone respected John so much.

But the John/Bismarck dilemma was soon forgotten when Ard Matthews, lead singer of the group Just Jinjer, sang the national anthem after the squad announcement had been made. On live TV, he managed to garble the lyrics, and eventually forgot them altogether. I felt really sorry for Ard, but there was also a lesson to be learnt. As proud South Africans, the least we can do is learn the words to our national anthem. It was unacceptable that he could appear on national television to sing the anthem without being properly prepared.

Ard later said that the moment had been too big for him, but the damage was done. Fortunately we had more important issues on our agenda: a proper Springbok team-building exercise. But at least it would not be a 'Kamp Staaldraad'!

The exercise kicked off with an interesting talk by Lewis Gordon Pugh, an extraordinary South African and the first person on earth to have swum distances of between 1 and 204 kilometres in every ocean on this planet, including the North Pole, where water temperatures dip below zero.

Pugh told us that his priority before attempting the North Pole swim in July 2007 was to rope in the most knowledgeable people to support him, or he might die. One of these experts was Pugh's psychologist, who was also a personal friend, and he gave Pugh three 'anchors' with which to brave the kilometre he would swim in water that was below freezing point:

1. Break the kilometre up into 10 units. For each 100 metres Pugh completed, the flag of a supporting crew-member's country would be hoisted. Although Pugh couldn't stop every 100 metres, with every raised flag he would think what that specific person meant to him, which spurred him on for the next 100 metres.
2. Think back on the difficult times in your career and focus on the positives that came from them.
3. Look ahead and think of the difference you can make if you successfully complete this challenge. (Pugh's issue was global warming, the damage humans do to the planet for their own personal gain and the difference that he can make.)

We could easily have applied Pugh's words to ourselves. For me, the most important point he mentioned involved the whirlpool of emotions he'd experienced just before entering the icy water. He'd asked his medical team to take him out of the water if he was in bad shape after 500 metres, but then his psychologist friend pulled him aside and said, 'If you dive in there with even the slightest thought of failure, you won't make it. You must know one thing for sure: if you take on this challenge, you either finish it or you die.'

Well, the World Cup might not have been a life-or-death situation, but I was nevertheless hoping that, when they boarded the aircraft to New Zealand, the squad would feel the same way Lewis Gordon Pugh did when he entered the water. None of the older players should think, 'We've won the Webb Ellis Cup, so it's okay if we can't do it again.' And by the same token, none of the junior players should say, 'We're still young. We'll get another chance.'

If anyone entertained such thoughts, we were in serious trouble. We had one chance to carve our names in the annals of rugby history as the first team to retain the World Cup title and win it three times. But we had two weeks to kick-off, so a team-building exercise was crucial to ensure that we were all on the same page.

On the morning of our departure for the camp we were divided into two groups. We flew to Skukuza in a pair of old cargo planes that dated back to 1942. I'd never before flown in a plane where the pilot rolled down the cockpit window in mid-air. It was rather scary! Some guys got quite airsick, while the rest of us chewed our fingernails. There was a universal sigh of relief when we touched down at the game reserve.

A tented campsite in the middle of the bush had been prepared for us, but not far from there lay a buffalo that had been brought down and killed by a pride of lions the day before. And what did we have as protection? Nothing but a very low electric fence! Some of the guys dragged the carcass even closer to our site, probably to about 50 metres from where our campfire was crackling.

Later, when the newly appointed coach of the Proteas cricket team, Gary Kirsten, addressed us, he found it rather difficult to concentrate with all the background noise generated by the lions and hyenas fighting over the buffalo carcass. You don't get to see lions and hyenas fighting over a kill every day. A cloud of dust started forming as the beasts alternately attacked and retreated with their fangs exposed and their eyes fixed on the prize. We learnt quite a valuable lesson from their struggle: each time a lion tried to chase the pack of hyenas away on his own, they stood their ground. But the moment the lions attacked in a group, the hyenas high-tailed it.

In 2011, Gary had coached the Indian national cricket team to World Cup glory on home soil for the first time since 1983. He talked to us about pressure in particular. According to him, we were actually in a good position, as everyone expected more from the All Blacks, the World Cup hosts, than from us. In order to rewrite the record books, he said, we should put ourselves under pressure, rise above mediocrity and do everything within our power to be well prepared.

After Gary's talk, he left with our coaches, and it was time for the guys to relax – but also to do some serious, straight talking. With the lions and hyenas still fighting over the carcass, we took our seats around the campfire to have our say. One of the most important issues raised was how the World Cup would offer players from South Africa the opportunity to unite an often divided nation.

We were still chatting away when the singer Robbie Wessels arrived with his guitar to provide some entertainment. We sat around the campfire till late, singing and talking. By 11 p.m. the lions had stuffed themselves and the hyenas moved in. Before we knew it, four of our teammates (whose names I'd rather not mention) had jumped over the electric fence and were leopard-crawling towards the carcass, intent on catching a hyena. They were about 10 metres away from one when John spotted them. On their return, they got a proper tongue-lashing from the captain. What they'd been about to do was not the brightest idea, John told them. I thought it was quite funny – boys will be boys!

That night we all had a good laugh and got to know each other better. Even though most of us had played together for eight years, there were a couple of new faces we didn't know all that well. At previous team-building exercises, it was always the same guys who lingered till the very end, but this time it was great that almost the entire squad stayed up until we called it a night.

In fact, it was an evening I will never forget. If the guys were ready to tackle a hyena, they were ready to take on the world!

We had some time off before getting together in Johannesburg the following Monday for our last week of preparation in South Africa. I could sense the excitement in the air – the guys couldn't wait to get to New Zealand. Practice was much more intensive and we put in some hard yards that week. We particularly worked on our play at the breakdowns, and at times the blood flowed. Nobody was holding back.

Unfortunately, Bakkies couldn't train with us. Where I had had a proper rest and was no longer concerned about my hamstring, the same could not be said about my lock partner and old friend. Bakkies had hurt his Achilles tendon and wasn't comfortable at all. Although the medical team was positive about his recovery, I could see the big guy wasn't convinced.

Although I hadn't had any problems with my back for a while, I still didn't want to leave anything to chance. The morning before we left, I saw Dr Mark Velleman for cortisone injections, just to make sure that my back wouldn't start acting up in New Zealand. I spent the rest of the day with my family. Although I was very excited to finally go, I also felt an emptiness in my stomach. I was going to be away from my wife and two beautiful girls for eight weeks, and I felt sorry for Monja, as staying at home to look after our two live wires was not going to be easy. I admired her for taking care of the girls on her own tour after tour, but at least this would be the last time.

I had arranged for Monja to join me in New Zealand if we reached the semi-finals, but we'd decided that Jaime and Giselle would stay behind in South Africa. It's a terribly long flight over all the time zones and it would have been hard on the youngsters. Before the 2011 World Cup, the longest I'd ever been away from my children was four weeks. I wasn't looking forward to the prospect of being away from them for eight. I wondered if they understood why their dad had to go away for so long.

Then it was time to say our goodbyes. With a heavy heart I left for Sandton, from where we would take the Gautrain to OR Tambo International Airport for our flight to Sydney. Although we knew that a lot of fans would come to wish us well, we didn't expect quite such a massive turnout: almost 40 000 people turned up! We were completely dumbfounded and humbled by the support.

And when the minister of sport and recreation, Fikile Mbalula, wished us well in Afrikaans (he told us to 'moer' the opposition), we not only had a good laugh, but also realised the immensity of the task that lay ahead. Once the speeches were over, we were sent off with thousands of fans shouting 'Viva Amabokke! Viva!' It took us about an hour to walk the 100 metres from Nelson Mandela Square to the Gautrain station, as we were stopped and asked to sign autographs and pose for photos all along the way. We felt unbelievably privileged to be able to bring the people of South Africa closer together. Just imagine what we as a nation can achieve if we stand together the whole time!

The waving, cheering and well-wishing didn't come to an end until we'd boarded the aircraft. As usual, the journey to Sydney was long and tedious, but when we eventually landed in Wellington, there were hundreds of people waiting to welcome us. The South Africans among them even started singing the national anthem! It was a touching moment and made us realise that we have supporters all over the world.

At last we were in New Zealand. Once again, we would try to win the World Cup for South Africa.

20

It starts with a green leaf

In Maori, the word describing New Zealand is 'Aotearoa', literally meaning 'land of the long white cloud'. These extraordinary white clouds are as much a part of the country as the Maoris and their culture. On 2 September, shortly after our arrival in New Zealand for the World Cup, we were welcomed in their traditional way.

Our entire squad was escorted to Wellington's waterfront, where Maori warriors performed the *haka*. The leader of the local tribe presented John Smit with a green leaf, which he laid on the ground in front of him. According to tradition, the leader of the visiting 'tribe' must pick up the leaf, after which the two leaders rub noses as a sign that the greeting – and the possible future challenge – is accepted.

This small ceremony is known as a *wero*, and although we often visited New Zealand (John and the other Sharks players in our group had visited New Zealand four times in 2011 alone), this was only the second time I had experienced this special occasion. Years ago, the Bulls were also welcomed in Christchurch with the *wero*.

We had eight days before out first game, against Wales, and after the welcoming ceremony we could start preparing for it in all seriousness. As I was still recovering from a hamstring injury and wasn't 100 per cent fit, the practices commenced without me. I was in a race against time to recover completely for our first World Cup encounter.

That Monday, Bakkies Botha, Danie Rossouw and I trained on our own next to the practice field, with one of our physiotherapists, Rene

Naylor, keeping an eye on us. We ran six 100-metre sprints in a row (it's called a set) with about 15 seconds' rest between each. We repeated the exercise three times – not easy for big guys like us!

We ran at about 80 per cent of our ability, and I felt good afterwards, so I was optimistic that the hamstring would heal in time for the opener against Wales. Unfortunately, Bakkies wasn't as lucky as me and he had to throw in the towel halfway through the session. His Achilles tendon was hurting like hell, and the medical team decided that it would be too big a risk to pick him for the Wales encounter.

Management decided to give Bakkies a few days' rest to fully recover from his injury, failing which they would have no choice but to send him home and call in a replacement. My old lock buddy wasn't a happy camper – he wanted to stay in New Zealand and help the Boks win the World Cup.

The next day, Bryan Habana also started having problems with his hammie, so he joined me next to the training field, where we could run on our own. We had to do three sets of six over 60 metres, but this time as fast as possible. The first set went well, and I was running at about 90 per cent of my ability.

I ran the second set a bit faster. I was trying to keep up with Bryan so that I could see what would happen if I ran flat out, but that was a mistake. My hamstring started hurting and I stopped immediately. After consulting with the medical team, the decision was made to rest me for two days, so I did nothing (except work on this book!). That Friday – two days before the Wales game – I would run again and a final decision would be made.

The situation was unbelievably frustrating. The World Cup kick-off on 9 September was around the corner. I would play for South Africa for the last time in this tournament, and I wanted to wear the green and gold and represent our nation with pride on the rugby field. As a team, we had the opportunity to rewrite the history books by becoming the first nation to win the Webb Ellis trophy three times *and* be the first to successfully defend the title. And there I was, nursing a painful hamstring!

That Thursday, Peter picked the most experienced Test side at the tournament for the game against Wales. The guys in the starting line-up had an accumulated tally of 815 Tests under their belt. Schalk Burger was back at flank forward after recovering from a hand injury; Frans Steyn was at fullback; and Danie came in at lock for the injured Bakkies. I was his lock partner, even though we still weren't sure whether I would be able to play.

Friday, two days before kick-off, I warmed up on my own and then joined the team for practice. My hamstring felt much better, but it still wasn't 100 per cent. However, the team doctor was satisfied that I could take on the Welsh. Had it been any of our other group games, I would not have played, but as this was our most important encounter, the coaching team wanted me on the field.

Later that day, minister of sport Fikile Mbalula handed out our jerseys. Kgalema Motlanthe, South Africa's deputy president, accompanied him. For the second time in a week, Minister Mbalula impressed me tremendously. He supported us wholeheartedly and was working very hard to unite all South Africans behind the team. Four years before, in 2007, we were threatened with having our passports revoked because the Springbok team wasn't representative enough, but this time round the government backed us all the way.

At last the months of waiting were over. Our 2011 World Cup campaign started against Wales in Wellington on Sunday 11 September. And we had a brilliant start when Frans Steyn crossed the try line early in the game. Even my hamstring wasn't acting up. But the rest of the first half was equally contested. At the turn we were leading by only four points (10-6), but we were nevertheless satisfied, as we felt we could increase the lead in the second half. Unfortunately, we lost Jean de Villiers early in the game to a rib injury, but we were certainly not panicking.

Five minutes after the start of the second half, I tried to tackle Shane Williams and I immediately felt my hamstring tightening. I didn't want to take any chances and informed the medical team that it would be better if I left the field. It might have been only a small tweak, but if I carried on playing, it could have resulted in a full-blown tear, which I didn't want to risk. I was replaced by Johann Muller.

But we just couldn't get going in the second half. It felt as if we were half asleep and were giving them far too many opportunities to attack.

Then Wales kicked a penalty and scored a goal, and suddenly they were leading 16-10, with 25 minutes left on the clock. On the sideline, Jean and I said to each other that we still had enough time; we could turn the game around and beat them.

Shortly after Wales took the lead, Peter de Villiers replaced John, 'Beast', Pierre and Bryan with Bismarck, Gurthrö, Willem and François Hougaard. All four made a major impact and played brilliantly. With John, Jean and me following the match from the bench, Fourie du Preez and Schalla took over the captaincy on the field.

With 15 minutes left on the clock, we were awarded a penalty close to Wales's 22-metre line. I could hear the spectators urging us to kick for posts, but if I had been the captain that day and was forced to make the call, I would have gone for touch to try to score a five-pointer. And Fourie made exactly the same call.

If we hadn't gone on to score a try, we would surely have been crucified afterwards. If Fourie had had his own interests at heart, he probably would have gone for posts. The only thing that mattered to him, though, was to secure a victory. It's an interesting aside that the same three players who had been responsible for the Bulls' try in the 2010 Super 14 final against the Stormers were again involved in scoring the Boks' winning try.

A line-out on the right-hand side of the field allowed us to move the ball left and then right again. Right under the posts, Danie first ran an excellent wide line to pull in the Welsh defenders. 'Hougie' then sped past Fourie just as he secured the ball from the ruck, received the short pass and flew over the try line. It was the same 'Soweto move' of 2010. After Morné Steyn's conversion, we led the Welsh 17-16.

With about three minutes left to play, we had an important decision to make when we were given a penalty barely within Morné's striking range. Many others probably thought we should have gone for posts, but I knew immediately what Fourie would do, as we had discussed similar scenarios in the past.

One option was to try to get the three points, but there was the possibility that we might miss the kick, which would give our opponents possession and an opportunity to launch a counter-attack. And even if we kicked the ball over, there would be enough time for Wales to restart the game, win back possession and throw caution to the wind in an effort to score a try.

You 'waste' a lot of time kicking for touch. Then all you have to do is secure the line-out ball and protect possession for two minutes and they would have no chance of winning. Yes, they could win the line-out ball, but then they'd have to run from deep within their own territory across the length of the field to score.

So Fourie decided to kick for touch. We won the line-out, protected the ball and won the game. Schalk deserves a lot of credit here. Fourie told me afterwards that he was quite gutted after Wales had scored a try, but Schalla was the one who motivated him again.

Perhaps it was not a pretty victory – and Wales did play very well, but the character the Bok team showed that evening in Wellington was pivotal. For old times' sake, and as this was my last game against Wales, I really wanted to shut up their 'clever coaches' with the way we played. Before the game, Wales coach Warren Gatland had said that the Boks 'did not play rugby', and that we had a boring approach to the game. Well, winning is never boring.

I'm very happy that I never played in a Springbok team that lost against the Red Dragons. Of course, we weren't at all surprised when we read in the newspapers the next day how badly we'd performed against Wales and that our chances of winning the World Cup were basically zero. The media even predicted that we would struggle to beat Fiji in our next encounter. In the past we had often been written off after mediocre performances, but for us, securing victory was all that counted.

Yes, I would have to agree that I was a bit nervous about the match against the Fijians – we hadn't forgotten how difficult it had been to beat them in the quarter-finals in 2007. But at the same time we also knew they would be no match for us if we played to the best of our abilities.

Because of my hamstring injury, I was forced to take it easy for the first couple of days after the Wales game. The decision was made that I would not play against the South Sea Islanders, allowing our fitness trainer, Neels Liebel, to help me recover as quickly as possible during my rehabilitation period.

So for the first time since my 2000 debut Bok tour, I was among the players who were not being considered for the upcoming Test; I was now a member of the extended squad. We call these non-players the 'dirties', derived from the term 'dirt trackers'.

I felt terrible not being part of the Test side, and I was also missing my family back home more than usual. To make matters worse, Jaime had injured her foot so badly that she had to have a cast fitted. My heart ached for my little girl back in Pretoria, and I wished I could be there to give her a big hug.

Luckily, Jean de Villiers and Butch James were also among the 'dirties', and with those two clowns in the mix, things were never boring. According to tradition, the 'dirties' usually went out for a meal the night before a Test. We made a few toasts to wish the team well; then we just relaxed and had some fun.

The game against Fiji started at an intense pace, and after 20 minutes the score was 3-all. However, the Boks soon turned up the heat and took control of the match. Quite a few players made use of the opportunity to shine, but Danie Rossouw, in particular, excelled.

In 2007 he'd had to replace Pierre Spies at short notice and did so very successfully. This time round he was wearing my No. 5 jersey. One of his tasks was to make the line-out calls, which made a couple of guys quite nervous. Not me, though. 'Danna' often called the line-outs when the Bulls played and I knew he was up to the job. And, boy, did he silence the critics! He went above and beyond the call of duty, and in the end he also scored a brilliant try. I wasn't surprised when he was picked as Man of the Match.

Danie is one of the most special guys I've ever played with. He knows the game, he runs great attacking lines and he has the ability to read the opponents' defensive structures. He isn't the kind of player you find round every corner. Fourie often said that if he had the final say, he would pick Danie in any starting line-up, no matter which team it was for. Danie had much to offer on attack and was a master at creating space for his teammates to run into. Unfortunately, because he could play in so many positions and got moved around a lot, he was often seen only as a versatile impact player.

After the World Cup, Danie will join Fourie to play club rugby in Japan, but I hope he doesn't disappear off the South African rugby radar, as I firmly believe that he can still be of value to the Boks in the next couple of years.

In the end, we beat Fiji 49-3, scoring six tries and conceding none. As in 2007, when we beat England 36-0, this victory gave the team a huge confidence boost just as the tournament started gaining momentum.

***

Next, we would face our African neighbour, Namibia. We were slightly more casual than usual in our approach the week before the game, and our new home base had a lot to do with this. We had left bustling Wellington and relocated to the much more relaxed Taupo, situated on Lake Taupo, about 300 kilometres south of Auckland.

Wellington, New Zealand's capital, is home to about 400 000 people (the entire national population numbers a mere 4.5 million); Taupo, on the other hand, has a population of just over 30 000. For two weeks we stayed at the Bayview Wairakei Resort just outside town. Because none of South Africa's five Super Rugby teams had ever set up camp at Taupo before, we knew little of that part of New Zealand. But with all the stunning golf courses within spitting distance, I was quite chuffed to be there.

On the Sunday of our arrival, we were invited to visit the local Maori tribe where, according to tradition, the All Black *haka*, the 'Ka Mate', has its origin. Opotaka, where the Ngāti Tūwharetoa tribe lived, was close to Turangi and about an hour's drive from our hotel. Some of the guys who had played against the Fijians the day before were pretty pooped and not very enthusiastic about the trip, but with Jean de Villiers and Jaque Fourie on the bus, there wasn't a dull moment!

In the end it was an enjoyable visit, as after 24 Tests against the All Blacks, it was interesting to actually go to the place where the *haka* had originated. According to legend – as relayed by the tribe's chief, Tumu Te Heuheu – Opotaka on Lake Rotoaira, next to Mount Tongariro, is the place where the warrior Te Rauparaha first performed the 'Ka Mate' *haka*, the exact same ritual the All Blacks repeat to this day.

Chief Te Rauparaha was being pursued by his enemies when he arrived in Opotaka. He asked the chief of the local tribe for shelter, and was hidden in the place where the tribe stored their food, while the chief's wife guarded the entrance. Te Rauparaha feared for his life and called out 'ka mate, ka mate' ('I'll die, I'll die'). But after a while, when he heard his pursuers departing, he shouted 'ka ora, ka ora' ('I live, I live'). He left his hiding place and performed a war dance that would later become known as the *haka*.

In the week leading up to the Test against Namibia, we had only one team training session. I had three runs with Neels. My hamstring felt much better and I was confident that I would be ready for Samoa in our last group encounter.

We played Namibia on Thursday 22 September at the North Harbour Stadium, north of Auckland, where the Bulls sometimes play Super Rugby matches. Although the Boks were slow out of the starting blocks, we soon picked up the pace. We beat Namibia 87-0 in an obviously one-sided affair, which made it difficult to take anything positive from the match. But we felt proud that it was the second Test in a row in which we didn't concede a try.

Peter gave us time off on the Friday and Saturday, and we were only scheduled to be back at our hotel in Taupo on the Sunday to start preparing for Samoa. Whereas the rest of the squad were planning to fly back from Auckland, Jean had the brilliant idea of taking a 'road trip' to Taupo. A few of us rented a minivan, which we immediately christened 'Gertjie' after the deputy minister of sport and one of our biggest fans, Gert Oosthuizen, because, somehow, the van looked like him.

So Jean, Fourie, Danie, John, Schalla, Butch, Pierre and I hit the road from Auckland that Sunday at 10 a.m. We'd all become firm friends over the years. Usually we were the last guys around the campfire at team-building exercises or the ones who would chat for hours in the team room after a game. And as there was room for one more in the van, we invited 'Mr Bones', also known as Willem Alberts, to join us.

We organised some music and provisions for the road: we had a cooler box stuffed with thirst-quenchers and some food. Pierre was the designated driver, which allowed the rest of us to relax a little. The locals said the trip to Taupo would take us no longer than three hours, but in the end we arrived there nine hours later!

It was a very special trip for me, as it was one of the last opportunities I'd have to spend quality time with my best rugby mates. In the eight years we'd played together, we'd lived through a lot of highs and quite a few lows, and it was great to reflect on those moments along the way … and be a bit silly as well.

Our road trip was taking place halfway through the World Cup, rugby's 'biggest spectacle', and in a small country like New Zealand nothing goes unnoticed. Somewhere along the way we 'borrowed' a red traffic cone, but somebody saw us and informed the police. We were pulled over at a roadblock and one of the guys tried to hide our 'loot'.

The police asked our designated driver if we had stolen a traffic cone. Pierre is a guy who can't tell a lie. 'Maybe' was the best he could come up with before he started giggling. Then Jean spilt the beans and accused *me* of being the mastermind behind the 'theft'. He pleaded with the cops to arrest me on the spot and lock me up. Fortunately, the cops had a sense of humour. Our 'sentence' was to pose with them for a few photos. They were friendly chaps and it was a pleasure to have our pictures taken with them.

In the next town, Matamata, we stopped for lunch. It was time to have more fun, so we pretended that we were going to appropriate a billboard outside a local sports bar. However, a woman in the bar saw what we were doing, stormed outside and confronted us.

It was all a big joke. The billboard wouldn't even have fitted into the van, and we immediately handed it back to her. You can imagine our surprise when we saw the newspapers the next day, which accused us of trying to steal a billboard. The papers even said that we would have got away with it had an eyewitness – the woman – not reacted so quickly. Fortunately, everyone saw the funny side of the story. The woman later sent the billboard to us in Taupo, where we signed it and sent it back. We heard that they were planning to sell it at a charity auction.

The people in the small towns welcomed us with open arms, and we really enjoyed seeing the New Zealand countryside. We posed for pictures with the locals in restaurants, signed autographs, ate some great meals and had a jolly good time. But, yes, when our little prank made the newspapers, we realised that rugby players can't slip off the radar during a World Cup. It was very funny.

With the weekend free, we had two days to explore the golf courses around Taupo before we would start preparing for the tough Samoans, who were waiting for us in our last group match (again in the North Harbour Stadium). We needed one more point on the log to avoid catching an early flight home.

Peter had decided to give John a rest against Samoa and start with Bismarck at hooker. I would captain the team and, unlike a few weeks before in Port Elizabeth, John and I were both comfortable with the decision. John supported me wholeheartedly throughout that week. Even though I was captaining the side and John was on the bench, his input remained invaluable. The team sheet might have looked different, but it didn't change the way we approached the game. We were an experienced group who had worked together for long enough to adapt to any changes with ease.

But I would lie if I said that I didn't feel the pressure. I'd watched the previous two games from the sidelines and the team had performed well. Now we were on the brink of our last group game, against a Samoan side that had beaten the Wallabies two months earlier, and it was my responsibility to prepare the guys for this crucial encounter.

We had serious training sessions on the Monday and Tuesday. We'd picked up that the Samoan forwards targeted the breakdowns, so all the players who weren't going to start in the upcoming Test were asked to act like our opponents at the practice and make things as difficult as possible for us. After a couple of days' rest, the guys were fresh and ready to give their best.

***

On the day before the Test, Rassie Erasmus, our technical coach in the management team, handed out our jerseys. It was interesting to see his approach to this ritual. Rassie said he had had the honour of playing in

36 Tests for the Boks, but he couldn't help South Africa win the World Cup. 'I'll tell you what I did wrong in my career,' he said.

First of all, he said, unlike most of us, very few players of his generation could choose when they wanted to terminate their careers. They either called it a day because they were injured, or they were simply dropped. 'The most important thing is to enjoy every single game to the full,' Rassie said, 'because nobody *deserves* the Bok jersey; it's simply an honour to wear it.'

When he looked back on his career, Rassie realised that he had sometimes thought himself bigger or more important than the game itself. 'Maybe I was impossible to coach. Maybe I was difficult to manage if things didn't work out how I wanted them to.'

Rassie also mentioned his 'misplaced loyalty' to Gary Teichmann and Werner ('Smiley') Swanepoel. 'I was really upset with Nick Mallett for not picking Gary for the 1999 World Cup and that Joost van der Westhuizen had got the nod ahead of my big buddy Smiley.

'As a result, I didn't put in the extra effort I usually did. If I'd walked that extra mile for the team, if I'd perhaps come up with a plan or a new idea, I might have made a difference. Maybe, just maybe, I could have helped us win the World Cup that year too.'

As tradition dictated, the captain normally thanked the presenter of the jerseys, so I had the honour of saying a few words. I said that we had no chance of making a success of the tournament if each player didn't give everything he had to make a difference.

'Guys, we shouldn't have any regrets when we look back on this year's tournament,' I said. It was time for each and every one of us to ignore our personal ambitions and do everything in our ability to make the team a success.

Then I addressed Rassie. I said that he might have made mistakes in his career, but when I was still a youngster, with little experience in professional rugby, he was the player who had influenced my career the most, precisely because he'd worked harder than almost anyone else. I was actually struggling to contain my emotions. Then I thanked Rassie and presented him with a small gift.

My nerves were shot before the match, as I knew that this game could potentially be my last in the Bok jersey if we lost to Samoa. The

Samoan team had grown into a solid unit and their rugby had greatly improved over the past few years. Even though we knew how to beat them, I was still worried. Luckily, we started the match strongly. We gave them a hard time in the line-outs and scrums, and as a result they couldn't get any decent possession. At half-time we were leading 13-0 after Bryan had scored a magnificent try in the corner.

Unfortunately, the second half was a different story. It seemed to me as if the guys had gone to sleep. Or perhaps they were distracted. All of a sudden, Samoa had all the possession and we were defending like crazy. One of the Boks' strong points since the start of the World Cup campaign had been our defensive play. We took great pride in our strong defence, as instilled in us by our new defensive coach, Jacques Nienaber. By the end of the game, we'd made more than 150 tackles on Samoa and they had scored only one try. And it was only the second try we'd conceded in New Zealand – not too shabby after 320 minutes of rugby!

We led by eight points throughout the game, but I believed that we could step up a gear. Unfortunately, that didn't happen, but nevertheless we still won this important encounter (13-5). We never panicked, even though it was our most physical game yet in the tournament. Samoa were involved in a lot of off-the-ball stuff, probably in an attempt to provoke us. But we kept our cool. Our discipline was exemplary and I was really proud of the boys. Everyone realised that we couldn't afford to be distracted from the much bigger task that still lay ahead of us.

There were many aching bodies after the game, especially among the backs. Bryan had received a hard knock on the thigh, JP Pietersen had injured his knee and François Hougaard had been out cold for a second or two after his head had accidently collided with a Samoan knee during a tackle. Luckily, none of these injuries was serious, and because the quarter-final match against Australia would only take place the following Sunday, we had enough time to fully recover.

But Frans Steyn wasn't as fortunate. He'd seriously injured his shoulder late in the game, which threatened to end his involvement in the tournament. I'd been worried about his fitness even before the start of the World Cup, but Steyntjie had had four brilliant Tests and had scored three tries, which only underlined his tremendous talent.

Finishing the group encounters unbeaten had been our first goal. Now our mission was accomplished, as we'd finished top of the log in our group. Besides the 21 tries we'd scored, we'd conceded only two tries in our four games, and we'd also won many new fans with the way we played. Everyone in the squad had had a chance to play, and even though there was the odd injury, we were ready for the quarter-final against Australia.

In the weeks before the final game in the opening round, local journalists had hardly mentioned the Boks as serious contenders for the title; now they were saying we were the only team that could beat the All Blacks.

21

A shattered dream

Games between Ireland and Italy hardly ever attract attention in South Africa, but the World Cup encounter between these two Six Nations teams (with South Africans Gert Smal as Ireland's assistant coach and Nick Mallett as Italy's head coach) was different. On 2 October we were glued to the TV, hoping against hope that Italy would surprise everyone by beating the Irish, because that meant that the Boks would play Italy, and not Australia, in the quarter-finals.

But the miracle didn't happen, and Ireland continued their impressive performance in the tournament, winning 36-6. Ireland had unexpectedly beaten Australia (15-6) earlier in the group stages, which put them at the top of the log in Group C, above the Aussies. As winners of Group D, we had to face the runners-up in Group C.

Playing Australia in the quarter-finals was most definitely not an easy road to World Cup glory.

It was a long week. The previous Friday we'd played Samoa, and now we'd have to face the Wallabies a week later. The Saturday after the Test against Samoa, we travelled back to Wellington, where Peter de Villiers gave us time off on the Sunday and Monday to recover from a very physical encounter. On the Tuesday, we got together to start preparing for the weekend's crunch game.

The two-day break was a blessing, as quite a few players were nursing injuries of various degrees. Luckily, my hamstring problems were no more, but Frans Steyn, Bryan Habana, JP Pietersen, François Hougaard and Heinrich Brüssow weren't 100 per cent fit.

Above all, Bakkies Botha still hadn't recovered from a recurring

Achilles-tendon injury, and we knew it would be touch and go whether he'd be fit enough to play against the Wallabies.

Of all the injured players, Frans had the biggest hurdle to overcome. He had hurt his left shoulder late in the game against Samoa. The next day, our medical team gave us the bad news: Frans could play no further part in our World Cup campaign.

It was sad to say goodbye to him. This youngster doesn't wear his heart on his sleeve, but we could see that it was really tough for him to pack his bags and head home. He was a key player in our backline and had scored tries against Wales, Fiji and Namibia. And, of course, we could no longer rely on his kicking boot to slot over penalties from 55 metres and more. His departure was a massive blow to the side.

Two days later, we were hit by another setback. During training it looked as if Bakkies had at last overcome his injury, but at our first line-out, he hurt the same tendon in the heel that had kept him sidelined for most of the tournament. I immediately realised that my old lock partner was in a bad state.

Bakkies had a chat with Peter that evening and told him he wouldn't be able to give his all for the team. He asked to be sent back to South Africa for an operation.

Bakkies broke the news to us during our Bible-study session the next morning. I was shattered because old Bakke and I had a fantastic partnership in the scrums, and his withdrawal meant that he wouldn't be there when I played the last Test of my career. I ended the session with a prayer and used the opportunity to thank the Lord for what Bakkies had offered the team – and me, personally – over the years.

I had a lump in my throat, but I knew that such situations were part of life and rugby.

Later that day, Bakkies told the team that he was going back to South Africa. He was very emotional, and we understood how much the Bok jersey meant to him. Our own 'enforcer', one of the hardest men in international rugby, had tears welling up in his eyes. Although Bakkies didn't officially retire from Test rugby, he made the decision that he would resume his career at Toulon, the French club I had played for in 2008.

I think Bakkies realised that he'd probably already played his last game in the green and gold. And he wouldn't have the opportunity to conclude an amazing Bok era in the team with John Smit, Danie Rossouw, Fourie du Preez and me.

But there wasn't much time to ponder the harshness of life. We had to prepare for the Wallabies, who had beaten us in four of our last five Test encounters.

The rest of the week went according to plan, and all the injured players, except Heinrich, who was still nursing a sore rib, recovered in time. Heinrich is as tough as nails and told the doctor just to give him an injection for the pain so that he could play. Then he would be ready to give the Aussie ball fetcher, David Pocock, a run for his money.

That week, the media went on about the threat the Wallaby backline posed and how the 'older and slower' Boks wouldn't be able to withstand the pressure if our forwards couldn't dominate and force our opponents onto the back foot. We knew we had to control the game from the front, but it was never an issue because we approached all our games that way.

With Frans out of the equation, Jean de Villiers was back at inside centre. It was great to have a level-headed player in a key position in the backline. Jean was one of the leaders in the team and brought calmness to the backs, where he and Fourie planned all the moves.

A day before the game, it was my turn to speak to the media. The same questions I'd heard so often over the past 10 years were posed again: 'Are you ready for the challenge?'; 'What about an unpredictable player like Quade Cooper?'; 'They've beaten you so regularly the past two years – do you have any plans to turn the tables?'

My answer, quite simply, was nothing that had happened in the past between South Africa and Australia mattered in this World Cup. All that counted was the 80 minutes on Sunday. The team that played with the most intensity, that could best handle the pressure and make the right decisions would win.

Although there were more and more South Africans arriving in Wellington, we knew that there would be massive support for our opponents too. Walking through the streets of the New Zealand capital that week, we got the feeling New Zealanders wanted us to win rather than the Wallabies. But we weren't being naive. We knew it was purely a matter of which side the New Zealanders liked the least: the Australians or us.

Even before the game that Sunday, we realised it was likely to be a long day on the pitch with New Zealand referee Bryce Lawrence officiating. I asked him specifically about Australia's line-out tactics – how they often come in from the side to slap the ball from the jumper's hands. It's considered against the rules, but Bryce said that he wasn't going to penalise it, as there's nothing wrong with it. I asked him whether this tactic contravened the laws, but he stood by his opinion. Neither John – who was standing next to me – nor I could believe the arrogance with which Bryce answered the question.

Match day arrived. We started strong and soon had them under pressure, but after 10 minutes they got their hands on the ball and kicked it into touch deep inside our half. We'd been in this situation many times before and decided to go for the safe option: win the line-out, pass the ball to one of our strong ball carriers – Schalk Burger, in this instance – to take it up a few metres, force the ruck and get Morné Steyn to kick it safely into touch.

This time, though, the plan didn't work. Schalla was brought down, and one of the Wallabies kicked the ball from the ensuing ruck. It popped out on their side and the Wallaby captain, James Horwill, barged over for a try – against the run of play.

A few minutes later, they had another good run in our half and forced a penalty, which James O'Connor slotted over to stretch the lead to 8-0.

Two early mistakes had given them the opportunity to score, but there was plenty of time to recover and we were in total control of the game. We pinched at least six line-out balls on their throw-ins. We had the upper hand in the scrums and pinned them down in their half of the field. The only area of play where we were put under pressure was at the breakdown, especially when Heinrich's rib injury started acting up again and he was forced to leave the field after 20 minutes.

Pocock was brilliant in mastering the ball on the ground, but we were baffled by the way Bryce handled this critical aspect of the game. Even in an ideal situation, the breakdowns are a grey area, as the interpretation of the laws differs from one ref to another. On this day, however, Lawrence's approach to the breakdown was even stranger than usual. He allowed everything – he never told defending players to roll away or release the tackled player in possession of the ball.

But we didn't allow this to break our stride, as we'd decided months earlier not to get distracted by the referee's decisions. And besides, Lawrence wasn't the type of referee with whom you could have a constructive discussion during a game.

By half-time, we were trailing just 3-8. The feeling in the changing room was positive. Although Morné had missed two difficult penalty kicks at goal, we believed that if we kept them under pressure, their defensive structure would eventually crumble and we would score a couple of tries, which would break their spirit.

In the 45th minute, our first real opportunity came when Jean hit a gap in their backline and sent a flying Pat Lambie towards the Aussie goal line. But Bryce judged the pass to be forward ... by a few centimetres, perhaps?

Five minutes later, Peter sent on Bismarck du Plessis and François Hougaard, two of our most outstanding impact players, as replacements. They gave it their all, but things still didn't go our way. We had the opportunities, but time and time again we lost the ball or were stumped by a forward pass. Morné added another penalty and drop goal, and with 20 minutes to play, we were leading 9-8 – not a lead that would put any team at ease. And we just couldn't land the knockout punch.

With about 15 minutes left, we had them under tremendous pressure again after a scrum close to their goal line. The ball popped out, Fourie got hold of it and went for the try line, but was tackled by two Wallaby defenders. They punted the loose ball downfield. It wasn't out, and Pat Lambie fielded it and launched a drop kick. It missed the target by a few centimetres.

In the 71st minute, they had a line-out in our half and threw the ball to Radike Samo at the front. I competed, but Samo secured the possession. As he came down, he jumped over Danie Rossouw, and the big Aussie with the Afro hairstyle hit the turf with a thump.

Play continued, but assistant referee Romain Pointe had his flag out and informed Bryce that Danie had taken Samo's legs from under him. It was a critical decision. A penalty was awarded and O'Connor added three points: Australia 11, South Africa 9.

There was still enough time on the clock, and we knew if we could penetrate their half we could force a penalty or get Morné in a position to take another drop kick. But things just didn't work out that way.

François Louw had a strong run with the ball, but was stopped with a tackle around the neck. Many referees would have awarded a penalty for a high tackle without hesitating, but Lawrence decided that the Aussies had formed the ruck and because we couldn't get the ball back, they were awarded the scrum.

Moments later, Bismarck tackled O'Connor with ball and all and held him off the ground, but the ref decided that this wasn't a ruck and awarded the Wallabies the put-in at the ensuing scrum. There was nothing we could do about it.

Time had run out. Will Genia picked up the ball from behind the scrum and booted it into touch. Lawrence blew the final whistle. Our World Cup campaign was over.

We had undoubtedly played better than the Aussies, but the only thing that counted was the scoreboard after the final whistle. It still read Australia 11, South Africa 9. Slowly but surely, reality set in. Our chance to take the Webb Ellis trophy back to South Africa was gone.

And my rugby career was over.

A few of the Wallabies came over to congratulate me on my career. It meant a lot to me. I'll particularly cherish the words of the locks, Nathan Sharpe and Dan Vickerman. Sharpie and I had had numerous encounters over the years. 'It was always a great honour to play against you,' he said. 'You're the best player I've competed against.'

Even Dan, not always the friendliest opponent, shook my hand and said that he'd always enjoyed our battles and that it was a great honour to have experienced them.

I couldn't help but feel good about myself after these compliments. What the newspapers and other people say pales in comparison to what your teammates and opponents say about you. It is by their words that you know whether you were successful in your rugby career or not.

We left the field and headed to the changing rooms. It was dead quiet and almost unreal. There we sat, after one of the best Bok performances in a long time, but as the losing team. We had come to the end of our World Cup road.

John and Peter said a few words. The rest of us decided we'd rather head off to our hotel, where we'd have a proper chat.

Again I had to face an army of journalists. I immediately sensed that they also couldn't fathom how we had lost the game. What could one say? We had beaten them in every aspect of the game, but we'd still lost. And that was all that counted.

One of the scribes wanted to know whether this had really been the last game of my career. 'Yes, this is it,' I said, but I suddenly wondered whether it was indeed the right decision.

I was satisfied with my performance on the day, and felt that it had been one of my best games in a Bok jersey in a long time. And by the sound of it, the Wallabies only had good things to say about me. Did I really want to end my career on such a note? But it wasn't the right time to contemplate the issue. I was way too emotional for that.

Instead I chose to talk about my plans for the future. I would soon be joining the SuperSport team, and I wanted to get more involved in WAD Finance, the business my sponsors and partners – Willem Britz, Antoine van Buuren and Daan van Rensburg – had been running and developing for the past few years.

My dream is to be involved with the Boks again some day, not as a player but as a coach, and to hopefully drink from the Webb Ellis trophy again. Rugby is in my blood; it's my life, and I know I would never be able to completely turn my back on this wonderful game.

We went back to the hotel, where we gathered in the team room. Everyone had the opportunity to say a few words. The overall sentiment was that although we'd lost to Australia, the game wouldn't define us as a team or as individual players.

Many guys also mentioned the fantastic environment we'd created over the past four years in the Bok camp. We'd grown closer as teammates, but, more importantly perhaps, also as friends. Even if we went our separate ways, we would stay in touch.

A lot of the guys thanked John and me for what we had meant to the team. It was a humbling experience to hear South Africa's best players say such kind words about me. Then it was my turn to say something. I stood up and cleared my throat, but I found it difficult to get the words out.

I thanked every player for the roles they had played in my career – from Fourie, one of my best friends, and Pierre, who had taught me so much on a spiritual level, to my youngest teammate, Pat, who had shown me the meaning of the word modesty.

'For me, rugby has been a journey,' I said, 'and I can say with the greatest confidence that I wouldn't swap either the good or the bad times for anything else.'

I thanked Peter and the management team for the best four years of my Springbok career, and then, on behalf of the rest of the guys, turned to John. I thanked him for his leadership over the past seven years. I told him that we appreciated how he never failed to support the rights of the team and the individual players. Every time management did something the players didn't like, John ensured that our rights were protected. He never once put his interests above those of the team.

I asked everyone to stand up and drink a toast to a wonderful friend – and, as far as I was concerned, the best Springbok captain in South African history.

Then John and Peter spoke. It was a very emotional moment for everyone. John thanked Peter for the wonderful environment he had created for the team over the past four years. He had kind words for the management team – they had put in such hard work. Peter said it had been the best four years of his life and that it was an honour to have worked with such quality players.

The first flight from Wellington to South Africa was the next morning at 6 a.m. I had to cancel Monja's ticket to New Zealand and then quickly pack my belongings for the long journey home. I joined the other guys in the team room, where most of them were relaxing. We would be driven to the airport at four in the morning.

As usual, it was a long journey back to Johannesburg. But what awaited us at OR Tambo on the Monday afternoon – not more than 30 hours after the final whistle had sounded on my playing career – was nothing short of amazing. We were expecting a handful of spectators, journalists and our families, but we entered the international arrivals terminal to find it was packed to the brim. It looked like we'd just won the World Cup.

I struggled to reach Monja and my children. The only small ray of light from our quarter-final defeat was that I could sweep Jaime and Giselle into my arms two weeks earlier than planned.

Carrying my two beautiful daughters, I wended my way through the crowd. The whole team was cheered on; supporters patted us on our shoulders and told us how proud they were of their heroes. It was the first time in my life I'd experienced such a welcome. Usually after losing, most supporters are critical and distant, but it was very different this time.

I know that many fans were angry and disappointed when we were knocked out of the competition – we were too – but not one person I spoke to had an unkind word to say. Everyone just thanked us for our contribution. I believe they appreciated both the way we had played against Australia and the quality of the players who had represented South Africa at the World Cup.

Most of the questions at the press conference shortly afterwards concerned Peter's future. His four-year contract as Bok coach would terminate at the end of 2011. Previously, he had told me that no one at SARU had spoken to him about his future, and he accepted that it was the end of the road for him as national coach. He wouldn't apply for the position again, but if they offered it to him, he would seriously consider it.

The media asked me what I thought of our World Cup campaign. I told them that I had no regrets about anything. We had been well prepared, the team spirit had been amazing and even though we might argue about certain team selections, I believed they had been spot on.

But the two biggest talking points after the World Cup remained our management team and the selections they had made. Did we have the best management team possible? I think we did, especially with the additions of Rassie Erasmus and Jacques Nienaber. We were 100 per cent prepared for every game, and with Rassie and Jacques as part of the coaching staff, our individual roles were crystal clear. For the first time in four years, I felt that every coach in the squad supported the game plan we had decided on.

Rassie was in control of our overall tactics – our kicking plan, our attacking strategy; Jacques was in control of our defensive strategies, and his passion and energy were obvious to everyone. I could now understand why the Stormers had defended so well in the Super Rugby series. Jacques eats, sleeps and dreams rugby, especially defence. He added unbelievable value to the team: in five World Cup games, we conceded only three tries, probably the least of any team at the tournament.

Dick Muir oversaw the backline players' individual skills, and the guys were happy working with him. Gary Gold was in charge of our scrums and line-outs, and I think it was our best scrum performance in all my years with the Boks. Percy Montgomery took the goal-kickers under his wing and did a stellar job.

And Peter?

His biggest attribute was that he never displayed any ego and never pulled rank; he allowed each player to go about his business without unnecessary interference. Peter steered the ship and saw to it that the operation was managed in the best way possible. With so many strong personalities involved, everyone wanted to stake a claim, but Peter made sure we all melded together both as individuals and as a team. In the bigger scheme of things, he did a superb job.

As far as team selections are concerned, the hooker position was the most contentious issue. John or Bismarck? It came down to the discussion John and I had had in Port Elizabeth, when I'd assured him of my support and told him that he was the only person who would know whether he was still good enough for the team. Nobody will ever know how things would have turned out if we'd approached this issue differently.

I thought John played excellent rugby in New Zealand. By the same token, Bismarck was brilliant every time he was given a chance to play. Regarding the dynamics in the team, I think Peter handled the situation very well. If an opportunity could have presented itself to leave John out of the team and appoint a new captain, it would have been perhaps at the end of 2009, or even before the start of the Tri Nations series in 2011 – but not shortly before the World Cup tournament.

One thing is certain: we didn't lose the World Cup because John had been the first-choice hooker. I believe most of the players supported Peter's decision to stick with John, and I take my hat off to Bismarck and his brother, Jannie, for handling the situation so well. They could easily have been disgruntled and jeopardised the team spirit, but they didn't.

A Springbok victory was not meant to be. Now we had no other choice but to let the matter rest.

22

A new dream

It's Tuesday 11 October 2011. I've just woken up in my house in Pretoria knowing that our dream of winning the World Cup has not come true. It feels unreal. We should still be in New Zealand, preparing for our next game, but we're not. I'm not sure what to do with myself.

Because of the jet lag, I didn't sleep well. So I do what most dads my age do: I help the children get dressed and drop them off at school. It is a chore I missed terribly in the month I was away from home, so it's great to do the school run again. I decide to stop off at the gym, because that's what I'm used to doing. Most of the people are surprised to see me there ... I am, after all, a retired rugby player who's supposed to take it easy.

I expected people to show their disappointment with our performance by avoiding me, but everyone I speak to is very supportive. They all want to know what exactly Bryce Lawrence tried to accomplish with his performance as referee. I can't give them any answers, because I still don't know.

The words of support are very special and mean a lot to me, but the fact is, we are no longer in the World Cup, and it hurts like hell. I feel empty, nauseous.

The next day, I feel a little better. I help the kids get ready for school, drop them off and once again head for the gym. Afterwards, I have a two-hour meeting with my partners at WAD Finance. I have to learn the ins and outs of the business, and they hand me a dauntingly thick file to study in order to prepare for our next meeting, in two days' time. So this is how things work in the business world.

WAD Finance involves a few businesses, among them some restaurants and a pharmaceutical company. The plan is that I will be in charge of one specific business. This is my new life, and although it's a bit of a culture shock to my 'sportsman's system', I look forward to the new challenges. I hope I can make a success of the business.

In the coming weeks, I'll chat to Heyneke Meyer about my future as coach with the Blue Bulls. I've also come to an agreement with SuperSport to participate in their rugby talk shows and appear in studio discussions during games. Because of this agreement and my involvement with WAD, I can't immediately start coaching full time. Hopefully, though, I'll get the opportunity to help out once a week at the Blue Bulls.

People want to know whether I will specialise as a line-out coach, but it would frustrate me to focus only on this integral aspect of the game. My passion for rugby stretches beyond jumping for and catching a ball. In fact, I find the art of attacking play very interesting in several aspects. I'd love to be head coach one day, but for now, it's important that I stay abreast of the tendencies in the game so that I don't fall behind in this ever evolving sport.

When I look back on my career, I realise what an unbelievable journey it has been. There were many highs and quite a few lows, but if I had to do it all over again, I wouldn't change a thing. Even those six months in Toulon were invaluable. It was wonderful to be there with my family, and it also reminded me of the reasons why I played rugby, and confirmed the passion I had, and still have, for the Bulls and the Boks.

Years ago, I was a little boy with big dreams of playing for the Blue Bulls or the Springboks one day. Now I can look back on a professional career spanning 14 years, with 110 Tests for my country and more than 100 games for the Bulls. During this time, I was involved in winning the World Cup, two Tri Nations, three Super Rugby and three Currie Cup titles. If someone had told that shy little boy from Pietersburg that he would achieve all that one day, he would have said that it was a totally preposterous notion.

Over the years, rugby has gone through many changes, but it's basically still the same game it always was. Excuse me if I sound a bit like

Peter de Villiers, but I believe if a former player returns to top-level rugby after an absence of a year or two, he'll struggle to grasp the finer details of the game, which could mean the difference between winning or losing a match at the highest level.

And yet the cornerstones of rugby will always remain the same. If you don't apply the basics in the scrums, line-outs, kicking and tackling, you can forget about achieving success at any level.

Professional rugby requires a lot of hard work. The longer it is amateurs who make the decisions at management level, the longer we'll struggle to overcome certain challenges. One only has to look at the successes of soccer and American gridiron as examples of fully professional sporting disciplines that are managed like proper businesses.

Rugby will have to follow suit, or the game will suffer in the long term. During the 2011 World Cup, the All Blacks threatened to withdraw from the next tournament in 2015 if the commercial model doesn't change to benefit participating teams. Although I don't think we'll ever see this sort of 'strike' actually happening, New Zealand's threat was a wake-up call for rugby administrators worldwide.

I saw what was possible if a club is run solely by its owner when I was with Toulon. It's the owner's team and the owner's money, and if the owner manages the club well, a team in the third league can eventually be good enough to play in the European league. Success means that the value of the club increases and the business grows. And then it becomes an attractive investment opportunity. Isn't that how all businesses are supposed to work?

In South Africa, outside investors can't buy a bigger share than 49.9 per cent of a rugby union. A few partners and I invested in the Boland Union, but no matter how hard we work, it'll always be tough for a team like the Cavaliers to compete with the five major unions in the country. They'll never have the opportunity to play Super Rugby and will therefore never be able to entice top players to move to Wellington in the Western Cape.

Smaller unions should be given the opportunity to move up. If they play well in the Premier League, they should be given the chance of playing in a promotion/relegation match against the team at the bottom of the Super Rugby log. This will ensure that the competition remains strong and that the opportunity exists for a small union to grow into a bigger one if the business is managed properly.

Don't get me wrong: rugby at amateur level is very important, because that's where the future stars begin their careers. However, I do believe guys coming from the amateur side of the game shouldn't be allowed to make decisions on a professional level. A lot of things can still be done to make South African rugby healthier than it is right now.

For many people, 'transformation' in South African rugby is still a contentious issue, but from a personal perspective, it was unbelievable to experience the unquestionable love and unconditional support South Africans from all walks of life have for the game. People from all races would chat and congratulate us after games, whether we won or lost.

Our biggest task is to develop the big pool of hugely talented players from disadvantaged communities. We need to coach them so that they can play at the highest level one day. I believe the sooner we accomplish this, the sooner there will be less political interference in the composition of teams at both the provincial and national levels.

To have played rugby at such a high level for so long was a blessing for me. Besides the wonderful experiences on the field, I was fortunate enough to see the world and meet amazing people. We were privileged to have had the best facilities, the tastiest food and top-class hotels wherever we went.

But with the good, there is always the bad.

I wasn't there when Jaime lost her first tooth. I also missed her first pre-school concert. And the pressures in professional rugby are immense. The better you get and the more success you enjoy, the higher the expectations of the supporters. The Bulls are a classic example. When we finished sixth in the Super 12 series in 2003, our fans were ecstatic, but after we won the Super 14 title in 2007, nothing less than first position was going to be good enough.

Then there are the high expectations people have of you as captain. They expect you never to falter; you have to be perfect, and that, of course, is impossible. John and I often spoke about these expectations, and when the pressure reached breaking point sometimes, we would wish that we could just be transported to some remote island where we could spend lazy hours with our families, where we could get up in the morning and not worry about combing our hair and do whatever we felt like. A pipe dream, of course!

Attending media conferences was also stressful; you were only ever allowed to say what was safe. You couldn't voice your disapproval of the referee, or SARU or the International Rugby Board, because that was not in line with the 'spirit of the game'. You always had to be diplomatic, even when you were itching to tell the truth or voice your own opinion, like guys do around a braai.

If you disrespected a weaker opponent, you were considered arrogant; if you sang their praises, the media portrayed you as insincere or claimed that you had a hidden agenda. And then, of course, there was the question I always struggled with: 'Victor, are you guys ready for Saturday's game?' Honestly? Did someone really think I was going to say, 'No, our preparation is a shambles and the guys think we don't stand a chance'?

Besides these unpleasant aspects of life as a professional sportsman, I wouldn't swap my rugby career for anything in the world. That is why I want to say the following to young players: Always have a dream, but know that it's not good enough if it stays only a dream.

Heyneke Meyer taught us that if you have a dream and you want to fulfil it, write down your dream and the steps you're going to take to achieve it. I did exactly that after my first year as captain of the Blue Bulls. Then, after you've written down your goals and how you plan to achieve them, you have to focus on what needs to be done and put in the hard yards. Remember, champions train when the others rest.

That's not to say you won't have any setbacks. But the burning ambition to reach your goal must carry you through the tough times.

I was lucky enough not only to learn a lot from the game, but also to learn life's lessons through the game. For me, the most important lesson was not to compromise my principles. Believe in what you stand for. Although this doesn't mean that someone who has a different opinion from yours is wrong. In a team sport like rugby, where there are many different personalities, you sometimes have to take a back seat for the greater good. I had to do this in 2004, when Jake White sent me home from Australia.

As I sit here now, with birds chirping in the garden, I know my rugby journey didn't end the way I wanted it to, but the final word has not been spoken yet.

The Bulls had a very tough season in 2011. We didn't even reach the knockout stages of the Super Rugby series. And then the Boks were sent packing in the quarter-finals of the World Cup tournament.

But – and this is the point – my teammates and I aren't defined by the last game we played. And the way in which South African supporters welcomed us home makes me believe that they agree with me. They, too, see the bigger picture.

My rugby journey made me the person I am today – from the once shy Pietersburg boy to the professional rugby player who had an influence on the lives of millions of people around the globe; someone who was a part of remarkable events in our country's history, like the Super 14 games in Soweto; who experienced moments that will last in his memory forever, like the road trip through the New Zealand countryside with lifelong friends; who spent time on a deserted beach in St Tropez with his wife, Monja, and firstborn, Jaime; who sat in the middle of the pitch at Loftus with friends and teammates to watch as the sun rose over the north and east pavilions while the Currie Cup stood next to them. Cups may come and go, but thanks to rugby, no one will ever be able to take these memories away from me.

Now I have a new dream: to arrive at the airport one day as the coach of the Springboks with my captain and my team, bringing the Webb Ellis Cup back to South Africa …

Victor Matfield's Test matches for South Africa

	Date	Age	Position	Opponent	Result
1	30 Jun 01	24	Reserve	Italy	W: 60-14
2	21 Jul 01	24	Lock	New Zealand	L: 3-12
3	18 Aug 01	24	Lock	Australia	D: 14-14
4	25 Aug 01	24	Lock	New Zealand	L: 15-26
5	10 Nov 01	24	Lock	France	L: 10-20
6	17 Nov 01	24	Lock	Italy	W: 54-26
7	24 Nov 01	24	Lock	England	L: 9-29
8	1 Dec 01	24	Lock	USA	W: 43-20
9	8 Jun 02	25	Lock	Wales	W: 34-19
10	6 Jul 02	25	Lock	Samoa	W: 60-18
11	20 Jul 02	25	Lock	New Zealand	L: 20-41
12	27 Jul 02	25	Lock	Australia	L: 27-38
13	10 Aug 02	25	Reserve	New Zealand	L: 23-30
14	7 Jun 03	26	Lock	Scotland	W: 29-25
15	14 Jun 03	26	Lock	Scotland	W: 28-19
16	28 Jun 03	26	Lock	Argentina	W: 26-25
17	12 Jul 03	26	Lock	Australia	W: 26-22
18	19 Jul 03	26	Lock	New Zealand	L: 16-52
19	2 Aug 03	26	Lock	Australia	L: 9-29
20	9 Aug 03	26	Lock	New Zealand	L: 11-19
21	11 Oct 03	26	Lock	Uruguay	W: 72-6
22	18 Oct 03	26	Lock	England	L: 6-25
23	1 Nov 03	26	Lock	Samoa	W: 60-10
24	8 Nov 03	26	Lock	New Zealand	L: 9-29
25	12 Jun 04	27	Lock	Ireland	W: 31-17
26	19 Jun 04	27	Lock	Ireland	W: 26-17
27	26 Jun 04	27	Lock	Wales	W: 53-18
28	14 Aug 04	27	Lock	New Zealand	W: 40-26
29	21 Aug 04	27	Lock	Australia	W: 23-19
30	6 Nov 04	27	Lock	Wales	W: 38-36
31	13 Nov 04	27	Lock	Ireland	L: 12-17
32	20 Nov 04	27	Lock	England	L: 16-32
33	27 Nov 04	27	Lock	Scotland	W: 45-10
34	4 Dec 04	27	Lock	Argentina	W: 39-7
35	18 Jun 05	28	Lock	France	D: 30-30
36	25 Jun 05	28	Lock	France	W: 27-13
37	9 Jul 05	28	Lock	Australia	L: 12-30

Venue

Venue	
EPRFU Stadium (Boet Erasmus), Port Elizabeth	
Newlands, Cape Town	First Test start
Subiaco Oval, Perth	
Eden Park, Auckland	
Stade de France, Paris	
Luigi Ferraris Stadium, Genoa	First Test try
Twickenham, London	
Robertson Stadium, UH, Houston	
Free State Stadium, Bloemfontein	Second Test try
Loftus Versfeld, Pretoria	Third Test try
Westpac Stadium, Wellington	
Wooloongabba, Brisbane	
Kings Park, Durban	
Kings Park, Durban	
Ellis Park, Johannesburg	
EPRFU Stadium (Boet Erasmus), Port Elizabeth	
Newlands, Cape Town	Fourth Test try
Loftus Versfeld, Pretoria	
Suncorp Stadium (Lang Park), Brisbane	
Carisbrook, Dunedin	
Subiaco Oval, Perth	RWC 2003
Subiaco Oval, Perth	RWC 2003
Suncorp Stadium (Lang Park), Brisbane	RWC 2003
Colonial Stadium (Telstra Dome), Melbourne	RWC 2003 – quarter-final
Free State Stadium, Bloemfontein	
Newlands, Cape Town	
Loftus Versfeld, Pretoria	
Ellis Park, Johannesburg	
Kings Park, Durban	Fifth Test try – SA Try of the Year 2004
Millennium Stadium (Cardiff Arms Park), Cardiff	
Aviva Stadium (Lansdowne Road), Dublin	
Twickenham, London	
Murrayfield, Edinburgh	
Velez Sarsfield Stadium, Buenos Aires	
Kings Park, Durban	
EPRFU Stadium (Boet Erasmus), Port Elizabeth	
Stadium Australia (Telstra), Sydney	

	Date	Age	Position	Opponent	Result
38	23 Jul 05	28	Lock	Australia	W: 33-20
39	30 Jul 05	28	Lock	Australia	W: 22-16
40	6 Aug 05	28	Lock	New Zealand	W: 22-16
41	20 Aug 05	28	Lock	Australia	W: 22-19
42	27 Aug 05	28	Lock	New Zealand	L: 27-31
43	5 Nov 05	28	Lock	Argentina	W: 34-23
44	19 Nov 05	28	Lock	Wales	W: 33-16
45	26 Nov 05	28	Lock	France	L: 20-26
46	10 Jun 06	29	Lock	Scotland	W: 36-16
47	17 Jun 06	29	Lock	Scotland	W: 29-15
48	24 Jun 06	29	Lock	France	L: 26-36
49	15 Jul 06	29	Lock	Australia	L: 0-49
50	22 Jul 06	29	Lock	New Zealand	L: 17-35
51	5 Aug 06	29	Lock	Australia	L: 18-20
52	26 Aug 06	29	Lock	New Zealand	L: 26-45
53	2 Sep 06	29	Lock	New Zealand	W: 21-20
54	9 Sep 06	29	Lock	Australia	W: 24-16
55	26 May 07	30	Lock	England	W: 58-10
56	2 Jun 07	30	Lock	England	W: 55-22
57	16 Jun 07	30	Lock	Australia	W: 22-19
58	23 Jun 07	30	Lock (C)	New Zealand	L: 21-26
59	15 Aug 07	30	Lock (C)	Namibia	W: 105-13
60	25 Aug 07	30	Lock (C)	Scotland	W: 27-3
61	9 Sep 07	30	Lock	Samoa	W: 59-7
62	14 Sep 07	30	Lock	England	W: 36-0
63	22 Sep 07	30	Reserve	Tonga	W: 30-25
64	30 Sep 07	30	Lock	USA	W: 64-15
65	7 Oct 07	30	Lock	Fiji	W: 37-20
66	14 Oct 07	30	Lock	Argentina	W: 37-13
67	20 Oct 07	30	Lock	England	W: 15-6
68	7 Jun 08	31	Reserve	Wales	W: 43-17
69	14 Jun 08	31	Lock	Wales	W: 37-21
70	21 Jun 08	31	Lock (C)	Italy	W: 26-0
71	5 Jul 08	31	Lock	New Zealand	L: 8-19
72	12 Jul 08	31	Lock (C)	New Zealand	W: 30-28
73	19 Jul 08	31	Lock (C)	Australia	L: 9-16
74	9 Aug 08	31	Lock (C)	Argentina	W: 63-9
75	16 Aug 08	31	Lock (C)	New Zealand	L: 0-19
76	23 Aug 08	31	Lock (C)	Australia	L: 15-27
77	30 Aug 08	31	Lock (C)	Australia	W: 53-8

Venue	
Ellis Park, Johannesburg	
Loftus Versfeld, Pretoria	
Newlands, Cape Town	
Subiaco Oval, Perth	
Carisbrook, Dunedin	
Velez Sarsfield Stadium, Buenos Aires	
Millennium Stadium (Cardiff Arms Park), Cardiff	
Stade de France, Paris	
Kings Park, Durban	
EPRFU Stadium (Boet Erasmus), Port Elizabeth	
Newlands, Cape Town	
Suncorp Stadium (Lang Park), Brisbane	
Westpac Stadium, Wellington	50th Test
Stadium Australia (Telstra), Sydney	
Loftus Versfeld, Pretoria	
Royal Bafokeng Stadium, Rustenburg	
Ellis Park, Johannesburg	
Free State Stadium, Bloemfontein	
Loftus Versfeld, Pretoria	
Newlands, Cape Town	
Kings Park, Durban	First Test as Bok captain
Newlands, Cape Town	
Murrayfield, Edinburgh	
Parc des Princes, Paris	RWC 2007
Stade de France, Paris	RWC 2007
Stade Felix Bollaert, Lens	RWC 2007
Stade de la Mosson, Montpellier	RWC 2007
Stade Velodrome, Marseilles	RWC 2007 – quarter-final
Stade de France, Paris	RWC 2007 – semi-final
Stade de France, Paris	RWC 2007 – final
Free State Stadium, Bloemfontein	
Loftus Versfeld, Pretoria	
Newlands, Cape Town	
Westpac Stadium, Wellington	
Carisbrook, Dunedin	First Bok win in NZ in 10 years
Subiaco Oval, Perth	
Ellis Park, Johannesburg	
Newlands, Cape Town	
Kings Park, Durban	
Ellis Park, Johannesburg	

	Date	Age	Position	Opponent	Result
78	8 Nov 08	31	Lock	Wales	W: 20-15
79	15 Nov 08	31	Lock	Scotland	W: 14-10
80	22 Nov 08	31	Lock	England	W: 42-6
81	20 Jun 09	32	Lock	Britain	W: 26-21
82	27 Jun 09	32	Lock	Britain	W: 28-25
83	4 Jul 09	32	Lock	Britain	L: 9-28
84	25 Jul 09	32	Lock	New Zealand	W: 28-19
85	1 Aug 09	32	Lock	New Zealand	W: 31-19
86	8 Aug 09	32	Lock	Australia	W: 29-17
87	29 Aug 09	32	Lock	Australia	W: 32-25
88	5 Sep 09	32	Lock	Australia	L: 6-21
89	12 Sep 09	32	Lock	New Zealand	W: 32-29
90	13 Nov 09	32	Lock	France	L: 13-20
91	21 Nov 09	32	Reserve	Italy	W: 32-10
92	28 Nov 09	32	Lock	Ireland	L: 10-15
93	5 Jun 10	32	Lock	Wales	W: 34-31
94	12 Jun 10	33	Lock	France	W: 42-17
95	19 Jun 10	33	Lock (C)	Italy	W: 29-13
96	10 Jul 10	33	Lock	New Zealand	L: 12-32
97	17 Jul 10	33	Lock	New Zealand	L: 17-31
98	24 Jul 10	33	Lock	Australia	L: 13-30
99	21 Aug 10	33	Lock	New Zealand	L: 22-29
100	28 Aug 10	33	Lock	Australia	W: 44-31
101	4 Sep 10	33	Lock	Australia	L: 39-41
102	6 Nov 10	33	Lock (C)	Ireland	W: 23-21
103	13 Nov 10	33	Lock (C)	Wales	W: 29-25
104	20 Nov 10	33	Lock (C)	Scotland	L: 17-21
105	27 Nov 10	33	Lock (C)	England	W: 21-11
106	13 Aug 11	34	Lock	Australia	L: 9-14
107	20 Aug 11	34	Lock (c)	New Zealand	W: 18-5
108	11 Sep 11	34	Lock	Wales	W: 17-16
109	30 Sep 11	34	Lock (c)	Samoa	W: 13-5
110	9 Oct 11	34	Lock	Australia	L: 9-11

Matches: 110 (17 as captain)
Wins: 69 (12 as captain)
Losses: 38
Draws: 2
Tries: 7

Venue	
Millennium Stadium (Cardiff Arms Park), Cardiff	
Murrayfield, Edinburgh	
Twickenham, London	
Kings Park, Durban	
Loftus Versfeld, Pretoria	
Ellis Park, Johannesburg	
Free State Stadium, Bloemfontein	
Kings Park, Durban	
Newlands, Cape Town	Sixth Test try – record of 57 Tests between tries
Subiaco Oval, Perth	
Suncorp Stadium (Lang Park), Brisbane	
Waikato Stadium, Hamilton	
Stade Municipal, Toulouse	
Stadio Friuli, Udine	
Croke Park, Dublin	
Millennium Stadium (Cardiff Arms Park), Cardiff	
Newlands, Cape Town	
Puma Stadium, Witbank	
Eden Park, Auckland	
Westpac Stadium, Wellington	
Suncorp Stadium (Lang Park), Brisbane	
FNB Stadium, Soweto	
Loftus Versfeld, Pretoria	100th Test – third Bok to reach this, 16th player overall
Free State Stadium, Bloemfontein	
Aviva Stadium (Lansdowne Road), Dublin	
Millennium Stadium (Cardiff Arms Park), Cardiff	Seventh Test try
Murrayfield, Edinburgh	
Twickenham, London	
Kings Park, Durban	
Nelson Mandela Bay Stadium, Port Elizabeth	
Westpac Stadium, Wellington	RWC 2011
North Harbour Stadium, Auckland	RWC 2011
Westpac Stadium, Wellington	RWC 2011 – quarter-final

Index